W9-BYZ-577

History
of
Warships

FROM ANCIENT TIMES TO THE
TWENTY-FIRST CENTURY

James L. George

Naval Institute Press • ANNAPOLIS, MARYLAND

Library of Congress Cataloging-in-Publication Data

George, James L.
    History of warships : from ancient times to the twenty-first
century / James L. George
       p.   cm.
    Includes bibliographical references and index.
    ISBN 1-55750-312-5
    1. Warships—History. I. Title.
V750.G46 1998
623.8'25'09—dc21   98-3376

To my United States Naval Academy classmates
of the great Class of 1961
who gave their lives serving their country in Vietnam:

Lieutenant Frank M. Brown Jr., USN

Captain Sterling K. Coates, USMC

Lieutenant Commander James L. Connell, USN

Lieutenant Gene R. Gollahon, USN

Lieutenant Commander Robert S. Graustein, USN

Captain Henry Kolakowski Jr., USMC

Captain W. Dale Marshall, USMC

Lieutenant Terence M. Murphy, USN

Captain John L. Pritchard, USMC

Lieutenant John D. Prudhomme, USN

The strength of the ship is the Service,
And the strength of the Service, the ship.

RONALD A. HOPWOOD, *The Laws of the Navy*

The backbone and real power of any navy are the vessels
which, by due proportion of defensive and offensive powers,
are capable of giving and taking hard knocks.

ALFRED T. MAHAN, *The Interest of America in Sea Power*

Contents

Tables

Preface

AVIES ARE ABOUT warships, many different kinds of warships. Armies are not just about tanks or artillery or helicopters or, in the past, about cavalry or even infantry, but navies are about warships. And though it is true that air forces are about warplanes, there are two major differences. First, the history of warplanes is still less than a century old while that of warships stretches back many millennia. Perhaps more important, whereas there once were several different types of planes, in all but a few air forces of the world today the inventory consists of only multi-role fighter-bombers. Even smaller navies, however, have several very distinctly different types of warships: surface combatants, probably both destroyers and frigates, submarines, mine craft, perhaps a small helicopter or V/STOL carrier with at least a few amphibious and underway replenishment ships. Armies can be described by barely mentioning their equipment and air forces with a few generic references to warplanes, but navies can be described only in terms of their many different warships.

There are several good books and even series on ship types. Time-Life published a series on ships in the late 1970s. In the early 1980s, the British National Museum printed ten slim volumes under the general title *The Ship,* covering everything from rafts and boats from prehistoric times to modern dreadnoughts and nuclear submarines. Conway Maritime Press has published what it calls a twelve-volume encyclopedia history from the evolution of boats into ships to navies in the nuclear age. There are also excellent books on individual countries' warships such as Norman Friedman's illustrated design histories of U.S. warships. Another naval writer, Anthony Preston, has done a first-rate series on major warship types. However, therein also lies the problem. Few people have the financial resources to buy, or even the time to read, some fifty-odd books to learn the complete history of warships. That is the primary purpose of this book—to cover in one volume the history of warships from ancient times to those for the forthcoming twenty-first century.

There are a few single-volume books on the history of warships, but with few exceptions, most are coffee-table picture books. This is not necessarily meant to be a criticism. Most of these books contain excellent paintings and photos necessary to appreciate the history of warships. Words alone cannot adequately describe the multitude of ship types. With all due respect to soldiers and airmen, a tank is a tank and a plane is a plane. There are obviously differences between World War I, World War II, and modern tanks as there are between the biplanes of World War I, the many fighters and bombers of World War II, and today's jets. But with a dozen or so photos, one could adequately illustrate the complete history of either tanks or airplanes. It would take at least a dozen times a dozen pictures, however, even to start to illustrate the history of ships from early craft to Greek triremes and Viking long boats of the Age of Galleys to the progression of early sailing ships from cogs and galleons to the magnificent hundred-gun ships of the line in Nelson's time in the Age of Sail, followed by the hodgepodge of vessels of the Age of Ironclads to all the various types today. It is for this reason that this book also contains representative illustrations. In short, these coffee-table books with their beautiful pictures of ships—and ships truly are beautiful— fill a very useful gap in the literature.

However, most of these books are slim and do not adequately explain each type and its evolution, and many categories are missing altogether. Except for Greek triremes, ancient warships are usually given scant attention, and important modern types such as mine craft, amphibious ships, and service ships are often totally ignored. Invariably, because these books concentrate on pictures, the ship's operational uses are not explained, nor is there space for analysis of the various types and how they were used.

In fact, there seem to be two types of naval books, which leads into the second purpose of this book. On the one hand, there are the coffee-table and design history books that emphasize the warship descriptions. On the other are the operational histories on seapower, which sometimes barely mention the warships themselves. This single volume will also attempt to bridge that gap, not just by describing the evolution of the warships, but also briefly discussing how they were used, concentrating on the major sea battles of each era.

Finally, the book will also attempt to bridge another gap. *History of Warships* is intended for both the interested general reader and the naval expert. Although naval engineers and architects might consider the necessary generalizations on warship designs and evolution a little fundamental, and naval strategists may find the summaries of operational uses way too brief, this work attempts to cover enough common ground between the two to make the book unique. Even experts might find the analysis and summary tables of some use. To the best of my knowledge, no similar work exists in the literature today, which is the real purpose behind this book. I have been looking for a single-volume book on warships for over twenty years and finally decided to write it myself. Whether I succeed will be left to the reader.

Acknowledgments

I would like to thank several people, either for supplying me with information or taking the time to read and comment on the book. They are Rear Adm. Ze'ev Almog, Israeli Navy (Ret.); A. D. Baker III; Bob Dulin; Larry Cavaiola; Tim Francis; Rear Adm. Franco Gay, Italian Navy (Ret.); Dick Garritson; Cdr. James Goldrick, RAN; Frederick Hocker; Tom Hone; Steve Keller; Andrew Lambert; Reuven Leopold; Ed Marolda; Paul Martineau; Spence Johnson; Rear Adm. Francesco Pascazio, Italian Navy (Ret.); Craig Symonds; Milan Vego; Stan Weeks; and David Winkler. Special thanks to the Naval Institute Press and especially Mark Gatlin, J. Randall Baldini, Sara Elder, and Trudie Calvert, who had the tedious chore of editing the book. Finally, I would like to thank my beloved proofreader and coffee maker, my wife, Jeanne.

Abbreviations

THERE ARE LITERALLY dozens, perhaps even hundreds, of abbreviations used by the world's navies. Below are some of the more frequently used, and although most of these are actually United States Navy abbreviations, they are now generally accepted worldwide, at least in the Western press.

AA Antiair
AAW Antiair warfare
ACR Armored cruiser
AE Ammunition ship
AF Stores ship
AFS Combat stores ship
AIP Air-independent propulsion (for submarines)
AO Oiler
AOE Fast combat support ship
AOR Replenishment oiler
APD High-speed transport (modified DDs and DEs)
ASDIC British name for sonar (for Anti-Submarine Detection Investigation Committee)
ASuW Antisurface warfare
ASW Antisubmarine Warfare
ASTOVL Advanced short takeoff/vertical landing (airplane)
BB Battleship
BC Battle cruiser
CA Heavy cruiser
CAG Guided missile heavy cruiser
CC Command ship
CG Guided missile cruiser

CGN Guided missile cruiser, nuclear powered
CIC Combat Information Center
CL Light cruiser
CLG Guided missile light cruiser
CMB Coastal motorboat
CTOL Conventional takeoff and landing (airplane)
CV Aircraft carrier
CVA Attack aircraft carrier
CVE Escort carrier
CVN Aircraft carrier, nuclear powered
CVS ASW aircraft carrier
DD Destroyer (non-guided missile)
DDE Destroyer, ASW
DDG Guided missile destroyer
DDR Radar picket destroyer
DE Destroyer escort
DL Destroyer leader (frigate in USN before 1975)
DLG Guided missile frigate
FAC Fast attack craft
FF Frigate
FFG Guided missile frigate

"G" Guided missile designation; e.g., DDG—guided missile destroyer

LCAC Landing craft air-cushion

LCVP Landing craft vehicle and personnel

LHA Amphibious assault ship

LHD Amphibious assault ship

LPD Amphibious transport dock

LPH Amphibious assault ship (helicopter)

LSD Dock landing ship

LST Tank landing ship

MCM Mine countermeasures ship

MHC Mine-hunter, coastal

MSO Minesweeper, ocean

MTB Motor torpedo boat

"N" Nuclear designation; e.g., SSN—nuclear-powered submarine

OPV Offshore patrol vessel

PC Protected cruiser

PC Patrol craft

PT Torpedo patrol boat

RN Royal Navy

SAM Surface-to-air missile

SLBM Submarine-launched ballistic missile

SS Submarine, conventional powered

SSBN Ballistic missile submarine, nuclear powered

SSG Guided missile submarine, conventional powered

SSN Submarine, nuclear powered

STOVL Short takeoff/vertical landing (airplane)

SWATH Small waterplane-area twin hull (ship)

TBD Torpedo boat destroyer (early destroyer)

TT Torpedo tubes

UNREP Underway replenishment

USN United States Navy

VERTREP Vertical replenishment (by helicopter)

VLS Vertical launch system (for missiles)

V/STOL Vertical and/or short takeoff and landing (airplane)

Conversion Ratios

1 inch = 25.4 mm
1 meter = 3.3 feet

Some Standard Gun Sizes

3 inch = 76 mm
4.7 inch = 120 mm
5 inch = 127 mm
6 inch = 152 mm
8 inch = 204 mm
11 inch = 280 mm
12 inch = 305 mm
15 inch = 381 mm
16 inch = 406 mm

History of Warships

Introduction

1

MAN WENT TO sea for four basic reasons: first, for food, second, for the classic "because it was there," which led to the third reason, exploration, and, finally, for commerce. Shipping by water was, and remains to this day, the most efficient, cheapest way to transport goods and troops, with the latter considered the origin of the first use of ships for military purposes. This led to the development of warships in two stages. The first were armed merchantmen to protect that commerce. Pirating was rampant throughout ancient history, continuing off and on until the early nineteenth century, and at least a few armed merchantmen were needed to protect shipping. Although pirates might be stopped with armed merchantmen, nations started building fleets, which led to navies and a second stage, the building of specialized ships for war. Thus began the history of warships.

The long history of warships is usually divided into four periods or "ages": the Age of Galleys, the Age of Sail, a short transitional period called either the Age of Steam, Ironclads, Steel, Shell, or some variation of those words, and finally the Modern Age. The Age of Galleys is thought to have started around 2500 B.C., with the first recorded sea battle in 1190 B.C. The famous Battle of Lepanto in A.D. 1571 is usually cited as the end of the age, although galleys took part in Mediterranean sea battles for another 150 years and were still in use until the mid-nineteenth century in the Baltic.

Although the era of fighting sail can be traced to around A.D. 1200 with the use of armed merchantmen, "fighting cogs," the start of the Age of Sail is usually cited as the running Spanish Armada–English sea battle in 1588, only seventeen years after Lepanto. The last major engagement of the age was the Battle of Navarino Bay in 1827, and sailing warships still played major roles until the early 1850s. The start of the transitional Age of Steam and Ironclads began in 1814 with the launching of Robert Fulton's *Demologos*, but it was not until the mid-1850s that steam vessels starting replacing sailing ships of the line. Even then, most steam warships also carried sail into the 1880s. While modern warship types such as battleships, cruisers, destroyers, and even submarines can be traced to the 1880–90 time frame, the launching of the famous *Dreadnought* in 1906, making "all else obsolete," is usually cited as the beginning of the Modern Age.

In short, and as will be explained in more detail in the appropriate chapters, although there are some generally acceptable dates and conventions, there are, in fact, no simple starting and ending points between the ages and there is considerable overlap. That is not the only problem in writing a history of warships. While the book will attempt to point out firsts and lasts, largest and smallest, and some unique warship types, the primary purpose is to examine the most common types and the most common interpretations. But the reader should be forewarned of four caveats. First, for every common type, there is at least one exception, usually several. Second, over the life of most warships, changes were inevitably made. Even during the Age of Galleys, a ship's configuration would often change, and that is the standard practice for all modern ships. Third, even in common classes, especially large classes, the first and last are often different in some manner. For example, in the large sixty-two-ship U.S. Navy *Los Angeles* submarine class, there are three very distinct variations. Finally, for every common interpretation there is invariably at least one contrary viewpoint. In the larger scheme of things, however, these differences are usually minor and where they are significant, for example the upgrading of the Japanese *Mogami* class of the World War II era from a light to heavy cruiser, they will be noted.

Finally, some notes and caveats on terminology that unfortunately sometimes adds to the confusion. The two most confusing are a ship's dates and their weights or displacement as it is called in nautical terms. The problem with dates is not enough information in ancient times and then too much during more modern periods. There is a paucity of exact information for most of the Age of Galleys and even into the early years of the Age of Sail, which is the reason for rounding dates in most cases. Starting with the large ships of the line in the eighteenth century and especially with modern ships, the problem is sometimes too much information and the use of several different dates: when they were authorized, when started or keels laid, when launched or put into the water, when completed, and finally when they joined the fleet or were commissioned. For most modern ships, there is at least a year between each of these events. Europeans usually cite launch dates as a ship's beginning, Americans commissioning date, but there are no standards. I will try to be specific, but readers who have seen other dates should not assume one or the other is necessarily wrong.

The issue of weight or displacement is sometimes even more confusing, but it is important to understand because, along with weapon systems, most navalists consider tonnage rather than length and width a better measurement for comparisons since it indicates amount of armor and weaponry. For example, both British World War I light cruisers and 1890s-era first-class armored cruisers were around 450 feet long, but the light cruisers with little armor and 6-inch guns were only 4,200-odd tons, the armored cruisers with 6-inch armor belts and up to 9-inch guns over 10,000 tons. Because most people can visualize length and width more easily than tonnage, they will also be listed occasionally, usually written 300 by 50 feet, that is, 300 feet overall length with a 50-foot beam.

Then there is the issue of the weight itself. Traditionally, most books listed the "standard displacement," which is the ship's weight *minus* water and fuel but including ammunition. This definition stems from the interwar naval treaties in which "standard" displacement was used. Standard displacement varies from the actual or deep load, and the differences can be significant. For example, the British *Kent*-class heavy cruisers were listed at 9,800 tons standard to conform to the Washington Treaty, but their real or deep load was about 13,500—a significant 30 percent difference.

These technicalities can be important. A 7,000-ton "light" cruiser with 6-inch guns was quite a different matter—especially for an opponent—from a 13,500-ton "heavy" cruiser with 8-inch guns and the various *Los Angeles*-class upgrades, and distinctions can be important in certain situations. Yet most of these differences are minor in the larger picture and certainly beyond the scope of this book to detail except when they are truly significant. The reader should be aware of these more technical issues such as displacement, dates, differences within common classes, and the like, which unfortunately are not usually explained in most books, sometimes causing confusion later.

THE BOOK WILL proceed in chronological order through the ages, with concentration on the Modern Age for one simple reason. There are more significant differences between warship types during the Modern Age. There were, of course, differences during the earlier ages. In the Age of Galleys there were at least a dozen identifiable types. Not too many years ago, many books cited virtually no changes between ships of the line from 1700 to 1850, but recent scholarship has proven otherwise. Yet the differences between the types in these early ages are relatively minor, especially when compared to those between a battleship, a submarine, and an aircraft carrier. This concentration on the Modern Age does not, incidentally, necessarily mean they were more important. In fact, without question, the greatest influence of warships on the history of the world came during the Age of Sail.

Finally, while the book will attempt not to be overly parochial, for reasons of both available records and dominance during certain periods, concentrations on certain navies is unavoidable. For example, one reason for the concentration on the Greeks during ancient times, besides the fact they were a great people with an interesting history, is that they left extensive records, whereas the Phoenicians, also great seafaring peoples, left very few. Again, one reason for the concentration on the Royal Navy during the Ages of Sail and Ironclads was their dominance, but another is that there are better records and books, at least in the English language. This dominance, however, does not necessarily mean they were the most important in the development of warships. For example, many consider that the French built better ships during the Age of Sail, whereas during the Age of Ironclads many of the innovations came from the lesser navies, but invariably England, with its greater industrial capacity, was able to adapt these new ideas more readily.

From dugouts to dreadnoughts, skin boats to submarines, coracles to aircraft carriers, understanding warship evolution is important and not just for navy history. Throughout history, warships have been the most complex piece of machinery of their day. During the Age of Galleys the weaponry crammed aboard these small ships would, on a comparative basis, put a sophisticated modern ship to shame, and they were considerably more complex than any land equipment. It was not until the invention of the airplane in 1903 that another intricate piece of weaponry would join inventories. Yet, even today, with the possible exception of the space shuttle, warships are still the most complex piece of "self-sustaining" weaponry able to operate for days, weeks, and even months on end. But more important, understanding navies and seapower requires understanding the history of warships.

EARLY HISTORY

The Age of Galleys
2

THE AGE OF GALLEYS was by far the longest, lasting for at least 2,500 to over 4,000 years, depending on definitions. Although galleys played minor roles through the eighteenth century in the Mediterranean and the mid-nineteenth in the Baltic, there is general agreement that the age ended with the Battle of Lepanto in A.D. 1571, the last major sea battle fought between galleys. The problem is pinpointing the beginning. What some scholars consider the first true warships, or what today would be called surface combatants, galleys built with rams, dates to around 900 B.C. The addition of a ram also, for the first time, required special construction differentiating war from merchant ships.

On the other hand, the first use of ships to transport troops dates to at least 2450 B.C. Since galleys beached, these could be considered the first amphibious ships, warships by most definitions. In between these two dates are others. The first navy is usually attributed to the Minoans, who ruled Crete from 2000 to 1500 B.C. The first recorded engagement at sea took place in 1475 B.C., the first naval blockade around 1370 B.C., the first standard warship, the penteconter, about 1250 B.C., and the first major sea battle in 1190 B.C. In short, the reader can pick a date, but surely the ram definition from 900 B.C. is too narrow since both the military uses of ships and navies date much earlier.

Besides dates, there are three other problems. First, the historical evidence on warship construction during the Age of Galleys is sketchy, relying mostly on a few reliefs and pictures on broken pottery with little archaeological evidence and only the briefest of written descriptions. This paucity of information has led to a second, definitional and nomenclature problem that has occupied scholars. Terms like *penteconter, trireme,* and especially the various polyreme designations of the "super-galleys" era have caused confusion in determining galley specifications. In one case these terms refer to the total number of oars, in another to the levels or banks of oarsmen, in still another to the number of rowers per oar, but there are exceptions, adding to the confusion.

Finally, for the galley, "it is difficult to trace the story of its development as a straightforward, self-contained whole," as one author put it.[1] In the other ages, the development of warships was generally larger, faster, more efficient, and more powerful. For the history of galleys, development is somewhat up and down, making it almost impossible to draw straight-line conclusions. There are, however, some fairly discernible subages or eras of galley types that make the story somewhat manageable. Before turning to these, first let us take a brief look at the very earliest history of water craft before the development of warships.

Early Rafts, Boats, and Ships

There were, of course, rafts, boats, and even seagoing ships for other uses long before their development into fighting machines, warships. This early development can be broken down into three broad periods.

IN THE BEGINNING: 200,000–4000 B.C.

Early man probably first went to sea, or more likely a quiet river, clutching a log sometime during the Lower Paleolithic period from 700,000 to 200,000 B.C. The first "sea battle" undoubtedly took place when two cavemen from different tribes met in midstream and the winner knocked the loser off his log. The next step up from logs is more conjectural. Earlier most believed a dugout was probably the next stage, but many now feel a skin boat came first and that this improvement took place during the Upper Paleolithic, Mesolithic, and Neolithic periods from 40,000 to 8000 B.C. The oldest known boat pictures dating to 8000 B.C. are Norwegian rock carvings of skin boats. One author deduces that such boats could have been built as early as 16,000 B.C.[2]

Evidence also exists from this period suggesting the migration of people between continents, either by then existing land bridges or primitive rafts and boats, as early as 30,000 B.C., and there is more definitive proof of movement between mainland Greece and the island of Melos from 11,000 to 8000 B.C. Pieces of obsidian, a hard volcanic stone found on Melos, have been unearthed on mainland Greece. Speculation has varied that these voyages were made either on dugouts, bundles of reeds, rafts of logs, inflated animal skins, or perhaps even frameless skin boats. A replica of a reed raft has made the journey. The earliest water craft that would have kept a person both afloat and dry was probably a skin boat called a coracle built with hides stretched over a light frame of branches. The earliest solid evidence of a vessel is a dugout, a hollow pine log, found in the Netherlands dating to 6315 B.C.[3]

THE RIVERINE PERIOD: 4000–3000 B.C.

The next period might be called the riverine era because most of what is known took place along rivers, by the Egyptians along the Nile and by the Mesopotamians in the fertile crescent of the Tigris and Euphrates. There is also some indication of similar activity in the Indus River culture and by the ancient Chinese along the Yellow River.[4] Sometime after 4000 B.C. the early Egyptians learned to waterproof the reeds (bulrushes) of the Nile, probably first into bundles lashed together and then later rafts. By 3500 B.C. they had shaped the reeds into simple boats. These early vessels were long and slender, pointed at each end, often described as spoon or crescent shaped. They were propelled with paddles and had a steering oar (also called quarter rudders) on the side. They were usually on the right side; this "steering side" is the derivative of the nautical term *starboard* for "right." To protect the quarter rudder, ships in port were docked on the other side, the derivative of the nautical term *port* for "left." Side-mounted quarter rudders would remain the method for steering throughout the Age of Galleys.

Sails were also used during this early period, and by 3500 B.C. they had developed into the familiar square-sail that became standard throughout ancient times. The earliest picture of an Egyptian boat on a vase dated around 3500 B.C. shows a sail. Development also began in Mesopotamia (modern Iraq) at about the same time. A clay model, probably of a Mesopotamian skin boat (coracle), has been dated to 3400 B.C. This riverine period continued through the fourth millennium and perhaps as late as 2700 B.C.[5]

EARLY SEAGOING VESSELS: 3000–2500 B.C.

Sometime after 3000 B.C., three important innovations took place. These were the appearance of wooden planked vessels, the first evidence of seagoing ships, and then the switching from paddles to oars. Thus was finally born the seagoing galley.

The first step was the building of boats entirely of wooden planks. A main chronicler of this ancient period, Lionel Casson, theorizes that early planked boats were dugouts with their sides built up with boards and frames later inserted for strength. There is some indication that the planks on these early boats were sewed together. These planked boats might have appeared first in the Aegean areas, where wood was more abundant. The best evidence for these, however, dates from around 2700 B.C., when the Egyptians developed a stone architecture requiring sturdier vessels than reed boats to carry the stone.[6]

The ancient peoples developed a construction method that was to last over four thousand years. This was what modern scholars call the "shell"

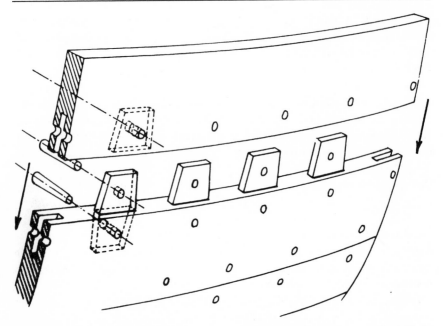

FIGURE 2.1 The mortise-and-tenon joint system used for the shell construction method. Plank seams were attached by tenons that fit into mortises and were then secured with dowels. (Drawing by John Coates)

method. Unlike today's boats that are built with the internal frame work first, followed by the attachment of planks, the ancients took the opposite approach. That is, a keel would be laid with planks attached and built up as an integrated shell and frames later inserted for strength. The boards were fastened edge-to-edge with an intricate tongue-in-groove arrangement of mortises and tenons as shown in figure 2.1[7] (Later this edge-to-edge arrangement would be called the "carvel" planking method as contrasted to an overlapping or "clinker" method, which was used in northern Europe.)

The Egyptians also early on solved a difficulty that plagued larger wooden boats when they went from calm rivers to more rough seas. This was the problem of the ends drooping, or "hogging," as it is called in nautical terms. The Egyptians used a rope cable that ran from the bow to the stern with a Spanish windlass, a tourniquet-like device, for tightening the ends to resist hogging. Perhaps ironically, the hogging problem, which generally restricted all wooden ships to less than 200 feet, would not be completely solved until the early nineteenth century, on the eve of the Age of Ironclads and Steel, when it was no longer needed.

The next step was the first evidence of seagoing vessels for carrying cedar logs from the Levant (modern Lebanon) since Egypt did not have the appropriate wood for building ships. By 2600 B.C. trade was so well established between Egypt and Byblos (near modern-day Beirut) that early merchantmen were called "Byblos-ships." There was also trade between Mesopotamia and Persian Gulf countries and perhaps even India. And there is evidence of sea-going vessels in the Aegean during this period.

Finally, sometime after 2500 B.C., oars started to replace paddles, an important, more energy-efficient step for three reasons. Rowing allows the muscles of the lower body to be used, not just the upper back and arms used in paddling, and the oarlock device allows for more energy efficiency to propel the ship. Furthermore, while a paddler must sit close to the water, oarsmen have more flexibility. They can be placed inboard and, more impor-tant, they can either be on different levels or several men can be put to a single oar, generating more speed.

Thus, by the mid-third millennium B.C., the stage was set for the emer-gence of seagoing fighting galleys. Although the shape of ships would change many times during the Age of Galleys, the basic building method of shell construction and side-mounted steering rudder with usually some type of antihogging device was well established. With only slight modifications, this construction method would last for over four thousand years, not changing until around A.D. 1200–1300 of the medieval period.

The Mediterranean Galley

Although galleys were constructed in other areas, most of what is known took place in the Mediterranean. The story of the Mediterranean galley can be broken down into the following stages.

THE PENTECONTER AND OTHER EARLY WARSHIPS: 2500–900 B.C.

Not surprisingly, the first military use of ships was for the transportation of troops, and since vessels in those days beached, they would today be consid-ered amphibious ships. Although it can probably be safely assumed that ancient man very early on deduced the utility of using ships for transporting troops, solid evidence for such use does not exist until 2450 B.C. Around that time, Pharaoh Sahure built a fleet to transport an army to the Levant and later had this event documented by carvings on the walls of his pyramid. This is also the earliest picture of a seagoing ship and clearly shows the cable device to prevent the hogging. Whether these were specially designed troop transports or modified merchantmen is unknown.

Warships also appeared in the Aegean Sea around 2500 B.C. Lead models and ships portrayed on terra-cotta "frying pans" found on the Aegean Sea islands of Naxo and Syros show low, slender boats that were probably meant to carry troops and not cargo.[8] According to Thucydides, however, writing in the fifth century B.C.: "Minos is the first to whom the tradition ascribes the possession of a navy. He made himself master of a great part of what is now termed the Hellenic Sea; he conquered the isles of the Aegean and was the first colonizer of them." For years Minos was thought to be simply an ancient myth repeated by Thucydides. In A.D. 1900 diggings began in Crete, and subsequent findings confirmed Thucydides' writings. Thus, to the Minoans who ruled Crete from approximately 2000 to 1500 B.C. usually goes the distinction of having the first navy.

One painted frieze uncovered on the volcanic island of Thera dating to 1600 B.C. shows a long, slender decorated galley with approximately twenty paddlers. Since oars were in use by this time, there is some speculation that this might have been a ceremonial vessel. Another part of the broken frieze shows what appears to be a galley with low parapets at the bow and stern with a lone marine, spear in hand, standing watch on the bow.[9] These longer and more slender craft were clearly not merchantmen. Later, galleys would become known as "long" and sailing merchantmen as "round" ships.[10]

There are, unfortunately, few records of the Minoan navy, but it was clearly powerful. Further excavations have concluded that the Minoan cities were not walled—an extremely dangerous practice in those violent ancient times—indicating that this island nation relied solely upon its navy for protection. The lack of walls might have eventually led to the Minoans' downfall. They traded with the Mycenaeans of Greece, who over the years grew stronger, eventually invading and conquering Crete around 1450 B.C. Without walled cities for protection, the Minoans might have challenged the Mycenaeans on the beach, perhaps making this the first opposed amphibious landing.

The Mycenaean Age lasted from approximately 1500 to 1200 B.C. This was also the age of the Homeric epics, at one time considered myths. Now, stories such as Agamemnon's attack on Troy are thought to be true if somewhat exaggerated. Although a powerful city-state, Troy apparently had no navy, so the Mycenaeans could attack at their leisure. While the Minoans might have been foolish not to have walled cities, the Trojans were equally foolish not to have a navy—early examples of the dangers of relying on one-dimensional defenses.

More important for the history of warships, to the Mycenaeans goes the distinction of developing the first standard warship—the penteconter. In both the *Iliad* and the *Odyssey,* the Mycenaean galleys described by Homer are twenty- and fifty-oared with the latter the desired size for transporting troops. This was the "fifty-er," *pentekontoros,* or *penteconter,* as it is usually written in English (sometimes spelled with an "o"—pentecontor). The pente-conter was described as a galley with a total of fifty rowers, twenty-five to a side. There is later evidence of a triacontor, a thirty-oared galley. The pente-conter, which appeared some time between 1300 and 1200 B.C., became the somewhat standard war galley until the appearance of the trireme around 500 B.C. and would never completely disappear. Based on space requirements for oarsmen, it has been estimated that the penteconter was approximately 125 feet long and 13 feet wide.[11]

The Egyptians never disappeared from the seas, and to them must be credited three important firsts: the first recorded incident at sea, the first naval blockade, and the first sea battle. During the time of Thutmose III, from 1504 to 1550 B.C., Egypt once again reasserted its influence in the Levant, using galleys to transport its armies. On their return from his fifth campaign around 1475 B.C., ships of Thutmose's fleet seized two ships which Casson calls "the first act of piracy on record."[12] A hundred years later around 1370 B.C., one of Thutmose's successors refused to come to the aid of Byblos. An enemy fleet seized their ships and later imposed a blockade, forcing Byblos to capitulate—the first recorded sea blockade.[13]

This attack on Byblos was carried out by people called sea raiders or rovers, who began to appear around 1400 B.C. These sea rovers have been compared to the hordes that would later come out of Eurasia. By 1200 B.C. they became more dominant and brought on an ancient "dark ages" period (now sometimes debated) that lasted until around 900 B.C. Little is known about these raiders, especially one group simply called the "Sea People."[14] They are important, however, because they precipitated the first recorded sea battles. According to one scholar, the first recorded sea battle took place in 1210 B.C. when the king of the Hittites defeated and burned an allied Cypriot–Sea Peoples fleet.[15]

The much better known (and usually cited as the first) recorded sea battle took place around 1190 B.C., when an Egyptian fleet defeated a Sea Peoples fleet. This victory was carved in detail on a great temple near Thebes, the only picture of a sea battle from the ancient world. The Egyptian ships have a curved hull with a low prow and stern and a single bank of oars. The Egyptians are shown using bow and arrow. The Sea Peoples' ships appear smaller, less curved, with higher stem and sternpost, both with a bird's head as an ornament. The lack of oars on their boats has been interpreted to indicate the Sea Peoples were caught off guard, not that these were sailing ships. This was an important, perhaps even a major, "strategic" sea battle. The Sea Peoples had come out of the eastern Mediterranean sweeping many of the other empires before them. Had they not been stopped by the Egyptians, world history might have been quite different.

RAMS AND BIREMES: 900–500 B.C.

Sometime after 1000 B.C., probably around 900 B.C., an event took place that Casson describes as being as revolutionary as the introduction of cannon at sea. This was the appearance of the ram. For the first time, warships were no longer merely troop transports but became what today would be called surface combatants. The first solid indication comes from an 850 B.C. ornamental pin found at Athens with Greek vases dating from 850 to 700 B.C. also showing galleys with rams. This important development also came as the world was in the transition from the Bronze to the Iron Age.

One scholar even dates the start of the Age of Galleys from introduction of the ram.[16] There is some justification for this definition. Although the Minoans, Mycenaeans, and others built war galleys, most were really troop transports. The distinction between ship types was not really significant, and merchantmen often were pressed into service as warships during emergencies. Now, for the first time, ships had to be built differently and considerably stronger to support this new weapon. No longer would a modified merchantman suffice. In addition, only the richer states could afford to build these ships, which might have been at least one reason why the introduction of the ram coincides with the demise of the sea raiders and the end of the ancient dark ages. Sea raiders could build small, swift boats for pirating and raids, but they might not have had the skill and especially the resources to build the larger ships. These stronger, ram-fitted galleys would probably have made short work of any remaining sea rovers and pirates still sailing with old, light galleys. In short, though using the introduction of the ram to date the start of the Age of Galleys might be too limiting, it nevertheless was a major threshold in the development of warships.

Two other changes occurred during this period. The first was the development of two types of galleys, one open, the other with a superstructure. The open galleys or "aphracts," had a lighter hull with a low rail along the sides and a less massive brow. These aphracts are thought to have been only troop carriers because they are never pictured in combat. Rather, those shown in combat have a raised deck superstructure that runs the length of the ship, protecting the oarsmen while providing a platform for the warriors. This latter type also served as a transition to the next major change, the introduction of two-banked biremes.

The ram required strong and fast ships to support and use this new weapon. For strength, one step was addition of a full-length deck that reinforced the hull, and another was building up the prow for the ram. For speed for ramming, more oars, oarsmen, or both had to be added, and thus the two-level galley or bireme was developed. The bireme's exact origins are obscure but took place sometime during the eighth century, probably around 775 B.C. From the scant evidence available, it appears that bireme development went through two stages. Painting on pieces of broken pottery from around 750 B.C. indicate that a second bank of oarsmen was simply placed on the superstructure deck above those already at the sheer (or gunwales in modern terms). This was a top-heavy arrangement that left little room for marines. Later versions show the upper level at the sheer with the lower oars worked through small ports in the hull. To conserve space, the levels were then staggered, not one atop the other. A relief of Phoenician biremes from the palace of Sennacherib, who reigned from 705 to 681 B.C., seems to show this two-level staggered arrangement, leaving the superstructure deck for the marines. The staggered arrangement also meant that a galley could be more compact and stronger for ramming. The standard was still the penteconter, but instead of twenty-five oars to each side in a single row, the bireme had them in two levels. The galley could thus be shortened considerably to about 65 feet from the 125 for the single-level penteconter.[17]

Unfortunately, no records exist of these Phoenician biremes in battle, but since Phoenicia was the dominant power until the revival of the Greek states in the seventh century, there were undoubtedly at least a few. The bireme remained the main ship of the line for over two hundred years before being replaced by the trireme around 500 B.C., and it never fully disappeared from ancient fleets. (Two-banked liburnians became the backbone of the later Roman navy.) While the Greek trireme usually receives the most attention, in fact, in the history of warship development, this period with the introduction of the ram and the bireme was probably more important.

THE GREEK TRIREME: 725–400 B.C.

The Greek trireme is by far the most famous of the ancient galleys for several reasons. Its use as the standard warship starting around 500 B.C. coincides with two great struggles in ancient times: between the Greeks and Persia at the beginning and then the Peloponnesian civil wars at the end of that century. In both these conflicts, triremes played crucial roles. It was also the time of the world's first historians, Herodotus and Thucydides, author of *The Peloponnesian War,* so for the first time detailed accounts exist. Some naval inventory records have also survived although none describe the trireme in blueprint detail, which led to a debate about their actual construction called the "trireme question" in the literature.

According to Thucydides, "The Corinthians were the first to turn to ship-design that was very close to the modern fashion, and the earliest Greek triremes were built in Corinth." This was thought to have taken place as early as 725 B.C. No description of these first triremes exists, but probably another layer of oarsmen was simply added to the existing biremes, perhaps by placing them on the superstructure deck. These early triremes played only minor roles with their main development coming around 500 B.C.

To the Corinthians, however, goes another first that bears brief mention. Corinth was the first Greek state to reemerge from the ancient dark ages. By 600 B.C. their interests had become so far-flung that they were faced with what today would be called a two-ocean problem. Although its location on an isthmus made commerce in two directions easier, Corinth was unable to afford two fleets to protect those interests. The Corinthians first thought about a canal but gave it up as too expensive. Rather, they built a primitive railroad called a *diolkos* complete with tracks and wheeled carts pulled by oxen that could transfer the galleys between the two seas.[18]

The term *trireme* is an English translation of the Latin *triremis*, which means three-oared. The Roman and Greek navy men, however, used the term *trieres*, translated as "three-fitted." What "three-fitted" exactly meant led to some confusion. The term *triaconter* (thirty-er) referred to the total number of oarsmen in the crew. Since the term *trieres* was clearly different from triaconter, it was thought to have a different meaning, probably indicating three levels. During the sixteenth century, scholars questioned the feasibility of three levels (and especially the fours and fives that began to appear during the Age of Polyremes to be described below). Based on their own sixteenth-century galleys, they speculated that "three-fitted" meant three oarsmen on the same row. The debate has now been settled, and more recent scholars agree that a trireme was indeed a three-level galley. Further proof came through the reconstruction of a trireme called *Olympias* in 1987 under the supervision of another scholar of this period, John Morrison.[19]

Although exact details are still unknown, according to naval inventory records, much is clear, including the names and numbers of oarsmen on each level. There were twenty-seven rowers on the bottom level, called thalamites because they were seated in the hold or *thalamos*. They worked their oars through small ports in the hull only 18 to 30 inches above the waterline. To keep out the water, a leather bag was fitted around the oar. On the next level were twenty-seven zygites, so named for the *zygos*, the beam on which they sat. They also worked their oars through holes in the hull just below the sheer of the ship. What differentiated the trireme from the bireme was a third level of thirty-one rowers called thranites because they sat on a *thranos*, who worked their oars from an outrigger or *parexeiresia*. This outrigger (not to be confused with the South Pacific island canoe outrigger) was actually more an overhang which allowed for a third level without increasing the height of the ship. Finally, for compactness, the triremes, like the biremes, had staggered banks.

As can also be seen from the picture of the *Olympias*, these were extremely cramped quarters. All told, the crew of a trireme numbered about 200. There were 170 oarsmen—27 thalamites and zygites each and 31 thranites to each side. In addition, there were 5 officers: a captain, who in Athenian times was usually a political appointee, the second in charge called the helmsman, the time-beater in charge of rowing, a fourth for various administrative duties such as paymaster, and finally the bow officer. Besides the rowers, there were a handful of other sailors, including carpenters and deckhands to handle the sails and quarter rudders. By this time the single steering oar had been

The *Olympias*, reconstruction of a Greek trireme.
(Paul Lipke, courtesy of the Trireme Trust)

replaced with two, one on each side. Finally, there were 14 marines, 10 with spears and 4 with bow and arrow.

About three feet above the upper (thranite) rowers was a full deck that stretched from prow to stern and to each gunwale. The deck served as a platform for the marines and also as a protective deck for the rowers. For further protection, a leather screen was hung from the deck to the gunwale to keep out arrows and other missiles. These "fenced-in" galleys were called cataphracts, as opposed to the aphracts or open galleys. Like all ancient ships, triremes were shell-built, had a cable device running from stem to stern to prevent hogging, and a flatter bottom for beaching.

The Athenians had a formal rating system that distinguished between new and old ships, later classified as "selects," "firsts," "seconds," "thirds," and "old" according to age. The life of a trireme was approximately twenty years. When not in use, they were hauled out of the water and placed in elaborate sheds. Much information on the trireme's dimensions comes from the ruins and records of these sheds. Based on the size of the shed's slipways, the *Olympias*'s measurements are 120 feet, 9 inches in length with a 17-foot, 9-inch beam.

There was also a formalized transportation force. Older triremes were used as "soldier-ships" (*stratiotis*), troop transports (*hoplitagogos*), and horse transports (*hippagogos*). For the soldier and transport ships, the two lower levels of oarsmen were not used; their seats were taken by troops. In the horse transports the lower-level seats were replaced with stalls.[20] Interestingly, there

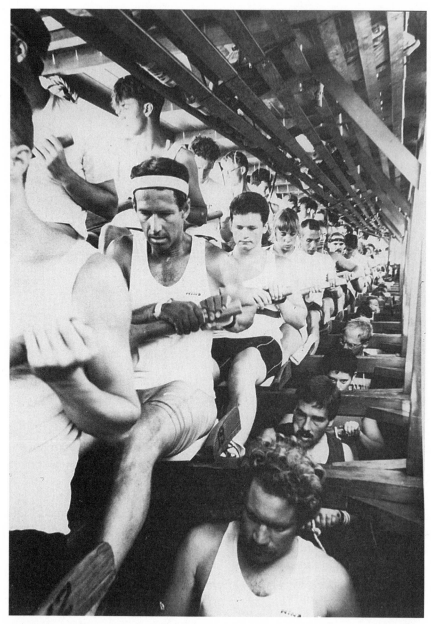

The interior of the *Olympias,* showing the three levels of rowers and the very confined quarters.
(Mary Pridgeon, courtesy of the Trireme Trust)

was no service force to supply the fleet, which meant that the navy, just like an army, had to live off the land. While galleys also put into shore each night for safety and comfort reasons, without a service force the traditional flexibility of a navy was limited. This deficiency would prove disastrous for Athens.[21]

The Greeks also adopted more formal fighting methods. The normal formation was for two opposing fleets to face each other line-abreast. Then, two main tactics were used: the *diekplus,* or "breaking through," and the *periplus,* or "sailing around." In the *diekplus,* the ship would dash through the enemy's line and then wheel around and ram him. The *periplus* was essentially a flanking movement in which the usually stronger side would send galleys around the end of the enemy line, then turn and hit him from the rear. These tactics required great skill, and, as a result, only the better navies, such as the Athenian fleet, used these maneuvers, whereas others stuck with simpler boarding practices. A third, more defensive move called the *kyklos* was also used. This was essentially a "circle the wagons" technique with sterns together and the prows and rams facing outward like the spokes of a wheel.

The ram also changed over the years. The early rams were pointed and, though effective, often endangered the attacker who found himself stuck in his opponent's hull. During the sixth century B.C. the shape was changed to a blunt face, which still damaged the enemy's hull but prevented the ram from becoming wedged. Still later a two-pronged device was used, finally developing into a fin-type design with three grooves, again, so as not to get wedged in an enemy's hull and to make a larger hole more difficult to fix.

In short, by the mid-fourth century B.C., the Athenian navy had developed into a very sophisticated force with different levels of fighting ships, new ram designs, complex tactics, a modern infrastructure, and even a transportation force. Not all states followed the Athenian lead. The Phoenicians, for example, accommodated the third level of oarsmen by adding to the height of the ship rather than using the outrigger. Tactics also varied with some navies still preferring old-fashioned boarding attacks rather than the more sophisticated ramming techniques. But the stage was now set for the full use of seapower.

THE FIRST DOCUMENTED use of the trireme occurred during the wars between the Greeks and Persia. The spark setting off the wars was the rising of the Ionians from Asia Minor against Persia in 497 B.C. The mainland Greeks came to their aid, and thus began a conflict that finally ended with the Peace of Callias in 448 B.C. The most famous campaigns, however, were the three major Persian invasions of Greece in 492, 490, and 480 B.C. The latter ended in what most historians consider the first great sea battle in history, the Battle of Salamis.

Besides great sea battles, these campaigns marked another first. To the Persians and a lesser extent the Greeks must go the honor of first conducting what today would be called combined land-sea operations. The Persian campaigns were very elaborate military efforts in which their huge army was supported by the navy. In fact, the first invasion of 492 B.C. was abandoned when the supporting fleet was destroyed in a storm off Mount Athos. In the third campaign, Xerxes would build a canal through the Mount Athos isthmus to avoid that problem. It was during this campaign that a pontoon bridge of ships was thrown across the Hellespont (Dardanelles).

Although there were several naval engagements throughout these wars, some as far away as Egypt, the most famous was the Battle of Salamis in 480 B.C. Salamis was not only a decisive tactical but also a strategic victory for the Greeks that essentially ended the Persian threat. Xerxes had invaded Greece with 180,000 troops and 1,300 warships, most from Phoenicia and Egypt. At the Battle of Salamis, a Greek force of only 300 opposed a Persian fleet of some 800 ships. The two sides lined up line abreast facing each other, but in the narrow straits the Persians could not bring their superiority to bear. The Greeks, with their greater skill in ship handling, were able to sink 200 Persian ships, losing only 40 of their own. Although Persia still had a large fleet, it withdrew, never again to threaten the Greek city-states.

The Greeks had been united against Persia, but in the years following they split into two alliances, the Attica League under Athens, the major sea power, and the Peloponnesian league under Sparta, the major land power. It was almost inevitable that a war would ensue. Thus began the Peloponnesian War, which lasted from 431 to 404 B.C. This was a classic struggle between a land and sea power. For many years Athens essentially conceded the land to Sparta, retreating behind the safety of its walls and those of the seaport, Piraeus, connected by a long wall. Athens relied on its fleet to keep the sea lines of communications open for trade and food and for many years was successful.

But Athens made two fatal mistakes that eventually led to its downfall. The first was the Sicilian Campaign against Syracuse, which started in 415 B.C. A contest Athens expected to be easy instead bogged the city-state down for two years ending with its fleet trapped and defeated in Syracuse's outer harbor. In the closed harbor waters, the Athenians were not able to conduct their usual *diekplus* (breaking through) or *periplus* (sailing around) ramming movements and were defeated by the Syracuse fleet, which relied more on boarding tactics. In addition, Syracuse had modified its galleys, strengthening the bows and fitting heavier rams which proved effective in the closed waters.

The Syracuse defeat was the beginning of the end, which came in 405 B.C., when an Athenian fleet, caught off guard, was destroyed while beached foraging for food. Casson rather bluntly attributes this defeat to two factors:

"the curious features of ancient naval logistics, the cavalier fashion in which the vital manner of feeding the crews was treated," exacerbated by a "bone headed admiral" who had landed on a remote beach with no near market.[22] The Spartans had noticed this, and when the Athenians left to forage for food, the Spartans attacked and destroyed the Athenian galleys. With no fleet, Athens was defenseless and surrendered a year later. Thus for the lack of what today would be called service ships, an empire fell. Athens would rebuild its fleet but never regain the dominance it had during the fifth century.

POLYREMES, CATAPULTS, AND LEMBOS: 400–31 B.C.

The next, and in some respects last, stage in ancient galley development from triremes to polyremes covers the so-called Hellenistic Age from the death of Alexander the Great in 323 B.C. to the famous Battle of Actium in 31 B.C. This period includes the Diadochi (successor) War after Alexander's death, the Rome-Carthage Punic War, and the early Roman Empire years. The era of polyremes—which is really just a convenient term for all galleys larger than triremes—with "fours" (quadriremes), "fives" (quinqueremes), and "sixes" all the way up to a "forty," is in many respects the most interesting of all the galley periods since there was no one standard ship size such as a penteconter or trireme. Also, besides these larger super-galleys, several smaller galley types were developed for other missions. In addition, new weaponry appeared such as catapults, fire pots, and two ingenious boarding devices. In short, instead of the normal quantitative arms races to see who could build the most ships, for the first time there was now a distinct qualitative aspect as well.

The origins of the polyremes can be traced to 399 B.C., when Dionysius, the ruler of Syracuse, began building fours and fives, although Pliny has written that "Carthage was the first to build a 'four.'" They did not gain full acceptance for another half-century and did not come into their own until the struggles over Alexander's empire after his death in 323 B.C. Casson traces development of the polyreme in three stages: "first, from the trireme to the 'six,' by the first half of the fourth B.C.; second, from the 'six' to the 'sixteen,' between 315 and 288 B.C.; third, . . . more powerful types culminating in Ptolemy II's 'thirty,' between 288 and 246 B.C."[23]

Although there was some question about what trireme or "three-fitted" actually meant, the greatest source of confusion over galley construction can be traced to the era of the polyremes, and the reader is forewarned there is no simple or even totally accepted explanation. For many years it was assumed that like the trireme's arrangement of one rower per oar in three staggered banks, fours, fives, sixteens, and so on simply meant four, five, and sixteen levels or banks of single oarsmen. But though a four- or maybe even a five-bank galley might have been possible, common sense and simple physics raise the question whether a ship really could have had sixteen levels of rowers. No surviving archaeological findings exist that indicate galleys were ever built with more than three levels.

Hence a second theory arose that the numbers referred to the total oarsmen all pulling the same oar. This was the method used by the sixteenth-century galleys. But because records indicate that two- and three-level galleys still existed during this period, a third and now generally accepted theory has evolved positing that it was probably some combination of the two, that is, more than one oarsman per oar in several levels. Thus, a "four" meant one of the levels, probably the upper (thranite) bank, had two oarsmen. A "five" probably had two rowers on the upper two levels, and a "six" indicated two to each. This explains the fours, fives, and sixes. But there is still the question of the larger "thirty" and especially the huge "forty" built by Ptolemy IV around 215 B.C. A Greek writer of the period describes the "forty" as "double-prowed and double-sterned," 420 feet long, 57 feet wide, with more than 4,000 oarsmen, 400 other crew, and 2,850 marines. Casson's conclusion was that "double-prowed and double sterned" meant it was probably two "twenty" hulls joined together, or what today would be called a catamaran.[24]

Despite all these explanations, however, there are still some inconsistencies. For example, while it appears that the fourth-century B.C. Roman "fives" were triremes with three levels of rowers, the first-century B.C. Roman "fives" were single level, with five rowers to a single oar. Yet both are "quinqueremes." In short, while the polyreme numbers refer to the number of oarsmen per side, the actual arrangement or number of levels is unknown. An "eight," for example, could have been either a three-level trireme with rowers in a three-three-two arrangement, a bireme with four rowers per bank, or a single-level galley with all eight pulling the same oar.[25]

While the solution to the riddles of these oar arrangements is important for scholars to pursue, equally important for warships is their weapons. During this same period, another major system was added to the galley's arsenal—the catapult. The first use of a catapult for land sieges against walled cities is attributed to Dionysius I's engineers around 400 B.C. These first catapults fired oversized arrows, but stone-throwing variations were soon developed. The first use from the sea is attributed to Alexander, who is said to have placed stone-throwing catapults on his older triremes for an assault against the walled Phoenician city of Tyre in 332 B.C. And the first use in a sea battle was a 307 B.C. engagement between Demetrius and Ptolemy I fighting over Alexander's empire. By this time, refinements had been made and catapults could fire arrows, stones, smaller darts, and even grappling hooks. Another device was the ballista, which threw arrows at low angles of fire whereas the catapult fired at a high angle.

Similar to the relationship between the ram and the development of the bireme and the trireme, there is a relationship between the catapult and the polyremes. Alexander's narrow triremes could accommodate only one or maybe two catapults, but the larger sixteens and twenties probably had enough deck space for a barrage and thus can be considered the predecessors to the Age of Sail's mortar ships, World War II rocket ships, and even the arsenal ship for cruise missiles once contemplated by the U.S. Navy. The larger deck of the polyremes also allowed for more marines, and boarding became more important. For greater height, collapsible towers were used, stowed during voyages and raised for battle. The first recorded use of towers was at the Battle of Chios in 201 B.C. Around 190 B.C. Rhodes came up with fire pots that foreshadowed the infamous Greek fire first used by the Byzantine navies. The fire pots were hung from long poles from the bow, presenting a dilemma to enemy ships. If the enemy turned away to avoid the fire pots, he made himself susceptible to ramming, but if he did not move, the pots would be dropped on his deck. Also during this period the Romans developed two new boarding devices. The ram was still important, but the larger polyreme decks allowing for catapults, towers, fire pots, boarding devices, and more marines added flexibility to the Hellenistic galley. Considering the small size of even the larger polyremes, on a comparative basis the weaponry crammed on these galleys would put a modern warship to shame.

Finally, during this period smaller galleys were developed for various missions from controlling pirates to minor war-fighting. There had, of course, always been smaller ships. The smaller penteconters and triaconters had never fully disappeared, but by 200 B.C. those particular names disappeared and new types were built. One of the first was the *hemiolia,* meaning "one-and-a-half," originally a pirate vessel that is first mentioned around 375 B.C. It had one and a half banks of rowers. To counter the *hemiolia,* around 300 B.C. Rhodes developed the *trieremiolia,* a two-and-a-half-bank galley. There is some confusion as to the rationale for these one and two and a halfs. According to Casson, the "half" was to leave room for sail to overtake slower galleys, although John Morrison claims the "half" was for extra oarsmen placed at the broader midship without increasing the overall size of the ship.[26] Another small galley developed around 200 B.C. was the *lembos.* Described only as fast ships, these were built in both one- and two-level variants with from fifty to only sixteen rowers, and most had rams. The *lembos* at the Battle of Chios in 201 B.C. are described by Casson as destroyers that "would dart in among the enemy's heavier units to break up their formation, interrupt their tactics, even do damage to their oars."[27] Later, the Romans would develop another smaller type called *liburnians,* which became the standard warship during the Roman Empire days.

ALTHOUGH ALEXANDER THE GREAT from Macedonia had the Greek fleets at his disposal, most of his conquests were on land, and galleys played only minor supporting roles. To Alexander, however, must still go several firsts. He was the first to use catapults at sea as siege weapons. Then, at least according to legend, he was lowered into the seas in a glass jar that is often cited as the first "submarine." Finally, the first recorded use of fire ships happened during his time. During his siege of the Phoenician city of Tyre, the Tyrians used fire ships effectively against a causeway Alexander had erected to attack the city.

Two great struggles during this period involved polyremes. The first was among Alexander's successors, and the second was the Punic Wars between Rome and Carthage. After Alexander died in 323 B.C., his successors engaged in a fight over his empire, the greatest of which was between Ptolemy I of Egypt and Antigonus the One-Eyed and his son Demetrius of Macedonia. While during the fourth century there had been a slow increase in the size of galleys from triremes to "sixes," Alexander's death touched off the greatest quantitative and qualitative naval arms races in ancient history. Antigonus in 315 started building "sevens," and his son Demetrius built eights, nines, up to thirteens, and later a fifteen and sixteen. Ptolemy II later built a twenty and thirty. These Diadochi (successor) Wars raged on until 280 B.C., with fighting over control of the seas lasting until around 200 B.C., when Rome started to become the dominant power.

One of the most famous battles was another Battle of Salamis (but off Cyprus, not the Peloponnesus) in 306 B.C., which was also the first appearance of the larger super-galleys. Ptolemy had more galleys, 140, but all were fours and fives. In that battle Demetrius had 118 ships, including 50 fives and fours, but he also had some new sevens. The battle opened with both sides using their catapults, but eventually the two sides engaged. In addition to having heavier units, Demetrius had another new device, wooden platform towers. This combination proved deadly, and the Egyptians fled the field. Salamis touched off a naval arms race that raged on for another twenty-five years, with each side building even larger units, that ended only with the defeat of Demetrius' son in 280 B.C. Although the polyremes never fully disappeared from the seas, these larger units were simply too expensive to operate, and most were laid up with only a few maintained as flagships.

By the first Punic War between Rome and Carthage from 264 to 241 B.C., the quinquereme, a five, had become the standard size in most fleets. Rome had become a powerful land power by 264 B.C. but still had virtually no navy. Carthage (modern-day Tunisia), a former colony of Phoenicia, one of the greatest of the ancient sea peoples, was the preeminent sea power of the times. Fortunately, the Romans captured a Carthaginian quinquereme early in the war, which they carefully studied and copied. Rome quickly built a fleet of one hundred quinqueremes but made them slightly heavier than the originals and more sluggish and less maneuverable for ramming. Rome's military advantage was her soldiers, not sailors, and boarding, not ramming, was more important. To further aid in boarding, the Romans came up with a new boarding-bridge device called the *corvus*. The corvus, or "raven" as it was called by the Roman sailors, was essentially a gangplank, 36 feet long, 4 feet wide, with a heavy spike at the end that was dropped on the enemy's deck allowing the Roman soldiers to board quickly and easily.

In the first clash between the two fleets at the Battle of Mylae in 260 B.C., a Roman fleet of 145 ships faced a Carthaginian fleet of 130. Although outnumbered, the confident Carthaginians attacked, violating one of the most basic tenets of warfare—underestimating your enemy. The new corvus proved decisive, and Rome won. Carthage also lost the second major Battle of Ecnomus in 256, where again the corvus proved itself. In 250 B.C. Carthage finally reacted, building lighter and faster fives that were able to outmaneuver the larger Roman galleys. Once again, however, Rome captured one of these new quinqueremes, made modifications, including eliminating the corvus, which had made their ships top-heavy, and was able to respond, eventually defeating Carthage.

Thus, in the relatively short space of about ten years, both sides made major tit-for-tat qualitative changes in their warships and tactics that in some respects would not be duplicated until World War II, when constant changes were needed to counter aircraft and submarines. Many of these changes were made possible only because Rome was able to copy captured Carthaginian ships—a problem that still sends chills down military leaders' spines, especially when introducing new weapon systems.

In the second Punic War, from 218 to 202, although there were few sea battles, seapower still played a vital role. By this time Carthage had lost control of the seas. Although Hannibal was able to invade and then terrorize Rome for several years, wandering around the countryside, he was never able to win a final, decisive battle. Without control of the sea, he was finally forced to leave, and Rome eventually invaded and destroyed Carthage.

After the Punic Wars, the old struggles between Macedonia and Egypt over Alexander's empire continued, with Rome finally entering the conflict after 200 B.C. At least according to legend, one new weapon was introduced during this period. Supposedly during one engagement, Hannibal, now a mercenary admiral, flung a pot of poisonous snakes at Roman ships, which might be the first instance of psychological warfare at sea.

There is some indication that about this time all the galleys, although still called mostly fours and fives, had switched from three to single banks, that is, with four or five rowers on the same bench pulling the same oar. There were a few larger units, mostly sevens, but usually just as flagships. And sometime during the first century B.C., the liburnian made its appearance in the Roman fleet. Simply described as a smaller, swift galley with one or two levels, it would later become the standard ship of the Roman fleet.

Finally in 48 B.C. the Roman civil wars began, the most famous of which was the struggle of Octavian versus Anthony and Cleopatra, ending in the last major sea battle of ancient times, the Battle of Actium in 31 B.C. During this period, yet another boarding device was developed called the *harpax* or "gripper." The *harpax* was an iron grapple which was hurled by a catapult at the enemy ship, then hauled in with a winch. In the final battle, Octavian had some four hundred triremes and liburnians and a few large fours, fives, and sixes against Anthony and Cleopatra's two hundred, but larger units, including a ten to carry the flag. Anthony had burned two hundred of his smaller galleys. Most unusual, Anthony had kept his sails on board rather than leaving them ashore as was the normal practice. The battle itself was somewhat anticlimactic. The most famous maneuver was Cleopatra's sailing through Octavian's line, but instead of executing a *diekplus,* she simply sailed away, with Anthony soon following.

Actium was an important, even strategic battle. It was the end of the Ptolemaic line and of the Egyptian Empire that had been a major power for four thousand years. It was also the start of the Roman Empire that lasted somewhat peacefully until late in the second century and did not completely end until the fifth century A.D. And it was also the end for the large fighting galleys for over a thousand years.[28]

ROMAN TRIREMES AND LIBURNIANS: 31 B.C. – A.D. 450

Actium in 31 B.C. was the last major sea action until the battle between Constantine and Licinius in A.D. 324, a period of over 350 years. Because there was no need for large battleships, except for a handful kept as flagships, the polyremes disappeared from the seas. A Roman-designed trireme reemerged as the largest standard ship for the main fleets, with the smaller liburnian the main unit for the provincial fleets. Both these ships originated in the earlier era but were then overshadowed by the larger units.

Sometime around 100 B.C., the Romans modified the original Greek trireme design, no longer using the outrigger for the upper (thranite) level of oarsmen but placing the thole pins through the hull of the ship as the Phoenicians did. But the outrigger, or at least some projection remained. Casson theorizes that this was kept as protection for the oars. One of the main tactics was shearing off an enemy's oars, and this projection might have "served as a massive bumper to shield the oarsmen."[29] Further modifications were made over the years. Around A.D. 150, the single-pointed ram reappeared, and then around A.D. 200, a large forecastle for marines was placed on some galleys. About this time the era of Pax Romana was starting to break down, piracy was escalating, and these modifications might be an indication that more sea battles were taking place.

The liburnian, first mentioned as taking part in the 36 B.C. Battle of Naulochus, probably also appeared sometime around 100 B.C. and is thought to have been a derivative of the *lembos*. They are described as small, open (aphract), two-bank galleys. The Roman fleet also maintained a handful of "fours" and "fives" in both single- and double-banked variations. During this period, captain's cabins became standard on most ships. Finally, although not a warship per se, perhaps the most unique vessel ever built, one that contributed to his reputation as one of the great scoundrels of history, must be credited to Nero. This was a collapsible galley designed to drown his mother. Although it apparently worked, she was able to swim safely to shore.

Rome developed a far-flung naval organization, with two main and several provincial fleets. The main fleet at Misenum in the Bay of Naples had 88 ships, including 1 "six," 1 "five," 10 "fours," 52 triremes, and 15 liburnians. The other home fleet at Ravenna in the northern Adriatic had 36 ships, including 2 "fives," 6 "fours," 23 triremes, and 4 liburnians. The provincial fleets that ranged from Germany and Britain in the Atlantic and throughout the Mediterranean into the Black Sea usually had one trireme as the flagship with the rest made up of liburnians.[30]

Because the Romans had no major powers as enemies, their navies were occupied clearing the sea of pirates and escorting grain ships from Egypt when Rome could no longer feed herself. The provincial forces acted as "fleets-in-being," sailing occasionally for "naval presence." There were no major sea threats to Rome until A.D. 254 when the Goths started appearing in the Aegean, and although most of the challenges came from land, there were a few sea battles. In A.D. 267 a Roman fleet defeated a Goth fleet of five hundred light galleys.

The end finally came when civil war broke out between the Roman leaders Constantine and Licinius. In A.D. 324 Licinius' fleet of three hundred-odd triremes faced Constantine's force of two hundred single-banked triaconters, and Constantine emerged the victor. It would be one of the few times that smaller ships would defeat larger ones, leading some historians to believe that Licinius' crews were not trained to handle the more complex triremes. Although usually not considered one of the major sea battles of history, this would turn out to be a major turning point. Six years later, in A.D. 330, Constantine (later called "the Great") moved the capital of the Roman Empire to the ancient Greek city of Byzantium, renamed it Constantinople (modern-day Istanbul), and thus began the approximately thousand-year Byzantine Empire. In A.D. 395 the Roman Empire was officially divided in two, and Rome was soon overrun by Goths, Franks, and Vandals while the Byzantine Empire would last until 1453, when Constantinople finally fell to the Turks.

Constantine's victory was a turning point for warships as well. The smaller liburnian would last for another hundred years, but the sea battle of A.D. 324 was the last for the trireme, the most famous of all the ancient galleys. The trireme in various forms had been a major warship type for almost a thousand years, from its invention around 700 B.C. by Corinth, and it was, perhaps, fitting that its demise should coincide with the end of the great Roman Empire.

DROMONS, GALEA, AND GREEK FIRE: A.D. 450–1250

With the passing of the Roman trireme, a smaller, single-bank liburnian became common until a new type, the dromon, or "racer," emerged sometime during the late fifth century. In various modes, the dromon remained the standard ship type until the appearance of the Venetian (or Mediterranean) galley in the thirteenth century. Unfortunately, very little is known of the dromon until the tenth-century writings of Leo VI the Wise. Another, smaller type also appears called the *galea,* more famous as the root for the English word *galley.* This period is perhaps best known not for any galley types but rather for a weapon system: Greek fire. Finally, during this time came an important construction change from the shell to the frame method and the first appearance of the triangular-shaped lateen sail.

Dromons are mentioned in late fifth-century writings, but the first details are from a Byzantine historian writing in A.D. 534: "And they had also ships of war prepared as for sea-fighting, to the number of ninety-two, and they were single-banked ships covered by decks, in order that the men rowing them might if possible not be exposed to the bolts of the enemy. Such boats are called *dromones* by those of the present time; for they are able to attain a great speed. In these sailed two thousand men of Byzantium, who were all rowers as well as fighting men." [31] The main source for dromons comes from the writings of the emperor Leo VI the Wise, who ruled from 886 to 911 but is better known for writing an extensive treatise on warfare, the *Tactica,* around 907.

The early dromons described by the Byzantine historian were single-bank, covered (cataphract), fast ships; there is some speculation that they might even have been liburnians with a new name. By the ninth century, dromons became larger, two-banked galleys in three sizes. The smallest was the *ousiakos,* so named because it carried one company or *ousia* of 108 men. Next in size was the *pamphylos* with 120 to 150 men, and finally the largest, the *chelandion,* or dromon with a crew of up to 300. Thus the term *dromon* was used both generically and specifically for the largest. Exact sizes are unknown, but based on arrangements of oarsmen, the dromons were probably 115 to 130 feet long. [32] To protect the rowers, a frame ran along the side to hang shields. The upper level of rowers sat above the main deck so they could join the battle in a boarding action. There also were parapet castles on both the forecastle and amidships for marines and various weapons.

More important from a construction viewpoint, sometime during this period shipbuilders switched from a strict shell method of building to a modified frame method. Instead of using thousands of pegged mortise-and-tenon joints to fasten the wooden planks, by the tenth century shipbuilders were relying more on frames.[33] This probably had another effect, the elimination of the ram, although the exact relationship is open to dispute. The older, more intricate, mortise-and-tenon method meant the galleys were able to absorb the shock of ramming. Once rammed, however, they were difficult to repair. Therefore, one author concludes, "The abandonment of mortise-and-tenon joinery may be another indication of the rarity of ramming, as the frame-based construction of the Byzantine period is poorly suited to distributing the shock of delivering a ramming blow."[34] Another takes the opposite opinion, speculating that the less intricate frame method of construction made damage control and repairs at sea easier, thus lessening the effect of ramming.[35] Later ships show rams above the water replaced by a prowlike device used for boarding. Also, by A.D. 880, the square sail in existence since 3500 B.C. had been replaced by the lateen, triangular-shaped sail, which had been introduced much earlier.

There were smaller ships called *moneres* and *galea,* described by Leo as "smaller and very swift dromons . . . quick and agile, which you use for patrol and other duties requiring speed." The *galea*'s lasting fame, however, was the Latin root for the English term *galley.* Another small type used by the Arabs was the dromonian.

During this period many new weapons appeared, including one of the most famous: Greek fire. The origins of Greek fire are unknown and may have been in the sixth century, but its first recorded use was by the Byzantines against the Arabs' initial siege of Constantinople from 673 to 679. The exact nature of Greek fire is also unknown, but it was probably some kind of naphtha mixture, perhaps similar to modern-day napalm. It was very effective and was successfully kept a state secret for over 150 years until a traitor disclosed the mixture to the Arabs in 827. Greek fire was used in two ways. The most common was a pump device located in the forecastle. Some of the larger ships also had two smaller, hand-held launchers for the sides. The other way was by catapults hurling an early version of a grenade that would explode when it hit the enemy's deck. There were other devices such as a crane that dropped large boulders through an enemy's deck and a pumping machine that filled his hold with water. Leo also writes about hurling pots of vipers and scorpions as Hannibal had done in ancient times. And there were still catapults hurling various weapons, including caltrops, small spiked devices with at least one point upward, which might be considered early versions of cluster mines.

Perhaps most interesting is the survival of Leo VI's *Tactica,* both a strategic and a tactical manual with topics ranging from preparation to battle, to tactical formations, to the use of signaling flags. Regarding strategy, Leo stressed prudence and preservation of the fleet, avoiding large sea battles, attacking the enemy only when his fleet was divided or even before they assembled.[36] Thus with Greek fire, viper pots, rock cranes, water pumps, catapults, crossbows, and a formal tactical and strategy manual, the dromon became a very complex fighting machine.

The period of the dromon covers the Byzantine Empire years from the era of Constantinople trying to defend the old Roman Empire through the rise of the Muslims after Mohammed died in 632, the conquests of Charlemagne and the Franks, the Crusades, and finally the emergence of the great Italian city-states such as Pisa, Genoa, and especially Venice. Throughout, seapower played a major role. Although there were many sea campaigns, among the most enduring throughout this period were those between Byzantine and the newly emerging Arab Muslims.

The Arabs were not seagoing people, but after they captured Alexandria with its shipyards in 640, they were able to build a fleet. Their ships, called *karabos,* were somewhat larger and slower but were generally similar to the various dromon types. In the Battle of the Masts in 655 the Muslims scored a major victory over the more experienced Byzantine fleet by chaining their ships together to form a floating fortress. They were then able to destroy the enemy ships with their boarding parties. This victory eventually led to a campaign that resulted in the first Muslim attack on Constantinople that was thwarted only when Kallinikos, a Syrian in Byzantine service, invented Greek fire, which surprised and decimated the invading Arab fleet.

Another assault on Constantinople from the East also deserves brief mention. In 865 early Russians of Scandinavian descent attacked using ships called *monozula,* which means a single piece of timber. Sometimes interpreted to mean dugouts, *monozula*s are thought to mean some kind of "clinker-built" craft similar to Viking longboats. Constantinople was able to withstand both these attacks by Muslims from the West and Russians from the East until finally succumbing to the Turks in 1453. While the walled city of Constantinople and the Byzantine armies were obviously important factors in keeping the invaders at bay for over a thousand years, the role of the navy was also important. The Byzantine navy and its control of the sea lines of communications kept Constantinople free for many years even when the city was surrounded by hostile land forces. For that purpose alone, the dromon was important. The Byzantine navy ceased to be an important aspect of defense after the eleventh century, as their borders retreated, which was one factor in their eventual downfall. But from a shipbuilding view, this was a crucial era during which the four-thousand-year-old shell construction method was replaced with the more flexible frame method.

THE VENETIAN GALLEY: A.D. 1250–1800

The Mediterranean galley would undergo one final evolution at the end of the thirteenth century that, with a modification of the oarsmen arrangement around 1550, would remain relatively unchanged until galleys finally disappeared at the turn of the nineteenth century. Most scholars agree, however, that the end of the long, four-thousand-odd-year Age of Galleys came not in 1800 but rather at the Battle of Lepanto in 1571, the last major sea battle fought between galleys. Another important change would take place during this time: the introduction of gunpowder and cannon at sea around 1350, but it would have only limited effect for another century and a half. Perhaps more important than any new warship design or weapon system was the development of the magnetic compass and the stern rudder during this period.

Although often referred to as the Venetian galley because Venice was the dominant power during the fourteenth and fifteenth centuries, this design was found in all the navies and for that reason the vessel is also sometimes called the Mediterranean galley. The exact origins of this last galley design have been lost to history, but it is known that the galley went through two phases based on the disposition of the rowers. The first was called *alla sensile* (or *zenzile*), which means "in the simple fashion," with each oar worked by a single oarsman, usually three all rowing from the same bench level. There is some indication that the early galleys had two rowers on the same bench, each with his own oar, but the standard developed by the mid-fourteenth century had three oarsmen. To facilitate this arrangement, with oars at different angles, the bench was angled, and as had been the case with ancient Greek triremes, there were outriggers which had a box shape when viewed from above. Galleys during this period were in the 152- by 16-foot range. This new oar arrangement has added to the confusion regarding galley nomenclature. Although the term *trireme* usually refers to the three-level arrangement, these Venetian galleys are also sometimes referred to as triremes, even though all three oarsmen were on the same bench.[37]

This *alla sensile* rowing system lasted for approximately three hundred years, replaced by the *a scaloccio* method in the mid-sixteenth century. The term *a scaloccio,* from *scala,* meaning "ladder" or "staircase," has caused some confusion for those looking for a literal meaning. As a practical matter, the term simply means the method was changed from each rower pulling his own oar to all pulling the same oar. Unlike the *alla sensile* method that required trained professionals with each to his oar, the *a scaloccio* oarsmen could be less skilled or even slaves and prisoners. In 1534, Venice experimented using three men to a single oar. While this proved less efficient than the *alla sensile* three-man oar arrangement, further experiments with four or five rowers to an oar proved successful. By 1570, all galleys had switched to this method. Four or five oarsmen was the standard, although a few larger flagship types had as many as seven.[38]

The other significant change during this period was the introduction of the cannon. The use of gunpowder in Europe has been traced to around 1320, and guns were carried on ships as early as 1337. Development was slow, however, and the presence of larger cannons was not apparent for another hundred years. Guns were not a significant presence until around 1500. Most galleys carried one large gun forward with two smaller guns on each side of the larger guns, still forward. Later, small guns on swivels were added along the sides. But cannon fire was still considered secondary to boarding until the seventeenth century. At the Battle of Lepanto, most of the attacks were boarding engagements.

The era of the Venetian galley covers the rise of the Italian city-states, the fall of the Byzantine Empire, the awakening of the Atlantic European countries, and the start of the Age of Discovery. In the Mediterranean there were many conflicts, including several between the Italian city-states, but the main struggle during the fifteenth and sixteenth centuries involved the European Christian countries trying to hold back the Ottoman Turks. The Ottomans under Selim I first consolidated all the Muslim countries in North Africa in the early sixteenth century. Sulieman the Magnificent, who ruled from 1520 to 1566, later concentrated on Europe.

The culmination of this Christian-Muslim struggle came at the Battle of Lepanto on 7 October 1571. A Christian coalition fleet of 210 galleys under the command of Don John of Austria met a Turkish fleet of 225 galleys at the entrance of the Gulf of Patrae on the Adriatic side of Greece. In the Christian fleet were a few of a new type of warship called galleasse. These were larger ships, made out of merchant galleys' hulls with a large forecastle for more cannons.

The two fleets met, and the Christians won a decisive victory, destroying or capturing 150 Turkish ships. Lepanto checked the Muslim advance, making it one of history's greatest strategic sea battles. More important for the history of warships, Lepanto was the last major sea battle fought between galleys. Just seventeen years later, in 1588, came the battle between the Spanish Armada and the English, which is usually considered the start of the Age of Sail.

Galleys did not, of course, immediately disappear, and, in fact, they played minor roles for another 150 years. In 1650, the start of the era of the sailing ships of the line, there were 220 to 260 galleys in Mediterranean fleets with 90 in 1740 and 6 still listed in 1800.[39] Galleys took part in Mediterranean sea battles throughout the seventeenth century. The Battle of Matapan in 1717 was the last major battle in which they participated. France finally did away with its galley service in 1748, but as late as 1797, galleys were

The Battle of Lepanto, 1571. The last major sea battle fought between galleys, it is usually cited as the end of the Age of Galleys even though such ships remained in some fleets for another 250 years.
(U.S. Naval Institute)

still being built by Venice and were present in the fleets of a few other smaller states. In 1798 some smaller 100-by 20-foot "half-galleys" were built. Napoleon used some of these for his expedition to Egypt in 1798, where they proved useful fighting on the Nile. The last half-galleys were built by the Sardinian navy in 1814.[40]

The last galley built in the Mediterranean was a reconstructed trireme for Napoleon III by the famed French ship designer Stanislas Dupuy de Lome in 1861. Perhaps somewhat fittingly, if ignobly, this trireme, the most classic of the ancient warships, met its fate as a target ship for one of the symbols of the dawning modern age, the then new torpedo.[41] Thus ended the Age of Galleys in the Mediterranean.

Galleys in Other Areas

There were, of course, galleys in other areas, although in no other region did they reach the full development or importance of the various Mediterranean war-fighting galleys.

THE VIKING LONG SHIP: A.D. 750–1200

After the Greek trireme, the Viking long ship or longboat is undoubtedly the best-known galley. Remains of northern warships have been found dating to 300 B.C.; the earliest example of a complete vessel dates to around A.D. 300. This so-called Nydam boat, excavated in a peat bog at Nydam, was double-ended with no deck, measured 78 feet long and 10.5 feet wide, and was propelled by fifteen oars to a side. Like most northern craft it was clinker (overlapping planks) built fastened with iron rivets.

It was not until the late eighth century A.D. that the Scandinavian Norsemen or Vikings swept down from the North to terrorize Europe off and on until the twelfth century. The ships used during the height of the Vikings' reign, from about 800 to 1050, were from 60 to 100 feet long. Their main warship during this period was the longboat, a sleek, open galley measuring approximately 76.5 feet long, 12.5 feet wide, with less than 3 feet of freeboard. Yet these relatively small galleys, comparable in size to the small Roman liburnian, sailed the seas throughout the North Atlantic through the Mediterranean and the Black Sea. It is now thought that those that traveled to North America were not longboats but a more sturdy, cargo-carrying type called a *knarr*.[42] Although there were several sea battles, the longboat was essentially a raiding ship. Around 1000, another type appeared, the larger *drakkars*, or dragon ships, some up to 150 feet long.

Unlike the Mediterranean ships, these Viking ships did not have rams. Although the larger dragon ships had raised platforms, throughout this era the Vikings fought with bow and arrows, spears, axes, and swords. During battles at sea, a standard procedure was simply to lash the longboats together in a fortress formation and essentially conduct land battles at sea. Although the Vikings did enter the Mediterranean during this period, there is no record of long-ship versus dromon battles, but the more fragile long ship might not have fared well.[43]

OTHER NORTHERN GALLEYS

The Vikings were not the only builders of galleys. England built a few galleys in the thirteenth and fourteenth centuries, although little is known of their design. Like all northern ships, they were clinker-built with a square-rigged sail. From the records available, we can ascertain that the ships were approximately 100 feet long yet had from 100 to 180 oarsmen. Since 50 oarsmen could not fit in such a space, these were probably biremes.[44] In 1515, Henry VIII built three classes of galleys. The most interesting was the *Great Galley,* a large ship with 207 guns. According to one account, she had 120 oars, to another 160. Originally clinker-built, the *Great Galley* was replanked carvel-fashion in 1523, although she was not the first to undergo what today would be called a major overhaul and refit. The *Sovereign,* also originally clinker-built in 1488, was rebuilt carvel fashion in 1509–10.

Except for the Viking longboats, galleys never played the major role in northern Europe that they did in the Mediterranean. In fact, on several occasions, the various rulers hired the fleets of Mediterranean city-states. For example, during the Hundred Years' War between England and France, from

1337 to 1453, the French several times rented a fleet of Genoese galleys. During the early Age of Sail, many of the smaller ships, including frigates, still carried oars (called sweeps) for maneuvering in port or when becalmed.[45]

It was in the northern, Baltic Sea waters, however, that galleys played their final role. Early in the eighteenth century, as galleys were being phased out in the Mediterranean, a mini–galley arms race was beginning in the closed waters of the Baltic between Sweden and Russia. Peter the Great launched his first large galleys in 1704, and the Swedes followed in 1712; the first major action between their galleys took place in 1714. Although the Russians built galleys up to 174 feet long and the Swedes at least one 154 feet long, most on both sides were around 100 feet. Sweden ceased building large galleys in 1749 and the Russians in 1796, although Russia continued building smaller rowing gunboats as late as 1854. (Other countries also built small oar-propelled gunboats in the nineteenth century, including the United States during the War of 1812.) The Russian gunboats were 74 feet by 17 feet, carried two guns, and were propelled by twenty pairs of oars. In August 1854 some of these gunboats engaged British ships off Turku in what was probably the last galley action. At about this same time steam-driven vessels started to appear. Unlike sailing ships, they could safely work in the closed, rocky waters of the Baltic. As one scholar notes, it was not sail but steam that finally ended the galley's long reign: "If it had not been for the coming of steam, the Baltic gunboat might well have become as nearly a standardized type as the Mediterranean galley had been in her day."[46] Thus, although the golden age of galleys had ended in 1571 at the Battle of Lepanto, galleys would serve in various minor roles for almost another three hundred years.

THE FAR EAST

There was some indication of riverine activity along the Chinese rivers from the earliest times, and the Chinese must be credited with several firsts. Starting in the second century A.D. the Chinese built ships with transverse bulkheads, the first indication of watertight compartmentalization that would not appear on Western ships until the nineteenth century. In the fifth century the Chinese developed a treadmill-propelled paddle-wheel boat. They early on used a compass and by the eleventh century also had navigation tables. The Kublai Khan may have had the largest armada in history when he gathered 3,500 vessels for an assault on Japan in 1281, which was stopped only by a typhoon-force wind—the *kamikaze,* or "divine wind," which destroyed most of his fleet, saving Japan.[47]

The Koreans, however, had the most interesting of all the ships in the long Age of Galleys. This was their "turtle ship," developed during the Japanese-Korean War from 1592 to 1598. The turtle ship was a galley with an iron-plated "turtleback" deck which provided protection against missiles and spikes to discourage boarding. The stem had a ram, and the sides had archery ports. It was the first "ironclad" warship and proved deadly in most of the Korean-Japanese sea battles.

Conclusion

There were at least ten identifiable standard, major warship types during the Age of Galleys in the Mediterranean: the early single level penteconter, the bireme, Greek trireme, various polyremes of which the most common were the five (quinquereme) and four (quadrireme), the Roman trireme and liburnian, the early and then later dromon types, and finally the Venetian galley. In addition, there were numerous smaller types such as the *hemiolia* and *lembos*. Although in some cases the basic design never changed, in others there are indications of major variations. For example, the early Hellenistic Age fives and fours were probably three-level, the later Roman galleys single.

Despite the different designs, there were many similarities. Most galleys were approximately 125 to 130 feet in length, their width varying from 12 to 20 feet, and, except for the few large polyremes, probably never displaced more than 100 tons. By comparison, today's frigates are approximately 400 feet long and 40 feet wide, displacing about 4,000 tons. Galley speeds varied depending on size and crew, as well as the winds and currents, but the normal cruising speed has been estimated at approximately 2 to 4 knots, with a top ramming speed of about 8 to 10 knots. By comparison, modern ships cruise at about 15 knots, and 30 to 35 knots is considered flank speed for most types.

The major differences between galleys were in the various oar arrangements, from single banks with one man to an oar to two and three levels with up to eight per oar. Unfortunately, the exact arrangements are often unknown and the standard nomenclature is sometimes confusing. For example, although the term *trireme* is usually associated with the three-level Greek and Roman galleys, later Venetian single-level galleys with three oarsmen to an oar are also described as triremes. The terms *penteconter* and *bireme* usually refer to the earliest galleys, yet throughout the Age of Galleys, there were galleys under different names, which had fifty oarsmen in both single- and double-level arrangements. This lack of exactitude is not necessarily limited to these ancient galleys. Terms such as *cruiser* and especially *frigate* have had different meanings at different times.

Although an in-depth analysis of personnel is beyond the scope of this book, two brief points deserve mention. First, despite the popular image of slave galleys from Hollywood movies, throughout most of ancient times, galleys were rowed by free men. Conditions were often harsh, but they were not much better ashore. And very often the rowers were quite skilled free men, which leads into the second point. Many historians feel the switching back and forth from single to multiple rowers had as much to do with available skilled oarsmen as with design changes. It was the lack of skilled personnel that led to multiple oarsmen arrangements. Single oarsman had to be skilled, but with multi-oarsmen, only one had to be experienced and the others simply applied muscle power.

VIRTUALLY ALL THE lessons of seapower can be found during the Age of Galleys from decisive battles such as Salamis and Lepanto, to more normal sea control and show the flag gunboat diplomacy as practiced by the ancient Mycenaeans, Phoenicians, Greeks, Romans, and Byzantines among others. On the tactical level, there are also many lessons: larger, stronger ships with well-trained crews and better tactics usually won, but there were exceptions. The better equipped and trained Athenians were beaten when bottled up in Syracuse harbor and finally lost when foraging for food. New inventions and concepts were also important, at least initially. The first appearance of a new weapon such as a corvus or Greek fire was often decisive, but opponents invariably learned to adapt. More likely, changes were incremental. For example, it was once claimed that the invention of the cannon doomed the galleys, leading to the Age of Sail, but the change was actually much slower and more subtle.

Finally, compared to land weapons, galleys were more sophisticated. The invention of the chariot and various siege machines pales in comparison with more complex galley designs and their weaponry. Some of the weaponry adapted for and then crammed on board these small galleys was comparable to that on modern warships. In sum, war galleys were the most sophisticated pieces of machinery of their day.

The influence of seapower on world history during the Age of Galleys was important but should not be overemphasized. Great nations like Mesopotamia, for example, barely went to sea. Others like Egypt and Rome were really land powers that also went to sea. As Chester G. Starr, in *The Influence of Sea Power on Ancient History,* writes: "Instead of viewing sea power as an important element in the course of ancient history, we must expect it to be a spasmodic factor, though at points it does indeed become a critical force."[48] There were exceptions. Seapower was crucial for Phoenicia, Athens, Carthage, Byzantium, and such Italian city-states as Venice and Genoa. And even though Rome was a land power, its fleet was important. As another author has noted: "We hear very much about the influence of Roman roads in promoting Roman civilization, but the influence of Roman fleets in bringing about that miracle has been almost totally ignored. Yet it is demonstrable that the Roman Empire depended quite as much on its fleets as on its roads."[49]

In sum, although the Age of Galleys in many respects is truly ancient history, usually overlooked by naval strategists, especially when compared to the Age of Sail's great influence on world events, there are still lessons for today. In fact, the lessons of seapower from the ancient era of Pax Romana might actually have more applicability to today's turn-of-the-century post–Cold War environment than that of the more modern Pax Britannica.

The Age of Sail 3

THE AGE OF SAIL was the second longest age, lasting for at least 250 to over 400 years, again depending on definitions. Although many steam warships also carried sails into the last quarter of the nineteenth century, there seems to be general agreement that the Age of Sail ended during the first half of that century. The Battle of Navarino Bay in 1827 was the last major sea battle fought exclusively between sailing warships, and they still played significant roles until the early 1850s. The problem, once again, is pinpointing the beginning. The first major sea battle between sailing warships was the English–Spanish Armada engagement in 1588, which many cite as the start of the Age of Sail. That date also fits in nicely with what most consider the end of the Age of Galleys, the Battle of Lepanto in 1571.

On the other hand, even the earliest galleys had carried sails, although they fought under oar, and merchant ships had long operated under sail. For this reason, some scholars use the term *fighting sail* to differentiate among galleys, merchantmen, and sailing warships. "Fighting cogs," which became common around 1200, are sometimes cited as the first sailing warships, but the advent of the three-masted so-called "full-rigged" carrack after 1400 is usually considered the first step toward the final development of the classic sailing ship of the line around 1650. Another important date is 1500, when gun ports appeared, with full-rigged man-of-war galleons first built around 1525. Galleons were the principal fighting ships in the Armada battle. In short, once again, readers can pick their own dates, but, using major sea battles as benchmarks, many consider that the Age of Sail started with the Armada in 1588 and ended with the Battle of Navarino Bay in 1827. If one considers warship types, the age started as early as 1200, but full-rigged sailing warships did not appear until after 1400, fighting galleons were not common until 1525, the classic ship of the line developed about 1650, and the end of the Age of Sail came around 1850. Before turning to the sailing warships, however, a brief overview of the use of sail during the Age of Galleys is necessary because many of the important characteristics of sailing ships were developed during this era.

Sail during the Age of Galleys

The wind was used early in human history as a labor-saving device to propel boats and ships and, probably even earlier, logs, rafts, and dugouts. There is some speculation these early sail devices were simply large, leafy branches, palms, or ferns. The earliest depictions of boats along the Nile, from 3500 B.C., show sails probably made of woven reeds or leaves.[1] These early Egyptian sails were rectangular shaped, higher than they were wide, and placed forward on the vessel. Around 2000 B.C., however, the shape of the sail changed from being higher than wide to the slightly wider than high "square shape," and over the years the location of the sail moved back until around 1900 B.C. it was midships.[2] Thus the familiar square-shaped sail located midships was developed very early on. Around 500 B.C. some ships show a second forward smaller foremast and sail probably used more for steering than power. Some depictions of triremes also show this smaller foremast.

The next major change occurred around A.D. 500 with the development of fore-and-aft rigs and the triangular-shaped lateen sail. The exact origins of the lateen rig are unknown but are often attributed to the Arabs since it became more popular on their craft. The fore-and-aft rigs are those in which the sail is set parallel with the keel (i.e., like most of today's sailing boats) rather than athwartships like the square sail (seen on many of today's so-called tall ships). Although fore-and-aft sails are less efficient than the square sail when going with the wind (i.e., with the wind to their back), their great advantage is that they are more proficient when heading into (or against) the wind. In nautical terms, they can sail "closer to the wind." This is why today's pleasure sailing boats are fore-and-aft rigs with triangular-shaped sails, more proficient for tacking back and forth into the wind. A disadvantage is that lateen sails require more sailors for tacking, making them more expensive to operate. Lateen sails became very popular in the Mediterranean during the medieval period, but the square sail remained the standard in the Atlantic.

While galleys carried sails from the beginning, they fought under oar stowing their sails for battle or even leaving them ashore. There are more indications of sailing warships in Atlantic waters. Julius Caesar's galley fleet fought an early sea battle off the coast of Brittany in 56 B.C. against Celtic sailing warships. But with few exceptions, galleys remained the dominant warship until the mid-sixteenth century.[3]

FIGHTING COGS, HULKS, AND NEFS: 1200–1400

Another exception from the Age of Galleys was a modified merchantman, the "fighting cog." The cog was important not just as the first step toward the development of sailing warships but also as the first to use a stern rudder rather than a steering oar and as the transitional ship type bringing together the North Atlantic and Mediterranean building traditions. There had, of course, been numerous types of sailing merchantmen throughout the Age of Galleys in both the Mediterranean and Atlantic. In the Atlantic, the early merchantmen were descendants of Viking and Celtic boats.[4]

Unlike the sleek Viking longboats, the cog was a very simple, flat-bottom boat with high sides and straight stern and stem posts. As is true of most early types, the exact origins of the cog have been lost to history. Coglike boats can be traced back to the lower Rhine River of 200 B.C. pre-Roman days. The earliest mention of the term *cog* is from ninth-century documentary records found at Utrecht, and there are indications that it was used as both a merchantman and a warship and might have also had oars.[5] Ninth-century coins show a small, flat-bottomed boat still with a side rudder.[6] It was not until around 1200, however, that cogs appeared in great numbers and many coastal towns depicted them on their official seals.

At the end of the twelfth century, two seemingly unrelated events occurred that had a great effect on ship development. The first was the formation of the Hanseatic League in 1159, and the second was the appearance of the stern rudder around 1180, considered "one of the most important steps in the history of the ship."[7] As can be expected, this invention had a major impact on ship construction. Until this time, most ships were "double-ended" with no difference in the shape of their bow or stern. That changed with the invention of the stern rudder since it was obviously easier to hang a rudder on a straight, rather than a curved, sternpost. Thus the stern became flatter over time. The stern rudder also made it easier to steer. Although this made little difference in early, smaller sailing ships, it would have a major effect when larger ships were built.

Another seminal event was the formation of the Hanseatic League among northern German cities for trade in the Baltic and Atlantic. This led to the need for larger cogs and, as often happens, warships to protect them. Within a short time, the Hanseatic League found itself in conflict with other area powers, which led to the development of "fighting cogs." At first, soldiers were simply placed on the merchant cogs, but around 1285 during a fight with the king of Denmark, temporary wooden towers were built on the bow and stern giving the soldiers and crossbowmen a height advantage. Later, the towers were incorporated into the ship's design and cabins were built into the larger aftercastle, giving the cogs a modicum of comfort. Up to that time, both crew and any passengers had stayed on deck and the more important cargo was stowed below.[8]

Fighting cogs played significant roles in two major conflicts of the period. First were those in the Baltic area between the Hanseatic League and the other powers of the area, mostly Denmark. The other, and more famous, was the Hundred Years' War between Britain and France from 1337 to 1453. While France used mostly galleys, often rented Genoese, the British used both galleys and cogs. Many of the British cogs were supplied by an association of English trading towns called the Cinque Ports, again illustrating the relationship between merchantmen and warships. The merchant cogs, now with fore and aft castles, were readily converted to warships. Of more than thirteen hundred English ships identified in the early years of the Hundred Years' War, 57 percent were cogs.[9]

Since fighting at sea in those days still consisted mostly of coming together and boarding, it would be hard to evaluate which was better, the French and Genoese galleys or the English cogs; however, the English did win many of the decisive engagements. The galleys were obviously better for close-in maneuvering, but the cogs with their higher sides had the advantage in drawn-out fights. Equally important, the cog became a major transport ship necessary for England to move troops and horses across the English Channel.

The cog served another important role, bringing together the northern and southern, or Mediterranean, building traditions. The cog was the dominant merchant ship in the North and around 1300 started entering the Mediterreanean, where it was quickly adapted. The cog introduced the stern rudder to the Mediterreanean, while the northerners started learning about both frame and carvel-built ships. Starting around 1000, the old shell method of building was replaced with the frame method in the Mediterreanean, where the edge-to-edge or carvel method of laying planks, rather than the northern overlapping or clinker method, had always been used. During the next few centuries, both the frame and carvel methods became standard throughout Europe. The cog itself was somewhat of a mixture of the two with carvel planking from the keel until the turn of the sides where traditional northern clinker construction began.

Although many seals and a few illustrations and tapestries have survived from this era depicting cogs, there are, unfortunately, no detailed descriptions. In 1962 a Hanseatic cog from around 1380 was uncovered in a river near Bremen, Germany, and is now preserved in a museum. This Bremen find is 76 feet long and approximately 60 tons, but it is thought to be a smaller cog. Other records indicate that larger cogs were over 100 tons and probably around 100 feet long.

While the cog was the dominant ship during this era, two others should be mentioned. A merchant type called a "hulk" was developed around 800. Unlike the cog, the hulk had a rounded bottom. Little is known about the hulk, but it replaced the cog as the main merchant ship starting in the fifteenth century. There are no records of "fighting hulks," but it remained an important merchant type for many years, finally replacing the cog completely by 1450. Unlike the hulk, the nef was a warship. There is some indication that *nef* was simply a generic term, although some inventories differentiate between cogs and nefs, and there is some speculation that Atlantic nefs were built in the older Viking style. The term *nef* is also applied to a few Mediterranean types.[10] Nevertheless, the dominant ship during the thirteenth and fourteenth centuries was the cog.

Rise of the Full-Rigged Ships: 1400–1650

While the cog was an important transitional type, it was still single-masted, not much differently rigged than those over four thousand years earlier. The major change occurred after 1400 with the development of the three-masted so-called full-rigged ship, which one scholar calls "arguably the most significant piece of technology created by man since the making of fire and the use of the wheel." Besides this technological achievement, "the three-masted ship made possible the voyages to the Indies. . . . Even more important it made possible the discovery by Europeans of the vast continent of the New World."[11] There were three important early types before the final development of the ship of the line around 1650. These were the carrack, the caravel, and the galleon.

CARRACKS: 1300–1525

The carrack is important in the progression of warship development for two reasons. First, it served as the transition from the single to the full-rigged three-masted ship after 1400 and second, after 1500, as the transitional ship for finally making guns at sea a significant factor. As with all these early types, the exact origins and even the term *carrack* are obscure. It is thought to have been derived from a Genoa cog derivative called a *coche* first mentioned around 1302. *Carrack* appears in the English language around 1350 referring to these Genoese ships, but its exact origins are unknown.[12]

The original *coche* was probably simply a carvel, frame-built modification of the clinker, shell-built cog with a square sail and stern rudder. As noted earlier, the cog was considered important in bringing the northern and southern traditions of shipbuilding together, and the carrack continued that transition. Around 1350 a second after-mast was added called a mizzen, and two-masted carracks were common for approximately seventy-five years. French-hired Genoese carracks captured by the English in the years 1416–17 were still two-masted. Around 1416 the English built the "great ship" *Grace Dieu* with a third mast, and that configuration became common after 1450. Although a few four-masted ships were built over the years, the three-masted so-called full-rigged ship remained the standard until the end of the Age of Sail in the 1850s.

Besides being the first three-masted ship, the carrack was also very large and imposing, called the "jumbo jet" of their days by one scholar of this period.[13] Medieval authors such as Chaucer used the carrack image to connote largeness; one called them "orrible, grete and stoute."[14] The 1416 *Grace Dieu* was 1,400 tons, estimated to have an overall length of 180 feet when most large ships were in the 125-foot range. The *Great Michael,* built for James IV of Scotland in 1505, was reportedly 240 feet long, over 100 feet larger than most ships of the day. Although that length is questionable, carracks were undoubtedly very large ships for their day.

What truly differentiated the carracks from both earlier and later ships, however, was their very high aft and especially forecastles, as clearly illus-

Model of the Scottish carrack *Great Michael,* built in 1511. Carracks were the first three-masted, "full-rigged" ships and are considered a major turning point in the development of ships.
(U.S. Naval Institute)

trated in the first drawing of a carrack dated to around 1470 by a Flemish artist. Although the feature is considered somewhat exaggerated in the painting, all carracks had this high, protruding forecastle, some fifty feet above the keel. In some regards, the start of the Age of Sail can be traced to the development of the three-masted carrack. Later ships were simply more streamlined versions of the original carrack with these castles becoming smaller and finally disappearing completely. Or, as one author put it, "the changes made during the subsequent 350 years . . . being refinements rather than innovation."[15]

Like all these early types, carracks were primarily cargo ships. The vessel was larger than the cog and with a square sail, cheaper to crew, but it also became the main warship. One author suggests that the high forecastle was designed for war-fighting. Since boarding was still the primary means of fighting at sea, this high forecastle was important for gaining height advantage for crossbows and other devices.[16] But they saw little action. The period after the Anglo-French wars ended in 1417 was relatively peaceful in the North Atlantic waters and the galley was still the major warship in the Mediterranean. Nevertheless, other countries also built these large ships as much for prestige, or deterrence, as for war-fighting. In that regard they might be considered the medieval equivalent of the ancient polyremes and the precedent to later battleships.

Around 1490 Henry V built two large carracks. One, the *Regent,* had 225 guns, but these were small guns and boarding was still considered the main tactic. Around 1500 a major change occurred in warships with the invention of gun ports. Guns at sea can be traced back to the early fourteenth century, but most were very small, carried on the upper decks and castles to assist in the boarding with only one or two larger cannon in the bow. That changed after 1500. Although a seal dating to 1493 shows a gun port, the invention is usually attributed to a French shipwright from Brest named Descharges in 1501. The hinged, watertight gun ports for the first time allowed larger guns to be placed below the main deck.

The gun itself was undergoing major changes during this period. Until the late fifteenth century, guns had been fairly small breechloaders, that is, loaded from the back of the gun (like today's guns) using a very complex mechanism that took some fifteen minutes to load. Around 1475 wrought iron gave way to bronze guns. Then, after the turn of the century, guns changed from breech to muzzle-loaders, which became standard by around 1520. Muzzle-loading was relatively easy, with a good crew able to fire off a round every three minutes or so. As a result of these changes, within a short time frame around 1500, guns went from being a minor weapon used mostly for assisting boarding to the main battery. As two authors commented, "It was the carrack, the musket and the ship's cannon that finally completed the process."[17] A ship was actually sunk by gunfire in 1513.[18]

These changes would have an effect on shipbuilding and eventually lead to the development of the galleon. The gun ports were also placed on the high towered carracks, with perhaps disastrous results. The 1545 sinking of the *Mary Rose,* originally built in 1510, has sometimes been attributed to her being top-heavy or perhaps having her gun ports open in rough weather. What is known is that soon after gun ports became common around 1525, the carrack gave way to the galleon. Thus, although the carrack took part in few major sea battles, it nevertheless played a major role in the evolution of the warship.

CARAVELS: 1400–1550

Another early sailing type deserves brief mention, not because it was a warship per se, although some served that purpose, but rather because it played such an important role during the fifteenth-century Age of Discovery. It was also, perhaps, the origin of the term *carvel-built.* That ship was the lateen-rigged caravel. The term *caravel* can be traced to Iberian fishing boats of the mid-thirteenth century and was probably derived from the *caravo,* or *qarib,* a lateen-rigged boat used by Muslims in both Iberia and North Africa, but the term died out during the fourteenth century.[19]

The caravel reappeared early in the fifteenth century to play an extremely important part in the Age of Discovery, which began around 1440, when Prince Henry of Portugal started using them for his voyages around Africa. The lateen-rigged caravel was particularly well suited for sailing back to Portugal against the generally northwesterly winds along the west coast of Africa. The main advantage of the lateen sail was its ability to sail into (or against) the wind. Caravels were also used on all of Christopher Columbus's voyages to America. The *Santa Maria* was a carrack, but the *Nina* and the *Pinta* were caravels. Columbus preferred the caravels, finding the *Santa Maria* sluggish.

Unfortunately, no good description or depiction of a caravel has survived. The early caravels were small fishing boats and coastal traders, probably simply open boats with one mast. Early in the fifteenth century, a decked caravel was developed with two and three masts, a small, low aftercastle, and no forecastle. Besides the lateen sail, the caravel was characterized by its long, narrow shape, estimated to have a length-to-beam ratio of around 5 : 1 or 4 : 1 when most other ships were in the 3 : 1 range.[20] As a result, these were considered fast ships. Although there was no one standard size, one author estimates that caravels had an overall length of about 50 to 60 feet, with a beam of about 18 feet.[21] While most caravels were fore-and-aft lateen rigged, during the late fifteenth century some were square-rigged. In fact, Columbus's caravels were square-rigged at various times for better performance in the open ocean.

The caravel might also be the origin of the term *carvel-built* (i.e, edge-to-edge), as contrasted to the northern clinker-built (overlapping) method of building ships.[22] The appearance and adaption of the Iberian caravel in northern waters after 1450 coincided with the end of the clinker-built ships in Britain. Iberia would have been a natural bridge between these Mediterreanean and northern traditions of building ships.

On occasion caravels were used as warships, especially for patrol and convoy duty, because of their speed. While the carrack was the standard warship during this period, "caravels, like the frigates of later times, were ordered out on special assignments or when speed was required."[23] The caravel became popular during the mid- to late fifteenth century when a series of recessions hit Europe and larger ships went out of fashion. Because their narrow length-to-breadth ratio gave them limited cargo capacity, they were eventually replaced by larger ships in the sixteenth century. To the caravel, however, must go the honor of being the principal type during the important early years of the Age of Discovery.

GALLEONS AND GREAT SHIPS: 1525–1650

Galleons are famous as the Spanish treasure ships that carried gold back from the New to the Old World and as the main fighting ship in perhaps the most famous sea battle in history—the battle of the Spanish Armada against the English, usually considered the first major sea battle between sailing warships and the first in which guns, not boarding, played the major role. Galleons were also the last transitional type leading to the battle ship of the line around 1650.

The exact origins of the term *galleon* are obscure. As the name implies, there was undoubtedly some connection to oared galleys, now lost to history. Iberian ships called *galeones* can be traced to the thirteenth century, but the term probably came from Venician oared *gallioni* used for river patrols in the fifteenth century.[24] Venice's first sailing galleon was built around 1528.[25] Galleasse were also developed about this same time by Venice, and although they are sometimes described as oar-powered galleons, there was a difference. Despite these Venetian origins, the galleon is mostly associated with Spain, especially as an escort ship for convoys to America during the sixteenth century. First French and then English attacks on Spanish ships in the Caribbean forced Spain to resort to convoys to protect its ships. Galleons were also used by other countries, sometimes under different names. The Netherlands' pinnas and whalers were galleons, or at least galleonlike ships.

In many respects the galleon was a streamlined carrack. The carrack's high forecastle superstructure was lowered and moved back into the hull, placed after the stem rather than being forward. Because guns were now starting to replace old boarding tactics, these high forecastles were no longer needed. This new arrangement also allowed for the galleons' most distinguishing feature: a large (galley derived) beakhead that projected forward from the stem. Although the beakhead was actually a platform to handle the foresails, it also became useful as a latrine, the derivative of today's nautical term *head*. The aftercastle consisted of a half-deck, quarter-deck, and poop deck aft of the mainmast. There were usually two full decks above the waterline for cannon. Another streamlining feature of the galleon was that the hull became longer and narrower. Whereas carracks had a keel-to-beam ratio of about 2:1, for the galleon it increased to over 3, even 4:1.[26] There were, however, no standard sizes, and galleons ranged from only 300 to over 1,000 tons, with lengths of about 150 to 180 feet. In the later sixteenth century, the English started building an even lower, more streamlined and maneuverable galleon sometimes referred to as race-built. These two variants, the higher Spanish and lower English galleons, would clash at the Battle of the Spanish Armada in 1588.

Since its introduction around 1525, the galleon had become the main warship for many countries and participated in several battles. Venician galleons had battled Turkish galleys as early as 1537, and Spanish escort galleons had fought off privateers. But by far the most famous battle of this era was the battle of the Spanish Armada. In 1588, Spain sent a huge armada of 130 ships to invade England. Of these, 20 were listed as galleons and 29 as *naos* armed for battle with the rest cargo ships. *Naos* was a general term for warship, and there is some speculation that these might have been older carracks.[27] Also included were four galleasse and four galleys, although the galleys turned back. Thus the Battle of the Armada is cited as the first between fighting sail.

The English victory over the Armada is usually attributed to their sleeker galleons, which stood off using their guns rather than closing the Spanish, who had planned to use boarding tactics. Opposing the Spanish Armada were 197 English ships, but most were small, and few were warships. Fifty-seven Spanish versus only 13 English ships were over 500 tons; most of the English ships, 150, were in the 100- to 150-ton range.[28] The Spanish galleons were also less sleek with length-to-beam averages of about 3.35:1 versus the English 3.77:1. Thus, as one scholar concludes, "The notion that the primary fighting ships in the English fleet were sleeker and faster seems borne out."[29] Most of the 34 Spanish ship losses were actually caused by storms. None of the galleons were sunk fighting, although some were damaged by gunfire and later floundered. Nevertheless, this was still a great strategic battle: the beginning of the end for Spain and, more important, the start of the rise of English seapower.

Somewhat ironically, although the smaller, sleeker English galleons had won the day using longer-range cannon, not boarding tactics, the navies of the first half of the seventeenth century reverted to building larger galleons called great ships. Many of these ships were built as much for show and prestige as for war-fighting ability. It was during this era that ships reached "their greatest beauty" with elaborate, usually stern, ornamentation.[30] The best known of these ships was the Swedish *Wasa,* lost on her maiden voyage in 1628, rediscovered, and restored in the early 1960s. Her sinking is usually attributed to instability caused by the addition of an extra gun deck at the behest of the king who was seeking prestige.

These great ships are also important as the final transition to the classic three-decker ship of the line. Although gun ports had been around for over a century, it was not until the the first half of the seventeenth century that two- and even three-deck ships were built. Two authors claim that the *Prince Royal,* 56 guns, built in 1610, was probably the first three-decker.[31] Most, however, cite the English *Sovereign of the Seas,* built in 1637 with 100 guns, as the first. The *Sovereign of the Seas* had a keel length of 127 feet, overall length of about 232 feet, a beam of 46.5 feet, and was the first to have 100 heavy guns. Some older ships had more guns listed, but they were lighter, mostly man, not ship, killers. A year later, the French responded with *La Couronne,* which was approximately the same size as the *Sovereign of the Seas* but had only 72 guns on two decks. In fact, although the three-decker was more famous, the two-decker with 70-odd guns would become the most common warship during the Age of Sail. Another important type also appeared during this period. This was the two-decker *Constant Warwick* built in 1646, usually considered the first frigate. Thus, after two hundred-odd years of transitional types, the stage was set for the final step in the Age of Sail: the classic ship of the line.

The Classic Ship of the Line: 1650–1850

Despite the development of two- and three-decked gun ships now carrying heavy guns, the standard fleet formation was to still sail line abreast, just as the Greeks had done over two thousand years earlier, and the ultimate battle tactic was still boarding. That changed during the first Anglo-Dutch War from 1652 to 1654 and brought on the last stage of the sailing warships. There were four main categories of ships during this time. Most important was the large ship of the line, followed by the frigate, then smaller sloops and corvettes, and finally specialized craft such as bomb vessels.

THE SHIP OF THE LINE

The main fighting tactic into the mid-seventeenth century was still the chase followed by boarding. That changed at the Battle of the Gabbard in 1653, during the first Anglo-Dutch War, when the British finally abandoned the old tactics and line abreast formations and instead formed in a single line ahead with one ship following the other. The opposing fleets were now beam-to-beam, broadside-to-broadside, rather than bow-to-bow. While this was clearly the best method for ships with guns along the side, there was also a major drawback: a small ship could find itself opposite a larger one. Thus only those ships "fit to lie in a line" were deemed sufficient for combat with the smaller ships "falling out of the line." Or, as the leading scholar of this period, Brian Lavery, states, a ship of the line was "a ship capable of forming part of a line of battle, and therefore able to stand up to the fire of the largest enemy ships and make an effective reply. This meant that she had to be a large ship for her times, stoutly constructed, and in practice carrying at least two decks of guns."[32] This also meant that the days when merchantmen could be pressed into service were over. In short, it was another turning point in the history of warfare at sea.

The number of guns required to stay in the line varied, and, as can be expected, grew over the years. Ships with the minimum number of guns to stand in the line over the years were as follows:[33]

1650—30 guns
1700—50 guns
1750—64 guns
1800—74 guns
1840—80 guns

These new line requirements also led to a more formal rating system for warships with some navies adopting six rates. While the rating system can be traced back to 1618 in the Royal Navy, when ships were divided into Royal, Great, and Middling classes, it became more formal and important after 1650. The ratings were based on number of guns and, again as can be expected, that number grew rapidly from 1650 to the early eighteenth century and then stayed relatively steady throughout the Age of Sail. Their ratings in the Royal Navy were:[34]

	First	Second	Third	Fourth	Fifth	Sixth
1650	60	50–60	40–50	30–40	24	16
1700	100	80–100	60–80	50–60	30–44	20–28

The first three ratings were generally considered the ships of the line, with the fourth the smallest to sometimes be accorded a place. The fifth rate were the frigates, and the sixth rate was the smallest ship in the Royal Navy commanded by an officer of captain's rank.

The ship of the line was in many respects simply a streamlined galleon. The upper works were reduced with only a slightly raised after quarterdeck area with a smaller poop deck. Thus, over the years, the main distinguishing features from the carrack to the galleon to the ship of the line was the streamlining of aft castles and forecastles. When broadsides rather than boarding tactics became more important, these castles with their height advantage were no longer needed. Another difference from the galleon was that the pointed beakhead was now shorter and stronger.

All of the large 100-gun first-class and most of the 80- to-90-gun second-class ships were three deckers, meaning they had three full decks of guns, not counting those on the quarterdeck, forecastle, or poop decks. The lowest deck had the largest cannon, usually 42-pounders or "cannon of seven" (for its 7-inch bore), or 32-pounders with 24-pounders on the middle and 12-pounders on the upper deck. The 42-pound round shot was considered the heaviest that could be handled by a man, but even this was considered awkward and many were later replaced by 32-pounders for more rapid fire.[35] Very few large, first-rate three-deckers were built. Most countries had only one or two, and even England never had more than a dozen or so at any one time. At the famous Battle of Trafalgar in 1805, for example, of twenty-seven British and thirty-three French and Spanish ships of the line, only four ships on each side had 100 or more guns.

HMS *Victory*, a 100-gun ship of the line built in 1765 and Admiral Nelson's flagship at the Battle of Trafalgar in 1805. The ship is still preserved at Portsmouth, England. (Ewing Galloway)

The most famous three-decker is Nelson's flagship *Victory,* still preserved at Portsmouth, England. The *Victory,* rated at 100 guns and launched in 1765, was 186 feet long and 52 feet wide. She was thus forty years old at Trafalgar. The largest of the day was the Spanish 116-gun *Santissima Trinidad,* built in Havana in 1769. She was rebuilt in 1796 with a full upper spar deck capable of carrying 140 guns and is often referred to as a four-decker. The larger three-deckers with 120 guns were actually built after the Napoleonic Wars. The *Pennsylvania,* 120 guns, launched in 1837, was the largest American sailing warship built. The French *Valmy,* 116 guns, 210 by 57 feet, launched in 1847, was the last large sailing warship built.

Most ships of the line were two-deckers. A few large two-deckers with 80 guns were built, but most were in the 60- to 80-gun range. Indeed, the most common ship during the height of the Age of Sail from about 1740 on was the third-rate 74-gun two-decker. At Trafalgar, of the twenty-seven British ships of the line, sixteen were 74s, and of the thirty-three French and Spanish, twenty-two were 74s. A typical 74 in the Royal Navy in the second half of the eighteenth century was about 160 to 170 feet long, had a beam of 47 feet, with 32-pounders on the lower deck, 18-pounders in the middle, and a few 9-pounders on the quarterdeck and forecastle.

There was a certain commonality of design throughout this whole period so captured ships were easily incorporated into fleets. In fact, many times even the same name would be maintained, which has caused some confusion for scholars. But there were also differences. The Dutch, for example, with fewer deep-draft harbors, built few three-deckers. The Spanish ships were often bigger and better built, as shown in one famous battle when the Spanish *Princessa,* 70 guns, was able to hold her own against three similar armed but smaller British 70s. While the Royal Navy was dominant during the Age of Sail, the French ships were usually considered better designed although the British were better built. British ships were generally considered too small for the number of guns they carried. The French ships were a little larger, which made them better gun platforms. American ships were also somewhat larger and considered overgunned by contemporary standards. The American 74, the *Independence,* launched in 1814, was 190 feet long when most British 74s were about 176 feet.

Finally, there has developed a myth that ships changed little during this period. While ships of the line were, in some respects, simply streamlined galleons, there were many differences. The greatest difference was the minimum number of guns needed to stand in the line, from only 30 guns in 1650 to more than double that number by Trafalgar as ships got larger over the years. In 1650, three-deckers were in the 1,500-ton range, increasing to about 2,000 tons by 1750 and 2,500 tons in 1800. Lavery notes twelve separate suberas of ship-of-the-line development in the Royal Navy alone.[36] On the other hand, most of these differences were modest; the basic design changed little and ships were generally in the 160- to 200-foot range throughout this period. Ironically, the greatest changes came after the Napoleonic Wars during the early years of the Age of Steam and Ironclads. In 1804 the British designer Sir Robert Seppings came up with an improved diagonal bracing system that finally solved the centuries-old hogging problem for larger wooden ships, enabling ships to be much larger and carry heavier guns. Another important change came in the early eighteenth century when the steering wheel was developed. Until then, a complicated "tiller and whipstaff" system had been used.

As can be expected, when guns replaced boarding, new tactics were developed. The basic tactic was for the two fleets to come together in parallel lines only a few hundred yards apart and simply blast away with broadsides. The attacking fleet approached from windward, that is, with the wind to its back. This was usually considered more advantageous because there was more choice, plus there was the military advantage of attacking rather than waiting. The fleet to leeward, however, had the option of withdrawing and could use its broadsides against the approaching fleet. Although it depended on the situation, the English generally preferred the wind, while the French preferred the lee. This coming together in parallel lines was called the formal tactic. The problem was that this tactic produced few decisive battles.

In contrast were melee tactics when the attacking fleet would try various maneuvers such as massing or doubling on the opposing fleet to obtain two-to-one advantage. Another tactic was breaking the line with one fleet going through the enemy's line. This became known as "crossing the T," when one fleet was able to bring all its broadside guns against the other's limited forward guns. But as the name of the tactic suggests, there was less control in these melee situations. For this reason, for many years the British stuck with the formal linear tactics. This situation finally changed in the late eighteenth century, resulting in many great British victories. Besides tactics, another difference between the English and French was in gunnery. The British tended to shoot at the hull while the French aimed for the rigging. Downing the rigging made a ship helpless and gave the French the option of tactical withdrawal. Few wooden sailing ships were ever sunk.

While scholars can debate whether there were minor or major changes in ship configurations during the Age of Sail, there is little debate that this was the age of the greatest "influence of sea power upon history," as the great naval strategist Alfred Thayer Mahan put it in his famous book.[37] Although there were only a handful of strategic sea battles during the four thousand years of the Age of Galleys, there were several in the much shorter Age of Sail, and many had worldwide implications. During the eighteenth century, England and France fought several important conflicts. English seapower prevailed during the Seven Years' War, from 1756 to 1763, and France lost Canada, but during the American Revolution, from 1775 to 1783, England temporarily lost control of the seas and the French prevailed at the Battle of the Virginia Capes in 1781, forcing the British to release the thirteen colonies. During the French Revolution and Napoleonic Wars, from 1793 to 1815, there were many sea battles, including three of the most famous, the Battle of the Nile in 1798, the Battle of Copenhagen in 1801, and the Battle of Trafalgar in 1805. In fact, during the era of the ship of the line, from 1653 through the end of the Napoleonic Wars in 1815, barely a year passed without a war. In all of these, seapower played major and in some cases crucial roles.

FRIGATES

Another important warship type during the Age of Sail—if for no other reason than that the name has survived—was the frigate. Today, frigates are by far the most numerous type found in most navies. During the Age of Sail, it was generally "considered to be the largest vessel that was not meant to lie in the line of battle,"[38] which usually meant the fifth and sixth rates. Nevertheless, frigates had important roles. The most important was reconnaissance or "eyes of the fleet," as it was usually called in the days before airplanes, radar, and overhead spy satellites spoiled everything. Another important role was *guerre de course,* or commerce raiding. The sailing frigate was also used for independent "cruising" operations and is considered the antecedent of the modern cruiser. Finally, the frigate has a particularly special place in American naval history as the earliest warship type as well as playing a role in some of the most spectacular one-on-one ship duels in history.

The exact origins and even the meaning of the term *frigate* has been lost to history. In the sixteenth century, small oared vessels used for carrying dispatches in the Mediterranean were called frigates, and in the early seventeenth century, many fleets had sailing warships called frigates, some quite large.[39] The 32-gun, 350-ton *Constant Warwick,* built as a privateer but taken over by the British Navy in 1645, is often cited as the first frigate. During the first Anglo-Dutch War, the British built several frigate classes, including thirteen of the large *Speaker* class, then rated third rate with 60 guns, which for their time made them fairly large ships of the line.

The role of the frigate changed when the focus of action switched from the relatively confined channel conflicts of the Anglo-Dutch Wars to the more far-flung English-French conflicts that began in 1689, continuing throughout the eighteenth and early nineteenth centuries. For these, a cruising ship was needed for the "increasingly global nature of naval warfare."[40] The French needed frigates to conduct their *guerre de course* against British merchantman, and the English needed them to protect and control their ever-expanding colonies. Although larger ships of the line were occasionally dispatched for colonial duties, they were too expensive so that role was normally left to the smaller frigate.

The frigate grew in size over the years. During the late seventeenth century, most were approximately 100 feet long, 500 tons; in the early eighteenth century, about 125 to 130 feet; after 1740, close to 150; and in the early nineteenth century, up to 175 feet and over 2,000 tons. Frigates carried lighter guns than ships of the line throughout most of their history. Late seventeenth-century frigates had only 8- and 9-pounders, increasing to 12-pounders in the early eighteenth century, then 18-pounders after 1780, 24-pounders in the late eighteenth century, and most carried 32-pounders after 1820. The number varied, with fifth rates carrying 28 to 44, even 50 guns in the early nineteenth century and sixth rates carrying 18 to about 28.[41]

While all the smaller sixth rates were one-deckers, some of the fifth rate had two and some even had a one and a half, or what the French called a *demi-batterie*. In that arrangement, one deck, usually the lowest, carried only a few guns. There were, of course, national differences with countries like Sweden preferring larger single-deck frigates over two-deckers. The French built a small or light sixth rate called a *fregate legere* while American frigates tended to be larger. But national differences were slight, with captured frigates easily incorporated into the victor's fleet.

Frigates played both a useful and a romantic role in warfare. Lesser powers found the frigate useful for conducting war on the enemy's commerce. France refined this strategy, still known by the French phrase *guerre de course,* although other sea powers also adopted the strategy from time to time. Perhaps the frigate's greatest role was for reconnaissance "eyes of the fleet." Admiral Lord Horatio Nelson, for example, had a ring of frigates outside French Mediterreanean ports that were able to sight and then relay messages by flags frigate-to-frigate in a short period.[42]

The frigate also played a major role in the early days of the United States Navy. In 1794 the United States built three very large 44-gun frigates, the *Constitution, United States,* and *President.* During the War of 1812–14, the American frigates generally got the better of British frigates in a series of famous one-on-one battles. The *Constitution* bested the *Guerriere* (38) and *Java* (44) and the *United States* the *Macedonian* (38). Another smaller American frigate, the *Essex* (32), wrecked havoc on British shipping in the Pacific before being bested by the *Phoebe* (36) and the sloop *Cherub* (28). This action is also famous for another reason. The *Essex* carried mostly short-range cannons called carronade, allowing the British simply to stand out of range and pound her into submission. Even an American frigate defeat has been heralded for the heroic last words of its captain. The *Shannon* (38) beat the *Chesapeake* (36) in 1813, but the dying Captain Lawrence

USS *Constitution*—"Old Ironsides." A large, 44-gun frigate built in 1797 and still preserved in Boston.
(U.S. Naval Institute)

uttered perhaps the most famous of all American naval sayings, "Don't give up the ship."[43] There was also a certain romance attached to these solitary sailing ships, and it is therefore not surprising that the novelist C. S. Forester has his hero Captain Horatio Hornblower sailing in a frigate in one of his books.

SLOOPS AND OTHER SMALL CRAFT

During this period there were smaller craft types below the six rates. In the Royal Navy these were often generically called simply "sloops," but in fact there were several types in many navies running literally from "A" to "Z." Alphabetically, these include advice boat, *aviso*, bark or barque, barque longue, barquentine, *batterie couverte*, boyer, brig, brigantine, *chasse-maree*, corvette, cutter, *fregate d'avis*, *fregate legere*, jacht, ketch, lugger, pink, schooner, shallop, sloop, smack, snow, and finally the xebex or zebec. Although some were quite similar, most had distinct variations in their hulls or riggings.

The roles and missions of these smaller ships varied widely from dispatch carriers like the advice boat and *aviso* to cutters, boyers, and jachts used mostly for coastal patrol to minor war-fighting missions for the sloops, corvettes, brigs, and schooners. In size they varied from small 30- to 50-ton craft, carrying only a few guns, to French light frigates, *fregate legere*, with twenty guns putting them in the sixth-rate category. The major types, such as the sloops and corvettes, grew in size over the years. Mid-nineteenth-century sloops and corvettes were quite large, up to 175 feet.

The most important of these smaller craft were the square-rigged sloop and corvette and later the brig. The term *sloop* in the Royal Navy has been traced to 1656 with the first purpose built in 1666. In the 1670s the French began building a comparable type called *bargues longue*. The largest was called *La Corvette*, and the term *corvette* gradually replaced the term *barques longue*. These early seventeenth-century sloops and corvettes were in the 40- to 60-feet, 40- to 70-ton range with only four to eight smaller 3- or 4-pounder guns. In the early 1700s they had increased to 60 to 80 feet, and about a hundred tons and carried ten to sixteen guns and by 1800 were over 100 feet, 400 to 600 tons, with some carrying 32-pounders. The American corvette *Constellation*, built in 1855, was 176 feet long, carrying twenty-four guns. Today, the term *corvette* survives, generally used for ships below the frigate category.

The numbers of sloops and corvettes varied widely over the years. Only the Royal Navy built them in any large number, but even the British built few during most of the Age of Sail. That changed around 1800. In 1795 the Royal Navy built the 100- by 30-foot sloop brig *Cruizer* with eighteen guns that became the prototype for the largest class of wooden warships of which 104 were built between 1803 and 1813. While the European small ships were in some engagements, once again it was in the young American navy that these small ships played major roles. Two American sloops, *Wasp* and *Hornet*, built in the early 1800s, played important roles in the War of 1812 and their names were later memorialized by World War II carriers. The crucial Battle of Lake Erie, which gave the Americans control of the Great Lakes, was fought between brigs and sloops. But overall, the roles and missions of these smaller ships were in support of the large fleet or independent show-the-flag operations.[44]

OTHER TYPES

Three other types deserve brief mention. These are fire ships, bomb or mortar ships, and finally the precursors of what today is called a service force. Fire at sea has always been dangerous, especially for wooden ships. Greek fire was a feared weapon for almost two centuries during the Age of Galleys. During the Age of Sail, fire ships became a part of many naval arsenals and saw some success during the early days of sail. In most cases, fire ships were old merchantmen or smaller warships stuffed with combustibles that were sailed alongside an enemy's ship with a skeleton crew and set afire. Although fire ship successes were limited at sea where ships could maneuver, they were often effective in harbors. The English used fire ships against the Armada when it pulled into Calais Roads, and although no ships were set ablaze, the Spanish were forced to sortie. The most successful was an English attack on Dutch ships anchored in the Vlie, where five fire ships caused the loss of some 170 ships. One of the most spectacular successes came during a sea battle when the Dutch used a fire ship to destroy the English hundred-gun first-rate *Royal James* in 1672.[45]

Another important type was the bomb or mortar vessel developed to overcome the difficulties ships had elevating their cannons to attack forts. That solution was putting mortars on ships. In 1682 the French built the first bomb vessel or *galiote a bombes,* to which the English responded with the *Salamander* in 1687. Most of the ships used for this purpose were ketch-rigged, and thus these were often called bomb-ketchs. While early ships had stationary mortars with fixed elevation requiring the ship to be maneuvered to aim, in the early eighteenth century mortars were placed on turntables and given trunions for elevation adjustments, which in some respects foreshadowed the turrets of the Age of Ironclads.[46]

Finally, during this period we see the beginnings of a service or support force to serve the fleet both in port and at sea. In port, one type was the sheer hulk, usually an old warship cut down and outfitted with capstans and cranes to fit masts on ships. Other hulks were used for prisons and barracks. In addition, there were small craft for transporting goods and personnel to ships. Larger sailing ships rarely docked because of the difficulties in maneuvering. Another type was a dredger. The Dutch had difficulties because their ports were so shallow, and they developed the first practical dredger in 1589. Finally, there were seagoing support craft such as troop transports and hospital ships. With sailing ships carrying their own stores, under-way replenishment was not needed.[47]

Conclusion

The Age of Sail was important in both the design of warships and the history of the world. From 1200 to around 1400, the technique of shipbuilding that had endured for some five millennia, the so-called shell-method, finally gave way to the frame procedure of construction. This allowed for the building of larger ships and development of the full-rigged warship—comparable to the invention of fire and the wheel in the history of the development of technology, according to one scholar. While that comparison might be slightly exaggerated, it nevertheless was a significant step leading to the Age of Discovery and the development of the large ships of the line that dominated world history for two hundred years before ending around 1850. There were other major ship design changes during this period. Northern clinker overlapping planking gave way to the carvel edge-to-edge method. More important was the development of the tiller around 1400, followed by the steering wheel around 1600. In sum, in a relatively short time span, shipbuilding went through major changes.

While early sailing warships were converted merchantmen, with the invention of gun ports around 1500 and later large three-deck great ships, the development of the ships of the line was not long in coming. Thus began the construction of the magnificent seventy- to one-hundred-gun ships of the line around 1650 that dominated the battle line until 1850. Although these ships of the line fought the major engagements, equally important were the smaller frigates and even smaller sloops, corvettes, and brigs that in most cases conducted the day-to-day operations throughout the empires.

Although an in-depth analysis of personnel is beyond the scope of this book, a few points deserve mention. While conditions aboard sailing ships were better than those aboard the cramped galleys, life was still hard. Several hundred men were squeezed into a small deck space, sleeping on hammocks. But living conditions were not much better ashore in the seventeenth and eighteenth centuries. And contrary to the popular image of press gangs being required to man the ships and floggings by harsh and tyrannical officers who commanded the dregs of society, most sailors were volunteers, and most officers well understood the need for good morale as well as discipline.[48]

This was also the age of the greatest influence of seapower on history, as Admiral Mahan so aptly put it. Starting with the Age of Discovery in the early fifteenth century, the European powers built far-flung empires and colonies that could be supported and maintained only though seapower. They would not have been discovered or maintained without the large, full-rigged warships. This was truly the golden age of seapower.

The Age of Steam, Ironclads, and Steel

4

FOR THE FIRST TIME—at least at first glance—there are specific dates for the next age of warships, the Age of Steam, Ironclads, and Steel. It started with the building of Robert Fulton's *Demologos* in 1814 and ended with the launching of Admiral Jackie Fisher's famous *Dreadnought* in 1906, a period of ninety-two years. One must add the caveat "at first glance" because while the building of the *Demologos* was a seminal event, sailing warships still predominated until the early 1850s. It was the use of explosive shells during the Crimean War of 1854–56 that doomed the wooden sailing ships. At the other end of the time spectrum, although the *Dreadnought* was another seminal event, most of today's modern ships can be traced to around 1890. Thus, in some respects, the age lasted barely forty years, from around 1850 to 1890. Despite this short period, this age is one of the most important, marked by dramatic technological progress. In just a few years warships, which in some ways had not changed for hundreds, even thousands, of years, were transformed almost overnight.

That rapid progress, however, causes a problem. Although the main purpose of this book is to cover the major, common ship types while pointing out firsts and lasts, during this transitional period from the Age of Sail to the Modern Age, virtually every year there were new types and firsts, resulting in a hodgepodge of warships difficult to categorize, especially for the period 1860 to 1890. Thus it is difficult to label this age. While the other ages can rather easily be described with a single word—galley, sail, or modern—no single term can adequately express this fascinating age known variously as the Age of Steam, Ironclads, Steel, Shellfire, Torpedoes, Screw Propeller, Paddle Wheel, or some combination thereof.

In spite of these difficulties, there are three broad periods with suberas that make analysis somewhat manageable. The broad areas are the early years that lasted from approximately 1815 to 1860 with two suberas for first, paddle-wheel warships and then the introduction of the screw propeller and early conversions. Next came the broad area of ironclads, steel, and other innovations with three overlapping suberas, first the early ironclads, then an experimental period, and finally the introduction of steel and other innovations. Last comes the pre-dreadnought or premodern period that started around 1890.

The Early Years: 1815–1860

THE PADDLE-WHEEL ERA: 1815–1865

Although the span of the paddle-wheel warships was the longest, lasting for thirty years from 1815 to 1845 with a minor role for another twenty years, the term *paddle wheel* is seldom included in this multinamed age. This is probably because they did not take part in any major battles and were used mainly as tugboats and packet vessels, although they did prove useful for amphibious operations and one is sometimes cited as the world's first "aircraft carrier." They were nevertheless an important transitional step in the development of the modern warship.

The beginning of the Age of Steam can be traced to James Watt's invention of the first practical steam engine in 1765. Almost immediately there were proposals to adapt this new technology for commercial ships. Frenchman Claude François, Marquis de Jouffroy d'Abbans, began experiments in 1778 and is credited with producing the first known successful steam vessel in 1783. The first practical steamer is usually attributed to William Symington for the towing ship *Charlotte Dundas* in 1801. Then, in 1807, Robert Fulton built the North River Steamboat or Steamboat No. 1 (better known as the *Clermont*), often cited as the first serviceable steamship.[1] All were paddle wheelers, which should not be surprising. While the principle behind the screw propeller was known, the paddle wheel was considered easier and more adaptable, and proposals that paddle wheels be used dated back to the Age of Galleys.

Plans for warships were not far behind. The Earl of Stanhope built the unsuccessful *Kent Ambi-Navigator* in 1793. Although there were a few other proposals, the first successful steam warship, the *Demologos,* was laid down by the imaginative Robert Fulton in 1814. The *Demologos* was actually a semi-catamaran with the paddle wheel protected between the hulls. Thus Fulton early on anticipated the two main problems with this type of warship, namely that the paddle wheels were vulnerable and took up space for broadside guns. Designed to carry thirty 32-pounders, she only carried 24-pounders, yet that was more than most paddle wheelers would ever carry. While often described as a warship, the *Demologos* (with a speed of only 5 knots) was really a mobile battery built to defend New York and Long Island Sound during the War of 1812–14 but was not completed until 1815.[2]

For the next twenty years the paddle wheelers went through what a leading scholar of this period, Andrew Lambert, describes as the "Tug and Packet Boat" phase.[3] Although there were exceptions, such as Andrew Jackson's use of them to move men during the war of 1812–14, most of the paddle wheelers built through 1830 were used either for towing the large ships of the line in and out of port or for so-called packet duty carrying mail and messages. In 1821 the Admiralty ordered its first steam vessel, the *Comet,* as a tug and in the same year the *Lightning* and *Meteor* entered service for the Post Office. The Royal Navy built the *Congo* in 1816 for exploration of the Congo River, and in 1818 the first French steamers, the *African* and *Voyager,* were built for service on the Senegal River.

Although these early paddle wheelers often carried one or two guns, they barely qualified as warships. There were exceptions, most built for foreign governments. In 1821 Lord Cochrane built the *Rising Star* with twenty guns in Britain for the Chilean war of liberation from Spain, but she arrived too late to take part. Thus to the British-built Greek *Karteria* of 1826 used in the Greek War for Independence (1825–29) goes the honor of the first use of steam in combat. The East India Company had used the small packet ship *Diana* to transport troops and also to launch rockets in the First Burma War of 1824. The U.S. Navy used the *Seagull* against Caribbean pirates. In 1824 a Royal Navy ship also named *Lightning* joined a naval expedition to Algiers, making her the first deployed overseas. HMS *Columbia* was given two 24-pounders in 1829, the first with larger guns.

Most steamers, however, were still built for towing and packet duty. That situation started to change in the 1830s with the construction of the *Dee* and especially the *Gorgon* in 1835. The *Dee,* commissioned in 1832, was the largest of the early steamers at almost a thousand tons, 166 feet long, and while sometimes described as the first practical warship, still carried only two 32-pounders. More important was the *Gorgon,* launched in 1837 as a first-class paddle sloop. She was 1,610 tons, 178 feet long, and carried six large guns, four 42-pounders, two on pivots, two stationary, and two even larger 68-pounders. The *Gorgon* was followed two years later by the *Cyclops,* rated a second-class paddle frigate of almost 2,000 tons, 190 feet long, carrying two 98-pounders and four 68-pounders. Eighteen *Gorgon* and seven *Cyclops* similar derivatives were completed through 1846. A few more sloops and frigates were built around the same time, including the largest, the 3,190-ton *Terrible,* rated as a first-class frigate with eight 56-pounders, eight 68-pounders, and three 12-pounders. The last paddle-wheel warship of this era in the Royal Navy was launched in 1852.[4]

From 1829 to 1839 France built twenty-three small 910-ton, 166-feet-long *Sphinx*-class *avisos* and then a few larger frigates in the early 1840s to match the British *Gorgons.* Although France actually built more paddle war-ships than England, most were smaller; still, concern over French plans fueled British building in the 1840s. In 1822 the creative Colonel Henri Paix-hans, better known as the inventor of the shell, wrote in *Nouvelle Force Maritimei* that a small force of steamboats armed with shell-firing guns could defeat the large British fleet. There were also fears that with steam vessels, for the first time a quick invasion across the channel was possible before it could be stopped by the mighty Royal Navy sailing fleet.

The paddlewheel steam frigate USS *Mississippi,* built in 1841.
(U.S. Naval Historical Center)

The United States also built a few during this period. A *Fulton II* for harbor defense was constructed in 1837, and in 1841 the navy built the large paddle wheelers *Missouri* and *Mississippi.* The latter became famous as Commodore Matthew Calbraith Perry's flagship in "opening Japan" in 1853. The *Mississippi* was 3,220 tons, 220 feet long, and carried two 10-inch and eight 8-inch guns. Paddle wheelers made a comeback during the Civil War, mostly for the river campaigns with some of the so-called double-enders (because the bow and stern were similar) used for coastal patrols into the early twentieth century.[5] As shown in table 4.1, most of the other powers built only a handful.

Paddle wheelers did participate in the few wars of the era, but in secondary roles. During the Crimean War paddle wheelers were often lashed to ships of the line for maneuverability, and during the American Civil War steam frigates were used for blockade and river operations. On occasion they participated in shore bombardments, but there were no paddle-wheel fleet engagements. Their greatest contribution was as river gunboats in the Civil War. They also proved useful as amphibious transports with special landing craft called paddle boats designed for storage over the paddle wheels. In 1849 the Austrian paddle wheeler *Vulcano* launched balloons with explosive charges, and some have cited her as the first "aircraft carrier."[6]

Screw propeller warships started to appear in 1845 and within a very few years became dominant. Paddle wheelers did not, of course, disappear immediately and they participated in both the Crimean and Civil Wars, but the advantages of the less vulnerable below-the-waterline screw that also freed up more space for guns was obvious. During both world wars the Royal Navy built paddle-wheel minesweepers. In World War I, Britain and Germany used paddle wheelers for seaplane tenders, and in World War II the United States converted two Great Lakes paddle wheelers into training aircraft carriers. Today, paddle wheelers are still found plying the Mississippi River as tourist boats although more for sentimental than practical reasons. Because only England and France built large paddle-wheel warships in any number and they did not participate in any major engagements, these ships are often overlooked. Nevertheless, paddle wheelers were the dominant type for over a third of the Age of Steam and Ironclads and deserve credit as an important transitional type.

THE SCREW PROPELLER AND CONVERSION ERA: 1845–1860

Proposals for a screw propeller date to Du Quet in 1729. Hand-operated experiments began as early as 1794. In 1800 a patent for a "perpetual sculling machine" using the ship's capstan to operate a propeller was granted to Edward Shorter. Test runs reached one and a half knots on the transport *Doncaster* in 1802. In 1825 Captain Samuel Brown of the Royal Navy won a prize for proposing a two-blade propeller, but at the bow, not stern. Others also had proposals, but it was not until 1836 that John Ericsson, originally from Sweden, and Francis Petit Smith of England both came up with more practical ideas. Ericsson, with a patent from 1836, tested his launch the *Francis B. Ogden* on the Thames on 19 April 1837 and is often credited as the first, although Smith tested his *Francis Smith* on 1 November 1836. Smith's was considered the better design, and he soon built another ship, the *Archimedes,* in 1838.[7] After trials on rivers, the *Archimedes* went to sea in 1839, making her the first seagoing screw vessel. Making 8 to 9 knots, the *Archimedes* performed well enough that the Admiralty ordered its first screw warship, the sloop *Rattler,* launched in 1843.

The *Rattler* was slightly over 1,100 tons, 176 feet long, carried one 68-pounder pivot gun on the bow and four 32-pounders, and could make approximately 9 knots. The *Rattler* was famous not only as the first screw warship but also for her participation in a series of tests against paddle wheelers culminating in her winning a famous tug-of-war with the paddle wheeler *Alecto* on 30 March 1845. This event was often cited as finally convincing the admirals of the advantages of screw versus paddle wheelers but is now considered more a publicity stunt, since the Admiralty had already made that decision. Nevertheless, it is still considered a defining event, and within a few years, paddle wheelers were rarely built.[8]

By 1850 screw ships had become dominant, but despite this major revolution in propulsion, there was in some respects a retrogression in warship design. Unlike the paddle wheelers, which required innovations like pivot guns on the bow and sometimes the stern, the warships built during the next ten years were essentially old ships of the line with machinery inserted. This should not be too surprising. Although guns were getting bigger with up to 68-pounders (from the previous 42- and 32-pounders) with some on pivots, the broadside was still considered the standard fighting procedure. While paddle wheelers had restricted broadsides, screw warships did not. Thus began a ten-year period that can best be described as a conversion era. While there was some new construction, most warships during this period were simply the old ships of the line with machinery backfitted and still considered auxiliary power to the sails. The first ships converted in 1845 were some old 74-gun ships of the line and 44-gun frigates for harbor and channel defense. HMS *Ajax* was the first, completed in 1846 for a planned attack on the French naval arsenal at Cherbourg. Although she is often cited as the first steam battleship, most analysts consider her more a blockship.

Despite the Royal Navy's lead, the French were the first to build a true large steam battleship, launching *Le Napoleon* on 16 May 1850. *Le Napoleon* was a large 90-gun two-decker, just over 5,000 tons and 234 feet long. She was immediately followed by the British *Agamemnon* of approximately the same size. Both were considered successful ships, and others were built. During the period 1850–60, the Royal Navy built eighteen new and converted forty-one ships of the line and the French built ten new and did twenty-eight conversions.[9]

As shown in table 4.1, only England and France built large steam warships and battle fleets, with other navies constructing only a few smaller frigates, sloops, and corvettes. The American corvette *Princeton,* built by Ericsson in 1843, was the world's second screw warship (after the *Rattler*), and the French built an experimental frigate, the *Pomone,* in 1845. The Royal Navy responded with its first screw frigate, the *Amphion,* in 1846. During the

Table 4.1 Paddle and Screw Warships Naval Balance, 1840–1860

Type	Britain	France	Germany	Italy	Russia	Austria	U.S.
Paddle frigates	16	19	3				3
Paddle corvettes		14	2	18			1
Paddle sloops	36	56				13	2
(Subtotal)	(52)	(89)	(5)	(18)		(13)	(6)
Screw three-deckers	16	6			3		
Screw two-deckers	37	31		1	6		
Screw frigates	28	16	4	9	9	3	7
Screw corvettes	22	15	4	4	18	3	6
Screw sloops	26	19			8		
(Subtotal)	(129)	(87)	(8)	(14)	(44)	(6)	(13)
TOTAL	181	176	13	32	44	19	19

NOTES: There were still sailing ships in many of the fleets, not listed above. Classifications varied widely from navy to navy, e.g., RN paddle sloops were in the 600- to 1,100-ton range, while French paddle sloops were in the 150- to 200-ton range.

1850s, there was a small arms race in steam frigates and ever larger ships were built. Some of them were over a hundred feet longer than the battleships, yet they were classified as frigates or corvettes because they had only one covered deck of guns and carried only forty to fifty guns. Some of the classifications were confusing, contributing to the hodgepodge of ship types that persists throughout the rest of this period. For example, the five American *Merrimack*-class frigates built in the mid-1850s were 5,300 tons, 257 feet long, and carried forty guns and were followed by the *Niagara,* which at 5,440 tons and 328 feet long was both heavier and longer, but since she carried only twelve 11-inch guns was called a spar-deck corvette. The largest of the period and the largest wooden warships ever built were the British *Mersey* and *Orlando* frigates at almost 5,700 tons, 336 feet long, carrying forty guns. They had a speed of 13 knots, considered very fast by contemporary standards.

One major war took place during this period. That was the Crimean War from 1854 to 1856. Although no major sea battles took place during the war, it is nevertheless cited as the end of the strictly sailing warship and the beginning of the end for wooden warships. The reason was not the use of paddle wheelers or even screw, but rather the first major use of shell-firing guns. In 1819, Major Henri Paixhans of France came up with the idea of high-explosive shells, which for the first time had the capacity to destroy wooden warships. The old cannonballs had great smashing capabilities, but they seldom sank ships. At the Battle of Sinope in 1853, a Russian fleet using shells had defeated a Turkish fleet. During the Crimean War, France responded to the new shells by building heavily armed ironclad floating batteries, while England built nearly three hundred gunboats. There were several ship-versus-fort exchanges with decidedly mixed results.[10] Nevertheless, the proverbial handwriting was on the wall for wooden ships as well as less mobile sailing warships. Sailing warships were still used for shore bombardments, but they often had steamers lashed alongside for maneuverability.

While the paddle wheeler was a passing transition type, the introduction of the screw propeller was a true revolution that has lasted to this day. During the period from 1850 to 1860, there had developed a wider spectrum of warships from large three-deckers to blockships, frigates, and sloops down to smaller gunboats. But the large wooden three-deckers were still considered the first-line warships. That was about to change with the emergence of the ironclad.

Ironclads, Steel, and Other Innovations: 1860–1890

Starting around 1860, warship design entered an approximately thirty-year period that was probably the most turbulent interval of its long history, witnessing a wide assortment of new types. While hard to summarize, since new types appeared almost yearly, there are three overlapping suberas of first, the early ironclads, followed by an experimental period, and finally the introduction of steel and other innovations.

THE EARLY IRONCLADS: 1860–1870

The launching of the Royal Navy's iron-hulled and armored frigate *Warrior* in 1860 was, along with the introduction of steam and the *Dreadnought* in 1906, one of the most important events in modern naval history. The *Warrior* has often been considered the first truly modern warship, although in some respects, there was nothing new about it since both iron and armor had been used for years and her design was really an enlarged, armored version of the wooden frigate *Mersey*. As is true of many creative events, however, it was the bringing together of the two concepts that counted.

Iron canal boats had been in use since the late eighteenth century, and in 1819, the iron passenger barge *Vulcan* was constructed for use on the Forth and Clyde Canal. The first oceangoing iron vessel was the *Aaron Manby*, built in England but then sailed across the Channel in 1822 for service on the Seine. The first iron-hulled warship was the East India Company's *Nemesis*, an iron paddle wheeler, 184 feet long with two 32-pounders, four 6-pounders, and rockets, launched in 1839 and used in the First China War of 1841–43. In 1840, the Royal Navy ordered its first iron ships for duties in Niger and the Great Lakes.[11]

There were two major problems with iron ships. First was their effect on the magnetic compass, which severely limited their use beyond rivers, lakes, and channel crossings. That problem was solved by the Astronomer Royal Sir George Airey in 1839.[12] The other, and for a warship more serious, problem was that iron was brittle, especially when cold. In a series of tests in the mid-1840s, iron-hulled ships did not fare well. One examiner concluded, "It has been proved that the disastrous effects of shot upon iron are so great that it is not a proper material of which to build ships of war."[13] The Royal Navy built a few more iron warships in the mid-1840s, but these were quickly converted to troop ships, and iron-hulled warships were essentially abandoned for the next fifteen years.

The answer to the problem of brittle iron was armor. The use of armor can be traced back to the Age of Galleys, with the most famous examples being the Korean "turtle ships" of the late sixteenth century, but armor was not really necessary until the invention of the exploding shell. During the Age of Sail, although the round shot had great smashing capabilities, few ships were ever sunk. But that changed with the introduction of shells. Armor was needed to counter shells. One of the first proposals was the American Stevens Battery of 1842, originally designed for harbor protection. The Stevens brothers had found that 4.5-inch plate stood up well to the large guns of the

HMS *Warrior*, completed in 1860, was the world's first iron-hulled ironclad.
(Courtesy of Imperial War Museum)

period, the 64-pounders, and in 1845 they began construction on the battery, but it was never completed. Both the English and French picked up the battery idea during the Crimean War. The French launched the first, the *Tonnante*, in 1855. The *Tonnante* was 1,500 tons, carried sixteen 50-pounders, and was protected by 4½ inches of wrought iron plates on a wooden hull. Three batteries took part in the bombardment of Kinburn on the Black Sea on 17 October 1855, sometimes cited as the first use of armored steam warships.[14]

Thus by the late 1850s, the stage was set. The great French designer Dupuy de Lôme planned the world's first ironclad, the *Gloire*, launched in 1859. The *Gloire* was 5,600 tons, 255.5 feet long, had an almost 44-foot beam, and carried thirty-six 6.4-inch guns. She was wooden hulled with a 4½-inch armor plate. While a major improvement, she was quickly overshadowed by the launching of the Royal Navy's *Warrior* in 1860 (preserved at Portsmouth, England). The *Warrior* was a huge ship, over 9,000 tons, 420 feet long, 58-foot beam, carrying forty guns, twenty-six 68-pounders, ten 100-pounders, and four 40-pounders, and very fast at 14 to 15 knots under steam. But the *Warrior*'s claim to fame was that she was the first armored iron-hulled ship, making her the first modern warship.[15] Sometimes also called the first battleship, with only one deck of guns, the *Warrior* was classified as a frigate although she probably would have made short work of the wooden three-deckers.

Both the English and French built more ironclads in the early 1860s. France built the only two-decker ironclads in 1861. These were two *Magenta* class, 6,700 tons, 282 feet long, with fifty-two guns. England followed the *Warrior* with the *Black Prince* and a few other derivatives. The largest were the three *Minotaur* class at almost 10,700 tons, 407 feet long, carrying thirty-six guns. Other powers built a few in the early 1860s, Russia some coastal ironclads, and both Italy and Austria-Hungary built wooden-hulled ironclads. While some were both iron hulled and armored, during this early period many ironclads still had wooden hulls, and even the Royal Navy built two new wooden-hulled ironclads to use up old stocks of wood.

The American Civil War

Although the Civil War saw the first clash of ironclads, of the approximately 650 ships in the Union navy in 1864, only 49 were ironclads. Most were screw steamers (113), followed by sailing vessels (112), paddle wheelers (52), and over 300 civilian steamers purchased and fitted for naval purposes.[16] Nevertheless, ironclads played important roles, especially in the river campaigns and, of course, in the famous *Monitor-Merrimack (Virginia)* duel, the first battle between ironclads. The Civil War also saw the first appearance of three other warships that would become important in the modern age: torpedo boats, submarines, and cruisers. The most important warships were the Union wooden steamers and paddle wheelers fitted with iron plate used in the river campaigns. These Union ironclads were able to deny the Confederacy the use of the major rivers, thereby cutting the Confederacy off from the West.

The most famous ironclad clash, however, was the *Monitor-Merrimack* duel off Hampton Roads. The Confederates had raised the frigate *Merrimack,* sunk by retreating Union forces, and turned her into an ironclad, renamed *Virginia,* with 4.5-inch armor plate. The Union responded, hastily building the *Monitor,* designed by John Ericsson. The *Monitor* was relatively small at 172 feet by 41.5 feet, built entirely of iron. Her main feature was an extremely low freeboard with a small revolving turret housing two large 11-inch Dahlgren smoothbore guns, prompting the nickname "cheese box on a raft." The famous duel between the *Virginia* and the *Monitor* took place in March 1862, when the two ships blasted away at each other for several hours before the *Virginia* finally withdrew. Although usually considered a tactical draw, it was a major strategic victory for the Union. Just the day before the *Virginia* had rather easily sunk the Union frigate *Congress* and sloop of war *Cumberland,* and there were fears that she would then proceed up the Potomac and shell Washington. With this famous duel, the age of wooden ships that had lasted for thousand of years finally ended.

The Union navy went on to build sixty-four more *Monitor*s and although some European countries followed suit, with their low freeboard and poor open-ocean sea-keeping capabilities, they had little lasting effect on naval shipbuilding. The original *Monitor* foundered and sank while being towed. Besides the *Monitor*s and river ironclads, only one seagoing armored ship, the *New Ironsides,* was built and completed during the Civil War. She was 230 feet long, with eighteen guns, carrying 4.5 inches of armor over most of her hull. The *New Ironsides* participated in several shore bombardments and although hit several times was only briefly put out of action when damaged by a Confederate torpedo boat.

Three other Civil War ship types deserve brief mention as forerunners of modern types. Both sides built what today would be called "small combatants," mostly because they could be built quickly. The Union navy, for example, built some labeled "ninety-day gunboats," indicating how fast they were built. The Civil War also saw the first use of what would later be called torpedo boats using spar torpedoes, usually detonated by direct contact. There were also the first semipractical use of submarines and semisubmersibles. Finally, there were the roots of the first modern cruisers. The Confederate raiders *Alabama* and *Shenandoah* are sometimes considered early cruisers, although the Union *Wampanoag,* the fastest ship of her day, is considered a more important precedent.[17]

EXPERIMENTAL PERIOD: 1860–1890

The era of ironclads continued for a few more years, but starting around 1865, it entered a new transitional phase, or what a leading scholar of this period, David K. Brown, calls the "Age of Uncertainty," that lasted until approximately 1890, the start of the pre-dreadnought era.[18] It might also be called the "Experimental Period" because during this time there was a major sorting out of ideas. Gun size grew considerably larger, from 8 inches to almost 18, and as a result armor got thicker, from 4.5 to 24 inches. Many consider this arms race between guns and armor the dominant feature of this period.

From a ship design viewpoint, however, one of the related aspects of the guns-versus-armor race was the sorting out of the position and types of gun mounts. The ironclad era had opened with a return to broadsides on the *Gloire* and *Warrior* but then went through some eight different variations before finally settling on the gun mounts we know today. The main reasons for the experimentation was the increasing power of the gun, which required greater thickness of armor, but since armor was heavy, it was no longer feasible to place it over the entire ship. Alternatives were needed to protect only the vital parts and especially the gun mounts. In general chronological order (although there was considerable overlapping), the alternatives for gun mounts explored were as described below.

The Monitor Turrets: 1862–1866

Two people are usually credited with coming up with the idea for armored turrets at about the same time. They were the Swedish American John Ericsson and Royal Navy captain Cowper Coles, both of whom made suggestions during the Crimean War. Coles made further proposals during the late 1850s, including an innovative plan in 1859 for a ship with ten armored cupolas, but none were built although an experimental turret was tested on the battery *Trusty* in 1861.[19] Thus Ericsson is usually credited with designing the first turret on the famous *Monitor* built in 1862.

These early turrets had two major problems. First, they were extremely heavy, restricting their placement high on the ship. As a result, the early monitors had low freeboard. The other problem was that sails were still needed because fuel consumption was high and turrets and sails with all their rigging did not mix well. Thus most early turret ships were used for coastal defense.

In 1866 the United States completed the *Miantonowoh* class of seagoing monitors, which made some ocean voyages, including one by the *Miantonowoh* across the Atlantic. For much of that trip, however, she was towed. In 1866, the Coles-designed ship *Prince Albert* was completed with more ship-like characteristics than the monitors, though she too was restricted to coast defense. Several other countries also built monitors or coastal defense ships during this period. Denmark had the *Rolf Krake* with four 8-inch guns built in Britain according to a Coles design. A similar ship, the *Huascar,* built for Peru, deserves mention because she was twice tested in battle, against two unarmored British cruisers in 1877 and two Chilean casemate ships in 1879. The *Huascar* still survives in Chile.

Central Battery and Casemate Ships: 1862–1882

Two other alternatives developed at about the same time were the central (sometimes called box) battery and casemate approaches. Although the terms are sometimes used interchangeably, there were slight differences. In both, the ship's battery was reduced so that the protecting armor was a short rectangular box in the center of the ship. The difference was that the early central battery ships had only a broadside configuration while the casemates had angled corner ports allowing greater arcs of fire.[20]

Although a few smaller central battery ships, mostly wooden conversions, were built in the early 1860s, the British *Bellerophon,* laid down in 1863 and completed in 1866, was the first major warship constructed. She was 7,551 tons full load, 300 feet long, and carried ten 9-inch and five 7-inch guns. The box casemate had 6-inch sides and 5-inch bulkheads. The *Bellerophon* was followed by ten more casement ships including the four-ship *Audacious* class, one of the few exceptions of a more than one- or two-ship class built during this experimentation period. Other countries also adopted the casemate ship design. The *Alexandra,* launched in 1875, was the last British casemate ship. France hung onto the design until 1882 with the completion of the *Devastation.* The main advantage of the casemate ships was that they essentially maintained the broadside tradition.

Seagoing Turret Ships: 1866–1870

In 1869 the Royal Navy completed the *Monarch,* its first large seagoing turret ship. The *Monarch* was 8,300 tons, 330 feet long, and the first to carry 12-inch guns (four), which became the common size for the Royal Navy until 1910. While generally considered a good design, she still carried sails that restricted the turret arcs of fire so she was also given 7-inch guns fore and aft. Captain Coles was critical of what he considered the *Monarch*'s high 14-foot freeboard and lobbied for another design, which resulted in the *Captain,* completed in 1870 with only an 8-foot freeboard. Although initial trials went well, while on channel duty later in the year the *Captain* was caught in a gale and capsized, taking 472 people, including Captain Cole, to their death. This accident cast serious doubt on these lower freeboard ships, and further construction was halted for many years.

Breastwork Monitors: 1870–1880

A new type described as monitors with a "breastwork amidships on which turrets were mounted, one at each end," was begun.[21] Like monitors, they had a low freeboard main deck but a higher armored deck in the center on which sat the armored turrets. Many were built as coastal defense ships. The *Cerberus,* 3,350 tons, 225 feet long, carrying four 10-inch guns, laid down in 1867 and completed in 1870, was built to defend Melbourne harbor. The *Devastation,* completed in 1873, was the first seagoing mastless ship and is often considered the basic pattern for all future battleships. She displaced 9,300 tons, was 307 feet long, and carried four 12-inch guns. The *Devastation* was followed by a sister ship *Thunderer,* but a third ship, the *Dreadnought,* was delayed for several years following the capsizing of the *Captain.*

Central Citadel Ships: 1876–1882

Then in the early 1870s came still another alternative. This was the central citadel arrangement with armored turrets placed midships. The honor of having the first such ship went to one of the emerging powers of the day. In 1873 Italy laid down the *Duilio* and *Dandolo,* which at almost 11,000 tons,

340 feet long, were large ships for their day. Their revolutionary feature was two massive twin-mount turrets with 17-inch armor placed amidships carrying 17.7-inch guns. The Royal Navy responded with the *Inflexible,* laid down in 1874 and completed in 1881. She was almost 12,000 tons, 320 feet long, carrying four 16-inch guns in turrets with 17-inch steel. The *Inflexible* was also the last British capital ship to carry a sailing rig. This "big gun" era lasted only a few years; most navies reverted to 12-inch guns until World War I.

The Barbette: 1877–1890

In the mid-1870s, the French came up with yet another idea, the barbette. This was simply an armored shield placed around a gun mounted on a turntable. The main advantage was that it was lightweight, which meant gun placement was no longer limited to lower levels and the center of the ship. The disadvantage was that these were open mounts, making the gun and its crew vulnerable to splinters and small gun fire. Although the French first introduced the barbette in the *Alma* in 1867 and the English had experimented with a barbette arrangement on the *Temeraire* in 1876, the first true

HMS *Devastation,* completed in 1873. A "breastwork" monitor, it is better known as the first mastless seagoing ship that set the pattern for later battleships.
(Courtesy of Imperial War Museum)

barbette ship was the French *Admiral Duperre,* laid down in 1877 and completed in 1883. She displaced 11,000 tons, was 319 feet long, with a main battery of four 13.4-inch guns. The barbette armor was 12 inches.

In 1876, Italy started construction of two large, fast *Italia*-class battleships, 15,400 tons, 409 feet long, with four large 17-inch guns in barbettes. These large ships with light armor are sometimes considered forerunners of the battle cruisers built in the early dreadnought era. The Royal Navy was slower adopting the barbette with the *Collingwood,* the first of the so-called Admiral class, laid down in 1880 and completed in 1887.[22]

Those described above are the most identifiable gun arrangements, but there were others. Germany developed the "reduit," which was an armored deckhouse arrangement, usually oval shaped with tracks to move one or two guns around to different ports. Other track arrangements were used to move guns at other locations, often on the bow and stern, for more flexibility. This gun-mounting problem was not resolved until the 1890s pre-dreadnought era, when an armored hood was placed on the gun mount, and they became known as the turrets still seen on today's warships.

THIS ERA OF experimentation and uncertainty dominated from the early 1860s until around 1890. There were many "one of a kinds" constructed, with perhaps a sister ship or two, but no large classes were built. The result was a hodgepodge of ship types that is hard to summarize. Perhaps nothing better epitomizes this experimentatal hodgepodge era than the two Russian *Popoffka* circular, 120- by 120-foot coastal defense vessels completed in the mid-1870s. Because of the expense involved in these experiments, only England and to a lesser degree France and Russia built capital ships during this period. Most of the other European powers built only a few and the United States none at all.

STEEL AND OTHER INNOVATIONS

Other important innovations occurred during this same general period that deserve brief mention. These are the introduction of steel ships, the final disappearance of muzzle-loading guns, the development of torpedoes, the re-emergence of the ram, and some new schools of naval thought.

Introduction of Steel

Steel, which was both stronger and lighter in weight than iron, had been in existence for years but until improved production began in the early 1870s was considered too expensive for shipbuilding. Once again, the French were the first with this innovation, laying down the *Redoubtable* in 1873, which was completed in 1878. The *Redoubtable* was a 9,200-ton central battery ship, 319 feet in length, 64.5 feet wide, with a main battery of eight 10-inch guns. The first British ships were the smaller dispatch boats *Iris* and *Mercury,* laid down in 1875 and 1876 respectively, both completed in 1879. These two ships are also sometimes considered prototypes for the modern cruiser and in the late 1880s were classified as second-class cruisers. They were 3,730 tons, 300 feet long, and carried thirteen 5-inch guns. Italy was another early convert, using steel in its new large *Italia*-class battleships. By the late 1870s, most navies had switched to all steel-hulled ships.[23]

Armor also underwent changes during this period. The original 1860 armor was hammered wrought-iron plates bolted on wood. Around 1865 rolled-iron armor on double layers of wood stiffened with iron girders and an inner skin of iron plate began to be used. Sandwich armor was introduced in 1870. This consisted of several layers of rolled iron plates alternated with layers of wood and an inner skin of two layers of sheet iron. A major change occurred in 1877 with the introduction of compound armor, steel-clad wrought-iron plates. Later during the pre-dreadnought era came more changes. First was the introduction of Harvey plate in 1890, which was nickel steel armor, steel plates with hardened surface of nickel and carbon. In 1895 Krupp introduced KC or Krupp-cemented steel, which was about 25 percent better than Harvey Steel, and in 1902 chromium nickel steel armor appeared.[24]

Emergence of Breech Loaders

The second major change during this period was the final disappearance of the old smoothbore muzzle-loading guns. Shells had been invented by General Paixhans in 1819 and by 1839 had been adopted by many nations. They had two problems, however. The first was that shells fired from smoothbore guns were inaccurate. This difficulty was solved by giving guns twisted internal grooves or rifling. Rifling had long been used in small arms to give bullets a spin that increased their accuracy. In 1846, Major Cavalli of Sardinia and Baron Wahrendorff of Sweden independently came up with the idea of rifling cannon, but that raised still another problem. Rifling complicated the loading of shells into guns from the muzzle. Cavalli and Wahrendorff developed crude breech-loading mechanisms that worked in tests, but they were less satisfactory in production.

It was not until the invention of the interrupted screw breech block that the problem was solved. With this mechanism the breech could be easily inserted, then, with a simple twist, screwed and locked into place. The originator was an American inventor, Ben Chambers, who patented a slotted screw in 1849. There were several modifications over the next few years, including one by French General Treuille de Beaulieu, who then played a major role in its adoption by the French navy in 1858. Breech loaders were placed on the first ironclad, the *Gloire,* in 1859.

Their adoption by the Royal Navy was not so smooth. In 1856 W. G. Armstrong built a rifled cannon using a more complicated system. These screw-guns were introduced in the Royal Navy in 1860 aboard the *Warrior,* but two years later aboard the British flagship *Euryalus* during the bombardment of Kagohima, Japan, there were several misfires and the Royal Navy reverted to muzzle-loaders for the next twenty-years. Although the muzzle-loaders performed as well or sometimes better than early breech loaders, by the late 1870s with improvements in gunpowders and shells, the differences were apparent, and in 1881, the Royal Navy finally switched to breech loaders.[25] Another era had ended.

One other major gunnery change took place during the pre-dreadnought era—the introduction of the quick-firing gun. Self-contained cartridges (that is, with both propellant and round), which had been available for repeating rifles and early machine guns since the mid-1860s, were developed for larger guns. This led to quick-firing cannon. The medium-caliber 4.7-inch quick-firing gun was tested on the Elswick yard cruiser *Piemonte,* built for Italy in 1887. It proved successful, and later a 6-inch rapid-fire gun was developed. Quick-firing guns had two major effects. First, they spelled the end of the torpedo boat threat. The quick firers also began a debate that would rage for years (especially during the interwar years) as to whether it was better to have a few slower-firing larger-caliber guns or more rapid-firing guns.

The Torpedo

While switching from muzzle to breech loaders and even the development of quick-firing guns might be considered evolutionary changes, the development of the self-propelled or locomotive torpedo by Robert Whitehead in 1866 was revolutionary. To this date so-called spar-torpedoes had been used, but they were nothing more than an explosive charge on a long pole. Towing or Harvey torpedoes (named after their inventor, Royal Navy commander Frederick Harvey) were also used. In 1866 Captain Luppis, retired from the Austrian navy, invented a surface torpedo with its own engine that was controlled by wires from shore. He took his invention to the English manager of an engineering works in Fiume, Robert Whitehead, who realized that, to be successful, the torpedo had to operate underway and independently of wires (although wire-guided torpedoes are still in use today). Whitehead is credited with inventing the "locomotive" or self-propelled torpedo, which ran submerged. In 1868 it was demonstrated to the Austrian government, which declined to purchase any (for lack of funds), but England bought two in 1870, and within a few years most navies had adopted the Whitehead torpedo. This soon led to the development of the torpedo boat and a whole new school of naval thought. The Royal Navy's first was the *Lightning*, TB-1, completed in 1877. The first use in combat of a locomotive torpedo was by the British frigate *Shah* against the Peruvian ironclad *Huascar* in 1877.[26]

Return of the Ram

A somewhat amusing event occurred during this period that is partly responsible for its being called an era of uncertainty. That was the return of the ram, not seen since ancient times. With steam giving ships maneuverability, starting around 1862 a few ships were built with rams, although generally their use was considered secondary. However, during the only fleet battle between ironclads, the Battle of Lisa on 20 July 1866, the Austrian ship *Erzherzog Ferdinand Max* rammed the Italian *Re d'Italia,* which sank in only a few moments. Even though the *Re d'Italia* had actually been dead in the water and thus vulnerable, this event sent shock waves through naval circles and rams were returned to most ships for the next twenty years. In 1867, even Sir John Colomb, considered one of the great maritime thinkers, wrote that "the ram was now the ultimate weapon." Most capital ships were fitted with rams and specially designed ships were built, some with greatly exaggerated rams that would have been the envy of the ancient Athenians. There were several accidental rammings and sinkings in fleet maneuvers, adding to the confusion over the ram's effectiveness. Though now considered one of the major naval faux pas in history, the ram was not without merit now that ships could maneuver without relying on wind, but the threat it presented was clearly exaggerated.

New Schools of Naval Thought

There were many new schools of naval thought during this period, none more provocative than *la jeune école* (the young school) under the leadership of French Admiral Théophile Aube. Aube argued that the torpedo had rendered the big gun superfluous and that a large number of fast torpedo boats might be used to attack battleships. This idea had great appeal for the country that had been trying to catch up with the Royal Navy for over three hundred years.[27] It dominated French thinking during the 1880s and has often found great appeal in other navies such as the Soviet navy of the 1920s and 1930s. Torpedo boats never really measured up, however, and were finally thwarted by the development of quick-firing guns and larger and faster torpedo-boat destroyers, the forerunners of today's destroyer. But the French were not the only ones to question conventional wisdom. In an article entitled "A Treatise on Future Naval Battles and How to Fight Them," published in 1885, Admiral Sir George Elliot argued that the torpedo and the ram were the dominant weapons of the day.[28]

The Premodern Age: 1885–1906

Starting in the mid- to late 1880s, the era of experimenting and uncertainty came to an end, warship design became more stable, and large classes once again were being built by 1890. Warships entered into what is usually called the pre-dreadnought era that lasted until the launching of the famous *Dreadnought* in 1906. More properly, it probably should be called the premodern era because besides dreadnoughts, the basic designs for cruisers, destroyers, and submarines also emerged. For continuity's sake, the premodern history of these types is included in their appropriate chapters in the next section so only brief summaries are given here. As is evident in table 4.2, however, this was one of the major periods of warship building.

Table 4.2 Pre-Dreadnought Naval Balance, 1890–1905

Type	Britain	France	Germany	Russia	Italy	Austria	U.S.	Japan
BATTLESHIPS								
First class	47	20	25	20	9	3	24	6
Second class	5	3	8	8	2	6	2	
(Subtotal)	(52)	(23)	(33)	(28)	(11)	(9)	(26)	(6)
CRUISERS								
First class								
Armored	35	25	8	8	6	4	15	9
Protected	21	28	7	11	5	2	2	11
Second class	60	1		4	8	3	17	7
Third class	50		25			1		7
(Subtotal)	(166)	(59)	(40)	(23)	(20)	(10)	(34)	(34)
Torpedo gunboats	33	16		17	5			2
Destroyers	147	55	54	120	15	8	20	23
Torpedo boats								
First class	100	66	115	97	109	39	32	17
Second class	74	369		98	48	26	4	69
TOTAL	572	588	242	383	208	92	116	151

NOTES: Approximate balance of those ships built from the late 1880s through 1905. Rating based on RN classes, with similar tonnage and armament used for other countries.

Cruisers

What many consider the first modern cruiser was the *Esmeralda,* laid down in 1881, launched in 1883, built in England for Chile. Also in 1883 the United States laid down the "ABC" cruisers, considered the start of the modern U.S. Navy. But, of course, it was the British who predominated in design during this period. In 1885 the Royal Navy began building seven *Orlando*-class armored cruisers followed by protected cruisers in 1888. During the 1890s three types were built: armored, protected, and unarmored.

The Pre-Dreadnoughts

By 1890 the experimentation period of gun mount placement was just about over and large capital ships or what became known as the pre-dreadnoughts started to appear. The Royal Navy's *Royal Sovereign* class, laid down in 1889, is sometimes cited as the first, although the *Majestic* class, laid down in 1893, is called the first "true" pre-dreadnoughts because they had greater protection. Other countries followed, but as usual, none matched the British.

HMS *Royal Sovereign,* completed in 1892. Ships of her class are usually cited as the first "pre-dreadnoughts."
(Courtesy of Imperial War Museum)

During this time a British policy dating to 1817 was restated in the Naval Defense Act of 1889: the famous "two power standard," or having a fleet the size of the next two fleets. Another famous act of the period was Germany's 1898 and 1900 Navy Laws implementing Admiral Alfred von Tirpitz's "risk theory" of building just enough ships to deter Britain.

Destroyers

During this period a completely new ship type emerged, the torpedo-boat destroyer (TBD), the predecessor of today's destroyer. Starting in the 1870s, small torpedo boats with the new Whitehead torpedo emerged. Some thought they could challenge, and perhaps even defeat, battleships. A new fast type was needed to defeat the torpedo boat, and thus was developed the TBD in the early 1890s.

Submarines

Finally, this period also saw the introduction of the first submarines. Serious experimentation had begun around 1875, and during the 1890s several designs were tried. Practical working models had been developed in both France and the United States by the turn of the century.

ALTHOUGH EXPERIMENTATION and uncertainty did not end during the 1890s, there was a certain settling down, as can be seen in the large size of the classes of ships. Whereas there were only a few three- and four-ship classes in the Royal Navy during the period 1865 to 1885, during the pre-modern era there were the seven-ship *Royal Sovereign* class, the even larger nine-ship *Majestic* class, and by far the largest class of the period, twenty-one *Apollo* second-class cruisers. In short, the admirals of the period were obviously satisfied with these ships. Unfortunately, virtually all were made obsolete with the completion of the *Dreadnought* in 1906.

For the first time in many years, some sea battles took place. In the Battle of the Yalu River in September 1894, during the Sino-Japanese War of 1894–95 over Korea, the two sides fought a major engagement mostly between armored cruisers. Although the battle was indecisive, the Chinese withdrew. The battle's real significance was the emergence of Japan as a major power. Similarly, during the Spanish-American War, the United States and Spain fought two minor sea battles, the Battle of Manila Bay in May and the Battle of Santiago in July 1898. Both were American victories, whose real importance was the emergence of the United States as a world power.

Although the above-mentioned sea battles were relatively minor with few lasting results, the Battle of Tsushima on the eve of the modern era in May 1905, during the 1904–5 Russo-Japanese War, was one of the major sea battles of history for several reasons. It was the only major sea battle during this entire age, but, more important, it was one of only two major battleship fleet engagements ever fought in history. (The other was the Battle of Jutland in 1916.) Not only did Japan decisively defeat the Russian fleet, it twice "capped the Russian T" in the classic tactic of the day. The lessons of Tsushima with gun exchanges at over 13,000 yards brought into question the need for smaller secondary batteries and was a major factor leading to the "all big gun" dreadnoughts.

This battle also pointed to the need for what later would be called a service force. The Russian fleet had journeyed from Europe, and the exhaustion from the months-long journey to the Pacific is usually considered a major contributing factor to their defeat. (In the interwar period experts would calculate that a fleet lost about 10 percent of its efficiency for each thousand miles traveled.) The Russo-Japanese sea battles also saw the first extensive use of mines and torpedoes. Coming on the eve of the modern dreadnought era, the Battle of Tsushima is now considered one of the great battles in history. It was also a fitting end to a truly fascinating era.

Conclusion

The Age of Steam, Ironclads, and Steel saw the greatest progress in the shortest time ever in history, comparable to the introduction of the airplane. Even the post–World War II period, when nuclear weapons and missiles were introduced, was in many respects evolutionary compared to the truly revolutionary changes during this period from wooden sailing ships of the line to dreadnoughts and submarines. Perhaps ironically, during much of this time the dominant navy, the Royal Navy, was often seen as resisting change, and it is not hard to find quotations from admirals resisting the introduction of steam or new weapons systems and designs. Many of the innovations were made by other navies. The French were the first with shells, ironclad batteries, and ironclads, and the Americans were the first with the turret and monitor and what some consider the first cruiser, the *Wampanoag*. But the British were never far behind, and during the era of experimentation from 1860 to 1890, most of those experiments were conducted on Royal Navy ships. Delays were usually only a matter of a year or two. In contrast, the introduction of new weaponry today takes anywhere from ten to twenty years. The U.S. Navy, for example, has been working on a new surface combatant type for almost ten years with the first scheduled for 2010. England had another unappreciated advantage. Many of the new types, though not built for the Royal Navy, were constructed in British shipyards. These include the *Rising Star* for Chile, *Karteria* for Greece, *Nemesis* for the East India Company, the ironclad *Huascar* for Peru, and the *Esmeralda* for Chile. All of these are considered important firsts.

This was also the era of some of the most important events in modern history, many relating to seapower. It was the time of the so-called Pax Britannica, the century of relative peace from the end of the Napoleonic Wars to the start of World War I that was maintained mostly through British seapower. This was also the golden age of balance-of-power politics, as well as the Age of Imperialism, the scramble for colonies that started around 1875. Both were dependent on seapower. And this period also saw the rise of new powers: Germany, Italy, the United States, and Japan, all of which, to varying degrees, spread their wings through seapower. This was also a golden age of naval thought, including the writings of Admiral Aube of France, the Colomb brothers, John and Philippe, and the most famous of all, American admiral Alfred Thayer Mahan, who wrote his classic *The Influence of Sea Power upon History* in 1890. Fred Jane and Earl Brassey also started their famous naval annuals during this time.

In short, though it lasted only a few years, the Age of Steam, Ironclads, and Steel was one of the most important in naval history. By the end of this age, virtually every modern warship type except aircraft carriers had been developed, new nations were emerging based on seapower, all backed up by what are now considered the masters of naval thought. This was also the last time that warship development would dominate military affairs. There were no similar advances in land weaponry. Repeating rifles, machine guns, and better artillery pieces were all invented during the nineteenth century, but these pale next to the proliferation of new ship types. And airplanes were not invented until the very end of the period in 1903. The Age of Steam, Ironclads, and Steel was truly a marvelous era for warships and seapower.

MODERN SHIPS

Overview of the Modern Age

5

A T LAST COMES the modern age, in which the complexity of the ships requires a separate chapter for each type. During the other ages, there were differences in warship types, some quite significant, but those differences pale in comparison with those of the Modern Age. Modern types such as aircraft carriers, submarines, mine craft, service ships, and specifically designed amphibious ships have no equals in the other ages, and even the contrasts among the three modern surface combatants—battleships, cruisers, and destroyers—are more pronounced than, for example, those between the three classes of dromons of the Age of Galleys or even the six ratings of the Age of Sail.

The Modern Age is usually divided into two general eras. The first is the dreadnought or "big gun" era that began with the building of the HMS *Dreadnought* in 1906 and ended with the close of World War II. The second is the post–World War II era that continues to this day. Sometimes called the nuclear era, it probably should more properly be called the era of missiles and electronics.

The Dreadnought Era: 1890–1955

By convention, the dreadnought or "big gun" era began in 1906 with the launching of HMS *Dreadnought* and ended in 1946, when most battleships and cruisers were retired, but there are problems with both the labels and the dates. In its series on warships, Conway's calls this era "The Eclipse of the Big Gun" because battleships and cruisers were eclipsed by both carriers and submarines in World War II. Though it might be more appropriate to call this the dreadnought, submarine, and aircraft carrier era, for most of this time, the big gun was considered more important, so labeling this the dreadnought era is probably appropriate, or at least adequate.

Then there is the question of dates. The launching of the *Dreadnought* in 1906 was indeed a seminal event. It made all existing battleships obsolete, and the battle cruisers made all the old armored and protected cruisers obsolete. Also around this same time, destroyers were emerging from being small craft to oceangoing ships, and second-generation, truly capable submarines were starting to be built. Yet most of today's modern types can be traced to the late 1880s and 1890s pre-dreadnought era. In sum, the period from 1890 to 1906 was not just a pre-dreadnought but a premodern period. Therefore, although 1906 was a significant date, the 1890–1905 pre-dreadnought period is also included in the following chapters on modern types for continuity's sake. At the other end of the spectrum, although many classic ship types were retired after World War II, major changes such as nuclear power and the introduction of missiles did not start until the mid-1950s.

The dreadnought era is fascinating for several reasons. It includes both world wars and the interwar period in which three naval arms control conferences laid down rules for ship types. These were the Washington Conference of 1921–22, which restricted battleship building and placed limits on future battleship, cruiser, and aircraft carrier construction; the First London Conference of 1930 that extended limits to cruisers, destroyers, and submarines; and finally the Second London Conference of 1935–36 that tried to continue these limits but finally broke down.

The period also saw the introduction of electronic systems that played a major role in World War II. These include radio, fire control, and sonar, all first used in World War I. Radar was developed in the late 1930s. The further development of these systems during World War II was crucial to the Allied success, and today many analysts consider electronics, not weaponry, a ship's primary weapons system. Unfortunately, the full story of electronics and its impact has yet to be written and is well beyond the scope of this book, but its importance should not be underestimated.[1]

Although the world wars, the interwar naval agreements, and the introduction of electronics are all important, from the viewpoint of warship building, this was truly the golden age of warship types. More different and distinct types were built in these relatively few years than at any other time in the long history of warships. For that reason alone, these types deserve separate chapters.

The Missile and Electronics Age: 1946–The Twenty-first Century

What many call the nuclear era began after World War II and continues to this day. Although this period is usually dated from 1946, new designs did not really appear until the mid-1950s, even the early 1960s. Besides the question of dates, there are problems with this era's label. The era has often been called the nuclear era for two reasons: first, to denote the introduction of new nuclear weapons, and second, because of nuclear power. Over time, however, both have proven disappointments. Except for sea-launched ballistic missiles (SLBM), nuclear weapons have disappeared from the sea. Nuclear bombs were placed on aircraft carriers in the 1950s, nuclear ASW weapons in the 1960s, and tactical sea-launched cruise missiles (SLCMs) in the 1980s, but all have now been removed (at least in Western navies). Nuclear propulsion has also been a disappointment. It has proven too expensive for more than a few surface ships, although it does remain a primary propulsion system for submarines.

Rather than the nuclear era, the post–World War II era should more properly be called the missile and electronics era because those developments have brought more significant and lasting changes. Few modern warships operate without both surface-to-surface missiles (SSM) and surface-to-air missiles (SAM), and today electronics are often considered the most important part of a ship's weapons suite. The most sophisticated ships in service today are the U.S. Navy's Aegis cruisers and destroyers. These "all big electronic" Aegis ships might look underarmed with few weapons showing, but they are as revolutionary as the "all big gun" *Dreadnought* that opened the Modern Age was in its day.

A BRIEF WORD about data: there is both a blessing and a curse of abundant data for the modern era. Starting in the pre-dreadnought era with the publication of *Jane's Fighting Ships* in 1898, there are many different sources on warships, but unfortunately they sometimes do not agree, which has often led to confusion on dates and certain data, especially displacement. For continuity, data from the excellent four-volume *Conway's All the World's Fighting Ships* series, which chronicles all warships since 1860, has been used. Although it sometimes differs from other sources, the differences are usually quite minor in the overall picture. Exceptions involve certain warship types such as service ships or mine craft, in which cases other sources such as Fahey's series *The Ships and Aircraft of the U.S. Fleet* have been used to fill in the gaps. Unless otherwise indicated, all displacements are rounded standard tonnage. In most cases only the warship's primary—that is, largest—gun battery is listed, but most ships also had several smaller or secondary batteries as well, and later even smaller guns for AAW. A battleship, for example, besides having a large gun, would usually have a secondary battery of 5- or 6-inch guns, then smaller 40- and 20-mm guns for AAW. A few secondary batteries are listed for illustrative purposes, but in general they are too numerous to chronicle for every type.

Battleships and Battle Cruisers　　6

ATTLESHIPS, BATTLE CRUISERS, DREADNOUGHTS—even for
people only vaguely familiar with naval affairs, these terms conjure
up something powerful and important, and they were, dominating
not just naval but all military affairs for almost half a century from
approximately 1890 to 1940. The launching of the battleship *Dreadnought*
in 1906 is seen as one of the defining events in naval history and the beginning of the modern age of warships. Virtually every other warship built
during this period was in support of the battleships in some manner or
another, usually for scouting or screening, "eyes of the fleet." Yet, for all the
time, effort, and expense spent on these behemoth ships—including a considerable amount of ink expended on writings about the dreadnoughts—
only one classic battleship engagement took place, the Battle of Jutland in
1916. In fact, most battleships were used in roles never envisioned.

Besides battleships, the now generic term *dreadnought* also includes battle
cruisers, perhaps the most controversial ship type ever built and the warship
behind a famous naval quote, "There seems to be something wrong with our
bloody ships today" as they were being blown up at Jutland. Yet every time
a new, large ship is built, it is quickly labeled a battle cruiser by the press. No
wonder most navalists are still fascinated by the dreadnoughts.

Early Dreadnoughts

Since ancient times there have been larger warships, but only a few would
be classified as dominant dreadnoughts. The earliest can be traced to the
polyreme era of the Age of Galleys from 400 to 250 B.C. Although the first
polyremes, the fours and fives, were only slightly larger than the common triremes, starting around 351 B.C. sixteens appeared and then around 288 B.C.
even larger twenties with one behemoth forty. During the dromon era that
began around A.D. 600, there were three warship sizes that are sometimes
compared to the modern battleship-cruiser-destroyer spectrum although the
differences among dromons were not that sharp. Some larger Venetian
"great" galleys were built in the sixteenth century, but the best example of

dreadnoughts during this stage of the Age of Galleys might be the few galleasse meant to anchor the battle line.

Clearer antecedents are found in the Age of Sail. The carracks that appeared around 1400 were described as large ships, and in both the early sixteenth and seventeenth centuries, countries built a few so-called great ships, as much for prestige as for war-fighting. But the clearest precedent were the large hundred-gun ships of the battle line that started to appear after 1650 and, indeed, the term *battleship* is simply a shortening of the phrase "ship of the battle line."

Although the first ironclads, the French *Gloire* of 1859 and the English *Warrior* of 1860, are sometimes called early battleships, the precursor of the pre-dreadnought design was the English breastwork monitor *Devastation,* the first mastless seagoing turret ship, laid down in 1869. The first with significantly large guns was the Italian central citadel *Duilio* with 17.7-inch guns begun in 1873. The lightly armored but fast *Italia*-class battleships laid down in 1876 are sometimes considered the forerunners of the battle cruiser. But it was not until the British *Collingwood* in 1882, which had high freeboard and guns in barbettes, that the basic battleship shape took form and set the stage for the pre-dreadnoughts.[1]

The Pre-Dreadnoughts: 1890–1905

By 1890 the early experimental period in ironclads had come to an end and the major powers were starting to build warships that looked like modern battleships. On 7 March 1889, Britain passed the Naval Defense Act, which set the "two-power" standard, meaning that the Royal Navy should be equal to the next two largest navies combined, which at the time were those of France and Russia. Several very large classes were laid down during this period. The first were seven *Royal Sovereign* class started in 1889 and completed by 1894. The decision was made that these should have higher freeboard for greater seagoing ability, and many consider the *Royal Sovereign*s the first pre-dreadnoughts. They were 14,150 tons, 410 by 75 feet, with four 13.5-inch guns and ten 6-inch quick-firing guns, and were heavily armored with 18 inches amidships.

The *Royal Sovereign* class was followed by the largest class of battleships ever built: nine *Majestic* class of almost 15,000 tons, with four 12-inch and twelve 6-inch guns, laid down starting in 1895 and completed in 1898. With better Harvey armor, fully enclosed armored turret hoods, and other improvements over the *Royal Sovereign*s, the *Majestic* class is sometimes considered the first true pre-dreadnoughts. Several other large classes were built during this period, including five *Canopus* class from 1896 through 1902; three *Formidable* class from 1898 through 1902; five *London* class from 1899 through 1904; and six *Duncan* class from 1900 to 1904. All of these ships were approximately 14,000 tons, 430 feet long, with four 12-inch and twelve 6-inch guns. The only major change came in the last large class of pre-dreadnoughts, eight *King Edward VII* class with four 12-inch, four 9.2-inch, and ten 6-inch guns built from 1903 to 1907. Some smaller second-class battleships for colonial duty with four 10-inch guns were also built. All told, from 1890 through 1905, the Royal Navy built forty-seven first-class and five second-class battleships.

The next two powers of the period, France and Russia, had much smaller shipbuilding programs. France finally abandoned the *jeune école* and in 1889 started building pre-dreadnoughts. The *Brennus*, 11,200 tons, with three 13.4-inch guns, was the first, but it was not until the three *Charlemagne* class, laid down in 1894 and completed at the turn of the century, that France matched the Royal Navy's designs. Russia began building pre-dreadnoughts in 1892, four battleships in the 11,000-ton range, all with four 12-inch guns. The largest class laid down at the turn of the century were five *Borodino* class at 13,500 tons with four 12-inch and twelve 6-inch guns. Three *Borodino*-class ships were sunk at Tsushima. During this period, France built eighteen and Russia twenty pre-dreadnoughts, compared to the British fifty-two. Although the two-power standard was not met, the Royal Navy ships in most cases were larger.

In 1888, the United States finally started building capital ships, laying down the *Maine*, originally designated an armored cruiser but later a second-class battleship. The first pre-dreadnought was the *Indiana*, BB-1, laid down in 1891 and completed in 1895. She was 10,200 tons full load, 351 feet long, with four 13-inch and eight 8-inch guns. During the next thirteen years, the U.S. Navy laid down twenty-three more battleships, ending with the *Idaho* BB-24. The largest classes in number were five *Virginia* class, 15,000 tons, 441 feet long, with four 12-inch guns and eight 8-inch guns, and four *Vermont* class at 17,600 tons and 456 feet long. Some experimenting still continued during this time. Among the most unusual were the *Kearsarge* and *Virginia* classes, built with a unique gun arrangement in which their secondary four 8-inch mounts were fixed on the roof of the 13-inch mounts.

In 1893, the emerging power Japan ordered two battleships from Britain similar to the *Royal Sovereign* class, then in 1896 four more comparable to the *Majestic* class. These six ships were the backbone of Japan's fleet during the Russo-Japanese War. In 1896 Germany laid down its first pre-dreadnoughts, the four 11,500-ton *Kaiser* class with four 9.4-inch guns. But more important was the appointment of Admiral Alfred von Tirpitz as secretary of state for the navy in 1897. The next year Germany passed the First German Naval Law, calling for nineteen battleships, followed by the Second Naval Law in 1900, calling for thirty-eight. Thus began the arms race that led to World War I. These plans were based on Tirpitz's "risk theory" of building enough ships to challenge the Royal Navy's two-power standard and thus deter England.

There was a great commonality to all these pre-dreadnoughts. Most carried four 12-inch guns (the Germans used 11-inch) with large secondary batteries of several 6-, 8-, or 9-inch guns and from 9 to 18 inches of armor.[2] Although large numbers of these early battleships were built, the pre-dreadnoughts are often overlooked for two reasons. First, even though most were not completed until the late 1890s and early 1900s, they became obsolete almost overnight when the *Dreadnought* was commissioned in 1906. Most participated in World War I but only in secondary roles. Second, there was only one major battle, Tsushima, and although considered an important, strategic sea battle, the major lesson of that battleship engagement was that the pre-dreadnought design with large secondary batteries was faulty. However, although it lasted only fifteen-odd years, the pre-dreadnought era was one of the most intense periods of shipbuilding the world had ever seen and was actually the longest era of battleships.

The Dreadnoughts: 1906–1914

Although one author traces the origins of the dreadnought to a conversation by Admiral Sir John "Jackie" Fisher in 1882,[3] most cite a series of events starting in 1900. In that year, the Italian naval constructor Vittorio Cuniberti wrote an article titled "The New Type of Armored Ship" calling for a moderate-sized ship with the "greatest possible armament," and Admiral Fisher began discussions with the chief constructor at Malta, W. D. Gard, on an all big-gun ship they called HMS "Untakeable." Many consider the most important article "An Ideal Battleship for the British Navy" by Cuniberti in the 1903 *Jane's Fighting Ships* calling for a ship with "very high speed—superior to that of any existing battleship afloat. . . . with medium calibers abolished—so effectually protected as to be able to disregard entirely all the subsidiary armament of an enemy, and armed only with twelve pieces of 12-inch."

The 1905 Battle of Tsushima seemed to confirm that theory. At the time, it was assumed that engagements would take place in the 3,000- to 5,000-yard range, where all ships' guns, including their secondary batteries—usually 6-, 8-, or 9-inch guns—were engaged as well as the larger 12-inch. At Tsushima, however, the two fleets started firing at almost 19,000 yards, scoring hits at 13,000 to 14,000 yards. Thus the need for secondary batteries was questioned.

The United States was the first on the drawing boards. On 3 March 1905 the United States approved plans for the world's first all big-gun ship, the *Michigan,* but it was not laid down until December 1906 (and not completed

HMS *Dreadnought*, completed in 1906, heralded the beginning of the modern age of warships. (Courtesy of Imperial War Museum)

until 1910). In the meanwhile, Admiral Fisher, who had become First Sea Lord in October 1904, soon after appointed a design committee with himself chairman which came up with the final design for HMS *Dreadnought*, laid down on 2 October 1905, launched only four months later on 10 February 1906, with trials beginning on 3 October 1906.[4] (Recent scholarship has revealed that Admiral Fisher had changed his mind regarding battleships, instead preferring battle cruisers and submarines, but he is nevertheless seen as the father of the *Dreadnought*.)[5]

HMS *Dreadnought* was 18,100 tons, 527 feet overall, 82 feet wide, and carried ten 12-inch guns, no secondary batteries with only ten 12-pounders (3-inch) for protection against torpedo boats. This was a major departure from the pre-dreadnoughts, most of which had only four 12-inch, but large secondary batteries of usually ten 6-inch quick-firers or 8- or 9-inch guns. Although generally praised, the dreadnought was not without its critics, including the father of naval strategy himself, American admiral Alfred T. Mahan, who claimed the lessons of Tsushima were that "the rain of fire" from the Japanese 6- and 8-inch guns won the battle, not the longer-range big guns. Many agreed, and 6-inch secondary batteries returned to the second generation of dreadnoughts. Besides the all big-gun feature, the *Dreadnought* was also the first large ship outfitted with turbines rather than reciprocating engines. The turbines were lighter and more durable, allowing for sustained high speeds. The *Dreadnought* could make 21 knots, about 3 knots faster than the pre-dreadnoughts. In short, with her all big guns and better speed, the *Dreadnought* truly did make "all else obsolete," as was often said. But the *Dreadnought* also "wiped the slate clean," meaning other countries now had a chance to catch up with the Royal Navy. However, it was not until 1910 that most would complete their first dreadnoughts, by which time the Royal Navy had already started building a second generation of super-dreadnoughts.

The *Dreadnought* was immediately followed by two three-ship classes, the *Bellerophon* and *St. Vincent* classes, laid down from 1906 through 1908. Slightly larger with some improvements, they were essentially repeat designs. One improvement was replacing the smaller 12-pounders (3-inch) with 4-inch quick-firers. In 1909 the *Neptune* was laid down. She was the Royal Navy's first with so-called superfiring turrets, one over the other, that would eventually allow all guns to be placed in the center line rather than having some on the wings, as in the original dreadnoughts.

In 1910, when other countries' first-generation dreadnoughts were finally starting to appear, the Royal Navy laid down its second generation, labeled "super-dreadnoughts," with ten 13.5-inch guns rather than the old 12-inch. The first were four 22,200-ton *Orion* class, completed in 1912, followed by four *King George V* class laid down in 1911, completed in 1913; and finally four 25,000-ton *Iron Duke* class in 1912, completed in 1914 just in time for the start of World War I. Starting with the *Iron Duke* class, a secondary battery of twelve 6-inch guns was reintroduced. The *Queen Elizabeth* class was also laid down in 1912. Although originally scheduled to have 13.5-inch guns, the main battery was changed to eight 15-inch following news that the United States and Japanese ships were moving to larger guns. The *Queen Elizabeth*s were also faster ships with speeds of 23 knots, versus twenty-one (or less) for most other battleships. The five 28,000-ton, 624-foot-long *Revenge* class laid down in 1913–14, completed in 1916–17, carrying eight 15-inch guns, were the last battleships built by the Royal Navy until after World War I. The Royal Navy did take over some battleships being built for foreign governments, including the largest of the period, the 28,600-ton, 661-foot-long *Almirante Latorre* (renamed *Canada*) being built for Chile. During this period and counting those taken over, the Royal Navy built or laid down thirty-five battleships from 1906 through 1914.

In 1907 Germany responded to the *Dreadnought* by laying down four 18,500-ton, 479-foot-long *Nassau*-class battleships with twelve 11-inch guns, completed in 1910. Germany then laid down four 22,400-ton *Helgoland* class with twelve 12-inch guns in 1908, followed by five 24,330-ton *Kaiser* class in 1910, and four 25,390-ton *Konig* class in 1911 with ten 12-inch guns. In 1913 two *Bayern*-class "super-dreadnoughts" were started with eight 15-inch guns. Germany went from 12- to 15-inch in one leap. The

Bayern class would be the last German battleships completed during the war. Germany built only nineteen battleships to England's thirty-five during this period.

There were considerable differences between the German and British battleships. The British had larger guns, with more 13.5- and 15-inch versus the German mostly 12-inch. British ships were longer, usually over 600 feet, while the German ships were all under 600 feet, yet in tonnage they were approximately equal. One reason was that the German ships had slightly more armor with more compartmentalization, allowing for better damage control. German guns were also considered superior because the British armor-piercing shells were defective. These characteristics are often credited for their subsequent victories over the British ships at Jutland.

While other European powers built dreadnoughts, none matched the race between England and Germany. France, for years the second naval power, became more concerned with land threats and was slow off the mark. In 1907, France starting building six 18,300-ton *Danton* class with some modern features, but with pre-dreadnought armament, four 12-inch and twelve 9.4-inch. France did not lay down its first true dreadnoughts until 1910, four 22,200-ton *Courbet* class with twelve 12-inch guns. They were followed by three more modern 23,200-ton *Bretagne* battleships in 1912 with ten 13.4-inch guns, but they were the last. Five *Normandie* class laid down in 1913–14 were never completed.

Russia, still reeling from its defeat in the Russo-Japanese War on the eve of the dreadnought era, had plans for battleships, but like France was soon concerned with land matters. It laid down only four large 23,400-ton *Gangut* class carrying twelve 12-inch guns in 1909, followed by three slightly smaller *Imperatritsa Mariya* class in 1911 before the war stopped construction. Italy laid down the 19,500-ton *Dante Alighieri* with twelve 12-inch guns, the first with large guns in a triple turret. She was followed by three 23,000-ton *Cavour* class started in 1910 and two *Doria* class in 1912 before World War I stopped further construction. Like France, Austria-Hungary laid down three 14,500-ton *Radetzky* class starting in 1907 with some modern features, but pre-dreadnought armament with only four 12-inch guns. It was not until 1910 that Austria-Hungary laid down modern dreadnoughts, four 20,000-ton *Tegetthoff* class with twelve 12-inch guns.

After Great Britain and Germany, the United States Navy built the most battleships. As noted above, the *Michigan,* laid down in late 1906, was actually planned earlier than the *Dreadnought* and in some respects was more modern with all center-line turrets, whereas the *Dreadnought* had some side turrets. The two *Michigan* class, however, under a congressional mandate that they have a 16,000-ton displacement, carried only eight 12-inch guns (versus ten on the *Dreadnought*). The tonnage limit was lifted for the next two classes, two 20,400-ton *Delaware* class with ten 12-inch guns laid down in 1907, completed in 1910, and two similar *Florida* class laid down in 1909 and completed in 1911. Two slightly modified 26,000-ton *Wyoming* class with twelve 12-inch guns were laid down in 1910 and completed in 1912. Starting in 1911, the United States switched to 14-inch super-dreadnoughts. First were two 27,000-ton *New York* class, laid down in 1911, and then two 27,500-ton *Nevada* class in 1912, all with ten 14-inch guns.

The *Nevada* class introduced the so-called all-or-nothing armor arrangement scheme, which was adopted by most other countries. The all-or-nothing arrangement had heavy armor for certain critical areas but then virtually nothing for others, based on the theory that since armor-piercing shells did not burst when piercing thin plates, it was better to have either very thick armor sufficient to stop the shells or nothing at all. The *Nevada* were followed by two larger 31,400-ton *Pennsylvania*-class ships with twelve 14-inch guns, started in 1913. They were essentially enlarged *Nevada* class. The United States also laid down and completed battleships during World War I. In 1915 three 32,000-ton *New Mexico* class were laid down followed by two similar *Tennessee* class in 1916. Both classes carried twelve 14-inch guns. Four essentially repeat *Colorado* class, but with eight 16-inch guns in twin turrets, were laid down immediately after the war. (One, the *Maryland,* was laid down in 1917.) The *Tennessee* and *Colorado* classes incorporated some of the so-called lessons of Jutland such as more armor and are sometimes referred to as a new generation of "post-Jutland" ships. All told, the United States laid down fourteen battleships before 1914 and five during World War I.[6]

Japan also started building dreadnoughts. The first were two 21,400-ton, 526-foot-long *Settsu* class with twelve 12-inch guns, laid down in 1909 and completed in 1912. They were followed by two large 30,600-ton, 665-foot-long *Fuso* class with twelve 14-inch guns started in 1912. Japan also laid down battleships during the war. First were two *Ise* class, laid down in 1915 with twelve 14-inch guns, followed by two *Nagato* class starting in 1917 with eight 16-inch guns. In Latin America, the "ABC countries" (Argentina, Brazil, and Chile) carried on a small dreadnought race. Brazil actually had the largest battleships of the day with two *Minas Gerais* class built in England in 1907 that carried twelve 12-inch guns. Chile responded with a larger 14-inch-gun ship, but it was taken over by Britain during the war. As an exception to the rule of minor navies having their capital ships built in Europe, the Argentines had two battleships, the *Moreno* and *Rivadavia,* built in the United States. Many of the smaller powers of the day also built or purchased a few battleships. Spain, for example, built two small dreadnoughts, and Greece purchased two small late pre-dreadnought American *Mississippi* class in 1914. Turkey ordered battleships that were never delivered, although during the war the German battle cruiser *Goeben* flew the Turkish flag. Norway, Denmark, and Sweden had smaller coastal battleships.

BATTLE CRUISERS

At the same time Admiral Fisher and Chief Constructor W. H. Gard were discussing a conceptual HMS "Untakeable," which would become the *Dreadnought,* they were also discussing a HMS "Unapproachable," which was to be a faster armored cruiser able to hunt down and overwhelm foreign armored cruisers. It would be more powerful than existing cruisers, with the speed to run from anything larger. By 1900 armored cruisers had become quite large, over 13,500 tons, with most carrying 9-inch guns. There was some thought to giving this new ship a slightly larger, 10-inch gun, but speed was considered most important to counter French commerce raiders. In 1904, however, England learned that Japan was building an armored cruiser with 12-inch guns and the innovative Italian Cuniberti had started two small *Regina Elena* battleships, also with 12-inch guns. Thus the decision was made to go with 12-inch guns, and since this was the beginning of the dreadnought era, it was decided to proceed with all big guns, eight 12-inch. To reach high speed, armor was sacrificed.

Although originally called armored cruisers when they first appeared in 1906, because of their large guns, they were quickly dubbed battleship cruisers and then simply battle cruisers in 1912. Thus was the genesis of the most controversial warship type in modern history, the battle cruiser. In brief, the controversy was whether they were fit to serve as ships of the battle line. Even at the time, Brassey's wrote: "Vessels of this enormous size and cost are unsuitable for many of the duties of cruisers; but an even stronger objection to the repetition of the type is that an admiral having *Invincibles* in his fleet will be certain to put them in the line of battle, where their comparatively light protection would be a disadvantage and their high speed of no value." And that is exactly what happened at Jutland.

In February 1906, just four months after the *Dreadnought* had been laid down, the first of three *Invincible*-class battle cruisers were started; all were completed by 1908. They were 17,400 tons, 567 by 78.5 feet, and carried eight 12-inch guns. The *Invincibles* were virtually the same size and actually longer than the 18,100-ton, 527-by-82-foot *Dreadnought,* which carried ten 12-inch guns. The main difference was in armor. While the *Dreadnought* had an 11-inch belt, the *Invincible* had only a 6-inch one. But as conceptualized, the *Invincibles* were much faster at 25 knots than the 21-knot *Dreadnought,* and they actually made 28 knots in trials. The *Invincibles* were also specifically designed with lower profiles and in that respect might be considered the first stealth ships.

In 1909 three *Indefatigable* class were laid down, essentially repeat *Invincibles.* Also in 1909, two larger 26,270-ton *Lion*-class battle cruisers were started, followed by the similar *Queen Mary* in 1911 and the 28,500-ton *Tiger* in 1912. They carried eight 13.5-inch guns and heavier armor, up to 9 inches. These were the last built before the war. During the war, two classes

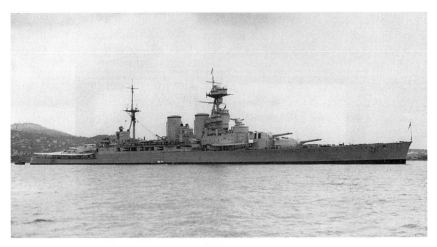

The mighty battle cruiser HMS *Hood,* completed in 1920, was the pride of the Royal Navy for two decades. She was sunk by the German battleship *Bismarck* on 24 May 1941. (U.S. Naval Institute)

were laid down. First were two 27,700-ton *Renown* class with six 15-inch guns, but only a 6-inch belt of armor laid down in 1915, completed in 1916, and two smaller 19,200-ton *Courageous* class with only four 15-inch guns. The *Courageous* class were classified as "large light cruisers" to overcome cabinet opposition to building more battle cruisers. A third large light cruiser, *Furious,* with two single 18-inch guns, was started but then converted to an aircraft carrier with the forward mount removed for a fly-off deck. And in 1916 the *Hood* was begun, but it was not completed until 1920. At almost 42,700 tons, 860 by 104 feet, with eight 15-inch guns, the *Hood* was the largest and most famous warship afloat for most of the interwar period.

In 1907 Germany laid down the 15,600-ton *Blucher* but with twelve 8.2-inch guns, she was really just a large armored cruiser. Germany's first true battle cruiser was the 19,000-ton, 563-by-87-foot *Von der Tann* in 1908 with eight 11-inch guns, followed by two 22,600-ton *Moltke* class with ten 11-inch guns laid down in 1908. They had 10-inch armor belts versus only 6 inches on the British *Invincibles*. In 1911 the *Seydlitz* was laid down with ten 11-inch guns but a 12-inch armor belt. In 1912 Germany finally moved up to 12-inch guns, building two *Derfflinger* class, followed by the single, similar *Hindenburg* in 1913. Germany started the larger 30,500-ton *Mackensen* class in 1915, but none were finished. Although the German battle cruisers carried smaller guns, they had more armor, answering the main criticism of these ships.

Besides England and Germany, only Japan built battle cruisers. It was the building of two Japanese *Tsukuba*-class 13,800-ton, 450-by-75-foot armored cruisers laid down in 1905 that prompted England to change the design of its battle cruisers. They were followed by two similar *Ibuki* class, also laid down in 1905. All four were classified as battle cruisers in 1912. Japan's first true battle cruisers were the four *Kongo* class, started in 1911. The *Kongo*, 27,500 tons, 704 by 92 feet, with eight 14-inch guns, was built in England, but the other three were built in Japan. The *Kongo* was the last Japanese capital ship constructed overseas.

None of the other powers built battle cruisers. Russia started four large 32,500-ton *Borodino* class with twelve 14-inch guns in 1913, but they were never completed. During the war the German battle cruiser *Goeben* was turned over to Turkey as the *Yavuz Sultan Selim*. She retained her German crew and had a colorful career, a constant worry to the French and Royal navies. Both the United States and Japan would start building large, over 40,000-ton battle cruisers with 16-inch guns after the war, but they were canceled as a result of the Washington Treaty.

The battle cruiser era was a very short one, lasting only ten years, from 1906 to 1916, although the *Hood* was not finished until 1920. Germany, France, and the United States would later build capital ships sometimes labeled battle cruisers, but the era really ended in 1918. Always controversial, the battle cruisers performed well when used as designed but failed in the most significant of the dreadnought battles at Jutland in 1916.

World War I

The dreadnought balance during World War I is shown in table 6.1. Often forgotten was that the fleets in 1914 still had large numbers of pre-dreadnoughts, many less than ten years old, usually considered young for a ship. They were still useful for certain duties, including convoy and shore bombardment, yet they were clearly obsolete. More important were the new dreadnoughts, the battleships and battle cruisers, most very modern, less than five years old. The Royal Navy was by far the largest with twenty-two battleships and thirteen more being built as well as ten battle cruisers. Second was Germany with fourteen battleships and five more building and six battle cruisers and two building. Thus the Royal Navy had almost a two-to-one superiority. Despite the existence of all these new ships, however, there would be only one classic dreadnought battle and four relatively minor battle cruiser clashes during World War I.

The sea war started fairly well for the Royal Navy, and especially its battle cruisers. In August 1914, a British force with five battle cruisers caught an inferior German cruiser-destroyer force off Heligoland Bight and sank three German light cruisers. The battle cruisers scored their greatest success in December. When the war started, Germany had two large armored cruisers, the *Scharnhorst* and the *Gneisenau,* and three smaller cruisers under Vice Admiral Maximilian Graf Spee in the Far East that began a journey across

Table 6.1 Dreadnought Balance in World War I

Type	Britain	France	Italy	Russia	U.S.	Japan	Germany	Austria
Pre-dreadnoughts	41	21	15	11	25	8	20	6
Battleships								
1914	22	10	3	4	10	2	15	6
Building	13	3	3	3	4	2	5	1
Built	0	0	0	0	2	2	0	0
(Subtotal)	(35)	(13)	(6)	(7)	(16)	(6)	(20)	(7)
Battle cruisers								
1914	9	0	0	0	0	6	5	0
Building	1	0	0	0	0	2	3	0
Built	4	0	0	0	0	0	0	0
(Subtotal)	(14)					(8)	(8)	
TOTAL	90	33	17	18	39	24	47	13
LOSSES								
Pre-dreadnoughts	11	3	2	2	0	0	1	1
Battleships	2	1	1	2	0	0	0	2
Battle cruisers	3	n.a.	n.a.	n.a.	n.a.	1	2	0

NOTES: Building are those building before that were commissioned by war's end. Built are those started and completed during the war. (Others were started but not completed.)

the Pacific. Off the coast of Chile, they ran into a British force of two armored cruisers and won the Battle of Coronel on 1 November 1914. The Admiralty immediately dispatched the battle cruisers *Invincible* and *Inflexible* and six cruisers to the South Atlantic. While the British were refueling at the Falkland Islands, the German force appeared, thinking the islands were undefended. Realizing their mistake, they started to flee but were gradually run down and sunk by the faster, more powerful British force. Both the Battles of Heligoland Bight and the Falkland Islands seemed to justify Fisher's concept of faster, lighter-armored battle cruisers with larger guns.

The next clash came only a month later, on 24 January 1915. Three German battle cruisers, the armored cruiser *Blucher,* and light cruisers and destroyers under Rear Admiral Franz Hipper had been sent to attack British trawlers and patrol boats off Dogger Bank. The British learned of the raid by breaking German codes and sent Vice Admiral Sir David Beatty with five battle cruisers, light cruisers, and destroyers to intercept. Outnumbered, the Germans tried to escape but were overtaken by faster British battle cruisers, which severely damaged and eventually sank the *Blucher*. Foreshadowing Jutland, however, the Germans scored major hits on Beatty's flagship the *Lion,* forcing him out of the line and ending the chase. The Battle of Dogger Bank was the first between dreadnoughts with hits being recorded at ranges of over 15,000 yards, again justifying Fisher's all big gun concept. Though it was a British victory, there was much dissatisfaction with the Royal Navy's performance. Only the German *Blucher* was lost and two of the German battle cruisers received three hits each versus sixteen scored on the *Lion* and six on the *Tiger*.

The only major fleet action of the war (and indeed of the whole battleship era) was the Battle of Jutland on 31 May 1916. It was truly a major battle involving 247 ships. In the British Grand Fleet were 28 battleships, 9 battle cruisers, 8 armored cruisers, 26 light cruisers, and 77 destroyers versus the German High Seas Fleet of 16 battleships, 6 pre-dreadnoughts, 5 battle cruisers, 11 light cruisers, and 61 destroyers. Total tonnage was 1,250,000 for the British and 660,000 for Germany and the total number in British crews was some 60,000 versus 45,000 for the Germans.[7]

The German main fleet had sortied hoping to catch the British in a trap, but once again, the British had intercepted a message. The battle began when Vice Admiral Beatty's battle cruiser force of six battle cruisers and four fast battleships met Hipper's scouting force of five battle cruisers around 3:30 in the afternoon. The two sides opened fire and within half an hour the British battle cruiser *Indefatigable* blew up, followed by the battle cruiser *Queen Mary* about an hour later, prompting Beatty's famous words, "There seems to be something wrong with our bloody ships today." The main fleets would engage later in the afternoon with the British losing yet another battle cruiser, the *Invincible,* and the Germans losing the battle cruiser *Lutzow.* In a controversial move, Admiral John Jellicoe broke off action at nightfall fearing submarine attacks, hoping to engage the next day, and although there were scattered destroyer attacks, the battle ended.

Overall, the British lost fourteen ships to the German eleven; in capital ships the British lost three battle cruisers to one German. Jutland is often seen as a slight German tactical victory, although Britain still ruled the seas. Perhaps more disturbing to the Royal Navy than the tactical loss was the apparent vulnerability of its ships, especially the battle cruisers. But they were being used in a way never intended. Although the sinkings were initially attributed to the "thin skins" of the British battle cruisers and better armor and damage control of the German battle cruisers, most analysts now attribute the cause to several factors, including inferior British shells. In a classic case of not realizing the meaning of what their own eyes were seeing, the British gunners were cheered by often seeing the bursts of their armor-piercing shells striking the German ships. Actually, the shells had been defeated by the German armor and were detonating *outside* the German ships. These losses would haunt the Royal Navy during the interwar period, and although corrections were made, during World War II once again the battle cruisers would prove vulnerable.[8]

The two fleets would never meet again. Later in the war, at Heligoland Bight on 17 November 1917, three British battle cruisers chased off some German light cruisers until two German battleships appeared. During most of the war, both the British Grand Fleet and the German High Seas Fleet would stay in ports as "fleets in being" acting as deterrents to each other. On the British side this was somewhat understandable. As Winston Churchill said, "Jellicoe was the only man who could lose the war in an afternoon." Although probably overdrawn, there was some truth to that statement since England did need to keep its sea lines of communications open but Germany did not. Foreshadowing their main use in World War II, both sides used battleships for gunfire support. During the ill-fated Gallipoli campaign, England and France would use eighteen battleships and battle cruisers and many pre-dreadnoughts. Similarly, Germany used ten battleships for Baltic landing support. When the war ended, the German High Seas Fleet sailed to the British base at Scapa Flow. While they were awaiting final surrender agreement terms, the Germans would eventually scuttle these ships.

Thirty-five battleships and battle cruisers were lost during the war, but most, twenty-four, were older pre-dreadnoughts sunk by mines and torpedoes. Considered obsolete, they were often placed in more vulnerable positions than the newer dreadnoughts. Overall, only five were sunk by gunfire, fourteen torpedoed, nine mined, six sunk by internal explosions, and one scuttled. While the utility of dreadnoughts was clearly overrated during the prewar period, in some respects they fulfilled their mission and design expectations. The battle cruisers proved disappointing at Jutland, where they probably did not belong, but when used properly as in the Falklands and Dogger Bank operations, they performed well.

The Interwar Period

When the war ended, the old European order was gone and the major sea power of the day, England, was spent. England, which with few exceptions had built two or three capital ships per year for almost three centuries, finished the battle cruiser *Hood* but laid down no more immediately after the war even though all its dreadnoughts were now considered to be an obsolete, pre-Jutland, design. Only the United States and Japan built more after the war was over. The United States laid down three more *Colorado* class in 1919–20 and then six 43,200-ton *South Dakota* class with twelve 16-inch guns in 1920, followed by six 43,500-ton *Lexington*-class battle cruisers with eight 16-inch guns in 1920–21. Japan completed two 33,800-ton *Nagato*-class battleships with eight 16-inch guns in 1920–21 and laid down two 39,900-ton *Kaga* class with ten 16-inch guns in 1920. Japan also planned a major so-called eight-eight program to build eight more each of modern battleships and battle cruisers.

Despite their plans, there was a movement for a "return to normalcy" in the United States, and Japan faced financial problems. With Europe spent, there was thus little resistance to the call by the United States for the Washington Naval Conference of late 1921–22, which set the rules for battleships for the next fifteen-odd years. The Washington Treaty established 5:5:3:1.66:1.66 ratios between England, United States, Japan, France, and Italy. Tonnage limits for dreadnoughts were placed at 525,000 each for the United States and England, 315,000 tons for Japan, and 175,000 tons each for France and Italy. In addition, there was a ten-year "naval holiday" on construction with any new battleships limited to 35,000 tons standard displacement and 16-inch guns. As the saying sometimes went, more ships were lost at the Washington Naval Conference than in any major battle in history. England gave up the most in number, but they were older types. In some respects the United States lost more: the six *South Dakota* class under construction, two almost completed, and six *Lexington*-class battle cruisers building. But the old colony achieved parity with the mother country England in the treaty. Another era had ended.

The Admiralty was not happy but had little choice in light of postwar budget constraints. Japan was also upset, wanting parity with the United States and England, but also faced budget constraints. France, with worldwide obligations, felt it should have more than Italy.[9]

With two exceptions, battleship construction ceased during the 1920s. The exceptions were two 33,300-ton, 710-by-106-foot *Nelson*-class battleships with nine 16-inch guns laid down by England in 1922, completed in 1927. Since England had not built any battleships during the war, it was allowed two "post-Jutland" designs. The *Nelson* and *Rodney* were the strangest looking battleships ever built. To conform to the new tonnage limits, all three 16-inch gun turrets were placed forward of the bridge, giving them a cutoff bobtail look. They were known as the "cherry tree" class in reference to Washington's cherry trees.

The Washington agreement was renewed at the First London Conference of 1930 by the United States, England, and Japan. France, however, refused to sign—and for a good reason. In 1929 Germany laid down the first of three so-called pocket battleships. In response, France started the first of two small 26,500-ton, 704-by-102-foot *Dunkerque* class with eight 13-inch guns in 1932. With speeds of almost 30 knots, the *Dunkerques* are sometimes referred to as battle cruisers, although they were considered fast battleships. Since France did not sign the London Treaty, Italy also dropped out and in 1934 laid down two 40,700-ton 780-by-107-foot *Littorio*-class battleships with nine 15-inch guns. France then started the 35,000-ton *Richelieu* that had eight 15-inch guns in 1935 and was almost completed when France surrendered in 1940.

With these exceptions, the Washington Treaty lasted until 1934 when Japan gave notice that it was pulling out of the treaty. At the 1935 Second London Conference, efforts were made to revive the agreement, but with Germany starting to rearm and Japan walking out, the negotiations broke down and all the major powers once again began capital ship construction.

England, as could be expected, laid down the most battleships immediately after the collapse of the second London talks, starting five 36,700-ton *King George V* class in 1937. They were smaller than the Italian and German ships because England was still adhering to the 35,000-ton standard. Somewhat ironically, they reverted to 14-inch guns. Two were commissioned before World War II started in 1939 and three after. The Royal Navy would start two 40,550-ton *Lion*-class ships in 1939 but later canceled them. In 1941, England's last battleship, the 44,500-ton *Vanguard* with eight 15-inch guns (left over from World War I) was started, but it was not completed until 1946.

Germany had entered the race with interesting designs. In 1929, Germany had started the first of three 11,700-ton *Deutschland* class with six 11-inch guns. Although designated *panzerschiffe* (armored ships) to avoid violating the Versailles Treaty, they were quickly labeled "pocket battleships" by the press. Later they were classified as commerce raiders and were generally considered heavy cruisers. In 1935 Germany laid down two 35,000-ton, 754-by-98-foot *Scharnhorst* class. Although heavily armored, they carried only nine 11-inch guns and with a speed of 32 knots are often considered battle cruisers. Finally came two large, 41,700-ton, 814-by-118-foot *Bismarck* class with eight 15-inch guns laid down in 1936, completed in 1940 and 1941. These were Germany's only true battleships.

Japan, which had pulled out of the agreement in 1934, did not actually begin battleship construction until 1937 but then built the world's largest, the 62,315-ton, 863- by 121-foot *Yamato* with nine 18-inch guns completed in December 1941. Three more were laid down, but only the *Musashi* was completed in 1942. One, the *Shinano,* was later converted to an aircraft carrier.[10]

Only the United States would build battleships in any number. In 1937 the United States started building two *North Carolina* class, followed by four *South Dakota* class in 1939. They were designed using the 35,000-ton standard, coming in at 37,500 and 38,000 tons respectively and both carrying nine 16-inch guns. In 1940, the United States abandoned the old limits, laying down the world's last battleship class, the four 48,100-ton, 887- by 108-foot *Iowa* class with nine 16-inch and twenty 5-inch guns. An even larger 60,500-ton *Montana* class with twelve 16-inch guns was designed but never laid down. In 1941 the United States laid down three and completed two 29,800-ton, 808-by-91-foot *Alaska*-class "large cruisers" (designated CBs) with nine 12-inch guns. Like the similar sized German *Scharnhorst* class, they are often considered battle cruisers.[11]

Thus, for another very short, approximately five-year period starting in the mid-1930s, some twenty-six more battleships and battle cruisers were started, but it would be the dreadnoughts' last hurrah. During the interwar period, the battleship's primacy had been challenged by the new aircraft

The Japanese battleship *Yamato*, completed in 1941. She was the largest and most heavily armored battleship ever built at 62,315 tons and with nine 18.1-inch guns. She was sunk by American airplanes on 7 April 1945.
(Courtesy of J. Blumenfield, via the U.S. Naval Institute)

USS *Iowa*, completed in 1943. She and her three sister ships were the last class of battleships built.
(U.S. Naval Institute)

carrier force. On the eve of World War II, however, most naval strategists still considered the battleship the primary capital ship. Writing in 1940, the man who would go on to become American's preeminent strategist, Bernard Brody, wrote that the battleship was still the main ship. That illusion was challenged, however, once the war began in 1939 and would be completely shattered by two events in December 1941.

World War II

The dreadnought balance for World War II is shown in table 6.2. Just as the pre-dreadnoughts are often forgotten in determining the World War I balance, often forgotten in World War II balances was that the old, slow, World War I–era dreadnoughts still were predominant. In fact, there were only a handful of "modern" fast dreadnoughts on hand when the war started in September 1939. By December 1941, three of the five *King George V* class would be completed by England but only the two *North Carolina* in commission for the United States. The only capital ships actually started and completed during the war were the two *Alaska*-class CBs.

World War II would be the greatest war in history. The Battle of the Atlantic was a crucial factor in the European theater, and the war in the Pacific one of the few truly naval wars in all of history, the outcome completely dependent on naval forces. Yet the main capital ship, the battleship, played a

Table 6.2 Dreadnought Balance in World War II

Type	Britain	France	USSR	U.S.	Germany	Italy	Japan
WW I era							
Battleship	10	7	3	15	4	4	6
Battle cruiser	3						4
Modern							
On hand 1939							
Battleship	2					2	
Battle cruiser		2			2		
Building or built							
Battleship	5	1		10	2	2	2
Battle cruiser				2			
TOTAL	20	10	3	27	8	8	12
LOSSES							
WW I–era battleships	2	1	1	2	1	1	5
WW I–era battle cruisers	2						4
WW II–era battleships	1				2	1	2
WW II–era battle cruisers		2			1		
TOTAL	5	1	1	2	4	2	11

NOTES: Building or built are those building before and during the war, that were commissioned by war's end. Those listed as modern battle cruisers included the French *Dunkerque*, German *Scharnhorst*, and U.S. *Alaska* classes.

relatively minor role. There were only a handful of minor battleship engagements, some quite spectacular, but nothing to compare to Jutland. Rather, in the Atlantic, the submarine would become predominant and in the Pacific, the aircraft carrier.

Perhaps somewhat apocalyptically foreshadowing events in the Atlantic, early in the war on 14 October 1939, U-47 penetrated the British anchorage at Scapa Flow and sank the battleship *Royal Oak*. But by far the most dramatic dreadnought engagement in the Atlantic and probably the whole war was when the mighty *Hood* and new British battleship *Prince of Wales* met the new German battleship *Bismarck* and heavy cruiser *Prinz Eugen* in the north Atlantic on 24 May 1941. The *Hood* blew up after only five minutes, and the *Prince of Wales* was hit and forced to break off. Although the *Hood* was actually a twenty-year-old battle cruiser at the time, her sinking was considered a major blow. Three days later, after being slowed by British torpedo airplanes, the battleships *King George V* and *Rodney* would extract revenge, sinking the *Bismarck*. Later, in December 1943, a British force with the battleship *Duke of York* sank the German battle cruiser *Scharnhorst*. Germany would sortie her battleships and battle cruisers a few times for commerce raiding but there were no more battles.

In the Mediterranean, English and Italian battleships clashed indecisively in small fleet engagements, but, as will be explained in chapter 7, this was mostly a cruiser war. There were, however, four significant battleship events. On 3 June 1940 British battleships shelled and damaged the French battleship force at anchor at Oran to prevent their falling into German hands. Then, on 11 November 1940, in what some consider a dress rehearsal for Pearl Harbor, British planes attacked Italian battleships at Taranto, sinking two and severely damaging another. The Italians extracted some revenge when their frogmen placed charges under two British battleships in Alexandria harbor on 19 December 1941, putting them out of action for months. Finally, in a harbinger of the postwar missiles era, Germany sank the Italian battleship *Roma* with a remotely controlled guided bomb while it was en route with other Italian fleet units to surrender to the Royal Navy.

It was in the Pacific that the battleships played major roles. Virtually every analyst agrees that while the sinking of the eight battleships at Pearl Harbor was a major propaganda blow to the United States, strategically it had little influence. All the battleships were old and too slow to keep up with the carriers. But if there was ever any doubt about the outcome of the battleship versus carrier debate, it was resolved only three days later, when the new British battleship *Prince of Wales* and old battle cruiser *Repulse* were rather easily sunk by Japanese airplanes. Although battleship losses at Pearl Harbor could be attributed to a sneak attack, the British force was at sea ready for combat. In short, any doubts that the Pacific would be an air rather than a battleship war were removed in December 1941.

There were a few battleship engagements in the Pacific. Both American and Japanese battleships took part in the mostly cruiser engagements around Guadalcanal in November 1942. In the first night battle off Guadalcanal on 12 November, the Japanese battleship *Hiei* was damaged and sunk the next day by aircraft. Then, two nights later, the *South Dakota* was badly damaged, but the *Washington* sank the *Kirishima*. (Both *Hiei* and *Kirishima* were originally built as battle cruisers but were modernized in the 1930s with heavier armor; thereafter, they were usually considered battleships.) The major Pacific battleship engagement occurred during the Battle of Surigao Straits of 24 October 1944 when two Japanese battleships engaged six American. The *Fuso* was sunk by torpedoes from American torpedo patrol (PT) boats and destroyers, but the *Yamashiro* was sunk when Rear Admiral Jesse Oldendorf crossed the "T" using old battleships, mostly Pearl Harbor victims raised and modernized. Japan would lose most of its battleships, including the *Yamato* and *Musashi*, to American planes.

The battleships' major role in the Pacific was for gunfire support missions during the numerous "island-hopping" amphibious operations. The Navy-Marine Corps team learned very early on that in most cases, unless the

U.S. Navy battleships practicing the battle line. In fact, there has been only one classic battleship engagement in history, the Battle of Jutland in 1916.
(U.S. Naval Institute)

landings were preceded by heavy shore bombardments, the assaults would be more difficult. Battleships also performed similar shore bombardment duties in the European theater, but they were crucial for the war in the Pacific.

Thirty-five dreadnoughts were sunk in World War II, but that number includes four French ships scuttled. Most, sixteen, were lost in air attacks, followed by seven scuttled, four by both gunfire and torpedo, four by torpedo alone and two gunfire alone, and one each by internal explosion and remote glider bomb. While the overall number lost was the same as in World War I, the toll was devastating for Germany and Japan, who lost all their capital ships.

Post–World War II

With the war over, all the World War I–era battleships were immediately scrapped, as were most of the others built in the 1930s. England completed the *Vanguard* in 1946 and France the *Jean Bart* in 1949, but there would be no new constructions. The Soviet Union had postwar plans for both battleships and battle cruisers, and in 1951 it laid down the first of three 36,500-ton *Stalingrad*-class battle cruisers with nine 12-inch guns; they were never completed. There was little question that the era of the battleship had passed. The *Vanguard,* the last Royal Navy battleship, was kept in the reserves as a training ship until the mid-1950s but finally retired. Somewhat shamefully, not one of the magnificent Royal Navy dreadnoughts has been kept as a memorial.

The four American *Iowa*-class battleships saw service during the Korean War, where they provided valuable gunfire support. They were then retired, with the *Iowa* and *New Jersey* the last to go, in 1958. The *New Jersey* was recommissioned from 1967 to 1969 for Vietnam, where she again performed shore bombardment, and then all four were once again recommissioned in the 1980s as part of the buildup in the U.S. Fleet. The *Wisconsin* and *Missouri* participated in the Persian Gulf War of 1991. With the end of the Cold War and decline in military budgets, once again they were placed in the reserve fleet with the *Missouri,* the last, going out in 1992. In early 1995 all four were stricken from the list and offered up as museums, but Congress placed a hold on two. Currently there are efforts to recommission at least one for gunfire support missions or as a multinational NATO flagship and trainer, but that seems unlikely for these expensive, manpower-intensive ships.

Conclusion

Although the battleship was the penultimate warship, its life span is one of the shortest on record, from the pre-dreadnoughts starting around 1890 to the end of World War II in 1945, but they had actually been displaced by the

Table 6.3 Dreadnought Comparisons

Class	Navy	Year	Displacement	Dimensions	Armament	Armor belt	Speed
Royal Sovereign	RN	1893	14,150/15,580	410.5 × 75 × 27.5	4-13.5 inch/10-6 inch	14-18 inch	16.5
Dreadnought	RN	1906	18,100/21,845	527 × 82 × 31	10-12 inch	4-11 inch	21.0
Invincible (BC)	RN	1908	17,400/20,078	567 × 78.5 × 26	8-12 inch/16-4 inch	4-6 inch	25.5
Iron Duke	RN	1914	25,000/29,560	623 × 90 × 29.5	10-13.5 inch/12-6 inch	4-12 inch	21.25
König	Gr	1915	25,390/29,200	575.5 × 97 × 27	10-12 inch/14-5.9 inch	3.2-14 inch	21
Nevada	USN	1916	27,500/28,400	583 × 95.5 × 28.5	10-14 inch/21-5 inch	8-13.5 inch	20.5
Hood (BC)	RN	1920	42,700/45,200	860 × 104 × 28.5	8-15 inch/12-5.5 inch	5-12 inch	31
Nelson	RN	1925	33,300/41,250	710 × 106 × 33.5	9-16 inch/12-6 inch	13-14 inch	23
Dunkerque (BC)	Fr	1937	26,500/35,500	704 × 102 × 18.5	8-13 inch/16-5.1 inch	6-10 inch	29.5
Littorio	It	1940	40,700/45,500	780 × 107.5 × 31.5	9-15 inch/12-6 inch	3-11 inch	30
Bismarck	Gr	1940	41,700/50,900	814 × 118 × 28.5	8-15 inch/12-5.9 inch	10.5-12.5 inch	29
King George V	RN	1940	36,700/42,076	745 × 103 × 29	10-14 inch/16-5.25 inch	4.5-15 inch	28
Yamato	Jp	1941	62,315/69,990	863 × 121 × 34	9-18.1 inch/12-6.1 inch	16.1 inch	27
Iowa	USN	1943	48,100/57,540	887 × 108 × 36	9-16 inch/20-5 inch	12.1 inch	32.5

NOTES: Year = year completed. Displacement = standard/deep load in tons. Dimensions = overall length by width by draft in feet. Armament = primary/secondary.

aircraft carrier in 1940—a truly brief fifty-odd-year period. Not counting the fifteen-year pre-dreadnought era from 1890 to 1905, there were four very short generations of modern dreadnoughts. The first were the original dreadnoughts built from 1906 through 1912, followed by a second generation of super-dreadnoughts built until 1916. These were followed by a few third-generation post-Jutland types, and finally the fourth generation, started in the late 1930s and built through World War II. Most were laid down during an even shorter period from 1906 to 1916, but they still dominated naval thinking right up to World War II.

Yet they had somewhat spotty records in both world wars, at least as originally envisioned as fighting in major Mahanian "decisive" battles. Does this mean the battleship was a failure? Although there were few major engagements, they still played major roles in gunfire support missions, a role advocates of recommissioning still point out is sorely needed for amphibious and littoral operations. Perhaps more important, however, was their symbolic role as measurements not just of military but of national power. In that regard they have sometimes been compared to intercontinental ballistic missiles for their deterrent value.

Even more controversial were the battle cruisers, yet every time a new, large ship is built, it is labeled a battle cruiser. The U.S. 14,000-ton nuclear cruiser *Long Beach,* commissioned in 1961, and the proposed 1970-era "strike cruiser" have sometimes been called battle cruisers. The large Russian *Kirov*-class cruisers, first laid down in 1974, with only small guns but many different missile systems, are usually called battle cruisers and, at 24,000 tons, probably deserve that label.

But the era of the dreadnoughts—those magnificent battleships and battle cruisers—is over, at least in our time. Interestingly, many science fiction writers label their military spacecraft battleships or—more likely—battle cruisers.

Cruisers

7

CRUISERS ARE PERHAPS the most interesting of all warships. In size, ships called cruisers have ranged from over 40,000 tons with 15-inch guns, larger than most battleships, to only a few hundred tons with guns smaller than those found on most destroyers. There have been belted, protected, armored, torpedo, scout, small, auxiliary, first-, second-, and third-class, and even battle cruisers in just their early years until the designations settled down into the categories of "light" and "heavy." The terms began to change again in the 1960s, when cruisers were designated, and sometimes redesignated, to create another confusing cacophony of terms.

Missions for cruisers have varied from solitary independent operations and patrols, *cruizing,* to commerce raiding, scouting "eyes of the fleet," the world's first aircraft carriers, convoy protection, and from both first- and second-line capital ships to simply running errands, dispatch boats. Cruisers were the key ships, the "gunboats," during the late nineteenth-century Age of Imperialism, the workhorse during World War I, crucial in World War II, and the capital surface combatant during the Cold War, yet today they have virtually disappeared from the seas. Cruisers were also the first modern ships built by today's most powerful navy, and, at least according to myth, a cruiser was instrumental in sounding the start of the twentieth century's greatest revolution. Cruisers were the subject of the first arms control summit, and a cruiser played a key role in ushering in the nuclear age. And it was the Soviet cruisers, not submarines, that changed perceptions of the Cold War naval balance in the late 1960s.

Early Cruisers

There is some confusion about the actual origins of the cruiser because it has few precedents. In the Age of Galleys ships often went on solitary patrols but were not specifically designed for that task. During the dromon era there were three standard sized warships of which the midsized might be considered a precedent, as the modern cruiser is usually considered the middle surface combatant between battleships and destroyers. Most analysts, however, agree that the cruiser is the lineal descendant of the large wooden sailing frigate, which had duties such as scouting, commerce raiding, and conducting isolated patrols.[1] The word *cruizing* was more "a description of function, not a classification of a ship-type" although in many cases these were frigates.[2]

The real problem is tracing the lineage during the Age of Ironclads experimental period until the term *cruiser* came into general use in the 1880s. As *Conway's Fighting Ships* from this era states: "The problem of classification in this period is acute—particularly for cruising ships—and it has not been possible always to find a suitable subheading. In many cases a subheading such as 'Masted Cruisers' or 'Unprotected Cruisers' included ships classified as frigates, corvettes and sloops."[3] Or, as another author states, "The path from the single-decked sail frigate to the First and Second World War cruiser, however, is rather tortuous."[4]

Many authors consider the Union navy ship *Wampanoag* the first cruiser type. "The beginning of the true cruiser probably came with the American Civil War" when the *Wampanoag* was started in 1863 in response to the Confederate commerce raiders, another traditional cruiser mission.[5] When completed in 1868, the 4,215-ton *Wampanoag*, with three 5.3-inch guns and a speed of 17 knots, was the fastest ship in the world. The Royal Navy responded in 1866 with the 5,780-ton *Inconstant* class carrying ten 9-inch guns.

The first "armored cruiser" with armor belts on the side was the 5,030-ton Russian *General Admiral* with six 8-inch guns laid down in 1870 and completed in 1875 (and not actually stricken until 1938). The British responded with the 5,670-ton *Shannon* with two 10-inch guns, laid down in 1873 and completed in 1877. The *Shannon* is usually credited as the first with a "protected" deck, that is, an armored deck to protect the machinery and magazine spaces. The British also built a third, "unarmored," type, two smaller 3,730-ton cruisers, the *Iris* and *Mercury,* mounting thirteen 5-inch guns. Completed in 1879, they were the first Royal Navy warships to be constructed of steel. But this was the experimental period of the Age of Ironclads, and all these ships still carried full sail rigging. Most originally were rated as frigates, corvettes, or even *avisos,* a French word for dispatch boats.[6]

Pre-Dreadnought Era Cruisers: The First Golden Age

If one had to pick a starting date for the modern cruiser, it might be 1883 for several reasons. In that year, the 2,950-ton, 270- by 42-foot *Esmeralda* with two 10-inch guns in barbettes fore and aft and sixteen 6-inch guns along the sides was completed in Britain for Chile. The *Esmeralda* was the first constructed without sails or side armor, instead having a continuous and complete armored (or protected) deck and is therefore often cited as the first modern cruiser.[7] She was also the first of the "Elswick" (shipyard) export cruisers built during this period for several countries, including Japan, China, Greece, and Italy.

Also in 1883, the U.S. Congress authorized the so-called ABC cruisers, *Atlanta, Boston,* and *Chicago,* usually considered the start of the modern U.S. Navy. While the *Atlanta* and *Boston* were fairly small 3,190-ton ships with two 8-inch guns, the *Chicago* was almost 5,000 tons with four 8-inch guns. Finally, in 1883, Great Britain launched two cruiser classes: four 4,300-ton *Leander* with ten 6-inch guns, originally classified as dispatch vessels although later rated as second-class cruisers, and the larger *Imperieuse* class armored cruisers of 8,500 tons with four 9.2-inch guns. Several other powers of the day laid down cruisers around the same time. As an offshoot of its *jeune école,* France in 1885 officially stated that it would avoid fleet actions pursuing an antitrade strategy dependent on cruisers. The Elswick cruiser *Piemonte* built for Italy in 1887 was the first fitted with quick-fire (QF) guns carrying six each 6- and 4.7-inch guns.

Another crucial year was 1888. The Russian armored cruiser *Admiral Nakhimov* was completed and, although still fitted with a full sailing rig, she was the first to carry main batteries in turrets. Considered more important was the French *Dupuy de Lome,* laid down in 1888 but not launched until 1893. The speedy 19.7-knot *Dupuy de Lôme* with both a protected deck and a narrow belt of armor caused quite a sensation. Also in 1888 the United States authorized its first armored cruiser, *New York,* as well as the protected cruiser *Olympia.* Finally, 1888 saw the completion of the largest class of cruisers for this early period, seven British *Orlando*-class 5,600-ton armored cruisers with two 9.2-inch guns.

Also in 1888 two cruiser classification systems were started. The first was the distinction between "protected" and "armored" cruisers. A "protected" cruiser was one with an "armored" arched deck over the vital parts of the ship such as the machinery and magazines. An "armored" cruiser was one with vertical side armor on the sides and sometimes superstructure.[8] The term *unarmored* was used for smaller cruisers with no armor.

The other method started by the Royal Navy in 1888 was to divide cruisers into three classes based on size.[9] The first-class cruisers ranged in size from the nine 7,350-ton *Edgar*-class protected cruisers to the three large 14,600-ton *Minotaur*-class armored cruisers laid down in 1905. Most of the first-class cruisers had 9.2-inch guns as their primary battery with 6-inch guns as secondary. The second-class cruisers were generally in the 3,000- to 5,000-ton range and usually carried 6-inch guns. The four *Mersey* class completed in the late 1880s had two 8-inch guns. All second-class ships were "protected," that is, they had armored decks but little or no vertical armor. The largest group of second-class cruisers in the late 1880s was the twenty-one ships of the *Apollo* class with two 6-inch guns and six 4.7-inch guns. Finally were the third-class 2,000- to 3,000-ton cruisers, many listed as "scout" cruisers. Most carried 4-inch guns and were unprotected, that is, they had no armor. Despite these classifications, as one author noted, "These distinctions were sometimes narrow ones, and even overlapped."[10]

This three-class system in the Royal Navy lasted until the eve of World War I. On 31 January 1913 all first-class armored and protected cruisers were redesignated as simply cruisers with second and third class designated as light cruisers.[11] Other countries generally followed suit. This system fore-shadowed the classifications "heavy" and "light" used after the Washington Naval Conference of 1921–22 through the 1950s.

After building a few armored cruisers in the late 1880s, most countries switched to building protected cruisers in the 1890s, believing that side armor offered little protection from plunging shells. Then, with the development of lighter Harvey and Krupp steel in the mid-1890s, countries once again switched back to building armored cruisers. First-class protected cruisers built by England in the early 1890s included two 9,150-ton *Blake* class, completed in 1892–94, nine 7,350-ton *Edgar* class built in 1893–96, two large 14,200 ton *Powerful* class, 1897–98, all with two 9.2-inch guns, and finally eight 11,000-ton *Diadem* class with sixteen 6-inch guns. The armor deck in these protected cruisers ranged from 4 to 6 inches. Then, starting at the turn of the century, Britain again switched to building armored cruisers. A total of thirty-five in seven different classes were built through 1906. The *Monmouth* class with ten ships, laid down from 1899 to 1901, commissioned in 1903–4, was the largest class in number. The last and largest armored cruisers in the Royal Navy were the three 14,600-ton *Minotaur* class laid down in 1905, commissioned in 1908–9, mounting four 9.2-inch and ten 7.5-inch guns. There were five different second-class cruiser classes with almost half of the forty-seven built in the twenty-one-ship, 3,400-ton *Apollo* class. The third-class cruisers were a mixture of dispatch boats, torpedo cruisers, and scout cruisers. The largest in number were eleven 2,135-ton *Pelorus* class with eight 4-inch guns commissioned from 1897 to 1901.

In Germany it was not until the late 1890s, after Kaiser Wilhelm II came to power, that cruiser construction began in earnest with the laying down in 1896 of the five 6,390-ton *Victoria Louise* class protected cruisers carrying two 8.2-inch guns and then in 1897 ten 3,030-ton *Gazelle* light cruisers with ten 4-inch guns. Germany built only eight more heavy cruisers of which the best and most famous were the 12,800-ton *Scharnhorst* and *Gneisenau* completed in 1907–8 and mounting eight 8.2-inch guns.

France, which had always been considered the second naval power until the Kaiser decided to challenge Great Britain, built twenty-two armored cruisers, most in the 9,000- to 13,000-ton range. The last and most powerful, laid down in 1905–6 and completed in 1911, were two almost 14,000-ton *Edgar Quinet* class mounting fourteen 7.6-inch guns. France built only a

The German armored cruiser *Scharnhorst*, completed in 1907. She was sunk by Royal Navy battle cruisers at the Battle of the Falkland Islands on 8 December 1914. (U.S. Naval Institute)

handful of smaller protected cruisers. Italy built six smaller armored cruisers around the turn of the century. The three 7,230-ton *Giuseppe Garibaldi* class were considered the best armed and protected ships of their day on a relatively small displacement with one 10-inch, two 8-inch, and fourteen 6-inch guns.

Russia built only a handful of armored and protected cruisers and was to pay the price during the Russo-Japanese War. Russia did have the distinction of building the largest armored cruiser. This was the 15,190-ton *Rurik* mounting four 10-inch and eight 8-inch guns. Japan had only a few armored and protected cruisers, but some were of historical interest. She purchased the original *Esmeralda* from Chile and then several "improved" *Esmeralda* and *O'Higgins*-class Elswick cruisers.[12]

The U.S. Navy built twelve armored cruisers starting with the 8,200-ton *New York* mounting six 8-inch guns in 1890, followed by the *Brooklyn* in 1893. They were followed by two classes, sometimes collectively called "the Big Ten." These were six 13,700-ton *Pennsylvania* class with four 8-inch and fourteen 6-inch guns, most completed in 1905, followed by the four *Tennessee* class, 14,500 tons, with four 10-inch and sixteen 6-inch guns, laid down in 1903 and completed between 1906 and 1908.

The United States had a harder time deciding on smaller, protected cruisers. The 5,900-ton *Olympia* with four 8-inch guns commissioned as a fast commerce raider was considered a success, and there were continuous calls for follow-ons, but only a few were built. The largest class was the six 3,200-ton *Denver* with ten 5-inch guns. In 1905, the United States laid down the three 3,750-ton *Chester* "scout cruisers" with only two 5-inch guns. They were designated CS1 through 3, starting the U.S. Navy's cruiser sequential numbering system (regardless of size) that lasted until 1949, ending with heavy cruiser *Newport News* CA-148.

THIS PRE-DREADNOUGHT PERIOD was the height of the Age of Imperialism and the age of "gunboat diplomacy." In the forefront in that role were the cruisers because the large pre-dreadnoughts were considered too valuable to be sent far from home waters. In the first modern cruiser action, the Battle of the Yalu River during the Sino-Japanese War of 1894–95, a Chinese fleet of two old battleships and eight armored cruisers was defeated by a Japanese fleet of nine armored cruisers. Both sides used follow-on variations of the original *Esmeralda*. The Spanish-American War in the Far East was a cruiser war. The American squadron under Commodore George Dewey on board the *Olympia,* accompanied by the cruisers *Baltimore, Raleigh,* and *Boston,* easily defeated the Spanish fleet of two old cruisers and a few gunboats. Although battleships were prominent in the Battle of Tsushima in 1905, the eight Japanese armored cruisers played key roles in the mop-up action after the initial engagement.

The cruisers of this period are often overshadowed by the pre-dreadnoughts, but there were more interesting and unique cruiser types, from very large armored cruisers, the size of second-class battleships, down to small third-class scouts, than there were battleship designs. This was truly a golden age of cruisers.

The Modern Era: 1906–1914

As the *Dreadnought* made all the previous battleships obsolete, the laying down in 1906 of the large, fast, 18,000-ton *Invincible*-class battle cruisers, originally called armored cruisers, with 12-inch guns made the older, slower armored cruisers, most with 9-inch guns, obsolete. Cruiser construction was reevaluated, interrupted, in some cases temporarily, in others permanently. Both the United States and France stopped building cruisers altogether, and after the *Invincible* only smaller light cruisers would be built. Italy built four smaller scout and colonial cruisers. Russia also suspended cruiser construction but then in 1913 laid down ten smaller cruisers though only two were built during the war. Japan built five smaller cruisers during this period in the 3,000- to 4,000-ton range with 4- to 6-inch guns. Germany built a dozen light cruisers after 1908 in the 4,500- to 5,000-ton range, most carrying only 4-inch guns. Interestingly, most of the early airplane experiments were conducted on cruisers, including the first flight by Eugene Ely off the American cruiser *Birmingham* in 1910.

The situation in England was even more confused because Admiral Fisher did not like light cruisers, feeling that the large 2,170-ton *Swift*-class destroyer flotilla leaders could take their place and that nothing else was needed between capital ships and destroyers. His views were not shared, and after his departure in 1908, the Royal Navy in 1909 started a series of four classes collectively known as the "Town" class because they were all named after

British towns or cities. These were five *Bristol* class, four *Weymouth,* six *Chatham,* and four *Birmingham,* all around 5,200 tons, 453 by 48 feet, carrying eight or nine 6-inch guns (except for the *Bristol* class, which had only two). In 1912, eight smaller 3,750-ton *Arethusa*-class light scout cruisers with two 6-inch guns were built. Then, in 1913 the Royal Navy started the first of six classes collectively known as the "C" class: six *Caroline,* two *Calliope,* four *Cambrian,* two *Centaur,* four *Caledon,* and five *Ceres,* all completed during the war with others completed afterward. The "C's" were all in the 4,200-ton range, 446 by 41.5 feet, with from two to five 6-inch guns.

In late 1913 all British cruisers were reclassified into "cruiser" and "light" categories, but on the eve of World War I, their roles and missions were in doubt. As *Conway's* for this pre–World War I era states, the "flaw in Fisher's doctrines was his conviction that there was no longer any need for cruising ships, whether cruisers or escort class."[13] This view was shared by other navies, and many stopped building cruisers or built only very small scout cruisers. The Great War would prove that decision to have been a mistake.

World War I

Cruisers played important, although sometimes unappreciated, roles in the Great War at sea. Most books focus on the then new submarine warfare and, of course, the Battle of Jutland. Cruiser warfare, if mentioned at all, focuses on the German raiders such as the cruiser *Emden* and auxiliary cruisers, that is, merchantmen, often fast liners, fitted with guns. Both these roles were minor, although they did cloud thinking concerning cruisers during the interwar years. Rather, the importance of the cruisers was in the day-to-day work, unfortunately mentioned only in rare books such as Paul Halpern's *Naval History of World War I* that emphasize such operations. This was a role cruisers would share with destroyers in World War II, but during World War I, the cruiser was more important because the early destroyers were too small and did not have the endurance for more than a few days' operations. Table 7.1 shows the approximate cruiser naval balance in 1914 listed in accordance with their original designations. One must say "approximate" even with the help of *Conway's* and *Jane's* because not all navies used the same cruiser classification system. The "old" light cruisers were those built before 1906, usually classified as third class, the "new" those built after 1906. Britain had the largest cruiser force, outnumbering the Germans approximately four to one in heavier armored and protected cruisers and two to one in the light cruiser category. Light cruisers were the largest warships built in any quantity during the war.

Cruisers played key roles in the opening days of World War I, one most cruiser men would probably rather forget. The first Royal Navy casualty of the war was the cruiser *Amphion,* sunk by a mine on the first day of the war.

Table 7.1 Cruiser Balance in World War I

Type	Britain	France	Italy	Russia	U.S.	Japan	Germany	Austria
PRE-DREADNOUGHT ERA								
Armored	34	22	10	10	12	8	8	3
Protected	19	3	0	7	10	6	6	2
Light (old)	41	11	3	1	12	5	22	6
(Subtotal)	(94)	(36)	(13)	(18)	(34)	(19)	(36)	(11)
MODERN LIGHT								
1914	30	0	4	1	3	6	20	3
Built	28	0	2	1	0	0	12	1
(Subtotal)	(58)	(0)	(6)	(2)	(3)	(6)	(32)	(4)
TOTAL	152	36	19	20	37	25	68	15
LOSSES								
Armored	10	4	2	2	1	0	5	0
Protected	2	0	0	1	0	0	0	0
Light (old)	2	0	0	0	0	0	7	1
Light (new)	5	0	0	1	0	0	14	0
TOTAL	19	4	2	4	1	0	26	1

NOTE: Built = Those building before or built and commissioned during the war.

On 14 August, the *Birmingham* rammed and sank *U-15*, the first submarine sunk, but then on 5 September the German submarine *U-21* retaliated, sinking the old British scout cruiser *Pathfinder*. On 22 September, however, an event occurred involving cruisers that forever changed warfare at sea. On that date, the lone German submarine *U-9* in one hour sank three turn-of-the-century English armored cruisers, the *Aboukir, Cressy,* and *Hogue,* one of the major sea tragedies of the war. Many cite this as the start of the modern submarine warfare era. Naval warfare would never be the same even though a closer examination showed major mistakes. These old cruisers were patrolling at slow speed when the *Aboukir* was hit. The others were picked off when they stopped to rescue survivors.

One of the first duties of the Royal Navy was running down the few German cruisers that were still on the high seas at the start of the war. The most famous was the German light cruiser *Emden* that sank some 101,000 tons of shipping in the Indian Ocean before being sunk by the Australian cruiser *Sydney* on 9 November 1914. The most spectacular action was conducted by the German armored cruisers *Scharnhorst* and *Gneisenau* in company with three small cruisers that defeated a British cruiser force in the Battle of Coronel off the Chilean coast before being sunk themselves at the Battle of the Falklands by British battle cruisers. Although chasing down these German cruisers stationed overseas was often exciting and spectacular, within the first six months of the war they were all eliminated.

Cruisers played key roles in the main theaters in the North Sea and Channel areas carrying out most of the constant patrols. Some became famous such as Commodore Tyrwhitt's Harwich force (which also included destroyers) and especially Commodore Goodenough's light cruiser force, which was continually coming to the rescue like "light cavalry," as one author put it.[14] Cruisers also often acted as destroyer leaders. And the main fleets never ventured forth without a cruiser screen. In short, the cruiser became the workhorse of World War I.

Cruisers also played key roles in the few major actions of the war. The first significant sea battle of the war on 28 August 1914 at Heligoland Bight began as a cruiser-destroyer skirmish in which the Germans lost three light cruisers they could ill afford. Cruisers played a major role in the famous Battle of Jutland. The British Grand Fleet contained eight armored cruisers and twenty-six light cruisers, many of the latter serving as the main scouting force. The German High Seas Fleet had eleven light cruisers. Of the fourteen British ships lost, three were battle cruisers and three armored cruisers, and of the ten German ships sunk, one was a battle cruiser and four were light cruisers.

Despite participating in these few major engagements, however, the cruiser generally played three major roles. First was the day-to-day patrols and second was screening the main battle fleets. They also played a third, sometimes confusing, role as second-line capital ships, perhaps leading to the relieving of one admiral and the criticism of another. In the Mediterranean, Rear Admiral Ernest Troubridge, commanding the First Cruiser Squadron consisting of four armored cruisers, was court-martialed for failing to engage the German battle cruiser *Goeben* on its way to Turkey. Although acquitted, he was never again given a sea command. Just a few months later, Rear Admiral Sir Christopher Cradock with two older cruisers (and aware of Troubridge's berated inaction) was criticized for taking on Vice Admiral Spee in command of the modern German armored cruisers *Scharnhorst* and *Gneisenau*.[15]

Cruisers were also involved in two tragedies. In 1916, Lord Kitchener, the secretary of war, was drowned on his way to Russia when the cruiser *Hampshire* struck a mine; his loss had a great effect on British morale. And, at least according to myth, it was the old Russian protected cruiser *Aurora*, firing a blank round to signal the attack on the Winter Palace on 7 November 1917, that began the Russian Revolution.

Cruisers suffered relatively high losses in the war. The Royal Navy lost twenty, twelve armored and protected and eight light, while Germany lost twenty-six, five armored and nineteen light. Other countries also lost a few, including the U.S. armored cruiser *San Diego* that was mined off New York on 19 July 1918. Japan also lost a cruiser while on convoy escort duty. In addition, Britain lost seventeen armed merchant auxiliary cruisers, most torpedoed by German submarines.[16] Though generally overshadowed by the mighty dreadnoughts and new submarines, on a day-to-day basis, the cruiser was probably more important.

The Interwar Period: The Second Golden Age of Cruisers

The period between the world wars was another Golden Age of cruisers. Because battleship construction was restricted, the future roles of both the submarine and the aircraft carrier were generally unappreciated, and destroyers were in abundance from World War I buildups; virtually every other ship type during this period became secondary to the cruiser. However, while it is difficult to summarize cruiser construction during the first Golden Age from 1883 to 1905, which saw many types from large armored and protected to various light cruisers, during the interwar period there were essentially only two types built: "heavy" 10,000-ton cruisers with 8-inch guns and "light" cruisers with 6-inch guns.

Section XI of the 1922 Washington Treaty stated that "no vessel of war exceeding 10,000 tons standard displacement, other than a capital ship or aircraft carrier" or one with a "gun with a caliber in excess of 8 inches . . . shall be acquired." This restriction led to the construction of so-called treaty cruisers of—not surprisingly—10,000 tons with 8-inch guns. These restrictions were a challenge to ship designers, which they sometimes mishandled. Some of the large armored cruisers of the early 1900s were 15,000 tons, so the new limits amounted to a 50 percent reduction. The main result was that armor was sacrificed, and these interwar cruisers were subsequently labeled "tin-clads."

Besides the design problems, there were other concerns about cruisers during this period. First was the debate, often bitter, between the United States and Great Britain over the numbers. This issue was settled by the world's first arms control summit between Prime Minister Ramsay Mac-Donald and President Herbert Hoover. Then there was the cruiser arms race between major powers Britain, the United States, and Japan, and another in the Mediterranean between France and Italy. Finally were weapons debates between advocates of the 6- versus 8-inch guns. All told, it was a most fascinating period.

With two exceptions, cruiser shipbuilding started slowly after World War I. Britain completed light cruisers already under construction but then stopped. The two exceptions were Japan and the United States. Japan laid down two classes of light cruisers, five 5,500-ton *Kuma* class in 1918–19 and six 5,570-ton *Nagara* class in 1920–21, both with seven 5.5-inch guns. More significant because the United States had not laid down a cruiser since 1904 was its initiation of the ten-ship, 7,050-ton full-load light cruiser *Omaha* class with

HMS *Kent,* completed in 1928. She was the first of the Royal Navy's "treaty" cruisers at 10,000 tons and with eight 8-inch guns.
(U.S. Naval Institute)

twelve 6-inch guns. These ships, designed as scout cruisers, reflected prewar designs and were the last class to carry old-fashioned casemate gun mounts.[17]

After the Washington Treaty agreement, however, all countries started building new 10,000-ton, 8-inch "treaty" cruisers. During the 1920s, the Royal Navy built fifteen, starting with seven *Kent* class in 1924. All carried from six to eight 8-inch guns. The United States laid down eight, two *Pensacola* (CA 24) class starting in 1926 with ten 8-inch guns and six *Northampton* (CA 26) class with nine 8-inch guns in 1928. Japan laid down three classes, two *Furutaka* class and two *Aoba* class, both with six 8-inch guns, and four *Nachi* and four *Takao* class, both with ten 8-inch guns. France laid down six heavy cruisers in two classes: two *Duquesne* class and four *Suffren* class, both with eight 8-inch guns. Not to be outdone, Italy responded with six heavy cruisers also in two classes: two *Trento* and four *Zara* class, both with eight 8-inch guns. Italy, alone of all the major naval powers of the day, built new light cruisers well after the Washington Treaty went into effect. These were the four *Giussano* class with eight 6-inch guns begun in 1928. In sum, with a few exceptions, the 1920s was an era of heavy, 10,000-ton cruisers with 8-inch guns. In length they varied from 560 to 668 feet.

Debates over cruisers continued in the 1920s with numbers being the biggest issue. The Royal Navy had a requirement for seventy cruisers, explained at the 1927 Geneva Conference by Admiral of the Fleet Jellicoe (who was actually representing New Zealand): "It is a generally accepted view that in a fleet five cruisers are required for every three capital ships. With a British fleet of 15 capital ships the number of cruisers needed for fleet work, therefore, is 25, and 45 out of 70 are therefore left for direct trade protection. Of this number we must expect 12 to be refitting or fueling at any given moment. With lines of communication 80,000 miles in length, this gives one cruiser for every 2,500 miles of communications."[18] The United States did not buy this argument, and as a result, "the Naval Disarmament Conference of 1927 was one of the most dramatically unsuccessful international gatherings of the twentieth century."[19] Relations were smoothed over only by a personal visit by Prime Minister MacDonald to the United States. This could perhaps be called the first arms control summit, setting a pattern that would become standard in the Cold War years between the United States and the Soviet Union.

Another issue that constantly arose was over auxiliary cruisers, or merchantmen, which could carry a 6-inch but not an 8-inch gun. Six-inch shells at around 100 pounds were considered the largest that could be manhandled. Since the British had the largest merchant fleet, they did not want restrictions on auxiliary cruisers. The Americans felt otherwise and preferred an 8-inch gun to overcome the auxiliary's 6-inch. In retrospect, it was fallacious to think a merchantman with a few 6-inch guns could defeat a similarly armed warship, but this argument came up constantly in the arms talks. (During World War II the German raider *Kormoran* would sink the Australian light cruiser *Sydney,* which had foolishly let the raider close with being properly challenged.) A related issue was the debate over whether it was better to have fewer, larger 8-inch guns with firing rates about three per minute or more rapid-firing 6-inch guns at about ten per minute.

Because of the presummit diplomacy, these issues were resolved at the First London Naval Conference of 1930. The British agreed to allow the Americans more heavy cruisers, eighteen to fifteen, for the British having a larger overall limit, 339,000 to 325,000 tons. The Japanese were unhappy with their allotted twelve heavies, but this problem was resolved when the United States delayed the last three cruisers on a one-per-year schedule starting in 1933. Finally, the ad hoc system of light and heavy cruisers was codified into two categories (a) and (b) of 8- and 6-inch guns respectively. The British had also wanted tonnage limits of 10,000 for (a) and 6,000 to 7,000 for (b) cruisers to save money, but this proposal was not accepted. The second London Conference held in 1935–36 extended these limits, but the system soon broke down although these limits were generally adhered to by the United States and England into the late 1930s.

Britain immediately began building light cruisers and never again built a heavy. At first they built traditional light cruisers in the 6,000- to 7,000-ton range, the five *Leander* class started in 1931, followed by the three *Perth* class in 1933, both with eight 6-inch guns, and the four even smaller *Arethusa* class of only 5,220 tons with six 6-inch guns, also started in 1933. With one exception, starting in 1934, Britain began taking advantage of the 10,000-ton limit, building larger light cruisers. These were five 9,100-ton *Southampton* class, three *Gloucester* class in 1936, and in 1939 the largest built by the Royal Navy, the two 10,550-ton *Edinburgh* and *Belfast* (still preserved as a memorial in London), all with twelve 6-inch guns. The eleven-ship, smaller 8,530-ton *Fiji* class was started in 1938. The only exception to the 6-inch cruiser was the eleven-ship 5,600-ton *Dido* class antiaircraft cruiser started in 1937, with most mounting ten 5.25-inch semiautomatic guns. After the war started, the five-ship antiair *Bellona* class was also built. Few light cruisers were built by Britain once the war began.

Japan built only a few more cruisers in the 1930s. The most famous were the four 8,500-ton *Mogami* class, originally built as light cruisers with fifteen 6-inch guns. There were problems with the design, and they were rebuilt several times, finally ending up as heavy cruisers at over 12,000 tons with ten 8-inch guns. The only heavy cruisers built during the 1930s were the two 11,215-ton *Tone* class with eight 8-inch guns. Two other light cruiser classes were built, the four-ship, 5,890-ton *Katori*-class training cruisers in 1938, mounting four 5.5-inch guns, and four 6,650-ton *Agano* class in 1940 carrying the usual 6-inch guns. Japan completed only one more light cruiser during the war.

The United States decided to build "up to treaty limits" in heavy cruisers starting with seven 10,000-ton *New Orleans* (CA-32) class mounting nine 8-inch guns in 1934. These were followed by the nine-ship light cruiser *Brooklyn* (CL-40) class just under 10,000 tons mounting fifteen 6-inch guns in 1935. After the war, several *Brooklyn* class cruisers were sold to Latin American countries, in whose fleets they remained into the 1970s and 1980s. One had the dubious distinction of being the last cruiser sunk in war. The *Phoenix* (CL-44) was sold to Argentina in 1951, renamed the *General Belgrano,* and was sunk by a British submarine on 2 May 1982 during the Falklands war. The United States, like Britain, decided to build an antiair cruiser. This was the eleven-ship *Atlanta* (CL-51) class of only 6,700 tons, with twelve or sixteen 5-inch guns.

The United States then began two large classes before World War II that were continued throughout the war. The first was the large, 11,750-ton *Cleveland* (CL-55) class light cruiser with twelve 6-inch guns, started in early 1940. Fifty-two were ordered with twenty-nine completed as cruisers, making them the most numerous cruiser class ever built. (Several became *Independence*-class light carriers.) They were accompanied by the 14,470-ton *Baltimore* (CA-68) class of heavy cruisers with nine 8-inch guns. Two other classes were laid down in 1945 and commissioned after the war: three very

USS *Cleveland* (CL-55), a light cruiser completed in 1942. Fifty-two of her class were ordered and twenty-nine were completed, making it the largest class of cruisers built. They were 11,750 tons and had twelve 6-inch guns.
(U.S. Naval Institute)

large, 17,255-ton, heavy cruiser *Des Moines* (CA-134) class with nine 8-inch guns and the large, 14,700-ton *Worcester* (CL-144) light cruiser class with twelve 6-inch guns. The *Newport News* (CA-148), commissioned in 1949, was the last classic gun cruiser built by the United States.

Throughout this period France and Italy conducted their own naval race. After matching each other with six cruisers apiece in the 1920s, the Italians forged ahead with several classes of heavy and light cruisers. The heavy cruisers included four 11,680-ton *Zara* class with eight 8-inch guns and the single *Bolzano*. Light cruisers included twelve variations of the Condottieri design ranging from 5,000 to almost 9,500 tons with from eight to ten 6-inch guns. There were twelve planned but only four completed of the smaller "Capitani Romani" class of 3,690 tons with eight 5.1-inch guns, called "destroyers of destroyers." During the 1930s, the French built one heavy cruiser, the *Algérie,* the single *Emile Bertin* light cruiser, and then the six-ship light cruiser *La Galissonnière* class of 7,600 tons mounting nine 6-inch guns. Although the anticipated Italian-French naval battles never took place, the Italian cruisers were a constant source of trouble for the Royal Navy in the Mediterranean.

The Germans built some of the most interesting cruisers of the interwar period. During the 1920s, they built a few traditional light cruisers, first a new 5,600-ton *Emden* laid down in 1921 with eight 6-inch guns, followed by three 6,650-ton *Königsberg* class mounting nine similar guns. Only two other light cruisers were built before World War II. Then, however, the Germans built heavy cruisers that outclassed all others of their day. First were the three famous *Deutschland* class started in 1929, dubbed "pocket battleships" by the West but really heavy cruisers. In the mid-1930s Germany built two classes of very large, heavy cruisers. The first were the two 14,050-ton *Admiral Hipper* class mounting eight 8-inch guns, followed by the even larger 17,000-ton *Prinz Eugen* class with similar armament.

These German ships obviously violated the treaty limits. Although the Treaty of Versailles allowed Germany ships with 11-inch guns, they were to be restricted to 10,000 tons. But Germany was not alone. Both the Japanese and Italians built cruisers above 10,000 tons, and all the countries found it difficult to build ships within the limits because armor had to be sacrificed. But despite these problems, for most of the interwar period, the cruiser was the dominant type built for a variety or reasons, including restrictions on battleships and lack of appreciation of submarines and carriers. The stage was now set for what would turn out to be the end of an era of classic sea battles, with most involving cruisers.

World War II

The role of the cruiser during World War II was once again overshadowed by other types of ships: the submarine and the aircraft carrier, both significantly unappreciated during the interwar period. Cruisers settled into their role as the daily workhorse, although it was one they would now share with destroyers. Thus, once again, the role of the cruisers is often overlooked in many accounts of World War II even though most of the major surface actions of the war were in fact cruiser battles.

Table 7.2 shows the cruiser balance in 1940, the year the war began in earnest. The Royal Navy had the largest cruiser fleet with sixty-eight, but

Table 7.2 Cruiser Balance in World War II

Type	Britain	France	USSR	U.S.	Germany	Italy	Japan
HEAVY							
1940	18	10	0	18	6	7	18
Built	0	0	0	9	0	0	0
(Subtotal)	(18)	(10)		(27)	(6)	(7)	(18)
LIGHT							
1940	50	7	9	19	6	12	38
Built	23	0	0	33	0	3	6
(Subtotal)	(73)	(7)	(9)	(52)	(6)	(15)	(44)
TOTAL	91	17	9	79	12	22	62
LOSSES							
Heavy	5			9	4	7	17
Light	22			3	3	6	22
TOTAL	27			12	7	13	39

NOTES: Built = Those building before and built during and commissioned during the war. British total of light cruisers on hand in 1940 includes 26 from World War I.

those numbers are a little misleading because they include twenty-six started during World War I. By contrast, the oldest American cruisers, the *Omaha* (CL-4) class, were built after the war. Only the United States constructed cruisers in any number during World War II. With very few exceptions, most of the British, Japanese, and Italian cruisers commissioned during the war had actually been started in 1938–39.

THE ATLANTIC THEATER

Once again, the early sea actions involved the Royal Navy running down German surface raiders. The most dramatic was the Battle of the River Plate on 13 December 1939, when the heavy cruiser *Exeter* with two light cruisers caught the German pocket battleship (heavy cruiser) *Graf Spee*. This battle might be one of the few that provides some evidence on the 8- versus 6-inch gun argument. According to the *Graf Spee*'s gunnery officer, although the rapid-firing 6-inch guns of the British light cruisers scored more hits, the 8-inch rounds of the *Exeter* caused more damage.[20]

Both British and German cruisers were involved in the most famous Atlantic sea battle of the war, resulting in the sinking of the battle cruiser *Hood*. The German heavy cruiser *Prinz Eugen* damaged the *Hood*, causing fires and permitting the *Bismarck* to obtain an accurate fire-control solution. In most of the other actions German surface forces were sent out as commerce raiders, and in many cases they were driven off by escorting British cruisers. In December 1940, for example, three Royal Navy cruiser escorts drove off the *Hipper*. Not all such actions were successful. On another occasion in July 1942, the British received word that a German force consisting of the battleship *Tirpitz* and cruisers *Admiral Scheer*, *Lützow*, and *Hipper* had put to sea against convoy PQ17. Even though there were four escorting British heavy cruisers, PQ17 was told to disperse with disastrous results—only eleven of the thirty-seven merchants made port. But these forays by the Germans would be few because Adolf Hitler was afraid to see his surface ships sunk. They were, however, constant threats as traditional "fleets in being" and continually tied up British ships, mostly escorting cruisers and destroyers.

THE MEDITERRANEAN THEATER

There were continuous clashes between the British and Italian fleets, most of them involving cruisers. The Italian navy had quite a few cruisers, considered by many commentators of the day to be among the best in the world. A major problem for the Italian navy was lack of air cover, in contrast to the British, who usually had at least one carrier involved in their actions.

Besides fleet engagements there were also a few cruiser-to-cruiser actions. In the first on 10 July 1940, the Australian light cruiser *Sydney* with five destroyers attacked and got the best of two Italian light cruisers, the *Barto-*

lomeo Colleoni and *Giovanni delle Bande Nere.* Most of the cruisers, however, were not sunk or damaged in surface engagements but by airplanes and submarines, which were most effective in these confined waters. The British antiair (AA) cruisers were used extensively in the Mediterranean and seventeen were lost. Italian cruisers also took heavy losses from British air and especially in convoy duties trying to resupply Axis forces in North Africa. Cruisers were also ideal for gunfire in the relatively shallow waters that might have been dangerous for battleships. Of the 314,298 tons of warships lost by Italy, cruisers accounted for the largest portion, 82,225, followed by 70,632 lost to submarines.[21] Similarly, of the 411,935 tons lost by the Royal Navy in the Mediterranean, by far the largest was in cruisers, 95,265 tons, followed by 73,260 tons for destroyers.[22] Thus in many respects the Mediterranean was a cruiser war.

THE PACIFIC THEATER

In the Pacific theater cruisers played a more dramatic role, at least initially, before settling into their more traditional one as the day-to-day workhorse. There were two series of major cruiser sea battles. The first was in February 1942 between the Japanese navy and the American-British-Dutch-Australian (ABDA) force under Dutch Rear Admiral Karel Doorman in the East Indies. The major action came on 27 February at the Battle of Java Sea. On paper, the two sides were fairly evenly matched. The ABDA force had two heavy cruisers, the USS *Houston* and RN *Exeter* of earlier Battle of River Plate fame, and three light cruisers, the Dutch *De Ruyter* and *Java* and the Australian *Perth,* and nine destroyers versus a Japanese force of two heavy and two light cruisers with eight destroyers. However, the better trained Japanese force (at least at this stage of the war) easily won the battles, which extended over three days. In the initial seven-hour engagement, the *De Ruyter* and *Java* were hit by torpedoes and sunk and the *Exeter* was badly damaged. Doorman went down on the *De Ruyter.* The next day the *Houston* and *Perth,* trying to escape through Sunda Straits, were caught and sunk by two Japanese cruisers and the *Exeter* was sunk by a Japanese cruiser-destroyer force the following day.

The second major series was the numerous engagements involved with the taking of Guadalcanal. In the initial night action off Savo Island the night of 8–9 August, four heavy American cruisers, the *Astoria, Quincy, Vincennes,* and *Chicago* and the Australian heavy *Canberra* were attacked by a Japanese force of seven cruisers. Only the *Chicago,* with her bow blown off, would survive. The Japanese lost the heavy cruiser *Kako,* sunk by a U.S. submarine.

In the second major surface action, the Battle of Cape Esperance on the night of 11–12 October, the Americans under Rear Admiral Norman Scott, with four cruisers and five destroyers, surprised a Japanese fleet with three cruisers and two destroyers. One Japanese cruiser was badly damaged and another sunk. The following month, however, at the first night battle of Guadalcanal on 12–13 November, the Japanese with a force containing two battleships defeated an American force led by Rear Admiral Daniel Callaghan with five cruisers. In this battle, both Admirals Callaghan and Scott were killed and the light cruiser *Atlanta* was sunk. The last battle took place the night of 30 November–1 December 1942, when an American force with five cruisers intercepted a Japanese destroyer force bringing supplies to Guadalcanal. As the Japanese destroyers turned away, they fired their torpedoes, hitting four of the five American cruisers. In February 1943 the Japanese finally evacuated Guadalcanal, ending this six-month campaign. Although there were larger actions in the war, none matched the ferocity of the cruiser sea battles around Guadalcanal.

There were other cruiser battles in the Pacific. The battle off the Komandorski Islands in the Aleutians in March 1943 is called the "last old-fashioned naval battle, line against line," with both sides firing "until their ammunition is exhausted."[23] Cruisers on both sides were damaged but not sunk. On 2 November 1943 in the Battle of Empress Augusta Bay, a Japanese task force of two heavy and two light cruisers and six destroyers tangled with an American force under Rear Admiral Anson Merrill of four cruisers and eight destroyers and lost the cruiser *Haguro*. This would be the final cruiser-versus-cruiser engagement in the Pacific.

Despite being involved in many engagements, as in the Atlantic and Mediterranean, the cruiser's primary role was protecting convoys and carrier battle groups. With the sinking of the battleships at Pearl Harbor, the heavy cruisers became the main surface combatant capital ship for about a year. The cruisers also had the speed to keep up with the fast carrier battle groups. Later, the cruisers were useful for the many gunfire-support missions in the numerous amphibious assaults of that theater.

One more cruiser incident deserves mention because it involves the start of the nuclear age and one of those historically interesting "what-might-have-beens." That was the torpedoing and sinking of the heavy cruiser *Indianapolis* (CA-35) after delivering the atom bombs that were later dropped on Japan. One can only wonder what the world would be like if she had been sunk before. Worse, her sinking went unnoticed for several days, resulting in the loss of most of the crew to exposure and sharks. Then the captain was court-martialed (for not zigzagging) with the chief witness the Japanese submarine skipper. The captain returned to duty but later committed suicide. The sinking of the *Indianapolis* was also the last major U.S. Navy war loss of World War II, unfortunately marring an otherwise generally heroic record.

Cruisers took a beating in World War II. Although most books note the horrendous toll in submarines, as a percentage, the cruiser losses were greater. Italy lost all of its heavy cruisers, Japan all but one. German losses probably would have been higher had its cruisers not been kept in port. The American losses in heavy cruisers was also high, lending some credence to the argument that the quick-firing 6-inch gun might have fared better in the Guadalcanal battles, but given the superiority of the Japanese in night engagements, their better long-lance torpedo, and the melee nature of the battles, that could never be proven.

Historically, these Pacific cruiser engagements would be the end of an era of fighting at sea that started in the sixteenth century. Although Sir Francis Drake, John Paul Jones, Lord Nelson, and all the other great seaman from the Age of Sail might have been somewhat bewildered were they to witness the new submarine and carrier battles, they would have easily recognized these cruiser fights.

Post–World War II Period

The golden era of cruisers continued for about five years into the Cold War with several cruisers started before and during the war completed. For example, the Netherlands completed the large, 9,500-ton light cruisers *De Ruyter* and *De Zeven Provincien,* both laid down in 1939. They were finished in 1953, operated for many years in the Dutch navy, and later were sold to Peru in 1973 and 1976. But the days of the traditional gun cruiser were coming to an end. Only the Soviet Union would build a new class of gun cruisers after World War II. These were the large 13,600-ton *Sverdlov* class mounting twelve 6-inch guns. Twenty-four were ordered, twenty laid down starting in 1949, and fourteen were completed from 1951 through 1955. Although fine-looking ships, they were already obsolete, described by Nikita Khrushchev as "floating coffins." The United States laid down the 5,500-ton *Norfolk* in 1949. Originally designated CLK-1, antisubmarine "hunter-killer" cruiser, the *Norfolk* was commissioned DL-1 (first destroyer leader and then frigate). She had eight 3-inch guns for antiair warfare.

While the gun age was coming to an end, the missile era was about to begin. Starting in 1952, the American heavy cruisers *Boston* (CA-69) and *Canberra* (CA-70) entered the yard to emerge as guided missile cruisers, CAG-1 and 2 in 1955 and 1956 respectively. From 1958 through 1960, six *Cleveland* class light cruisers were converted to CLGs with their after mounts replaced with either Terrier or Talos missiles. In the early 1960s three more heavies underwent more elaborate conversions with both fore and aft guns removed and replaced by the more sophisticated Tartar missile systems. These ships remained in the fleet, often as flagships, through the 1970s until the last was decommissioned in 1980.

One other American ship deserves mention because it was often considered the last "true" cruiser until the Soviet Union built the battle cruiser *Kirov* in the late 1970s. This was the large 15,100-ton, 721-by-23-foot *Long*

Beach CGN-9 laid down in 1957, commissioned in 1961. She was the first nuclear-powered surface combatant and originally carried no guns but three missile launchers, one Talos and two Terriers. Two 5-inch guns were added. Initially intended as a nuclear frigate, she was commissioned a cruiser. At 15,100 tons, the *Long Beach* was definitely in the cruiser class. She was also the first credited with shooting down aircraft with SAMs when she downed two MIGs over North Vietnam in May and June 1968.

Despite the *Long Beach* and American conversions, in 1962 an event took place that shook the complacency of Western fleets. In that year, the Soviet navy completed the first of four 4,400-ton *Kynda* class, designated "rocket cruisers" (RK), followed by four larger 6,000-ton *Kresta I* RK class starting in 1967. Then, starting in 1970, they completed ten *Kresta II*-class large anti-submarine warfare (ASW) ships (BPK), followed by the 6,700-ton, seven-ship *Kara* class, also designated BPK. These new Soviet cruisers bristled with missile systems in what was sometimes called a "fierce look." On closer examination, most were considered simply one-shot ships and many experts questioned the Western "cruiser" designation. But there was still great concern in the West and fears that the Soviet navy might actually be catching up with and even challenging Western navies. Although the main threat posed by the Soviet navy was still considered to be its large submarine force, for the first time it appeared that the Soviets were also challenging the West with a blue-water "cruiser" navy.

A partial solution to the emerging Soviet cruiser problem was found in 1975, when the United States Navy by the stroke of a pen redesignated twenty-two former American guided missile frigates (DLG) conventional-powered guided missile cruisers (CG) and guided missile cruisers nuclear-powered (CGN.) The new CGs were nine 5,150-ton *Leahy* (CG-16) class commissioned from 1962 to 1964 and nine 5,400-ton *Belknap* (CG-26) class commissioned from 1963 to 1965. The new CGNs were the 7,250-ton *Bainbridge* (CGN-25) commissioned in 1962, the 8,150-ton *Truxtun* (CGN-35) commissioned in 1967, the two-ship 10,150-ton *California* (CGN-36) class commissioned in 1974 and 1975, and the four-ship 10,500-ton *Virginia* class completed in the late 1970s. There were also plans for a new large so-called strike cruiser that would be capable of independent operations—a traditional role for the cruiser—but it was never built.

Other countries also built a few new cruisers after World War II. France constructed a guided missile cruiser in the 1950s, the 8,500-ton *Colbert*, and a helicopter cruiser, the 10,000-ton *Jeanne D'Arc*, commissioned in 1964. Italy built three helicopter cruisers with missile capabilities. These were two 5,000-ton *Andrea Doria* class, completed in 1964, and the single 7,500-ton *Vittorio Veneto*, completed in 1969. The Soviet Union also built some helicopter cruisers, first the two 14,400-ton *Moskva* class in the mid-1960s, followed by four 36,000-ton *Kiev* class in the 1970s, although the latter are really small carriers. The Royal Navy completed three *Tiger* class cruisers originally laid down in 1941 and 1942 after the war but built no new designs. The last to retire was the *Blake* in 1981, ending a hundred years of Royal Navy cruisers since the armored cruiser *Imperieuse* was laid down in 1881.

Only the United States and the Soviet Union have built cruisers in any quantity since World War II. During the 1980s both built interesting types. The Soviet Union built three, the 6,200-ton *Sovremennyy* and *Udaloy* classes and—perhaps the most interesting of all—the 24,000-ton *Kirov* class. Although designated RKR missile cruisers by the Soviet navy, the *Kirov*s are usually referred to as battle cruisers in the Western press and probably deserve that label. The *Kirov* is by far the largest surface combatant built by any navy since World War II. She carries five different missile and three gun systems as well as three helicopters. For the United States Navy, the most interesting are the twenty-seven almost 7,000-ton *Ticonderoga* (CG-47) Aegis-class cruisers first laid down in 1980, the last of which was commissioned in 1994. The CG-47s have two 5-inch guns and two helicopters and most have the vertical launch systems (VLS), but their primary weapon is their sophisticated electronics suite.

WITH THE DEMISE of battleships, cruisers became the major surface combatants during the Cold War and invariably became the flagships. During the Korean War, Allied cruisers conducted traditional gunfire support missions against North Korean targets. Again during the Vietnam War many of the gunfire support missions were conducted by cruisers. In fact, two American

USS *Monterey* (CG-61), an Aegis-class cruiser. Such "all big electronic" warships, first completed in the mid-1980s, are as revolutionary as the "all big gun" *Dreadnought* was in her day.
(U.S. Naval Institute)

Table 7.3 Cruiser Comparisons

Class	Type	Navy	Year	Displacement	Dimensions	Armament	Armor	Speed
Esmeralda	PC	Chile	1883	2950	270 × 42 × 18.5	2-10 inch/6-6 inch	2 inch deck	18.3
Apollo	2/c	RN	1892	3400	314 × 43 × 17.5	2-6 inch/6-4.7 inch	2 inch deck	18.5
Edgar	PC	RN	1893	7350	387.5 × 60 × 24	2-9.2 inch/10-6 inch	3-5 inch deck	18
Pelorus	3/c	RN	1897	2135	313.5 × 36.5 × 16	8-4 inch/8-3 pdrs	1-2 inch deck	18.5
Cressy	AC	RN	1901	12,000	472 × 69.5 × 26	2-9.2 inch/12-6 inch	2-6 inch belt	21
Rurik	AC	Ru	1908	15,190	529 × 75 × 26	4-10 inch/8-8 inch	4-6 inch belt	21
Konigsberg	CL	Gr	1907	3390/3814	383 × 44 × 17	10-4.1 inch/10-2 inch	1-2 inch deck	23
Caroline	CL	RN	1914	4220/4733	446 × 41.5 × 16	2-6 inch/8-4 inch	1-3 inch belt	28.5
Kent	CA	RN	1928	9870/13,540	631 × 68 × 20.5	8-8 inch/4-4 inch	1-4 inch side	31.5
Mogami	CL/CA	Jp	1935	8500/10,993	661 × 59 × 18	15-6.1 inch/8-5 inch	4 inch belt	37
Hipper	CA	Gr	1939	14,050/18,200	666 × 70 × 19	8-8 inch/12-4 inch	1-3 inch belt	32.5
Cleveland	CL	USN	1942	11,750/14,131	610 × 66 × 24.5	12-6 inch/12-5 inch	3.5-5 inch belt	32.5
Baltimore	CA	USN	1943	14,447/17,031	673 × 71 × 24	9-8 inch/12-5 inch	4-6 inch belt	33
Sverdlov	CL	USSR	1952	13,600/16,640	689 × 72 × 23	12-6 inch/12-4 inch	4 inch side	32.5
"Kresta I"	CG	USSR	1967	6000/7500	508.5 × 56 × 18	SSM/helo	none	34
Virginia	CGN	USN	1976	10,500/11,500	585 × 63 × 21	SAM/2-5 inch/helo	none	30+
Ticonderoga	CG	USN	1983	6560/8910	563 × 55 × 31	SAM & SSM/2-5 inch/helo	none	30

NOTES: Year = year completed. Displacement = standard/deep load in tons. Dimensions = overall length by width by draft in feet. Armament = primary/secondary. Japanese Mogami class started out as light cruisers but were later equipped with 10 heavier 8-inch guns.

heavy CAGs were redesignated as gun platforms to conduct gunfire support missions during the Vietnam War. Several American guided missile cruisers also scored hits on North Vietnamese MiGs with their SAMs.

During the 1956 Suez crisis, HMS *Newfoundland* sank the Egyptian frigate *Domiat* in what is sometimes called the last major surface action, and the Argentine cruiser *General Belgrano* was torpedoed in 1982 during the Falklands war with the loss of 321 lives. Then, during Desert Storm against Iraq, American cruisers took on a new role, launching deadly accurate Tomahawk cruise missiles against Iraqi targets. But the cruisers' main mission, like that of all major capital ships during times of peace, has often been more symbolic deterrence.

Conclusion

Cruisers have gone through four distinct phases. First was the pre-dreadnought era from around 1883 through 1906 characterized by three types of cruisers—armored, protected, and unarmored—followed by a second, light cruiser phase after 1906 that lasted through the end of World War I. Third was the interwar period with heavy and light cruisers, followed by the last, mostly missile cruiser phase of the post–World War II period. Throughout their existence, cruisers have often been the workhorses of the fleets.

Despite their importance over the years, cruisers may well follow the battleship into history. In an era when even building larger destroyers is rare, it would be surprising to see more cruisers built, at least by the smaller powers. Since both Russia and the United States have modern cruisers, they will undoubtedly last into the early twenty-first century, but beyond that is anyone's guess. The future of the Russian navy is completely up in the air, but one clear indication of Russia's direction as a major sea power will be whether it builds blue-water cruisers. The Russian navy has designs for a twenty-first-century cruiser but no money to build it. As the only power left with worldwide commitments, the United States will probably still be required to maintain at least a few larger ships in the cruiser range, although even that is not certain in times of decreasing defense budgets. Currently there are plans for a cruiser-size ship in the SC-21 family of surface combatants for the twenty-first century.

Despite their fascinating history cruisers, like a middle child, have often been overlooked. During most of their history, cruisers were generally overshadowed by the larger dreadnoughts at one end of the spectrum and the more dashing destroyers at the other. Yet in both world wars cruisers became the crucial day-to-day workhorses, and it is the day-to-day operations that are the key to success in seapower in both war and peace.

Destroyers and Frigates

8

DASHING, UBIQUITOUS DESTROYERS—they are probably the most romantic of the modern surface combatants for several reasons. Starting out as larger torpedo boats in the small craft range of ship sizes, they were usually the first commands for junior officers. Adding to the romance were the harsh "hard lying" living conditions. Later, when they grew in size, destroyers became the smallest in the surface combatant spectrum of battleships, cruisers, and destroyers and thus the first major command stepping-stone in any naval career. Few would advance to higher ranks without having first commanded a destroyer. Yet, as the smallest major combatant, they were still considered the most expendable warship, constantly sent in harm's way.

Starting out as single mission "torpedo boat destroyers" (TBD), they quickly became larger multimission ships but were still small enough to be built in the hundreds for both World Wars I and II, participating in virtually every operation of those wars. During the post–World War II period, after the battleships and most cruisers were retired, destroyers became the largest surface combatants in many navies, yet today, like the battleships and cruisers before them, they are slowly disappearing from the seas, replaced by smaller although in many cases still very capable frigates. Most navies are now becoming frigate fleets. For most of the modern era, however, destroyers and hardy destroyermen were considered the epitome of naval life.

Early Precedents

During the Age of Galleys, there were warships that might be considered destroyer precedents. Casson calls the smaller *lembos* of the Hellenistic Age, from 332 to 223 B.C., early destroyers, "dart[ing] in amongst enemy's heavier units to break up their formation, interrupt their tactics, even do damage to their oars."[1] During the dromons era, when the three types were based on size, the smallest might be considered early destroyers. And in the Age of Sail, the sloops and brigs would probably fall into a destroyer category by today's standards. These precedents from the Ages of Galley and Sail reflect more the later multimission destroyer and not its true beginnings, which can be traced to the 1880s and the Age of Ironclads.

The origins of the destroyer are directly related to the development of the self-propelled torpedo. During the early 1800s smaller craft used towing torpedoes and spar torpedoes, explosives at the end of a long pole that had to be directly attached to the enemy's ship, but the self-propelled or locomotive torpedo was not developed until the late 1860s. It was followed by the construction of torpedo boats in the 1870s and especially the 1880s. By 1890, France had 220 torpedo boats, Russia 152, Germany 143, Italy 129, and England 186.[2] This was the era of the French *jeune école* with thoughts that smaller, fast torpedo boats could defeat larger ships. As if to confirm the theory, in 1891 during a Chilean civil war, two torpedo gunboats sank the battleship *Blanco Encalada*. Thus even though England had many torpedo boats and indeed had developed the concept (explained in chapter 14), with her large fleet of pre-dreadnoughts and cruisers, she had the most to lose. Clearly, something had to be done to counter or destroy these torpedo boats.

In the 1880s there were some initial attempts, all built around the concept of "it takes a thief to catch a thief," to build a faster boat to "catch" the torpedo boats. These were simply larger and faster torpedo boats with guns, usually 12-pounders (3-inch) as well as torpedoes. In 1882 the torpedo ram ship HMS *Polyphemus* was completed, mostly for torpedo attacks. Because of her ram she is sometimes considered an early precedent to the destroyer, although she was too slow to catch the torpedo boats. More important was the English *Swift* in 1884, which inspired the idea for the torpedo boat catcher. The *Swift*, at 137 tons, 135 by 14 feet, was larger than existing torpedo boats and carried six quick-firing 3-pounders (1.9-inch). A private venture, the *Swift* was followed in 1887 by HMS *Rattlesnake* at 550 tons, 200 by 23 feet, called both a torpedo boat catcher and a torpedo gunboat. Sixteen follow-on *Rattlesnakes* were built, but all were too slow, with speeds around 19 knots, to catch existing 20- to 22-knot torpedo boats, and in the early 1890s the Royal Navy turned to private yards that finally produced the first successful torpedo boat destroyers.[3]

Pre-Dreadnought Destroyers: 1892–1902

On 27 June 1892 the Royal Navy ordered four new torpedo boat catchers, but starting on 8 August the term *torpedo boat destroyer,* or TBD, started to appear in official correspondence.[4] Although the full phrase *torpedo boat destroyer* was used officially by some navies into the 1920s, very soon the shortened term *destroyer* became common. The *Havock* at 275 tons, 185 by 18.5 feet, with one 12-pounder, three 6-pounders, and three 18-inch torpedo tubes, was completed in January 1894 by Yarrow. She is usually considered the first destroyer, although the Thornycroft destroyer *Daring,* completed in February 1895, was considered a better boat. With speed of around 26 knots, both satisfied a faster 27-knot requirement, and thirty-eight more "27-knotters" were ordered in 1893–94. They were followed by sixty-six faster "30-knotters" built through 1900. Although these vessels were considered fairly successful for their time, living conditions were miserable, leading to compensatory pay known as "hard-lying" money, which, of course, simply added to the romance of the destroyer for junior officers.[5]

Starting in 1896, the United States Navy built four larger ships officially classified as torpedo boats but generally considered the first U.S. destroyers. The first was the speedy, 30-knot, 279-ton, 214- by 21-foot *Farragut* with four 6-pounders. Then, in 1899, the navy ordered sixteen destroyers that in some respects were forerunners of modern types. The first were five *Bainbridge* class completed in 1902. The *Bainbridge* (DD-1) also started the American sequential numbering system for destroyers still used with the latest, the *Spruance*-class *Hayler* (DD-997), completed in 1983. At 420 tons, 250 by 24 feet, with two 3-inch guns, five 6-pounders, and two 18-inch torpedo tubes (TT), they had a raised forecastle rather than the so-called turtleback bow of most torpedo boats. The turtleback bows had a rounded shape sloping to the upper deck level, which in some respects was an early form of streamlining. Satisfactory in calm seas, turtlebacks were excessively "wet" in rough seas. Raised forecastles made them more seaworthy. All five *Bainbridge* class crossed the Pacific, spending most of their careers in the Philippines.[6]

Germany built ten large "division boats" or flotilla leader torpedo boats in 1886, the last six of which were considered early destroyers in the 400-ton range, and in 1898 Germany began building enlarged high-seas torpedo boat destroyers. Starting in 1899, France launched four 300-ton, 189- by 21-foot *Durandal*-class *contre-torpilleur,* followed by fifty-four more built through 1908. Japan purchased some English boats for use in the Russo-Japanese War. The first Japanese-built destroyers were the 375-ton *Harusame* class, completed in 1902. Russia built fifty-nine destroyers during this time and Italy twelve. By the turn of the century, the new torpedo boat destroyer with both guns and torpedoes had just about replaced the old torpedo boat in most navies, but they were still in the small combatant category with limited open-ocean capabilities.

Modern Era: 1902–1914

After the turn of the century, the destroyer entered a new phase and became more seaworthy. The Royal Navy's "River" classes (named after rivers) laid down in 1902 and launched in 1904 are considered the first. As *Conway's* comments, "These vessels marked the real break between the torpedo boat and the true destroyer, and set the pattern for destroyer development both in Britain and in most foreign countries until . . . the latter part of the 1914–18 war."[7] Most were around 550 tons, 225 by 24 feet, with four 12-pounders and two 18-inch torpedo tubes. Like the American *Bainbridge* class, they had forecastles and for the first time small cabins for officers. The "River" class was slightly slower at about 26 knots, sacrificing speed for seaworthiness, but an important engine improvement occurred during this time. In 1897 the experimental turbine-fitted *Turbina* made her appearance, demonstrating sustainable high speed, and in the early 1900s most destroyers were built with more reliable and faster turbines.

In 1904, Admiral Fisher became First Sea Lord, and he felt that large destroyers could replace light cruisers. The result was the 855-ton "Tribal" class (named after tribes) and the single large 2,170-ton "flotilla leader," the *Swift,* all considered unsuccessful. To supplement these larger ships, thirty-six small 250-ton *Cricket*-class coastal destroyers were built from 1906 to 1909, but the real fame for these ships, nicknamed "oily wads," was that they were the Royal Navy's first oil-fueled vessels. Later they were reclassified as torpedo boats.

With Fisher's departure, the Royal Navy built the coal-fired *Beagle* class in 1909, once again sacrificing speed for seaworthiness. In 1910 there was a return to oil with the construction of twenty 772-ton *Acorn* class, followed by twenty-six similar *Acheron*-class destroyers in 1911 and then twenty improved *Acasta* class in 1912. Starting in 1913, the first of twenty-two L (or *Laforey*) class were laid down followed by the M (first *Matchless*) and improved M classes that were built in various modifications throughout most of the war. These were all in the 1,000-ton, 273- by 27-foot range with three 4-inch guns and four 21-inch torpedo tubes. In 1914 the Admiralty started the *Lightfoot* class, the first of several large, approximately 1,500-ton flotilla leaders built during the war. The *Shakespeare*-class flotilla leaders launched in 1917 mounted a 4.7-inch gun, making them the heaviest armed destroyers at the time with the 4.7- to 5-inch guns becoming standard for most destroyers to this day.[8]

German destroyers were called *hochseetorpedoboote* (high sea torpedo boats) to accompany the fleet, as compared to small torpedo boats for coastal defense. Their primary mission, however, was to attack enemy capital ships, not destroy other torpedo boats, and most analysts consider them destroyers. They were in the 500- to 600-ton range during the early period, increasing to 800 to 900 tons on the eve of World War I. France built mostly smaller destroyers for coastal protection, none over 1,000 tons. The largest in number were twelve 800-ton, 248- by 25-foot *Bouclier* class with two 3.9-inch guns launched starting in 1911. Italy also built smaller destroyers in the

USS *Reuben James* (DD-245), one of the more than two hundred "four-pipers" or flush-deck destroyers built by the United States during World War I. Fifty were transferred to England in 1940.
(U.S. Naval Institute)

800-ton range, although it also had several larger "light scouts" considered flotilla leaders, from 1,000 to 1,800 tons. Russia had only a few destroyers, but one was the largest of the day. These included nine 1,100-ton, 322- by 31-foot *Bespokoiny* class launched in 1913–14, and the largest and fastest of the day was the 1,280-ton, 336- by 31-foot *Novik* launched in 1911, able to steam at 36 knots. Japan also built fairly large oceangoing destroyers before and during the war, many in the 1,300-ton range.

Although the honor of building the first modern destroyer usually goes to the Royal Navy's "River" class, the modern raised forecastle rather than turtleback bow had first appeared on the *Bainbridge* class commissioned in 1902. Considered the first fully seagoing U.S. destroyers, however, were the five 700-ton *Smith* class, launched in 1909, followed by twenty-one similar *Pauling* and *Monaghan* class, all collectively known as "flivvers" (slang for cheap autos). The eight *Cassin* class, first launched in 1913, were the first 1,000-tonners and carried four 4-inch guns. In 1917 the first of the famous "four-stackers," also known as "flush deckers" (without forecastles) were built, six *Caldwell* class. Then, starting in December 1917, almost three hundred mass-produced *Wickes-* and *Clemson*-class four-stackers started rolling out of the yards. They were all around 1,100 tons, 314 by 31 feet, with a speed of 35 knots, and carried four 4-inch guns and twelve 21-inch torpedo tubes.

World War I

Table 8.1 shows the destroyer naval balance for World War I. Destroyers and large torpedo boats were the most numerous warship type on the eve of the Great War and, equally important, they were the largest combatant built in any number during that conflict. The Royal Navy built almost 300 in four years, and the U.S. Navy punched out over 100 flush deck four-stackers in less than two years. Another 150 were completed after the war. Despite these numbers, all the admirals constantly called for more.

A destroyer had the honor of firing the first shot of the sea war. On 5 August 1914, HMS *Lance* sank the German auxiliary minelayer *Königin Luise* just thirteen hours after the declaration of war. Destroyers also took part in the first major sea battle, the Battle of Heligoland Bight on 28 August 1914. British destroyers and cruisers ensnared some German destroyers but in turn became entrapped themselves when German light cruisers appeared. Fortunately, Beatty's battle cruisers arrived in time. Except for overseas battles such as the Battle of the Falkland Islands, destroyers participated in all the major engagements of the war. At Jutland, of the 148 British ships, 77 were

Table 8.1 Destroyer Balance in World War I

Type	Britain	France	Italy	Russia	U.S.	Japan	Germany	Austria
PRE-DREADNOUGHT ERA	107	53	12	95	16	15	52	7
1914								
Destroyers	118	31	20	9	38	35	102	19
Destroyer leaders	3			1				
BUILT DURING WAR								
Destroyers	262	18	19	20	109	26	95	4
Destroyer leaders	27		9					
TOTAL	517	102	60	125	163	76	249	30
LOSSES								
Pre-Dreadnought	17	5	3	11	0	0	22	0
Modern	34	6	6	3	1	1	26	3
TOTAL	51	11	9	14	1	1	48	3

NOTES: The German pre-dreadnought DDs were listed as large torpedo boats around 400 tons but are usually considered destroyers. Some of these destroyers, especially those from the early pre-dreadnought era, served mostly as minesweepers.

destroyers; the Germans had 61 destroyers out of their total of 99. Jutland was the only battle in which the destroyer tactics of launching torpedoes against capital ships were put to the test, and though the results were generally disappointing, the destroyers still played major roles harassing the larger units with torpedo attacks, forcing them to turn away.[9]

Major sea battles were the exception, not the rule, in World War I, and though dreadnoughts stayed in port as fleets-in-being, the cruisers and destroyers conducted the daily operations. Most important were those operations in the English Channel successfully conducted by the destroyers of the Dover Patrol. Almost seven hundred convoys per year transported more than six million troops between England and Europe, but only one empty transport was ever sunk by German torpedo boats. The most famous Dover Patrol action came on 20 April 1917, when two British destroyers tangled with German torpedo boats, resulting in an old-fashioned boarding complete with cutlasses—perhaps the last in history.[10]

Destroyers also played key roles in other areas such as the Italian-Austrian conflicts in the Adriatic. As in the Atlantic, the major units of Italy and Austria-Hungary spent most of their time in port as fleets-in-being, leaving the fighting to light cruisers and destroyers. Both France and England also sent destroyer units to the Adriatic. Although there were a few minor clashes, again most operations consisted of daily patrols necessary to keep Austria off balance.[11] Sometimes overlooked was the participation of twelve Japanese destroyers sent to the Mediterreanean during the 1917 submarine crisis.

Destroyers played key roles in the early days of antisubmarine warfare because they had the maneuverability and speed to ram submarines, which was the preferred method at that time. Their shallow draft gave destroyers another advantage in that many torpedoes would pass underneath them. Later, destroyers would be outfitted with depth charges initially rolled off the stern. The first success of this practice came on 4 December 1916. In 1917 hydrophones appeared, followed by ASDIC (sonar) in 1918. But it was the convoy system instituted in 1917 that solved the ASW problem. Many of those escorts were destroyers.

During the Dardanelles operations, destroyers were used as troop carriers, gunfire support ships, and minesweepers. Because of their shallow draft, destroyers were pressed into service as troop carriers. (In World War II, older destroyers and destroyer escorts were modified and designated high-speed transports specifically for this role.) Then, after the loss of battleships from mines, they were withdrawn and destroyers often provided the only gunfire support. Another reason for withdrawing the battleships was the torpedoing and sinking of the old British battleship *Goliath* by the Turkish destroyer *Muavenet* on 12 May 1915, the most spectacular destroyer action of the war against a capital ship. Destroyers were also used as minesweepers in the swift current of the Dardanelles when the trawler-minecraft proved inadequate. They had the additional advantage of being able to fire back at harassing shore fire.

In short, destroyers played a key role in World War I participating in virtually every operation in a variety of roles. Their main limitation was their short range, restricting them to only three to four days at sea, which was one reason why the cruiser became the workhorse of the war. Most actions took place in close waters, however, so this was usually a minor problem. More important, destroyers proved to be versatile, participating in roles never envisioned such as minelaying and sweeping, troop transport, and gunfire support. Although there were no major engagements between destroyers as would take place during World War II, they still took major losses in the war. The Royal Navy lost fifty-one destroyers and Germany forty-eight.

The Interwar Period

After the war the major sea power, Britain, had many destroyers left over and thus did not start rebuilding until the late 1920s. Moreover, at the end of the war the Royal Navy had built several larger destroyer leaders, considered a good design as a result of wartime experience. The other major sea power of the day, the United States, was in even better shape with several hundred four-stackers, over a hundred of which were commissioned after the war. Even though in some respects the four-stackers were considered an old design, the United States had other priorities and did not recommence destroyer construction until 1934.[12]

Italy was the only major power to build new destroyers immediately after the war, although most were considered an old, small design. The first were four 875-ton, 269- by 26-foot *Palestro* class launched in 1919, followed by six even smaller 810-ton *Cantore* class in 1921. Four larger 1,200-ton *Curtatone* class were built in 1922. In the mid-1920s Italy built three more classes in the 900- to 1,000-ton range before finally building twelve larger 1,900-ton, 353- by 33-foot "Navigatori" class with six 4.7-inch guns in 1929. During the early 1930s Italy again built some smaller destroyers in the 1,200-ton range but then switched to larger 1,700-ton destroyers, including their largest class, nineteen "Soldati" class built on the eve of World War II and throughout the war.

France responded to Italy in 1923, building six then considered huge 2,126-ton, 416- by 37-foot *Chacal* (or *Jaguar*) class *contre-torpilleurs,* "destroyer of destroyers" but labeled "super-destroyers" by the press. (Destroyers over 400 feet would not become standard again until the 1950s.) These were followed by six 2,500-ton, 427- by 39-foot *Guépard* class in 1928. During the late 1920s to early 1930s France built more large *contre-torpilleurs* classes. Besides being large, they were also fast; the six 2,600-ton, 434- by 40.5-foot *Le Fantasque* class launched in 1933–34 was the fastest in the world. *Le Terrible* set a record of 45 knots that still stands.

Japan also built some super-destroyers. In 1927 Japan began twenty 1,750-ton, 388.5- by 34-foot *Fubuki*-class "special type" destroyers. With six 5-inch guns in the first twin mounts on destroyers and nine 24-inch torpedo tubes, they were considered the best armed of the day. Throughout the 1930s Japan built several more classes in the 1,900- to 2,000-ton range which were generally larger than comparable American destroyers. Destroyers were the only surface combatants built in any quantity by Japan during the war; twelve 2,700-ton 440- by 38-foot *Akitsuki* antiair class with eight 4-inch guns were completed by 1945. During the war, Japan also built thirty-two smaller 1,250-ton escort destroyers.

England started building destroyers again in the late 1920s launching nineteen A and B classes in 1928, followed by fourteen C and D classes in 1931, eighteen E and F in 1934, and twenty-seven G, H, and I classes in 1935, so named because the class names all started with the same letters. All were all around 1,350 tons, 325 by 34 feet, with four 4.7-inch guns and eight 21-inch TT. They were considered a little small for the time with limited range. Finally, in 1937 the Royal Navy launched the first of sixteen larger 1,850-ton "Tribal" class with eight 4.7-inch guns meant to take on larger destroyers such as the Japanese *Fubuki* class. In 1938, on the eve of World War II, the 1,700-ton, 356- by 36-foot J, K, and N classes were begun; they had six 4.7-inch guns and ten 21-inch TT. With some modifications, this basic design would be used for the bulk of destroyers built during the war. In 1943 Britain finally started building larger destroyers in the 2,300-ton range.

The first new American class were eight 1,360 ton, 341- by 34-foot *Farragut* class launched in 1934. They set the pattern for most prewar destroyers and were the first to use the dual-purpose (for both surface action and anti-air) 5-inch, .30 caliber guns, considered one of the best guns ever produced. They were followed by the eight 1,834-ton *Porter* class 381- by 37-foot "leaders" with eight 5-inch guns in four dual mounts. Five other classes of destroyers, all in the 1,500- to 1,750-ton range and one leader class at around 2,000 tons were launched from 1935 through 1939. In late 1939, the United States began the first of four very large destroyer classes. The first was the ninety-five-ship *Benson/Gleaves* class, built from 1939 through 1943. They were 1,840 tons, 348 by 36 feet, with five 5-inch and ten 21-inch TT. The *Benson/Gleaves* class were the last designed and built prewar destroyers.

Then, starting in 1942, the first of 150 *Fletcher* class built through 1944 were launched. At 2,325 tons, 376 by 40 feet with five single-mount 5-inch guns and ten 21-inch TT, the *Fletcher*s are considered one of the best destroyers ever built. They carried a major part of the destroyer war in the Pacific. They were followed by the 59-ship *Sumner* class built in 1943 and 1944 and then 105 similar *Gearing* class built in 1944 and 1945. The *Sumner*s were 2,610 tons, 377 by 41 feet, with six 5-inch guns in twin mounts. The similar *Gearing*s were fourteen feet longer and are sometimes called "long-hull" *Sumner*s. *Gearing*s and *Sumner*s remained in the United States Navy into the 1970s and foreign navies into the 1990s.

Germany, restricted by the Versailles Treaty, got into the destroyer game late. The first were four 1,625-ton, Z1 or "1934 type" launched in 1935 with five 5-inch and eight TT. The same essential design was followed in other German destroyers. They used a sophisticated high-pressure steam propulsion system that never worked properly, severely restricting their use. Although German battleships, cruisers, and submarines were usually considered among the best in the world, the same was not true for their destroyers, and they would pay the price during the war. Germany was also the only country that used numbers rather than names for its destroyers.[13]

In perhaps no other warship type was there such a confusion as to their roles and missions. Were destroyers still primarily torpedo boats or were guns now more important? This debate raged in the interwar period with most officers coming down in favor of torpedo tubes as the main armament. Considered less important at the time were the destroyer's ASW and antiair warfare (AAW) roles, but during the war these became paramount. The ASW problem was finally solved with numbers, and all countries quickly mounted more antiaircraft guns. Neither the British nor American AAW guns were

USS *Allen M. Sumner* (DD-692), built during World War II. Many *Sumner*-class destroyers remained in the U.S. Navy until the 1970s, and some can still be found in other navies. (U.S. Naval Institute)

considered satisfactory, with both using the Dutch 40 mm Bofors (originally developed by Sweden) and Swiss 20 mm Oerlikons.

The interwar naval agreements had little effect on destroyers. At the 1930 London Agreement destroyers were restricted to 1,500 standard tons (i.e., without fuel and water), but that caused few problems at the time. During the war, when it became apparent that even destroyers could not be turned out fast enough, many countries resorted to smaller ships called destroyer escorts, DEs in the United States, and escort destroyers, sloops, and even frigates in other navies. These were usually single-mission ships with a few guns in the 3-inch range built mostly for escorting ASW missions. Most were in the 1,000- to 1,300-ton range and under 300 feet, but some, like the American *Buckley* class, were almost destroyer size, about 1,500 tons and 306 feet long.

World War II

On the eve of World War II destroyers were again the most numerous warships by far and, more important, as shown in table 8.2, also again the only ships built in any quantity. Even these hundreds of destroyers would not be enough so several hundred more smaller DEs were built. The destroyers were even more important in World War II than World War I for three reasons. First, they were larger, better built, and for the first time had the capabilities to stay at sea for weeks rather than a few days although they still had some fuel restrictions requiring refueling at sea. Second, ASW became more impor-

Table 8.2 Destroyer Balance in World War II

Type	Britain	France	USSR	U.S.	Germany	Italy	Japan
WW-I era	127	0	16	71	14	34	43
1940	120	66	46	78	23	56	73
Built	165	0	11	392	19	6	40
(Subtotal DDs)	(412)	(66)	(73)	(541)	(56)	(96)	(156)
DEs	349			499	15	20	32
TOTAL	761	66	73	1,040	71	116	188
LOSSES							
WW-I era	17	n.a.	6	12	2	19	34
1940	67	14	20	22	15	39	69
Built	17	n.a.	0	22	8	3	34
DEs	32			12	8	8	10
TOTAL	133	14	26	68	33	69	147

NOTES: RN WW-I era DDs includes the 50 USN four-stackers. Some RN DDs were operated by Commonwealth countries. German WW-I era DDs include their large torpedo boats, usually considered in the DD range. Some Japanese WW-I era DDs listed in table had been rerated patrol boats before WW II. Included in the DE totals are frigates and larger patrol boats.

tant, and third, operations in World War II were truly worldwide and there were not enough battleships and cruisers to go around so the destroyer took up the slack. As a result, with the exception of a few early overseas engagements such as the Battle of River Platte between the German pocket battleship and Royal Navy cruisers, destroyers participated in virtually every surface operation of the war.

THE ATLANTIC

In the first major action of the war on 14 September 1939, Royal Navy destroyers sank their first submarine, protecting the carrier *Ark Royal.* In April 1940 the destroyer *Glowworm* was sunk by German shell fire after she succeeded in ramming and severely damaging the German heavy cruiser *Hipper.* Subsequent results, however, were mixed. In June 1940 the destroyer *Acasta* scored a torpedo hit on the German battle cruiser *Scharnhorst,* but against the *Bismarck* in May 1941 and then against the *Scharnhorst* and *Prinz Eugen* in their famous channel dash in February 1942, Royal Navy destroyer torpedo attacks missed. During the Battle of North Cape on 26 December 1943, destroyers did hit the *Scharnhorst* again with torpedoes.

The most decisive destroyer actions took place during the battle over Norway in early 1940. Germany used ten destroyers on 10 April to land troops at Narvik. The next day English destroyers entered the port, sinking two German destroyers before being run off. On 13 April, however, the battleship *Warspite* in company with nine destroyers sank the remaining eight German destroyers, leaving them with only nine overall. The resulting lack of destroyers compounded by their engine problems would haunt Germany throughout the war.

England also used destroyers to transport troops. They proved particularly useful at Dunkirk, removing the troops in that epic withdrawal across the English Channel. In the Mediterranean, both the English and Italians used destroyers for resupplying their troops. Although these few sea battles and troop transportations were exciting, once again the most important role of the the destroyers and DEs throughout the war was their day-to-day escort duties, especially for the crucial Battle of the Atlantic, protecting merchantmen against the German U-boats.

THE MEDITERRANEAN

While in some respects the Mediterranean was a cruiser war, destroyers were also important for several reasons. Cruisers would seldom venture forth without a destroyer screen; distances were shorter, lessening refueling problems, and on some occasions only the British destroyers had the speed to catch the faster Italian warships and besides, Admiral Sir Andrew Cunningham, the British commander, was an old destroyerman.[14] As a result, once again, destroyers participated in virtually all the operations from the main engagements such as the Battles of Calabria and Matapan to special operations such as troop movements. Destroyers played key roles in resupply to North Africa for both Italy and England and were the ships used by Britain to supply and then evacuate Crete. During the invasion of Italy, destroyers played major roles in gunfire support in the shallower waters, even becoming effective in antitank operations.

British destroyers had one of their greatest antiship successes when they attacked and torpedoed two Italian cruisers on 13 December 1941 in one of the few classic destroyer actions of the war. But as usual their greatest asset was in screening main forces and protecting convoys. For the English this was in the resupplying of Malta and for the Italians their forces in North Africa.

THE PACIFIC

It was in the great Pacific naval war that destroyers came into their own for both the Americans and Japanese. The first American shot of the war was fired by the old U.S. four-stacker *Ward,* which sank a midget Japanese submarine trying to sneak into Pearl Harbor very early in the morning of 7 December 1941. Unfortunately, this warning was ignored. Destroyers of the hastily assembled ABDA (American-British-Dutch-Australian) force in January 1941 carried out attacks on Japanese landing craft, but most American torpedoes failed to go off. This would be a recurring problem for American torpedoes throughout the war.

Until 1943, however, when lessons finally started to be learned, American destroyers generally took a beating. At the Battle of Java Sea on 20 February, the entire ABDA force of five cruisers and nine destroyers was sunk. Although generally known as cruiser actions, the sea battles around Guadalcanal also involved destroyers, and, in fact, revolved around the Japanese "Tokyo Express" attempting to resupply Japanese forces at Guadalcanal. Most of those Japanese express runs were conducted by destroyers, which were fast enough to make the round-trip during nighttime. Although American destroyer actions were sometimes disappointing because of their lack of night fighting experience and problems with torpedoes, they still played key roles harassing the Japanese. As Anthony Preston sums up, "Guadalcanal was the US Navy destroyer's equivalent of Jutland, a muddled series of actions in which they covered themselves with glory." Great praise also goes to Japanese Rear Admiral Raizo "Tenacious" Tanaka in charge of the Tokyo Express as "a remarkable destroyer man and [for] the skill of his crews."[15]

In 1943 the American destroyermen started to match their heroism with battle-learned skills and conducted a series of successful operations. In August

1943 at the Battle of Vella Gulf, U.S. destroyers sank three Japanese destroyers with no losses. Then in November 1943 a series of battles began starting with the Battle of Empress August Bay on 2 November and ending with the Battle of Cape St. George on 25 November during which Captain Arleigh "31-knot" Burke and his "Little Beaver" Squadron 23 became famous for their proficiency. After two years the American destroyermen finally matched the Japanese. The last major destroyer action was the U.S. sinking of the Japanese battleship *Fuso* and damaging the *Yamashiro* in the Battle of Surigao Straits. Although the Americans had continual problems with torpedoes, most ship-against-ship sinkings on both sides were by torpedoes, not gunfire.[16]

But despite these many spectacular engagements, as in the Atlantic and Mediterranean, the destroyers' main roles were as escorts. At the end of the war, both destroyers and DEs bore the brunt of the Japanese kamikaze attacks because they were on the perimeter, sometimes placed over sixty miles away from the main force as radar pickets. Thus it is little wonder that the dean of World War II historians, Rear Admiral Samuel Eliot Morison, writes in the conclusion of his *Two-Ocean War:* "One feels particular admiration for the officers of the destroyers, the 'tin cans' which operated in every theater of the war. They not only had to be first-rate seamen and ship handlers, but men of science to assimilate the new techniques of antisubmarine warfare and air defense. . . . These young officers maintained something of the port and swagger of oldtime frigate skipper, they were good for a lark ashore as for a fight at sea. In every theater and every kind of operation, as we have abundantly seen, destroyers were the indispensable component."[17] Although Morison was writing about United States destroyermen, his judgment also applied to all the other navies on both sides.

Post–World War II Period

After the war both England and the United States had hundreds of modern destroyers (DDs) and DEs on hand. England transferred many of its excess to Commonwealth countries, where some remained through the 1980s. The United States transferred its surplus to friends and allies throughout the world where a few can still be found. Their survival is a remarkable commentary for ships called "tin cans" built quickly during the war.

The end of the war was also the end of the classic destroyer because antiship warfare was no longer considered a primary mission. Rather, the destroyer's primary roles, already becoming apparent during World War II, became antisubmarine warfare (ASW) and antiair warfare (AAW). Initially this amounted to simply modifying destroyers such as replacing antiship with antisubmarine torpedoes and placing more AA guns on ships, but eventually two patterns emerged: guided missile destroyers (DDGs), for the AAW role and the deployment of helicopters for ASW. Finally, one last post–World

War II pattern has emerged. As destroyers became larger and more expensive, smaller, less expensive frigates have gradually replaced them in most navies.

The major early conversions were to antisubmarine DDEs and DDKs. The DDEs were faster ASW escorts to replace slower DEs with the DDK, a submarine "killer." In sum, they received more ASW weapons such as Weapon Alpha, hedgehogs, and depth charges and better sonar. The United States eventually dropped the DDE designation, but some countries such as Canada and the Netherlands have continued to use it for some of their new ASW ships. Most World War II American destroyers retained their DD designation until they were finally retired in the early 1970s. The United States also converted some destroyers to radar picket (DDR) to guard against possible Soviet air attacks.

There was, of course, also new construction. The British built the 2,830-ton, 390- by 43-foot *Daring* class in the late 1940s. Although slightly larger than World War II destroyers, it was still essentially an old design. The Soviet Union also began building an old design destroyer in 1948, the seventy-ship 2,320-ton *Skoriy* class, the largest destroyer class built by any country in the postwar period. In 1950 the Netherlands started four *Holland* class, the first European destroyers built without antiship torpedo tubes. And in 1951, the French laid down the 2,750-ton 422-foot *Surcouf* class called *escorteur d'escadre,* and Canada started construction of one of the handsomest ships of the period, seven sleek 2,000-ton *St. Laurent*-class DDEs with rounded bows somewhat reminiscent of the original turtlebacks.

The most radical changes in destroyer design were four American very large 3,640-ton, 490- by 48-foot *Mitscher*-class DLs, destroyer leaders, launched in 1952. Although considered underarmed with only two 5-inch and four 3-inch guns, they had extensive AAW electronic suites. They were followed by eighteen more conventional but still large 3,000-ton, 419- by 45-foot *Forrest Sherman* class built from 1955 through 1959. Handsome ships with rakish bows, the *Sherman*s were obsolete from day one because as they were being built, tests were being run on an old *Sumner*-class ship *Gyatt* redesignated DDG-1 for guided missile destroyer number one.

Those early missile tests proved successful, and in the late 1950s and early 1960s, most countries started building DDGs. The first were the ten American 4,170-ton, 512-foot *Coontz* class laid down in 1957, completed by 1961, followed by twenty-three smaller 3,300-ton, 437-foot *Charles F. Adams* class built from 1958 through 1964. Considered a successful design, *Adams* were built for Australia and West Germany, and Greece purchased four when they were retired from the U.S. Navy in the early 1990s. In 1958 the Soviet Union laid down its first DDGs, the 3,500-ton, 456-foot *Krupny* class. England followed in 1959 with the very large 6,200-ton, 522-foot "county" class DLGs, often considered in the cruiser class. During the 1960s, France, Italy, and the Netherlands all built DDGs.

DDGs continued to be built by most major naval powers through the 1980s, but construction has since fallen off due to costs. The last British DDGs were four 4,750-ton, 463-foot *Manchester* class built from 1978 through 1985; the last French were two 3,900-ton, 456-foot *Cassard* class built from 1982 to 1991, and the last Italian the 4,500-ton *Luigi Durand de la Penne* class built from 1986 through 1993. In 1993 China completed a single 5,700-ton "Luhu" class with perhaps more to be built. And Japan is finishing up four large 7,250-ton, 528- by 69-foot *Kongo*-class Aegis-class DDGs. The only country currently building DDGs is the United States. These are the large, 6,625-ton, 505- by 67-foot *Arleigh Burke* Aegis-class DDGs.

With few exceptions, all destroyers built after 1960 were DDGs. Those exceptions were ASW destroyers with embarked helicopters, the major trend for ASW since the 1960s. The largest class of ASW DDs are the thirty-one-ship American *Spruance* class built from 1972 to 1980. Although capable of carrying two helicopters, at a 7,800-ton full load, 563 by 55 feet, they have been severely criticized as being underarmed with only two 5-inch guns and the Sea Sparrow system. Several other countries have also built ASW destroyers. Canada, which had used the DDE designator, designated its

USS *Ramage* (DDG-61), an Aegis destroyer. This and other *Arleigh Burke*–class ships, first completed in the 1990s, are the world's most sophisticated destroyers. (U.S. Navy photo by JO₂ Todd Stevens)

HMS *Leander* (F-109), completed in 1963. She and her sister ships are often cited as the first large, modern class of frigates. Most navies are now becoming "frigate fleets." (U.S. Naval Institute)

3,550-ton, 423-foot *Iroquois* class helicopter destroyers (DDH). The Japanese *Yamagumo* class started in the mid-1960s were designated DDK; the *Haruna* and *Shirane* classes are called helicopter destroyers. They are the only destroyer-size ships capable of carrying three helicopters.

No country has built a large ASW destroyer since the mid-1980s, and DDGs are now also rare. This does not mean that surface combatants are disappearing from the sea. Rather, the cruisers and destroyers are being replaced by smaller frigates. Historically, frigates were fairly large warships, just below ships of the line, and the modern cruiser is considered the successor to the Age of Sail frigate. During the late interwar period, however, some countries started calling their smaller escort ships frigates. In 1943, Canada formalized the practice, and the Royal Navy followed suit in 1948. In 1955 the United States started calling its larger, cruiser-size destroyer leader, DLs, frigates, and though historically more accurate, the practice never caught on. In 1975 the United States finally gave up, redesignating its larger DLs "cruisers" and smaller DEs and DEGs "frigates."

As was the practice during World War II, the early 1950s European frigates and American DEs were usually small, single-mission ships in the 1,300-ton range. In 1959, however, the Royal Navy laid down the 2,350 ton, 372- by 41-foot *Leander* class, considered a "major landmark in modern design" by one naval commentator.[18] The *Leander* class was successful, with many adopted by Commonwealth and other countries. But, more important, it led to the building of larger frigates in other navies. The United States built the large forty-six-ship 4,000 full load, 438-foot *Knox* class (originally designated DE) from 1965 though 1974 and the fifty-four-ship 3,500-ton full load, 445-foot FFG-7 *Oliver Hazard Perry* class from 1975 through 1989. The United States Navy has never been enthusiastic about frigates and is currently retiring or selling most of the FFG-7s even though they are relatively new ships.

For both financial as well as current mission requirements, however, frigates have found favor in just about every other navy in the world. While some are small, barely larger than 1,000-ton corvettes, many are quite capable. The latest Royal Navy frigates in the 4,000-ton, 430-foot range are considered good ships, and Spain is currently planning to build a 6,000-ton Aegis-equipped frigate that really falls into the destroyer category. While most frigates are still considered primarily ASW ships, and most have helicopters, many also have limited SAM, even vertical launch systems (VLS) giving them limited multimission capabilities.

During the post–World War II era destroyers once again became the workhorse of most fleets, constantly deployed on station and various tasks. It would be hard to name a major operation at which a destroyer or frigate was not present either on its own or guarding carriers and amphibious groups. In both Korea and Vietnam they conducted daily patrols. During more recent actions destroyers and frigates were in the thick of it, often paying the price. Two British destroyers were hit by Argentina Exocet missiles and sunk while screening their carriers during the Falklands war. In the Persian Gulf, the American frigate *Stark* was hit by an Iraqi-launched French Exocet missile and almost sunk and the *Samuel B. Roberts* was mined. As shown in appendix D, destroyers and frigates are still being sent in harm's way.

Conclusion

No other major warship has undergone such a radical change over its lifetime as the destroyer. While battleships and cruisers were large ships even in the pre-dreadnought era of the Age of Steam, destroyers started out as less than 300-ton small craft, growing to 500 tons in the early modern era, then 1,000 tonners in the World War I era, 1,500 tons after the war to about 2,500 tons in World War II, to in some cases cruiser-size 8,000 tons in the post–Cold War period. Built in the hundreds for both wars, destroyers more than any other ship epitomized what navies were all about. Yet, on the eve of the twenty-first century, only the United States has concrete plans for a new destroyer class.

Table 8.3 Destroyer and Frigate Comparisons

Class	Type	Navy	Year	Displacement	Dimensions	Armament: Guns/Torpedo Tubes	Speed
Rattlesnake	"Catcher"	RN	1887	550	200 × 23 × 10	1-5 inch/6-3 pdrs/4-14 inch TT	19
Havock	TBD	RN	1894	275	185 × 18.5 × 7	1-12 pdr/3-6 pdr/1 3-18 inch TT	26
Bainbridge	DD	USN	1902	420	250 × 24 × 6.5	2-3 inch/5-6 pdr/2-18 inch TT	29
"River"	DD	RN	1904	550/620	225 × 23.5 × 10	4-12 pdrs/5-6 pdrs/2-18 inch TT	25.5
Acheron	DD	RN	1911	780/990	246 × 26 × 9	2-4 inch/2-12 pdrs/2-21 inch TT	32
S 49	DD	Gr	1915	800/1074	261 × 28 × 9	3-3.45 inch/6-19.7 inch TT	34
Wickes	DD	USN	1917	1090/1247	314 × 31 × 9	4-4 inch/2-1 pdrs/12-21 inch TT	35
Z1	DD	Gr	1935	1625/3156	391 × 37 × 13	5-5 inch/4-1.5 inch/8-21 inch TT	38
"Tribal"	DD	RN	1937	1850/1959	377 × 36.5 × 13	8-4.7 inch/4-2 pdrs/4-21 inch TT	36
Kagero	DD	Jp	1938	2030/2450	389 × 35 × 12	6-5 inch/4-1 inch/8-24 inch TT	35
Fletcher	DD	USN	1942	2325/2924	376 × 40 × 14	5-5 inch/4-1.1 inch/10-21 inch TT	38
Sumner	DD	USN	1943	2610/3220	376 × 40 × 14	6-5 inch/12-40mm/10-21 inch TT	36.5
Buckley	DE	USN	1943	1430/1820	306 × 37 × 11	3-3 inch/4-1.1 inch/2-21 inch TT	24
St. Laurent	DDE	Cn	1955	2000/2600	366 × 42 × 13	4-3 inch/2-40mm/2 ASW Limbo	28
Leander	FF	RN	1963	2350/2860	372 × 41 × 18	2-4.5 inch/2-40 mm/Helo	28
"Kashin"	DDG	USSR	1964	3400/4390	472 × 52 × 15	2 SA-N/4-76 mm/5-21 inch TT	34
Spruance	DD	USN	1975	5800/7800	563 × 55 × 21	2-5 inch/Sea Sparrow/6-12.75 inch TT/helo	30
A. Burke	DDG	USN	1991	6625/8315	505 × 67 × 20	90 cell VLS/1-5 inch/6-12.75 inch TT	32

NOTES: Year = year completed. Displacement = standard or light/deep load in tons. Dimensions = overall length by width by draft in feet. Armament = primary/secondary.

Frigates have now replaced the destroyer as the most numerous combatant in most navies. While many are adequate for current post–Cold War missions, there is some doubt whether they could survive in a modern, hostile war environment. This has been the United States Navy's main complaint about building these admittedly less capable ships. Yet with most missions still focused on naval presence rather than actual fighting, the frigates have performed well. In some cases, frigates with embarked helicopters have proved more flexible than more sophisticated but non-helicopter-capable DDGs.

Although destroyers are still important parts of most major navies' fleets, it will be interesting to see whether current ships are replaced as they start to age after the turn of the century. With only the United States currently planning to build destroyers in the future, it appears that, like the battleships and cruisers before them, destroyers could well become ships of the past.

Submarines

9

THE STORY OF THE submarine has come full circle during the twentieth century. After several hundred years of mostly disastrous experiments, at the start of this century navies finally developed vessels that could operate under the seas. There was, however, considerable question concerning their use. This was the dreadnought era, and submarines were looked upon as distractions. Despite this initial doubt, submarines became the most important offensive warships in World War I and then shared that distinction with aircraft carriers in World War II. During the Cold War, Western attack submarines were needed to counter the massive Soviet submarine fleet, and fleet ballistic missile boats were crucial for nuclear deterrence. Many analysts even considered the submarine the major capital ship of the Cold War era.

Now, almost a hundred years later, approaching the twenty-first century, there is once again considerable doubt, and even some disarray, about the future missions of submarines in this new post–Cold War era. The old Soviet threat has gone, and much of their once massive submarine fleet is literally rusting at the piers. The American submarine community that dominated the United States Navy during the Cold War is now struggling to maintain force numbers and qualitative standards, trying to justify increasingly expensive systems. Many other navies have also reduced their submarine forces. In short, the problem facing submarine forces at the end of the twentieth century is virtually the same as at the start—not capabilities but mission.

Early Precedents

The roots of the submarine can be traced to the Age of Galleys, when, at least according to legend, Alexander the Great had himself lowered into the sea in some sort of glass contraption that today would probably be called a diving bell. Throughout history many, including Leonardo da Vinci (1452–1519), mentioned and even sketched various submarine devices. There was more progress during the Age of Sail. The first practical design is attributed to Englishman William Bourne, who in 1578 had a plan complete with ballast tanks and moving walls to admit and discharge water for lowering and raising the vessel. The first operational vessel was built by Dutch doctor Cornelius van Drebbel in 1624. His design had oars protruding through leather gaskets, a compass, pressure gauge, and some system for providing air. In 1653, a French engineer, de Son, working in Holland, developed a design with a clockwork propulsion system that proved inadequate, and it was lost during a trial.

Although there were a few other proposals over the years, the next major event took place in 1776, when David Bushnell's *Turtle* attacked the British ship *Eagle* during the American Revolution. Though unsuccessful, it was the first use in war of an undersea vessel. The *Turtle* was a one-man, oval-shaped vessel with ballast tanks, pump, both horizontal and vertical screws, and even a crude snorkel device. The attack might have been successful, but there was no way to hold the *Turtle* against the hull to attach the charge.

In 1797 the innovative Robert Fulton offered a design to the French government which was finally built in 1801 and named the *Nautilus*. Unlike the small, oval-shaped *Turtle,* the larger *Nautilus* was more cigar-submarine shaped, had a three-man crew with a collapsible sail for surface movement, but was hand-operated when submerged. In an experiment on 8 August 1801, the *Nautilus* blew up an anchored ship, the first ship to be sunk in a submarine attack. Despite this success and the continuing British blockade, which the *Nautilus* was designed to end, France lost interest. Fulton moved to England to offer his services and, although supported by Prime Minister William Pitt, he found less enthusiasm in the Admiralty, prompting a famous quote by the First Sea Lord, Admiral the Earl of St. Vincent: "Pitt was the greatest fool that ever existed to encourage a mode of warfare which those that command the sea did not want, and which if successful would deprive them of it." Fulton returned to the United States, where he found similar disinterest before finally finding fame with the steamship *Clermont* in 1807 and the first steam warship *Demologos* in 1814.

In 1850 the Bavarian Wilhelm Bauer built a submarine, *Le Plonger Marin* (Sea Diver) at Kiel. Despite its limitations, *Le Plonger Marin*'s presence succeeded in keeping a blockading Danish fleet far off the coast—the forerunner of two oft-cited submarine missions: deterrence and coastal defense. During tests in 1851 she sank, but Bauer and the crew were able to make the first escape from a submerged submarine. In 1856 he built *Le Diable Marin* (Sea Devil) for Russia and at the coronation of Tsar Alexander II musicians on board played "God Preserve the Tsar."

During the Civil War the Confederacy developed semisubmersibles called *David*s. They did not fully go underwater but trimmed down until only a funnel and conning tower showed. Several of these steam-operated devices were built and used with limited success. More successful was the fully submersible, hand-operated *H. L. Hunley* with an eight-man crew. On 17 February 1864, the *Hunley* detonated a spar torpedo against the side of the

Union *Housatonic,* sinking both ships. Thus to the *Hunley* goes the distinction of the first successful wartime attack, although she paid the ultimate price. Another important event came in 1866 with the development of the self-propelled torpedo by the Englishman Robert Whitehead, originally for Austria-Hungary and later for Britain. The first success came in 1876, just when modern submarine development began. With the development of the self-propelled torpedo, the problems faced by the *Turtle* and *Hunley* would disappear.[1]

Pre-Dreadnought–Era Submarines: 1878–1904

The start of the pre-dreadnought or premodern era for submarines came in 1878. In that year the Irish-American John P. Holland and English clergyman George Garrett launched their first submarines. Although Holland's first venture was unsuccessful, it was the beginning of a series of experiments and prototypes that finally led to a successful design in 1900. Considered more important at the time was Rev. Garrett's *Resurgam* (meaning "I shall rise again"). A larger, 30-ton, *Resurgam II* was built in 1889. The concept caught the attention of Swedish arms manufacturer Thorsten Nordenfelt, who with Garrett built a 60-ton submarine in 1885, later sold to Greece. The *Nordenfelt No. 1* was the first with a Whitehead torpedo, and it carried a Nordenfelt machine gun on deck. *Nordenfelts* were later built in England for Turkey, Russia, and Germany, but all proved unsatisfactory.

The mid-1880s saw many countries join the submarine-building race. In 1886 Spanish naval officer Lieutenant Isaac Peral built the first successful submarine to run on batteries. Around the same time the French began a process that was to lead to what most historians consider the first successful submarine, the *Narval.* Noted French naval architect Dupuy de Lôme had started submarine designs, and when he died in 1885, the work was carried on by his disciple Gustave Zede. This work led to the *Gymnote* in 1888, the larger *Gustave Zede* in 1893, and then the *Morse,* launched in 1899, which was the first with a periscope.[2]

Then, in 1897 French designer Maxime Laubeuf won a contest that led to the building of the *Narval,* which displaced 117 tons surfaced, 202 tons submerged, and was 111.5 by 13 feet with four 17.7-inch torpedoes. She had a steam propulsion system for surface cruising, electric drive for underwater, and a double hull for water and fuel. With a range of 100 miles on the surface and 100 submerged, the *Narval,* completed in 1899, is considered the first with both offensive and defensive capabilities, setting the pattern for all future submarines. The *Narval* was taken into the service in June 1900.

Meanwhile, Holland had continued his experiments and after building the unsuccessful *Plunger* in 1897 according to U.S. Navy specifications, he started his own design. The *Holland* was completed in 1897, proved success-

The Royal Navy's Holland 1.
(Courtesy of the Royal Navy Submarine Museum, via the U.S. Naval Institute)

ful, and was purchased by the U.S. Navy on 12 April 1900. The *Holland* used a gasoline engine rather than steam. It was considered more reliable than the French *Narval* and, with a gasoline on the surface rather than steam engine, was smaller and could dive faster. The *Holland* was only 64 tons, 74 tons submerged, 54 by 10 feet, with one 18-inch torpedo tube and an 8-inch dynamite gun. Even though some considered the *Narval* superior, at the time the *Holland*s were viewed as better boats and were bought by other countries in the early 1900s.

After watching other navies' developments for several years, in 1901 the Royal Navy began building *Holland*s. In 1902 Russia took the plunge, followed by Italy in 1903 and Japan in 1904. Italy had earlier experimented with the submarine *Delfino* built in 1892. Ironically, considering the later significance for its navy, Germany was the last major power to order submarines, finally ordering the *Unterseeboot 1 (U 1)* from famed arms manufacturer Krupp in 1906. Except for Germany, by 1904 most countries were buying or building what can be considered the first generation of submarines.[3]

As has been true for virtually all new weapons throughout history, there were early attempts to outlaw submarines. At the First Hague Conference in 1899, one of the agenda items was outlawing submarines, or "plungers," but that proposal was defeated. Admiral Mahan on the American delegation took little interest in the debate but supported a ban providing it was unanimous, which proved impossible, and the issue was dropped. There would be more attempts to ban submarines during the interwar naval conferences.

The Modern Era: 1904–1914

These early turn-of-the-century submarines had limited capabilities and most navies considered them little more than experimental modes. Starting around 1904 more reliable second-generation submarines began being built, but they were still small, useful only for coastal patrols. The Royal Navy built thirteen 190-ton A class, most launched from 1902, followed by eleven 287-ton B class starting in 1904. Thirty-eight larger 238-ton C class launched starting in 1906 were considered a little more capable but still suitable only for coastal patrols. France built twenty even smaller 70-ton *Naïade* class in 1904 and then eighteen larger 398-ton *Pluviôse* class launched in 1907.

By 1910 most of the fundamental technical developments for submarines were well established, including the use of hydroplanes fore and aft and the system of ballast and trim tanks for diving and surfacing and both the periscope and gyro-compass. The torpedo had become the standard armament, and some submarines also had a deck gun. The only question remaining was propulsion. Until 1910, most submarines ran on the surface using either steam- or gasoline-fueled engines. Steam-powered submarines took at least fifteen minutes to switch off before diving, while gasoline engines were dangerous and also took some time to turn off. An alternative was needed, and that was the diesel engine, which was not only safer but, most important, could be turned off immediately for diving. The diesel engine had been invented in Germany in the late nineteenth century, and the French built the first diesel-powered submarine, the *Aigrette,* in 1904.

Around 1910 most countries switched to diesels and started building larger, oceangoing submarines. In 1908 the Royal Navy launched the first of eight 490-ton D class, most of which were completed in 1910–11. Besides being the first British submarines with diesel engines, they were larger and had other improvements and are considered the first with ocean capabilities. The United States built its first diesel submarine in 1911; the *U-19* in 1912 was the first German diesel. In 1912, the Royal Navy started the 655-ton E class, considered an excellent submarine, and Germany started the 669-ton *U-23* class in 1913, also considered a good boat. Thus by 1914, the design, propulsion system, and weaponry of the submarine was well established and, in fact, would change very little until after World War II.

Engineering, however, was only part of the problem. There was still the question of missions. France, still under the influence of the *jeune école,* supported submarines for their defensive capabilities. Perhaps ironically, submarines were also supported by Admiral Fisher, father of the *Dreadnought* and usually associated with the big-gun, high-seas fleet. The other battleship admiral of the day, German Admiral Tirpitz, was less enthusiastic about submarines, which accounts for the delay in their introduction in the German navy. Although there was some debate on their use, most admirals of the day saw submarines as useful for only coastal defense and perhaps for advance scouting, as "eyes of the fleet."

In short, on the eve of World War I, while the submarine was fully developed in the technical sense, there was still some confusion about its role and mission. The French had developed a notion for limited, defensive use, but most naval experts still assumed that the major fleet actions, as they had been for centuries, would be between the large ships of the line. That assumption was to change in a most dramatic way very early in the war.

World War I

Table 9.1 shows the submarine balance for World War I. The Royal Navy had the largest submarine fleet entering World War I with 73, over twice the number for Germany, which had only 35. But during the war Germany would order 800 and build 332. Second at war's beginning was France, which was not surprising considering its lead with the *Narval* and the influence of the *jeune école,* and third was the United States, again not surprising considering the influence of Holland.

During the war all sides would build better, larger boats with oceangoing types increasing from approximately 400 tons at the beginning to 900 tons by war's end. A typical German submarine, the *U-35,* was 212 by 20.5 feet, displaced 685/880 (surface/submerged) tons with two torpedo tubes each on her bow and stern carrying a total of six torpedoes. With two diesels, she had a speed of approximately 16 knots on the surface, 10 submerged, and a range

Table 9.1 Submarine Balance in World War I

Type	England	France	Russia	Italy	U.S.	Japan	Germany	Austria
1914								
Coastal	56	48	26	24	23	11	3	7
Ocean	17	7	8	0	15	0	32	0
(Subtotal)	(73)	(55)	(34)	(24)	(38)	(11)	(35)	(7)
BUILT IN WAR								
Coastal	9			25		2	228	19
Ocean	119	25	28	13	36	3	104	1
(Subtotal)	(128)	(25)	(28)	(38)	(36)	(5)	(332)	(20)
TOTAL	201	80	62	62	74	16	367	27
LOSSES								
1914	15	7	3	3	0	0	19	2
Built	18	2	10	4	0	0	142	5
TOTAL	33	9	13	7	0	0	161	7

NOTES: Coastal submarines were those generally under 400 tons. Ocean submarines were those over 500 tons, most around 600 tons at start of war and almost 1,000 tons at the end. Built = those building before or built during and commissioned during the war.

of 7,800 miles, although only 80 miles submerged. Most of the other countries' oceangoing submarines had similar characteristics.

There were some exceptions that deserve brief mention. The Royal Navy built three interesting special-purpose boat types: the K class fleet, M class monitor, and R class killer submarines. The K class was a large, 2,000-ton submarine with steam drive capable of 24 knots on the surface built to operate with the fleet. The M class monitors were also large, 1,600 tons, with a single 12-inch gun for attacks on the surface. In the 1920s, one was fitted with a hangar and catapult for a seaplane. The R class was specifically designed to kill other submarines. It had a high underwater speed with six torpedo tubes all forward for firing salvos. Italy built two so-called pocket classes of submarines for coastal warfare, one only 21 tons, the other 40 tons. Italy would build similar smaller submarines during World War II.

Germany also developed some interesting special types. In 1914 the Germans started a small 127-ton *UB-1* coastal class that could be broken down and transported by train. Several were built with the final 520/650 ton *UB 48* (or *UB III*) class considered the prototype for the famous Type VII of World War II. They also built 116 smaller *UC* classes in the 170- to 500-ton range as coastal submarine minelayers. Germany was the only country to continue building smaller coastal submarines after the war began. Germany also built larger 1,500-ton "cruiser" submarines used to carry cargo.

Germany's use of U-boats got off to a rocky start. In their first patrols, *the U-15* was rammed and sunk by the light cruiser *Birmingham* on 9 August 1914, and the *U-13* was lost, presumably to mines. On 5 September, however, the *U-21* drew first blood, sinking the British light cruiser *Pathfinder*. The British *E-9* responded, sinking the German light cruiser *Hela* on 13 September. The first sinking of a merchantman, the British collier *Glitra* by the *U-17*, did not occur until 20 October, and only three merchantmen had been sunk by the end of 1914. All analysts agree, however, that the most significant event signaling the start of a new era of naval warfare was the sinking of the three old British armored cruisers by the *U-9* on 22 September 1914, as described in chapter 7. With that event, naval warfare changed forever.

After the war began the British sent out their large submarine force, which had many victories. One of the most successful was their penetration of the Baltic, challenging the Germans in their own backyard. Several British and French submarines were also able to breach the Dardanelles and disrupt Turkish shipping in the Black Sea, although the price was high. Of twelve submarines that attempted the dangerous Dardanelles passage, seven were sunk. Italy similarly had victories in the Mediterranean and Adriatic Sea. But with Germany and Austria-Hungary keeping most of their merchant and naval fleets in port, overall Allied victories were comparatively few. Austrian Lieutenant Georg Ritter von Trapp (of later *Sound of Music* fame) in a small 270-ton submarine sank the French cruiser *Leon Gambetta*. He had more successes, becoming the highest-scoring submarine skipper in the Austrian navy.

By far the most important submarine operations during World War I were those conducted by the German U-boats, which almost won the war at sea, save for two reasons. The first was the small size of the U-boat force at the beginning, but perhaps the major reason was the on-again, off-again indecision by the German High Command on the question of unrestricted submarine warfare. On 15 February 1915, the Germans declared the waters around England to be a military area, but on 7 May 1915 the British liner *Lusitania* was sunk with the loss of 1,198 lives, including 124 Americans. This incident caused an international uproar, and as a result, Germany called off unrestricted warfare. The Germans would go back and forth between declaring unrestricted submarine warfare until finally proclaiming it for good on 1 February 1917, but by then it was too late. By 1917 the Royal Navy had finally adopted the convoy system, which turned out to be the best defense against submarines, and that same year the United States joined the fray. Some analysts feel that had Germany adopted unrestricted submarine warfare sooner, it might have won the sea war. On the other hand, unrestricted warfare might have brought the United States into the war sooner. Of the approximate 19 million tons of shipping sunk by German submarines, almost half, 9 million tons, was sunk in 1917.

The size of the German submarine fleet reached its zenith in October 1917 with 140, of which 55 were at sea, 39 in base, and 46 in overhaul and maintenance. The Germans lost 161 submarines in World War I but took a tremendous toll of approximately 31 ships sunk for every submarine lost, a more than acceptable ratio. (During World War II this ratio would drop to about two to one.) One can only wonder what might have happened if the Germans had started the war with 140 submarines.[4] England lost 33 subs.

The German U-boats were defeated by a combination of too little, too late, Allied use of convoys, development of antisubmarine warfare devices such as depth charges in 1916 and hydrophones in 1917, and new airpower.[5] Although hydrophones with microphones dipped into the sea to hear submarines were deployed in 1917, a real detection device, sonar—or, as the British called it, ASDIC (for Anti-Submarine Detection Investigation Committee)[6]—was not developed until the end of the war and thus never fully tested. This was to have an unfortunate consequence. During the interwar period, the British assumed that ASDIC had solved the submarine problem, one reason cited for their lack of preparedness in 1939. That was not the only problem, nor were the British the only ones to make mistakes.

The Interwar Period

The interwar period for submarines is interesting for several reasons. There were, of course, technological advances although in many respects the boats that fought in World War II differed little from those of World War I. More interesting were the political and strategic developments. On the one hand, the British made attempts to outlaw submarines at the interwar arms control conferences, and on the other, there was a misconception that sonar had solved the submarine problem. As a result, no strategy was devised on how to deal with submarines. The full story of ASW and submarine training during the interwar period has yet to be written, but it probably ranks as one of the great pre–World War II military blunders, along with the lack of appreciation and understanding of aircraft carriers and tank warfare.

The 1920s were dominated by the building of some interesting prototypes. The British built the large 2,325-ton XI experimental cruiser submarine with four 5.2-inch guns, launched in 1923, and in 1927 France started the larger 2,880-ton *Surcouf* with two heavy cruiser 8-inch guns and an airplane that had to be assembled. Not completed until 1935, the *Surcouf*, designed for long-range commerce raiding, caused quite a stir at the time. The United States also built three large submarines for minelaying in the 2,900-ton range, one, the *Argonaut*, launched in 1927, and two, *Narwhal* and *Nautilus*, launched in 1927 and 1930. During the war, the *Narwhal* and *Nautilus* were used to carry raiding parties.

Most submarines of the period, however, fell into two classes: either oceangoing fleet boats in the 1,300- to 1,500-ton range or smaller coastal submarines in the 600- to 700-ton range, although there were many excep-

U-977, one of more than seven hundred Type VII submarines built by Germany during World War II.
(U.S. Naval Institute)

tions. The Japanese, for example, built larger fleet boats in the 2,000- to 2,500-ton range, while Italy and Germany built fleet boats smaller than 1,000 tons. England, after building mostly larger fleet boats in the 1,300- to 1,500-ton range during the 1920s, switched to mostly smaller coastal class submarines in the mid-1930s. The Royal Navy's largest class, started on the eve of World War II in 1939 and built through 1943, were sixty-eight, 540-ton U and similar V classes.

Germany, restricted by the Treaty of Versailles, did not start building submarines until 1935. It settled on two basic classes: the 615/733-ton Type VII, the first *U-27* launched in June 1936, and the 1067/1162-ton Type IX, the first *U-37* launched in 1938. The Type VII would become the standard, of which over 700 were launched by the end of World War II. The last, Type VIIF mode were 1088/1181 tons. Although the Type VIIs were relatively small for oceangoing boats, in the coastal range size for submarines, and actually considered only slightly updated World War I era modes, they carried the bulk of Germany's fight.[7] By 1943 their inadequacy was becoming more apparent, and Germany did start some new types, but by then it was too late.

One other type deserves mention because it played such a large part in the war in the Pacific. On the eve of the war, in the fall of 1941, the United States started launching the first of 73 *Gato* class, followed by 132 similar *Balao* class in 1942, and finally 24 slightly larger *Tench* class in 1944. These fleet boats were all in the 1,500/2,400-ton range, 312 by 27 feet, with ten 21-inch torpedo tubes and one 3-inch gun. They were considered some of the finest submarines of the era and would prove deadly against the Japanese.[8]

The interwar naval agreements had little effect on submarines. The London Agreement of 1930 restricted submarines to 2,000 tons standard with

USS *Mingo* (SS-261), a *Gato*-class submarine built by the U.S. Navy in World War II. (U.S. Naval Institute)

5.1-inch guns, but most were well below this displacement and larger guns also were out of favor by then. There were, of course, many improvements during the interwar period. Hydraulic systems were developed in the 1930s, allowing for the rapid and remote control of valves and air vents that once required half the crew. Underwater depth limits were increased from the 150 to 250 feet of 1918 to 300 to 350 feet in 1939. New escape and salvage apparatus such as underwater respirators and radio-telephone buoys were invented.[9] Yet in some respects nothing had changed, with the lessons of World War I forgotten and not fully relearned until the spring of 1943.

World War II

As shown in table 9.2, unlike in 1914, in 1939 most of the major powers had sizable submarine fleets. The exception was Germany, with approximately 57, of which only 22 were oceangoing. Although this was almost twice the number Germany had on the eve of World War I, it was still far below the 300 Admiral Karl Dönitz felt he needed, and he was probably right.

During the war, most of the countries simply continued building modes already under way, but there are some exceptions that bear mentioning. By 1943 the small German Type VII was becoming obsolete. In June Germany began building new, advanced 1,595-ton Type XXI oceangoing and 230-ton Type XXIII coastal submarines with greater underwater speeds and other improvements. Hundreds were ordered, but the first were not launched until the summer of 1944. Germany also experimented and built a few so-called Walter boats with a closed cycle engine that did not require air from the outside of the boat as did the diesels. And late in the war they started using a

Table 9.2 Submarine Balance in World War II

Type	Britain	France	USSR	U.S.	Germany	Italy	Japan
WW-I ERA	10	0	5	37	0	7	6
1940	54	82	140	34	77	103	58
BUILT IN WAR	164	3	32	227	1133	42	118
TOTAL	228	85	177	298	1210	152	182
LOSSES							
WW-I era	2	n.a.	4	3	n.a.	1	0
1940	34	31	61	9	46	58	40
Built	35	1	6	35	706	26	90
TOTAL	71	32	71	47	752	85	130

NOTES: The Soviet Union also built 97 very small submarines in the 160- to 350-ton range. Italy also built 26 "midget" submarines in the 13- to 35-ton range. The Japanese army built 26 smaller submarines in the 270- to 400-ton range to supply its island garrisons.

snorkel (actually developed by the Dutch before the war), which permitted charging batteries underwater rather than having to surface, thus eliminating the submarine's greatest vulnerability. Some analysts have speculated that had these types been developed earlier, Germany might have won the Battle of the Atlantic. On the other hand, the Allies also made constant improvements in ASW throughout the war.

Germany's Axis partners also built some interesting types. The Japanese constructed some of their largest submarines, over 2,500 tons, after the war began, and Italy, once again, built some midget submarines. Generally, however, most of the submarines fabricated during the war were simply slightly improved late 1930s modes.

THE ATLANTIC THEATER

From Hitler's viewpoint, the submarine campaign got off to a less than auspicious start. On 3 September 1939, the *U-30* sank the British passenger ship *Athenia* bound for the United States with the loss of 128 lives. The British quickly accused Germany of waging inhumane unrestricted submarine warfare, and Hitler issued orders to cease firing on passenger ships. It looked as though World War II would become a repeat of World War I with on-again, off-again unrestricted submarine warfare, but after a few initial delays, both sides essentially waged unrestricted warfare. In the Pacific, the U.S. Navy immediately waged unrestricted warfare.

As in World War I, the German U-boats drew significant early first blood. On 16 September 1939, *U-29* sank the Royal Navy carrier *Courageous* off the west coast of Ireland, and then a month later, on the night of 13–14 October, German U-Boat ace Gunther Prien skillfully maneuvered his boat into the British anchorage at Scapa Flow and sank the battleship *Royal Oak*. These were the World War II equivalents of the sinking of the three cruisers early in World War I and quite naturally sent shock waves through the Royal Navy. During the war the Germans would sink three British aircraft carriers (*Courageous, Ark Royal,* and *Eagle*), two battleships (*Royal Oak* and *Barham*), and several cruisers.

But as in World War I, the main mission of U-boats was sinking merchant ships, not warships. While the few major surface sea battles such as the *Bismarck-Hood* engagement make interesting reading, their outcome had little overall effect on the war. It was the so-called Battle of the Atlantic (which also included the Mediterranean) where the outcome of the war rested. And again, as in World War I, the German U-boats with Italian assistance almost tipped the scales against the Allies. The most famous periods of success were the so-called happy times from June 1940 to March 1941, with a second in 1942, when German U-boats sank merchantmen almost at will.

The U-boat was defeated first by being too few and then later by a combination of Allied technological advances, including better sonar, sonar buoys, radar (which was extremely important because submarines attacked mostly on the surface at night), and better weapons, including not just advanced depth charges but also new weaponry such as hedgehogs, ASW mortars, and air-dropped torpedoes. But perhaps the two most important factors in the defeat of the submarines were the combination of Allied airpower and intelligence. The real change in the Battle of the Atlantic came when small escort carriers started to accompany convoys. The Allies also made two significant intelligence breakthroughs. The most important was the breaking of the German codes by British intelligence, and the second was the use of direction finders and intercepts. The German submarines made the mistake of talking too much, which in some respects was necessitated by the wolf-pack tactics that required Dönitz to send many boats to intercept convoys. More important, however, were Allied ASW airpower, long-range planes, and especially the eventual use of escort carriers.[10]

THE PACIFIC THEATER

The submarine war in the Pacific was quite different. Both Japanese and American uses have been severely criticized, although for entirely different reasons. The Japanese Navy, which generally performed well, even brilliantly in many respects, has been criticized by virtually all analysts for deploying its submarines against American warships rather than merchantmen and then later using them as supply ships for their island garrisons. There was no Japanese submarine battle of the Pacific comparable to the Battle of the Atlantic. Although some Japanese submarines did operate off the American West Coast and sink a few ships, in general they conducted little merchant interdiction, essentially giving the U.S. Navy and merchant fleets a free ride.[11]

American submarine operations are also interesting although unfortunately somewhat disturbing for two reasons. First was the apparent mental unpreparedness of some of the American submarine skippers, exacerbated by what can only be described as one of the darkest moments in the U.S. Navy's history—a severe torpedo problem that took over two years to solve and in some respects was still lingering until the end of the war. There was an assumption in the 1930s that ASDIC (or sonar, as the Americans called it) had solved the ASW problem, so the submarine's solution was to dive deep. This made firing torpedoes virtually impossible. Torpedo attacks had to be made either on the surface or at periscope depth and at short range. In short, skippers had to be aggressive. But even when skippers finally learned this lesson, the American torpedoes designed but *never* tested in actual conditions simply did not work. Worse, the skippers could not convince the brass, especially the Washington desk-bound brass, of the problem. Although some of the early skippers might not have been up to the job, others were probably unfairly branded because of the faulty torpedoes. It was not until 1943 that the problem was finally recognized by most, but still not all, admirals.

These problems were not unique to the American submarine force. The Germans also had torpedo problems early in the war, but they were recognized and solved. There were also some reported cases of German battle fatigue. Remarkably considering their staggering losses, German morale stayed high to the end. The British also had problems. In that typical British way of understatement, submariner Alastair Mars labeled this "early stage amorphism" where some of the early British skippers "found themselves faced with dangerous situations of which they had little knowledge . . . [which] . . . frequently leads to indecision." Mars notes that thought was given to relieving skippers over thirty-five (which today would eliminate virtually all submarine captains).[12]

Despite this "early stage amorphism" in the U.S. Navy and the continuing torpedo problems, the United States submariners performed admirably after the first few years and won their own battle of the Pacific against the Japanese merchant fleet. By the end of 1944, the American submarines had sunk so many Japanese merchantmen that they were reduced to sinking junks. In short, the American submarines did to the island nation of Japan what the German U-Boats failed to do to Britain.

ALTHOUGH IT IS IMPOSSIBLE to chronicle the literally hundreds of submarine operations of World War II, one deserves special mention because it had portents for the Cold War. On 9 February 1945, HMS *Venturer,* a 545-ton boat commanded by Lieutenant James S. Launders, while submerged, sank the German *U-864,* also submerged. To this day, this remains the only case in history of a submarine-versus-submarine submerged attack and sinking. Yet it is exactly this scenario that would become the assumption throughout the post–World War II era.

The submarine wars would take tremendous tolls. In the Atlantic, more than 2,000 merchantmen would be sunk for a loss of almost 800 U-boats. In the Pacific, the Americans would sink some 1,150 ships with an aggregate tonnage of 4,860,000 of Japanese shipping to a loss of 52 submarines. In rough terms, that was a ratio of one American submarine sunk for every 22 Japanese. Included in that total of Japanese ships sunk by American submarines were 1 battleship, 4 aircraft carriers, 4 escort carriers, 3 heavy and 8 light cruisers, 35 destroyers, and 26 submarines, including 1 German U-boat operating in the Java Sea.

Submarine loss rates were staggering for the three Axis powers: 130 out of 178 for Japan, or 73 percent; 781 out of 1,170 for Germany, or 66.7 percent; and 85 out of 145 for Italy, or 58.6 percent. The British submarine loss rate was 80 out of 225, or 35.5 percent, while that of the United States was 52 out of 313, or 16.6 percent. On a comparative basis, no other forces would take such losses.

The Post–World War II Period

In the immediate post–World War II era, many submarines, like all navy ships, were retired or placed in mothballs and older modes were scrapped. But the submarine force also immediately began modernization. In 1947 U.S. Navy experiments with captured Type XXI U-boats led to a program called Greater Underwater Propulsion Power (GUPPY), which increased battery capacity. Hulls were also streamlined. A GUPPY II program in 1948 would add snorkels to the ships, and then in 1953 the U.S. Navy would build the research submarine *Albacore,* with a streamlined, so-called teardrop hull. All countries have since adopted these basic designs with greater battery capacity and streamlined hulls.

This was also a time of experimentation. In 1947, the USS *Cusk* (SS-348) fired a Loon missile, which was essentially a German V-1. This led to the Regulus cruise missile program in the early 1950s. The USS *Tunny* and others were converted to carry the Regulus. Development of sea-launched ballistic missiles (SLBMs) ended the Regulus program. Another program, perhaps sarcastically called "Migraine," was begun, converting some submarines to radar pickets (SSRs) for early detection of Soviet bombers. This dangerous mission caused "migraine headaches" to the submarine community before being abandoned. The SSRs would have been sitting ducks for Soviet submarines.

There were also miscellaneous cargo conversions and other experiments. Some submarines were converted to oilers to fuel seaplanes first designated SSOs, later AGSS for miscellaneous auxiliary submarine, and then again AOSS, although some for transport kept the AGSS designation. In 1948, the *Perch* (SS-313) and *Sealion* (SS-315) were converted to troop "commando" transports with a hangar on deck for a LTV (landing vehicle track) jeep and eight ten-man rubber rafts. The *Perch* took part in operations in both Korea and Vietnam. In Korea, since the American forces were not then prepared for such operations, the *Perch* ended up landing British commandos. But the major conversions and missions for submarines in most navies became ASW against other submarines, with many designated SSK for submarine killer. Although the United States has since dropped the SSK designation, it is still used by other countries.

The most significant submarine events of the postwar era took place on 17 January 1955 and 20 July 1960. The first was the signal date from USS *Nautilus* "underway on nuclear power" and the second was the first firing of an SLBM from the strategic nuclear ballistic missile submarine (SSBN)

George Washington. As purists often point out, until 1955 there really were no "submarines." Up until that time, these vessels should have been more properly called "submersibles" because they had to surface to recharge batteries. Although the snorkel made them semisubmarines, snorkeling was detectable with conventional ASW tactics. Now, for the first time with the sailing of the *Nautilus,* submarines were truly independent underwater. The Soviet Union joined the nuclear club in 1958, Britain in 1963, France in 1971, and China in 1974. Other countries such as Canada and Brazil have looked at nuclear submarines but have been excluded from the "club" because of cost.

The other major event was moving ballistic missiles to sea starting in 1960 for the United States, 1962 for the Soviet Union (first on conventional submarines and then in 1968 with *Yankee* class SSBNs), 1967 for Britain, 1971 for France, and 1987 for China.[13] The invulnerable SLBMs on SSBNs have been the backbone of nuclear deterrence for years. Land-based intercontinental ballistic missiles (ICBMs) were considered extremely vulnerable from their inception. Placing them in hardened silos in the 1960s made them somewhat safer, but with the advent of larger, more accurate Soviet ICBMs in the late 1970s, they once more became vulnerable. For years ICBMs were justified for their accuracy, but with the advent of the accurate Trident II (or D-5) missile in the mid-1980s, the justification for ICBMs again became questionable and many have suggested moving to an all SSBN/SLBM force.[14]

Besides nuclear power and the building of ballistic missile submarines, the other major postwar change regarding submarines was the unprecedented buildup by the Soviet Union, whose inventory once numbered almost four hundred. The largest class in number were 215 1,050/1,340-ton "Whiskey" class conventional submarines built in the early 1950s. These were followed by other large classes such as the "Zulu" class in the late 1950s and "Foxtrot" in the 1960s. Then, in the 1960s the Soviet Union started to build nuclear-powered submarines. Although the numbers were of some concern, through the 1970s most Western analysts were not overly alarmed, noting that most Soviet submarines were conventional powered, required snorkeling to charge their batteries, and thus were fairly easily detected, with their nuclear modes extremely noisy, heard "an ocean away." That situation changed in the late 1970s with the emergence of the 4,900/6,000-ton "Victor III" that began a trend to quieter submarines. Unfortunately, much of the Soviets' success in reducing noise has since been attributed to the Walker spy case, in which a U.S. Navy warrant officer, John Walker, passed secrets to the Soviets. Although American submarines are still considered quieter, that gap has closed considerably. Submarines are considered the one area in which Russia might have a lead over the United States. Although American submarines are quieter, the Russian *Alpha* has reportedly reached speeds of 45 knots submerged and, with titanium hulls, reached greater depths than

Launch of USS *Springfield* (SSN-761). She is part of the *Los Angeles* class of nuclear attack submarines, built by the United States from the mid-1970s to the mid-1990s. (U.S. Naval Institute)

U.S. submarines. Currently, the only new ships being built by Russia are submarines.[15]

As can be expected, nuclear submarines have gotten larger. The U.S. Navy's *Skate* class launched in 1957 were 2,550 tons; the next *Skipjack* class of 1960, 3,070 tons; the mid-1960s *Sturgeon* class, 4,250 tons; and the 1980s *Los Angeles* class, 6,000 tons with the *Seawolf* class 7,470 tons. Other countries' nuclear submarines have also gotten larger with most in the 4,000-ton range. The largest in the world is the Russian "Typhoon"-class SSBN at 18,500 tons surfaced and 25,000 tons submerged. Conventional submarines have not disappeared; most countries operate at least a few. Two popular export modes found in many navies are the German-design Type 209 at around 1,100 tons and the larger Russian Kilo at around 2,300 tons. Smaller coastal submarines are also still being built. Germany, for example, has the Type 206 coastal submarine at only 456 tons. And some of the most exciting new developments are proposals to make conventional submarines self-sustainable. Sweden is building a so-called air-independent propulsion (AIP)

A Russian "Typhoon"-class SSBN. At 18,500 tons and 562.5 feet long, these are the largest submarines ever built.
(Royal Navy photo, via the U.S. Naval Institute)

submarine that would allow conventional submarines to remain submerged. There are actually several AIP modes, including closed-cycle systems for both diesel and gas turbine, the Stirling engine, and the use of fuel cells. There are also proposals for combination systems, sometimes dubbed SSNs, with small nuclear reactors to charge conventional batteries.

THE MAIN THREAT during the Cold War was the massive Soviet submarine fleet, which usually numbered around three hundred boats (versus approximately one hundred for the United States) and aroused legitimate fears of a third Battle of the Atlantic. After all, if Germany started World War I with only thirty-five submarines and World War II with fifty-seven and both times almost won, what would be the result if the Soviet Union started out with three hundred? For years the favorite war game at the U.S. Naval War College at Newport was holding the Soviet subs above the G-I-UK (Greenland-Iceland-United Kingdom) gap. Virtually every article on U.S.-Soviet naval relations during the Cold War included a commentary on the G-I-UK gap. Fortunately, that threat ended in 1990, and many of the once massive Soviet submarine force apparently are rusting at the piers, although again it should be pointed out that the only new ships currently being built by the Russian Navy are submarines.

Throughout the Cold War period there were only three classic submarine actions, none of which involved either the Soviet Union or the United States. The first was during a 1971 Indo-Pakistani war when the Pakistan submarine *Hangor* sank the Indian frigate *Khukri* in the Arabian Sea, and the other two occurred during the Falklands war. These were the sinking of the Argentinean cruiser *General Belgrano* by the Royal Navy submarine HMS *Conqueror* and the attacks by the Argentine diesel submarine on the British fleet. These are interesting actions for several reasons. First, they illustrate that minor, even Third World, countries are prepared to use their submarines. Submarine proliferation has now become the major worry of the United States as Third World fleets contain some three hundred-odd submarines.

Second and equally interesting are the attitudes of some Western and particularly American analysts to the Pakistan and Argentine uses. The former is virtually ignored and the latter often treated cynically. The Argentine attacks were unsuccessful, but there is some indication that the problem was faulty equipment. With only a razor-thin advantage and operating thousands of miles from Britain, the sinking of a few ships, especially one of its V/STOL carriers, would probably have forced London to call off the operation. Another ominous lesson was that the British ships expended considerable ASW ordnance—all to no avail. In short, if an untrained crew with faulty equipment can cause that much trouble for the well-trained Royal Navy, that is a worry.

The sinking of the old World War II–era cruiser *Belgrano* (former U.S. light cruiser *Phoenix* CL-46) is also interesting. On the one hand, it shows very effectively how a submerged submarine can still establish "presence," which has been one of the major criticisms against submarines. With that sinking, the Argentine navy pulled back, never to emerge. The Argentineans did have a small carrier, the *Veinticinco de Mayo,* that with some skill and a little luck might have caused considerable problems for the small British fleet. On the other hand, the British sinking has been severely criticized for several reasons, all with the underlying theme that this was somehow "unsporting."

Submarines have been involved in numerous operations during the Cold War, mostly as deterrents to possible Soviet submarine actions. There have also been many intelligence missions and some special operations. Unfortunately, except for a very few such as the *Perch's* actions during the Korean War, most were carried out in secret and remain classified to this day. Many in the submarine "silent service" community feel that in this new post–Cold War era, some of those operations should be declassified and disseminated to justify the submarines' existence.

In some respects, the need for submarines in the post–Cold War era got off to a good start. During Desert Storm, some of the first shots fired were

Table 9.3 Submarine Comparisons

Class	Navy	Year	Displacement	Dimensions	Torpedo Tubes/#T/Guns	Speed
Holland	USN	1897	64/74	54 × 10 × 8.5	1-18 inch/3	8/5
"E"	RN	1912	655/796	178 × 23 × 12.5	4-18 inch/8/1-12 pdr	15/9
U-51	Gr	1915	715/902	214 × 21 × 12	4-19.7 inch/8/1-2.45 inch	17/9
UB 48	Gr	1917	516/651	181 × 19 × 12	5-19.7 inch/10/1-3.45 inch	13.5/7.5
"T"	RN	1941	1090/1575	275 × 27 × 15	10-21 inch/17/1-4 inch	15/9
B1	Jp	1939	2200/3654	357 × 30.5 × 17	6-21 inch/17/1-5.5 inch	23.6/8
VIIC	Gr	1940	749/851	220 × 20 × 16	5-21 inch/14/1-3.45 inch	17/7.6
IXC	Gr	1940	1102/1213	252 × 22 × 15	6-21 inch/22/1-4 inch	18.2/7.3
Gato	USN	1941	1526/2410	312 × 27 × 15	10-21 inch/24/1-3 inch	20/8.75
"Whiskey"	USSR	1950	1050/1340	249 × 21 × 15	6-21 inch/12	18/13
Nautilus	USN	1955	3533/4092	324 × 28 × 22	6-21 inch	15/23
Sturgeon	USN	1966	4246/4777	292 × 32 × 25.6	4-21 inch	15/26
"Victor III"	USSR	1977	4900/6000	341 × 32 × 23	6-21 inch/18	15/30
Ohio	USN	1981	16,000/18,700	560 × 42 × 35.6	4-21 inch/24 SLBMs	15/25+
"Kilo"	USSR	1982	2300/2900	230 × 32.5 × 21	6-21 inch/12	12/25
"Typhoon"	USSR	1981	18,500/25,000	563 × 75 × 40	6-21 or 25.5 inch/20 SLBMs	15/25
Los Angeles	USN	1976	6000/6900	360 × 33 × 32	4-21 inch/VLS for SLCM	15/30+

NOTES: Year = year completed. Displacement = surface/submerged. Dimensions = overall length by width by draft in feet. Speed = maximum speed surface/submerged.

long-range Tomahawk SLCMs (sea-launched cruise missiles) fired from submarines. Another recent development justifies submarines. Although the old Soviet threat was disappearing, many Third World nations, including Iran, are purchasing conventional submarines. So-called brown-water ASW for shallower coastal waters has become a major concern.

Conclusion

Submarines have grown in size over the years from small experimental modes of less than 100 tons at the turn of the century, to fleet boats of just under 1,000 tons in World War I, to about 1,500 tons in World War II, to well over 4,000 tons for some of today's large nuclear attack submarines. The biggest change, however, was not size but the move to nuclear power in the late 1950s. And though the focus has usually been on the larger nuclear attack submarines, conventional types are still common and some still small submarines, less than a thousand tons, are used for coastal patrols. Thus in some respects, there is actually a wider spectrum of submarine types—from 600-odd-ton coastal types to 6,000-ton attack boats to over 16,000-ton ballistic submarines—than in any other warship type.

Despite this wide spectrum, however, approaching the twenty-first century, the submarine community in some respects is back to square one. The issue today, as it was at the beginning of the century, is not a submarine's capabilities but its mission. While Russia is still building sophisticated submarines that pose a potential threat, its once massive fleet has disappeared. There is a new fear of submarine proliferation, especially by rogue nations such as Iran and Libya, but they have only a handful. How this all sorts out in the twenty-first century may be one of the most interesting questions facing warships and seapower.

Aircraft Carriers

10

S TARTING OUT AS jury-rigged platforms on cruisers for a few daredevil aviators, the aircraft carrier has evolved into the undisputed capital ship of the modern era. While there was some question during the interwar period whether the battleship or carrier was more important, that debate ended abruptly on 7 December 1941. During the Cold War, submarines were often considered the primary capital warship, but their actions can be counted on one hand with the call, "Where are the carriers?" heard constantly. No other warship can match the power, dominance, and flexibility of a large-deck aircraft carrier with its embarked air group.

Yet despite this dominance, there are some ironies. At once powerful, they are also vulnerable with little inherent capabilities beyond their air group. Also, while all the powers of the day built dreadnoughts, only three countries—the United States, England, and Japan—built carriers in any number and only two—the United States and Japan—engaged in classic carrier sea battles. And today, though no one really questions their importance, only two countries—the United States and France—operate large-deck carriers. The reasons are their complexity and cost, mostly the latter. Although there has been somewhat of a renaissance in smaller V/STOL carriers, even they are too expensive for most fleets to have more than one.

Early Precedents

As would be expected, there are no real precedents for aircraft carriers in either the Age of Galleys or the Age of Sail. In 1798, France did embark a balloon unit of its Campagnie d'Aerostiers, the world's first organized military air arm, on the ship *Le Patriote* for duty in Egypt, but she ran aground and sank off Alexandria on 4 July 1798.[1] Thus to Austria-Hungary during the Age of Steam goes the honor of not just one but two firsts. During a siege of Vienna in 1849, Austria launched hot-air balloons carrying explosive charges calibrated to drop on the city, with some launched from the paddle wheeler *Vulcano*. Though unsuccessful, this can be considered as both the first flight and first bombing raid from a ship.[2] During the American Civil

War both the North and South used observation balloons, a few launched from ships. In 1861 the Union launched a balloon from the small steamer ship *Fanny,* and in 1862 the Confederates did the same from the tug *Teaser.*[3] During the late nineteenth century a few other countries experimented with balloons at sea, but no real progress was made until the modern era.

The Modern Era: 1903–1914

The age of flight started on 17 December 1903 with the Wright brothers' successful 852-foot, 59-second hop, and it was not long before proposals came to move aviation to sea. The Wright brothers approached the Royal Navy about buying an airplane in 1907 but were turned down.[4] In 1908 there were suggestions for tests on ships in the United States, and in the same year Wilbur Wright visited France, sparking interest in Europe. As so often happens, a farsighted dreamer forecast things to come. In 1909 Clement Adler wrote *L'Aviation Militaire* describing a future carrier complete with flat deck, island structure, elevators, hangar deck, and folded wings for planes. He was the first to use the term *aircraft carrier* (*porte-avions*) and wrote that the ship "will have to be cleared of any obstacles. It will be flat, as wide as possible, not conforming to the lines of the hull. . . . Servicing the aircraft will have to be done below this deck. . . . Access to this lower deck will be by means of a lift long enough and wide enough to take an aircraft with its wings folded. Along the sides will be workshops of the mechanics. . . . The speed of this vessel will have to be at least as great as that of cruisers."[5] It would be another decade before such a ship appeared.

Only a year later, however, came the first test, from, as Adler suggested, a cruiser. On 14 November 1910, Eugene B. Ely made the first flight from a 83-foot-long, wooden jury-rigged platform on the American cruiser *Birmingham*'s bow while she was steaming at 10 knots. His plane actually touched the water but was still able to lift off, landing on shore. Then, two months later on 18 January 1911, Ely made the first landing on the anchored armored cruiser *Pennsylvania* using arresting wires secured by sandbags on a 119-foot-long platform. He then flew off, the second recorded shipboard takeoff in history.

Despite these early successes with conventional planes, an event occurred in 1911 that would dominate naval aviation through World War I. That was the development of the float plane and later the flying boat. The float plane had floats or pontoon appendages attached externally to the fuselage while the flying boat used its fuselage to provide the flotation. The two terms are sometimes used interchangeably, but there was a difference. (The addition of wheels made them amphibians, able to function from either land or sea, but that would come later.) These early modes were actually known by the cumbersome word *hydroaeroplane,* and Winston Churchill claimed to have coined the term *seaplane.*[6] The Germans would take still another approach, developing their Zeppelins for longer-range overseas raids. During World War I, much of the cross-channel naval air war would be operations by English seaplanes raiding German Zeppelin hangars.

England finally got into the flying business in 1912 with some early experiments and in May 1912 established the Royal Flying Corps for all services. The Naval Wing of the Royal Flying Corps was established in 1914. Fly-offs were performed from battleships in 1912, and later the old light cruiser *Hermes* was converted to a parent ship with a platform fitted over her bow to launch float planes. The *Hermes* would take part in fleet exercises in 1913, but with war approaching, the platform was removed because it restricted her guns. The *Hermes* experiments were considered successful so a merchantman began conversion to a seaplane carrier. Named the *Ark Royal,* she is considered the Royal Navy's first aircraft carrier.

Other countries also carried out experiments, including building carriers. The French navy was the first to put an operational seaplane carrier to sea. This was the 6,000-ton, 390-by-66-foot *Foudre,* a former torpedo depot ship converted in 1912, able to accommodate eight seaplanes. In 1913 Japan converted the merchantman *Wakamiya* to carry three seaplanes and her planes carried out the first attacks in World War I. Italy also conducted some experiments in 1913, as did Russia. During the first Balkan war in 1913, a Greek seaplane reconnoitered the Dardanelles, the first use of a seaplane in war. In 1914 seaplanes from the battleship *Mississippi* during operations against Vera Cruz, Mexico, were fired on, marking another first. Thus on the eve of World War I, the stage was set for the carrier's first appearance.

World War I

World War I was important for the development of the aircraft carrier, not for its military contributions, which were, at best, minimal, but rather as a necessary transition period. In the early part of the war seaplane carriers were used, but their limitations were recognized and first forward fly-off platforms, then some so-called mixed carriers were built, followed by aft landing platforms and finally fully flush deck flattops. Thus in the short span from 1914 to 1918, the carrier we know today was developed, and it would go on to play a major role in World War II.

The need for aircraft carriers was recognized early in the war by England, and three old cross-channel steamers, the *Empress, Riviera,* and *Engadine,* were purchased in August and converted into seaplane carriers by September. The old light cruiser *Hermes* was once again reconfigured to ferry seaplanes but was torpedoed on 31 October 1914. What is usually considered the first significant carrier air raid was an attack on Zeppelin hangars at Cruxhaven on Christmas Day 1914 by seaplanes from the three former steamers. The Cruxhaven raid was unsuccessful and, worse, two Zeppelins spotted and bombed the British force, although none were hit. These raids against Zeppelin hangars would continue sporadically throughout the war. Japan actually gets the credit for the first aerial attack, with a raid by *Waka-miya* floatplanes on the German base at Tsingtao, China, in September 1914.

The three British converted channel-crossers should more properly be called seaplane tenders because they had to stop to lift their seaplanes in the water for takeoff, making them vulnerable to submarine attacks. Even worse, seaplanes could not take off in rough seas. These limitations had been recognized from the beginning, so most seaplane carriers were equipped with fly-off platforms. There was still the problem of recovery, which again made them vulnerable to submarine attacks. Three solutions were developed: the planes would fly off the ship and land ashore, return and ditch alongside while the pilot was fished out of the water, or, more commonly, land beside the ship and be hoisted aboard with a crane. It was not until 1917 that experiments began with after landing platforms.

Although preceded by the three former cross-channel seaplane carriers, the *Ark Royal,* finally completed in December 1914, is usually considered the Royal Navy's first true aviation ship because she underwent a more drastic conversion. At 7,080 tons, 366 by 51 feet, the *Ark Royal* could carry up to seven aircraft at a time when most ships could carry only three or four. In early 1915 three more civilian ships, the *Ben-my-Chree, Manxman,* and *Vindex,* were converted. A plane from the *Ben-my-Chree* (Woman of my heart) is often attributed with the first torpedo attack, sinking a Turkish supply ship on 12 August 1915, although a submarine in the area also claimed the kill. Unfortunately, the *Ben-my-Chree* also had the dubious distinction of being the only aircraft carrier sunk during the war. On 9 January 1917, she was set afire and sunk by Turkish artillery.

The *Vindex,* former passenger ship *Viking,* was the first of the mixed carriers with a hangar aft for five seaplanes and a launching platform forward for two planes with wheel undercarriages. She was the first Royal Navy ship to fly off a land plane, on 3 November 1915. Since most of these ships were too slow to operate with the fleet, an old former Cunard liner, the *Campania,* was converted in 1915 to provide aerial reconnaissance for the Grand Fleet, and to her sometimes goes the honor of being the first fleet carrier.

During the war the carriers had many roles. Usually considered most important was reconnaissance against both enemy surface ships and submarines. Very early on, these seaplanes were equipped with radios, but the results were sometimes disappointing. Seaplanes from the *Engadine* operating with Beatty's battle cruiser force during the Battle of Jutland actually spotted the German fleet, but the reports were not believed. Seaplanes were also used effectively during the ill-fated Gallipoli campaign and in several Middle East operations. Finally, they were used for ASW. Although many of these operations are interesting firsts, in the larger scheme of things they mattered little to the outcome of the war.

Rather, the real importance of carriers during World War I was their development into full-fledged aircraft carriers, and in some respects, nothing epitomizes that development more than what might be called the "curious *Furious* conversions." The *Furious* started out as one of Admiral Fisher's large light cruisers with little armor but two huge 18-inch guns. Considered a white elephant by most, she was offered up for conversion when Fisher retired. In place of the forward turret, the *Furious* received a long, 234-foot fly-off platform. Landing experiments were conducted with the pilot flying parallel to the ship and then swinging on board. Although the first attempt was successful, the second killed the pilot. The after turret was then removed for a landing platform, but wind swirls and eddies from the still large center bridge area made this dangerous, although it did lead to the conclusion that an unimpeded flush-deck flight deck was the answer. Carriers built in 1917 and 1918 were converted to flush decks, and the *Furious* herself was finally so reconstructed in the mid-1920s.

Thus by 1917 the answer for future aircraft carriers was becoming clear, and two conversions were done and one new construction begun. The first was the *Argus*, converted from the incomplete liner *Conte Rosso*. Originally planned, like the *Furious*, with a forward fly-off platform and aft landing platform, her design was changed in the course of building to a complete flush-deck carrier without even an island. Finally completed in September 1918, the 14,550-ton, 566-by-68-foot *Argus* was the world's first flush-deck carrier. In January 1918, the Royal Navy laid down its first carrier built from the keel up. This was the 10,850-ton, 598-by-70-foot *Hermes*, named after the original cruiser and not completed until 1924. Since the *Hermes* would not join the fleet for several years, in February 1918 the Royal Navy took over the incomplete Chilean battleship *Almirante Cochrane*, renamed her *Eagle*, and completed her as another flush-deck carrier. The *Eagle*, finally completed in 1920, was 21,630 tons, 668 by 94 feet. Unlike the fully flush-decked *Argus*, both the *Hermes* and *Eagle* had superstructure islands. All three would serve in World War II; *Hermes* and *Eagle* were sunk in 1942.

By late 1917, the shape of carriers became clear and would change little over the years. Equally important, considering some of the battleship-versus-carrier debates that would emerge during the interwar period, was the Royal Navy's appreciation for carriers. At the end of the war, Admiral Beatty was calling for six modern carriers for the fleet, and his successor called for three more. Thus, as one scholar states, it was really a myth to think the old battleship admirals did not appreciate this new airpower.[7]

Other countries also operated seaplane carriers during World War I. Germany is credited as being the first to use airplanes to accompany a task force using seaplanes from a cruiser for reconnaissance in the Baltic over the Russian coast early in the war. Russia had seven, France five, and Japan one seaplane carrier, but these were all smaller ships, really just seaplane tenders or depot ships. The United States continued with experiments, including testing catapults on the armored cruiser *North Carolina* in October 1915. No other country matched the Royal Navy's numbers or operations. All told, the Royal Navy operated eleven ships classified by *Conway's* as seaplane carriers. Four, the *Ark Royal, Argus, Furious,* and *Vindictive,* were listed as aircraft carriers and the *Eagle* and *Hermes* were being built. In short, although the United States Navy can claim to be the first to experiment with planes at sea, it was the Royal Navy that gave birth to the aircraft carrier.[8]

The Interwar Period

The Royal Navy was not the only navy to see the carrier's potential. Both Japan and the United States shared that view, yet only a handful were built through the mid-1930s for several reasons, mostly lack of funds. Another reason was that this was also the era of Italian Giulio Douhet's theory that bombers would make armies and especially navies obsolete. In the United States the main disciple of this notion was General Billy Mitchell, especially after he sank some stationary old German warships in 1921. No navy suffered more from these bombing devotees than the Royal Navy, however. The Royal Air Force (RAF) for all services was established on 1 April 1918. While a Fleet Air Arm was eventually reestablished in 1924, it would not become part of the navy again until 1939, with the result that RN carriers were still operating obsolete biplanes in 1941.

Despite these problems, carrier construction and conversion did not stop completely. HMS *Eagle* was finally completed in 1920 and *Hermes* in 1924. Japan is sometimes credited with the first keel-built carrier, beating the *Hermes* by a few months with the small *Hosho*.[9] Only 7,470 tons, 541 by 59 feet, the *Hosho* was the smallest carrier ever built, but she still managed to carry twenty-one planes. The Japanese also experimented with a mirror landing system on the *Hosho,* a method that would become standard in the 1950s. The United States converted the old collier *Jupiter* into the flush-deck *Langley* (known as the "covered wagon") in 1922.

All the other carriers built during the 1920s were conversions, most as a result of the 1922 Washington Naval Treaty. The treaty classified carriers as over 10,000 tons and restricted them to 27,000 tons, but the agreement also allowed the United States and Japan each to convert two large battle cruisers then under construction to 33,000-ton carriers. The United States converted the *Lexington* and *Saratoga,* completing both in 1927. They actually came in at around 37,000 tons. The treaty did allow 3,000 tons for improvements, which the United States liberally interpreted as allowing for the extra weight. Considered large white elephants at the time, they would prove invaluable in World War II and would not be surpassed in size until the *Midway* class, completed in 1945.

The Japanese conversions were also large 27,000-ton ships, capable of carrying almost ninety planes. They would be the largest Japanese carriers built until the *Taiho,* laid down in 1941. England also converted some former battle cruisers. The *Furious* went back for a final conversion in 1922, and two other former large light cruisers, the *Courageous* and *Glorious,* were converted starting in 1924. Besides the normal flight deck, all three were also given a second short flight deck over the bow, but that proved unsatisfactory and was eventually eliminated.

France built its only carrier, the *Béarn,* in the 1920s. She was converted from an incomplete battleship (*Normandie* class) hull in 1927. The *Bearn* was 22,150 tons, 599 by 89 feet, and capable of carrying forty aircraft. Although other countries had used wires and arresting tailhooks, at least according to one author, the French perfected this technique.[10] During the war she was interned at Martinique in 1942, finally outfitted in the United States, and then operated by the Free French. The *Bearn* was not retired until 1967, the only prewar carrier to survive postwar service. France laid down the 18,000-ton carrier *Joffre* in 1938, but she was never completed.

In an attempt to skirt the Washington Treaty 10,000-ton definition, Japan completed the small 8,000-ton *Ryujo* in 1933. In 1934 the United States also built a smallish carrier, the 14,575-ton *Ranger.* Both were considered failures. The United States would actually build a slightly modified repeat *Ranger,* the *Wasp,* in the late 1930s to keep under overall treaty limits for carriers. In the mid-1930s, countries finally started building larger carriers.

In 1935 the Royal Navy laid down Britain's most famous World War II carrier, the 22,000-ton, 800-by-95-foot *Ark Royal* capable of carrying sixty planes. Then, two years later, in 1937, England began three 23,000-ton *Illustrious*-class carriers capable of carrying thirty-three planes, followed by the similar *Indomitable,* modified for forty-five planes, and finally two kindred *Implacable* class capable of carrying sixty aircraft, laid down in 1939. Only the *Ark Royal* was completed when war began in 1939, with two *Illustrious*-class ships reaching completion in 1940. These would be the last large fleet carriers built by Britain during the war. The *Illustrious* class was the first to have armored hangars, considered a major improvement in carrier construction; none were sunk during the war.

Britain also built ten light fleet carriers before the war ended. In 1939 she laid down the single 14,750-ton *Unicorn* capable of carrying thirty-five planes and during the war four even smaller 13,190-ton *Colossus* class begun in 1942 and five 14,000-ton *Majestic*-class light carriers started in 1943. Five other ships were converted to small escort carriers, and thirty-eight more were obtained by lend-lease from the United States. In addition, nineteen former grain carriers and oilers were given jury-rigged flight decks and operated under the "Red Ensign" (merchant flag).

The United States also started building classes of carriers. In 1934 two

19,900-ton, 809-by-83-foot *Yorktown*-class carriers were started with a repeat *Hornet,* laid down in 1939. Carrying ninety-six planes, they are often
considered the U.S. Navy's first modern carriers. Then, in January 1941, the
United States began the first of twenty-six authorized (twenty-four built)
large 27,200-ton, 888-by-93-foot *Essex*-class carriers capable of carrying
over ninety planes. Perhaps more than any other ships, the *Essex*-class carriers were ultimately responsible for winning the war in the Pacific. The first
Essex class joined the fleet in 1942, followed by six more in 1943 and seven
in 1944.

The United States also built nine 10,660-ton *Independence*-class light carriers on converted *Cleveland* light cruiser class hulls. In addition, the United
States constructed some seventy-four smaller escort carriers (CVEs), sometimes nicknamed "jeep" carriers. The largest classes were eleven *Bogue* class
commissioned in 1942–43, fifty *Casablanca* class completed in 1943–44,
both around 10,000 tons, and then ten 18,900-ton *Commencement Bay*
class completed in 1944–45. These jeep carriers were large enough for
approximately thirty planes.

In contrast to the United States and Great Britain, Japan built a hodgepodge of both newly constructed and converted carriers. The largest new
construction class built before the war was two 25,700-ton, 845-by-85-foot
Shokaku class capable of carrying eighty-four planes completed in the fall of
1941, just in time to participate in Pearl Harbor. During the war, three
smaller, 17,200-ton *Unryu* class were laid down in 1942, completed in 1944.
Three of Japan's carriers were conversions from submarine support ships and
five were former passenger liners. Japan had by far the largest carrier of the
war, the 62,000-ton *Shinano* converted from the third *Yamato*-class battleship, but she could carry only forty-seven planes and was sunk in November 1944 before becoming fully operational. Japan was the only country
that continued building fully flush-deck flattops, that is, with no islands.
Ten of Japan's twenty-five carriers were flush-deck ones. Japan was also the
only country to build carriers, the *Akagi* and *Hiryu,* with a port- or left-
sided island. Experience had shown that pilots favored veering left when in
trouble, which was the reason for starboard (right) side islands.

Both Germany and Italy began constructing carriers, but none were completed. The most advanced was Germany's large, almost 27,000-ton, 820-
by-103-foot *Graf Zeppelin,* laid down in 1936 and launched in 1938. The
smaller 18,000-ton, former *Hipper*-class cruiser, the *Seydlitz,* was also laid
down in 1936; it was launched in 1939. During the war Germany made pre-
liminary plans for completing the French *Joffre* and converting some liners,
but they never took place. Italy began converting the former 23,130-ton liner
Roma into the carrier *Aquila* in 1941, but, again, it was never finished. Thus
there would be no carrier battles in the European theater.[11]

The interwar period was important for the development of carrier tactics
despite the ongoing fights between the old battleship admirals and the new

"air dales." While the battleship admirals were still dominant, there were enough visionaries in naval forces that carrier tactics and exercises were refined to show their potential. One such example was the U.S. 1928 Fleet Problem VIII raid on Pearl Harbor, foreshadowing things to come. Generally, however, the carrier was still seen as secondary to the battleship with its main role the familiar reconnaissance "eyes of the fleet."

World War II

Table 10.1 shows the carrier balance during World War II. While England, Japan, and the United States had approximately the same number of carriers in 1939, that would change drastically by the end of the war. The large American-built *Essex*-class carriers would win the war in the Pacific with the smaller carriers winning the antisubmarine Battle of the Atlantic.

Table 10.1 Aircraft Carrier Balance in World War II

Type	England	U.S.	Japan
FLEET CARRIER			
Start	5	7	6
Building	6	4	4
Built	0	17	3
(Subtotal)	(11)	(28)	(13)
LIGHT CARRIER			
Start	3	0	3
Building	1	3	4
Built	9	6	0
(Subtotal)	(13)	(9)	(7)
ESCORT CARRIER			
Start	0	1	1
Building	3	1	3
Built	41	74	0
(Subtotal)	(44)	(76)	(4)
TOTAL	68	113	24

LOSSES
RN: CV: *Eagle, Courageous, Glorious, Ark Royal*
CVL: *Hermes*
CVE: *Audacity, Avenger, Dasher*

USN: CV: *Lexington, Yorktown, Hornet, Wasp*
CVL: *Princeton*
CVE: *Block Island, Liscombe Bay, St. Lo, Gambier Bay, Ommaney Bay, Bismarck Sea*

Japan: Only Japan's original small carrier *Hosho* survived still operational
CV *Junyo* and CVL *Ryuho* survived but were damaged

NOTES: Start = Balance as of 1939 for England, end 1941 for the United States and Japan. Building = Building at start and completed during the war. Built = Started and completed during the war.

THE ATLANTIC

When the war started in September 1939, the Royal Navy quickly deployed the aging *Hermes* and *Furious* and newer *Courageous* and *Ark Royal* for Atlantic ASW operations, which proved a mistake since they were ill-equipped for such operations. The *Ark Royal* and her destroyer group did score an early victory, sinking a submarine on 14 September, but three days later disaster struck when the *Courageous* was sunk. The carriers were withdrawn and the ASW problem was solved only when small carriers joined convoys much later in the war.

Carriers took part in two other early Atlantic actions. The *Ark Royal, Furious,* and *Glorious* played important roles during the spring 1940 Norway operations, but again disaster struck. On 8 June, after skillfully landing some RAF planes with no tailhooks being withdrawn from Norway, the *Glorious* was caught and sunk by the German battle cruisers *Scharnhorst* and *Gneisenau,* giving her the questionable distinction of being the only large carrier sunk by gunfire. (The American jeep carrier *Gambier Bay* would be similarly caught and sunk by Japanese warships in the Battle off Samar.) The *Victorious* and *Ark Royal* would play critical roles chasing down the German battleship *Bismarck* in May 1941. The *Ark Royal*'s planes were credited with hitting her rudder, rending her uncontrollable.

It was the small escort carriers, the CVEs, however, that actually played the key role in winning the antisubmarine Battle of the Atlantic for the Allies. Their worth was noted early on. In December 1941, convoy escorts with the first British CVE *Audacity* proved successful, sinking twelve submarines; five sinkings were credited to planes. Lamentably, the *Audacity* was torpedoed in the process. Considered the crucial factor in solving the ASW problem were the CVEs, which joined the convoys in great numbers in the spring of 1943, causing the Germans to withdraw their submarines. While the larger fleet carriers were important in several engagements, overall it was the small CVE that won the crucial Battle of the Atlantic.

THE MEDITERRANEAN

Carriers played a significant role in the Mediterranean and often paid a price. The naval war in the Mediterranean was a war of convoys, with the British trying to supply Malta and Crete, and the carriers were involved in protecting those convoys. By far the most spectacular carrier operation of that theater was the daring British raid on the Italian fleet at Taranto, often cited as a dress rehearsal for Pearl Harbor. On the night of 11 November 1940, the *Illustrious* launched twenty-one old, slow Swordfish biplane torpedo-bombers against the Italian battleship fleet, severely damaging two and damaging one beyond repair. More important even than the substantial damage

HMS *Ark Royal* after being torpedoed in November 1941. Note the obsolete biplanes on the flight deck.
(Courtesy of Imperial War Museum)

was the raising of morale of the Royal Navy at a dark time, while considerably lowering that of the Italians.

The lack of adequate airpower would severely limit the Italian navy throughout the war, but the Germans moved in some dive-bombers, which took their toll. On 10 January German Stukas severely damaged the *Illustrious,* forcing her withdrawal. Then, on 26 May 1941, during the evacuation of Crete, German dive-bombers severely damaged the *Formidable.* Because of the lack of repair facilities, both *Illustrious* and *Formidable* were repaired in Norfolk, Virginia, taking them out of action for months. The worst blow to the Royal Navy, however, was the torpedoing and sinking of the *Ark Royal* on 13 November 1941 while returning to Gibraltar. This loss had a devastating effect on British morale, but she was the last British carrier to be lost in the European theater.

THE PACIFIC

Although carrier operations were important in the Atlantic and Mediterranean, they became absolutely crucial, indeed indispensable, in the Pacific for the island-hopping campaigns of both Japan and the United States. Any notion that battleships were more important than carriers ended on 7 December 1941 when planes from six Japanese carriers attacked and sank the American Pacific battleship fleet at Pearl Harbor. Fortunately, the two U.S. carriers *Enterprise* and *Lexington* were out on operations, or they undoubtedly would have also been sunk. Any lingering doubts that Pearl Harbor was successful only because it was a sneak attack ended three days later when the new RN battleship *Prince of Wales* and old battle cruiser *Repulse* foolishly tried to attack a Japanese force without air cover and were easily sunk by land-based Japanese planes.

During the early months of the war, carriers were influential for both sides. For the Japanese, carriers were needed to support their own island-hopping expansion south, capturing most of the Southeast Asian countries and islands above Australia. Darwin was severely bombed on 19 February 1942. The United States used the carriers for hit-and-run raids on the Marshalls and other islands. Though militarily insignificant, these pinprick raids boosted morale after Pearl Harbor. Considered most important for American morale and for its dramatic effect on the Japanese leadership was the famous Doolittle raid on 18 April 1942, when sixteen Army B-25s flew off the carrier *Hornet* and bombed Tokyo.

The Royal Navy and Japan almost participated in the first carrier-versus-carrier battle. In early April 1942, the Japanese sent a fleet with five carriers into the Indian Ocean. At the time, the Royal Navy had three carriers, but Vice Admiral Sir James Somerville wisely declined battle. Even though two were modern carriers, they all carried inferior planes. Unfortunately, the elderly *Hermes* was caught and sunk by the Japanese. With few exceptions, Royal Navy carriers operated in Indian Ocean waters during the war. One vital exception was sending the *Indomitable* to the Pacific in late 1942 when the United States was down to one operational carrier. After Germany surrendered, four Royal Navy carriers were sent to the Pacific, where they performed yeoman service, especially against Japanese kamikaze attacks. Americans were amazed at the beating the British carriers could take with their armored decks.

More important were the five American-Japanese, carrier-versus-carrier battles: Coral Sea, Midway, Eastern Solomons, Santa Cruz, and finally the Marianas "turkey shoot" at the Battle of the Philippine Sea.

The Battle of Coral Sea from 3 to 8 March 1942 was the first sea battle in history fought between warships without visual contact. Japanese forces on their way to take Port Moresby, New Guinea, consisted of two large and one small carrier, versus an American fleet with the *Yorktown* and *Lexington*. On 7 May the Japanese got in what they thought was the first blow, sinking the oiler *Neosho*, mistaking it for a carrier. While that was occurring, the Americans struck, sinking the small carrier *Shoho*. The main battle came the next day when the Japanese sank the *Lexington* and damaged the *Yorktown*. Both Japanese carriers were damaged but not sunk. During the confusion of battle exacerbated by rain squalls, some Japanese pilots got confused and tried to land on the *Yorktown*. Considered a tactical victory for Japan, which lost only the small *Shoho*, Coral Sea was a major strategic victory for the

United States because it stopped the Japanese thrust. And it will go down in history as the first carrier battle.

The Battle of Midway from 3 to 7 June 1942 is considered the most important sea battle in the Pacific and one of the most strategically important in all history. Admiral Isoroku Yamamoto was hoping for a classic decisive Mahanian sea battle to sink the remaining American carriers in the Pacific, but through good intelligence and even better luck, the Americans instead sank four large Japanese carriers. The Americans had broken the Japanese naval code and sent three carriers, including the *Yorktown,* still bearing battle damage from the Battle of Coral Sea, to ambush the Japanese fleet. The carrier battle began on 4 June when Japanese planes struck Midway. Even though the Americans had the element of surprise, the initial strikes by the lumbering Dauntless torpedo planes (TBDs) were disastrous, and Japan beat off five separate attacks. Finally, American dive-bombers (SBDs) attacked, sinking three carriers. Planes from the one remaining Japanese carrier did sink the *Yorktown* before herself being sunk. This "Miracle at Midway," as one author put it, was the beginning of the end for Japan even though the war would go on for over three more years.[12] Besides the loss of four carriers, Japan lost the cream of its flyers, and they were never fully replaced by Japan's slow, inefficient training pipeline system.

The next two carrier battles, the Battle of Solomon Islands on 23 to 25 August and the Battle of Santa Cruz Island on 26 October 1942, revolved around the struggle over Guadalcanal. Although the outcome of these battles was generally even, with Japan losing the *Ryujo* at Solomon Islands and the Americans the *Hornet* at Santa Cruz, this period proved to be the low point for the United States that Japan failed to exploit. When the *Wasp* was torpedoed on 15 September, for a time the *Hornet* was the only operational American carrier in the Pacific. HMS *Indomitable* was sent to the Pacific to help out, but a more important development was that the large *Essex*-class carriers started to join the fleet. The combination of too few experienced pilots and too many U.S. carriers proved disastrous for Japan at the last great carrier Battle of the Philippine Sea on 19 to 20 June 1944. Although Japan had five large and four small carriers opposing seven large and eight small American carriers, the real difference was in pilot training, leading to an overall strength disparity much greater that the 2 : 1 ratio implied by the number of ships. The inexperienced Japanese pilots were easily shot down in what became known as the Marianas turkey shoot.

One more battle deserves brief mention. At the Battle off Samar on 25 October 1944, part of the larger Battle of Leyte Gulf, a Japanese battleship-cruiser force caught a group of American "jeep" carriers under the command of Rear Admiral Clifton Sprague, sinking the *Gambier Bay* with gunfire and damaging others. But as they were on the brink of destroying the whole force,

USS *Essex* (CV-9) at anchor. The *Essex* class started to join the fleet in 1943 and were instrumental in winning the war in the Pacific.
(U.S. Naval Institute)

the Japanese withdrew, mistaking other escort carriers for Admiral William "Bull" Halsey's large fleet carriers (which were in fact out on a wild goose chase, hunting a Japanese decoy fleet).

Table 10.1 shows the carrier losses in World War II. Four of the five major Royal Navy losses (the *Eagle, Courageous, Glorious,* and *Hermes*) were old ships, all dating to the World War I era, and the last major U.S. Navy loss was the *Hornet* in October 1942. Although carriers are often portrayed as vulnerable, they proved very robust during the greatest sea war of all time.[13]

Post–World War II Developments

Despite the aircraft carrier's importance to the Royal Navy and its absolute critical necessity for the United States Navy, as after World War I, carriers once again came under attack by the zealots of strategic bombing, who this time were sure they had an ace up their sleeve—nuclear weapons. The U.S. Navy would survive this fallacious assault, but it would virtually destroy the proud Royal Navy.

The immediate problem, however, was how to cope with the new larger and faster jet aircraft. In November 1945, the Americans with a composite jet-piston engine plane on board the CVE *Wake Island,* and in December the Royal Navy aboard HMS *Ocean,* began experiments with jet aircraft. Further trials on board the *Franklin D. Roosevelt* with a FD Phantom in July 1946 proved that jets could operate from carriers, but there were several problems. Jet aircraft had to both take off and land at higher speeds and, being heavier than the old propeller-driven planes, faced a greater risk of accidents. Solving this problem led to two of the three major postwar improvements in carriers—stream catapults and angled decks.

Catapults were not new. They were developed during World War I and used in World War II for convenience to launch planes quickly. They now became a necessity, but the current hydro-pneumatic catapults were not powerful enough for the larger, heavier jet aircraft. In 1950 Britain experimented successfully with catapults run on steam from the ship's own boiler on board the *Perseus.* They were quickly adapted by the Americans, with the *Hancock* receiving the first in 1954.

Another innovation was the angled deck. The British came up with the idea at a 1951 conference as a safety feature for heavier jets that were not always stopped by arresting gear. The angled deck allowed those making bad landings to simply "touch and go," that is, fly off for another approach. (Parked planes on straight decks would have prevented this technique.) Touch and go experiments were conducted on the HMS *Triumph* and USS *Midway* in 1952, and the USS *Antietam* was outfitted with the first angled deck later that year. Starting out as a safety device for landing, angled decks also allowed for additional launching spots.

Finally, in the early 1950s the British came up with the third major postwar innovation, the mirror landing system, conceived by Cdr. H. Goodhard. In this system, the pilot sees his image in a mirror, making the necessary adjustments by keeping a main light or "meatball" aligned with rows of green lights on either side rather than using the old "bats-man" method with a landing officer flapping his bats trying to signal the fast jet. These postwar developments of the steam catapult, angled deck, and mirror landing device in conjunction with the prewar invention of the armored deck, all considered major milestones in carrier progression, were British inventions.

Both England and the United States finished several carriers started during the war. They would be the Royal Navy's last. Four (of eight) 13,190-ton *Colossus*-class light carriers originally laid down in 1943 and 1944 were finished in late 1945 and 1946. Several were loaned to other countries. Five similar *Majestic*-class light carriers originally laid down in 1943 were completed in the late 1940s and 1950s, and most were lent to other countries. The *Hercules* was purchased by India in 1957 and finally finished in 1961 as the *Vikrant.* Four slightly larger, originally 18,300-ton *Centaur*-class light carriers laid down in 1944–45 were finished at around 22,000 tons in the mid-1950s with modern features such as angled decks. The *Hermes* was converted into a V/STOL-capable carrier in 1977 and performed well during the Falklands War in 1981. In 1986 she was sold to India, which operated her as the *Viraat*.

Great Britain's last two fleet carriers, the *Eagle* and *Ark Royal*, laid down in 1942 and 1943, were completed in 1951 and 1955 respectively. Originally designed at 36,800 tons, when completed both were around 43,340 tons. Capable of operating about forty modern aircraft, they gave the Royal Navy good capabilities until retired in the early 1970s. In addition, the Royal Navy modernized the *Victorious*, although it took seven years, from 1950 to 1957. There were several plans for postwar large-deck carriers for the Royal Navy, but none were ever built.

In the mid-1960s the RAF's bomber and missile lobby finally did what the Spanish Armada, Napoleon, the Kaiser's High Sea Fleet, and Hitler's submarines never could do—they sank the once proud Royal Navy. In a 1966 White Paper, Defense Minister Denis Healy backed by Prime Minister Harold Wilson bought the RAF's erroneous argument for strategic deterrence and sacrificed the Navy's Fleet Air Arm. At the time the Royal Navy was planning to build a new 53,000-ton, 925-by-184-foot carrier designated CVA-01. Instead, the carrier was canceled and Britain's carriers were retired. The *Ark Royal*, the last, went to the breakers in 1978. After almost three and a half centuries of ruling the sea since its victory over the Spanish Armada in 1588, without aircraft carriers the once mighty Royal Navy was reduced to second-class status. Another era had ended.

The United States also completed carriers started during the war, including six more *Essex* class and, more important, three then considered huge 42,700-ton *Midway* class laid down in 1943–44 designated CVB for battle carriers. When finished, these large ships were initially considered white elephants, but they proved useful accommodating the new jet aircraft. Ten *Essex* class and the three *Midway*s were modernized in the 1950s. The last *Essex* class was retired in the 1970s and the *Midway* and *Coral Sea* were finally retired in the early 1990s.

Like the Royal Navy, the U.S. Navy was soon entangled with the newly separated U.S. Air Force in a bomber-versus-carrier dispute, mostly over nuclear weapons. Although the American USN-USAF debate was more colorful than the typically more reserved RN-RAF debate, the end result turned out better. On 18 April 1949, the United States laid down the new, large, flush-deck 66,500-ton, 1,088-by-125-foot *United States* that would have been capable of carrying planes large enough to carry nuclear weapons. About the same time, the Air Force was lobbying for a new bomber, the B-36. Secretary of Defense Louis Johnson sided with the Air Force and canceled the *United States* only five days after she was laid down, precipitating the famous "Admirals' Revolt" that ended with the resignation of Chief of Naval Operations Admiral Louis Denfeld.[14]

USS *Ranger* (CV-61) on the way to her retirement in 1993. These post–World War II large-deck carriers have proved indispensable to the U.S. Navy.
(U.S. Naval Institute)

It seemed that the Air Force had won the debate, but a year later the Korean War started. The first air strikes were carried out by the American carrier *Valley Forge* and British carrier *Triumph*. The value of the carrier was once more demonstrated (at least to the Americans), and in 1952, the keel was laid for the *Forrestal* (CVA-59), which essentially set the pattern for all American postwar carriers. The 61,200-ton, 1,039-by-129-foot *Forrestal*, capable of carrying ninety planes, was quickly followed by the *Saratoga* (CVA-60), also laid down in 1952, *Ranger* (CVA-61, numbered after the famous Naval Academy class of 1961) in 1954, and the *Independence* (CVA-62) in 1955. Starting in 1956, four similar *Kitty Hawk* (CVA-63)–class carriers were built. The major difference between the classes was that the bridge was moved aft with two elevators instead of one placed forward.

The building of the oft-called large-deck carrier was the first of two major American contributions. The other was the move to nuclear power. In 1958, the United States laid down the USS *Enterprise* (CVAN-65, the N for indicating nuclear). Costing twice as much as the *Kitty Hawk* class being built at the same time, the *Enterprise* was a one of a kind. The U.S. Navy switched back to building two more conventional-power *Kitty Hawk* class ships:

America (CVA-66), laid down in 1961, and *John F. Kennedy* (CVA-67), laid down in 1964. In 1968, however, the U.S. Navy again switched to nuclear power, starting the 74,000-ton, 1,088-by-134-foot *Nimitz* (CVAN-68). She was considered a better design than the *Enterprise* with two rather than eight reactors, allowing for more internal space. The *Nimitz* was followed by *Eisenhower* (CVAN-69) in 1970 and *Carl Vinson* (CVAN-70) in 1975. In the late 1970s, the Carter administration attempted to start a smaller 45,000-ton conventional-power carrier program designated a CVV, capable of carrying about fifty planes, but this plan was defeated, and Congress instead approved the *Theodore Roosevelt* (CVN-71). Since that time, all carriers have been *Nimitz* follow-ons. There are currently eight *Nimitz* class commissioned, with the *Ronald Reagan* (CVN-76) building and one more planned.

Two other carrier conversions deserve brief mention. In the 1950s the U.S. Navy converted several *Essex*-class carriers for ASW, designated CVS, to counter the massive Soviet submarine force. The CVS carried both fixed-wing and helicopter ASW aircraft. Attack carriers were designated CVAs. The last CVS was decommissioned in 1974, and in 1975 the CVAs were redesignated CV (or CVN), indicating a multi-role mission. While dropping the "A" for "attack" designation at the time was considered insignificant, in the new post–Cold War political environment it has proven a mistake and the Air Force now claims that "attack" role for deep-strike missions. The U.S. Navy could easily reclaim that role with a few buckets of white paint but has been caught up in the current "jointness" disease, fearing to take on the Air Force.

Only one other country, France, has consistently operated aircraft carriers since 1945. After the war, Britain and the United States transferred light carriers to France, which used them during the Indochina war. The *Arromanches* (former British light carrier *Colossus*) and *Lafayette* (former American CVL *Langley*) were used to support French troops at Dien Bien Phu, but the 250-mile trip made adequate air support impossible. In 1955 France laid down the 22,000-ton, 870-by-104-foot *Clemenceau,* followed by the similar *Foch* in 1957. Small even by late World War II standards, these two carriers have been adequate for France's limited purposes but are incapable of operating the latest aircraft. France is building a 34,500-ton CVN, the *Charles De Gaulle,* laid down in 1989 but not expected to be completed until the late 1990s. Worse, costs are projected at over $5 billion. A sister ship was originally planned but has been postponed indefinitely.

For a time it seemed that the Soviet Union would join the exclusive aircraft carrier club. In 1962 the Soviet Union laid down the first of two large *Moskva*-class ASW helicopter carriers, gaining some experience. These were followed by four larger, 36,000-ton *Kiev* class started in 1970. With an angled deck, they certainly looked like carriers, but they operated mostly helicopters and for a time VTOL Forgers. Then, in 1983, the 60,000-ton *Admiral Kuznetzov* was started, completed in 1991. She operates advanced fixed-wing planes, but uses a ski jump for lift. Another was laid down in 1985 but never completed. Finally, in 1988 the Soviet Union started a 65,000-ton carrier that most predicted would be a full-fledged large-deck carrier complete with catapults, but, caught up in the post–Cold War budget crunch, it was never finished. Currently, Russia is struggling to keep the *Admiral Kuznetzov* operational.

A few other countries have operated conventional carriers. Canada, Australia, and the Netherlands operated former British carriers through the 1960s. Both Argentina and Brazil still carry former British *Colossus*-class carriers on their books. While the Brazilian carrier renamed *Minas Gerais* is still operational, the Argentinean *Veinticinco de Mayo* has been in port for years. Currently Argentinean pilots train on the *Minas Gerais*. India also operates former British carriers as V/STOL ships.

There has been something of a renaissance for smaller helicopter and V/STOL carriers, and once again, the Royal Navy was in the lead. In 1960 it tested the first V/STOL (vertical and/or short takeoff and landing) plane that eventually became the Harrier—often called a "jump-jet" because it takes off vertically like a helicopter but then flies like a conventional airplane. There was only limited interest until the disastrous 1966 decision to do away with carriers. In 1967, the Royal Navy began plans for a helicopter-carrying

HMS *Ark Royal*, a V/STOL carrier with a "ski jump" for Harrier jump jets. (U.S. Naval Institute)

cruiser that led to the euphemistic "through-deck" cruiser *Invincible,* which when completed in 1980 looked remarkably like a small carrier, belying any myth that Royal Navy admirals have no sense of humor. The 16,000-ton *Invincible,* capable of carrying a mix of fourteen Harriers and helicopters, was followed by two more with traditional British carrier names, *Illustrious* and *Ark Royal.* A major contribution, again developed by the British, was the so-called ski-jump elevated flight-deck ramp that provides extra lift for the Harriers, allowing them to carry an extra 1,200 pounds for greater range or payload. (Taking off vertically expends considerable fuel.)

The United States looked at a small, 10,000-ton sea control ship (SCS) and a larger, 20,000-ton V/STOL support ship (VSS) in the mid-1970s, but they were never built. The SCS design was used by Spain for its 16,700-ton full load *Principe De Asturias,* completed in 1988, with a similar ship built by Spain for Thailand. In 1985 the Italian navy completed the 10,000-ton *Giuseppe Garibaldi,* then finally won a battle with its own air force allowing them to operate Sea Harriers. India operates V/STOL carriers with ski jumps. The United States has twelve large, 40,000-ton amphibious assault V/STOL-capable ships that operate Sea Harriers, but they do not have ski jumps for parochial reasons. The Marines fear they will be taken over by Navy air, while Navy Air fears Congress will force them to buy these ships at the expense of the large-deck *Nimitz* class. While these V/STOL carriers with their Sea Harriers are adequate for certain situations, as witnessed by their skillful use by the Royal Navy during the Falklands campaign, they are by no means front-line combatant ships.[15]

Carriers have proven very flexible in the post–World War II era. They provided some of the earliest responses during the Korean War. During the Vietnam War carriers were constantly on station, performing duties, and, unlike air bases, none were lost when North Vietnam took over South Vietnam. The British could not have conducted the Falklands War without the support of the V/STOL carriers. And at least once a year, the carriers have proven useful in responding to a crisis.

Conclusion

Starting out as jury-rigged platforms on old cruisers and merchantmen at the turn of the century, carriers have developed into the primary capital ship. During the early years of World War I most aircraft carriers were actually seaplane carriers, but by the end of that war the familiar flattop shape had appeared. In the 1920s development was boosted with the conversion of former large battle cruisers that allowed for greater capacity. Originally viewed as large white elephants, the large-deck carriers proved indispensable during World War II and became the standard in the postwar period. But their cost has restricted all but a few countries from building them.

Table 10.2 Aircraft Carrier Comparisons

Class	Type	Navy	Year	Displacement	Dimensions	Number Planes	Speed
Ark Royal	AVP	RN	1914	7,080/7,450	366 × 51 × 18	5 float, 2 land	11
Argus	CV	RN	1918	14,550/16,500	566 × 68 × 21	20	20
Langley	CV	USN	1922	13,990/14,700	542 × 65 × 21	30 wheel, 6 float	15.5
Lexington	CV	USN	1927	37,700/43,050	888 × 105 × 33	63	33
Béarn	CV	Fr	1927	22,150/28,400	599 × 89 × 30.5	40	21.5
Yorktown	CV	USN	1937	19,900/25,500	809 × 83 × 26	96	32.5
Ark Royal	CV	RN	1938	22,000/27,720	800 × 95 × 28	60	31
Shokaku	CV	Jp	1941	25,700/32,100	845 × 85 × 29	72	34.2
Essex	CV	USN	1942	27,200/34,880	888 × 93 × 147.5	91	32.7
Casablanca	CVE	USN	1943	8,200/10,900	512 × 65 × 108	27	19
Colossus	CVL	RN	1944	13,190/18,300	694 × 80 × 23	37	25
Ark Royal	CV	RN	1955	43,340/53,060	804 × 113 × 36	36	31
Forrestal	CV	USN	1955	61,200/78,500	1039 × 129 × 34	90	33
Clemenceau	CV	Fr	1961	22,000/32,780	870 × 104 × 28	40	32
Nimitz	CVN	USN	1975	74,000/91,440	1088 × 134 × 37	90	30+
Invincible	V/STOL	RN	1980	16,000/19,500	677 × 115 × 24	14	28
G. Garibaldi	V/STOL	It	1985	10,000/13,850	591 × 100 × 22	72	29.5
Asturias	V/STOL	Spain	1988	14,000/16,700	643 × 80 × 31	17	26
Kuznetzov	CV	Ru	1991	60,000/67,000	984 × 125 × 36	18 fixed, 12 helicopters	30
C. De Gaulle	CVN	Fr	1999	34,500/36,600	858 × 103 × 28	40	27

Notes: Year = year completed. Displacement = standard/deep. Dimensions = overall length by width by draft in feet. Airplane numbers can vary according to type.

The immediate future of the aircraft carrier is assured in both the United States and French (and perhaps also Russian) navies. The ten American *Nimitz*-class carriers built and building will last well into the twenty-first century, as will the French *De Gaulle*. But their costs are becoming prohibitive for most peacetime navies. Rumors of China building a carrier have circulated for years, but the building of the *Charles De Gaulle* illustrates the difficulties facing any country such as China and perhaps a resurgent Russia in building large-deck carriers. Even U.S. Navy officials comment that the carrier requested at the end of the 1990s will be "transitional." Currently there are efforts to develop an "advanced" or ASTOVL plane that could open up new possibilities for smaller carriers.

But it will be costs, not capabilities, that drive the carrier from the seas. No one questions their record during World War II or even their postwar record. At least once a year, the familiar "Where are the carriers?" is asked by a president looking to send a quick response to the latest crisis. While the U.S. Air Force has talked about the "virtual presence" of bombers, it is still the "real presence" of the carriers that makes the difference.

Amphibious Ships 11

AMPHIBIOUS SHIPS ARE both the oldest and newest of warships. They are the oldest in the sense that the earliest depiction of ships in the Age of Galleys shows them transporting troops, and, since galleys usually beached rather than docked, by today's terminology they would be considered amphibious ships. They are the newest because it was not until World War II, in fact well into the war in 1943, that specifically designed amphibious ships started to appear in any number. Yet they quickly became crucial to the Allies in Europe and especially the Pacific and by the end of the war were by far the most numerous warships, numbering in the thousands. Although there was some thought that the new post–World War II nuclear age would see the end of amphibious operations with their concentration of ships making easy targets for atomic weapons, they have survived and even flourished. One of the most famous amphibious landings, Inchon in 1950, took place after World War II, and today, the whole direction of the U.S. Navy is based on a quasi-amphibious "littoral strategy."

As implied by calling amphibious ships both the oldest and newest of warships, there is a need for definitions. Throughout history ships have carried troops and conducted landings, many even over the beach. The ships were not specifically designed for this task, however, but were simply other warships or merchantmen carrying troops. Also, most of these were unopposed "landings" using the ship's boats rather than opposed "assaults" requiring specifically designed landing craft. Thus an amphibious ship, as opposed to a troop transport, can be defined as a specifically designed ship usually with distinctive landing craft capable of carrying out an opposed amphibious assault.

Early Precedents

Throughout history ships have carried troops for landings. The earliest depiction of warships from ancient Egypt are vessels carrying troops, and the Sea Peoples from the 1200 B.C. era conducted landings on a continuous basis. There were even some slight modifications. The ancient Greeks jury-rigged older triremes for both horse and troop carriers, usually removing the lower one or two tiers of rowers to make room for horse stalls or benches for troops. The 490 B.C. Persian Campaign of Marathon against the Greeks is often cited as the first major amphibious assault, and in 480 B.C. the Athenians enlisted sea soldiers called Epibatae, sometimes referred to as the world's first marines. Throughout ancient times there were both large and small movements of troops by sea. More prevalent, however, were raids from the sea, with the Vikings conducting the most famous.

There were also many instances of amphibious operations during the Age of Sail. The early cogs were considered good troop carriers, and some were jury-rigged to carry horses. The Spanish Armada, often considered the start of the Age of Sail, was really a troop-carrying fleet to invade England. The Armada was to pick up more soldiers in Holland to be transported by barges but was thwarted by the English fleet. England formally organized marines in 1664; the Dutch followed in 1665. Peter the Great organized a naval infantry in 1705 and in 1713 skillfully conducted amphibious landings against Sweden using his galleys to outflank the Swedish army. Perhaps the most famous of all marines, the U.S. Marine Corps, mark their birthday on 10 November 1775, when Congress formally established two battalions. British general Sir Ralph Abercromby is sometimes considered the father of forced entry, conducting opposed amphibious landing against the Dutch in 1799 and later the French in Egypt.

There are, in short, many, many examples of what could be considered amphibious landings throughout history.[1] In all these cases, however, the ships were not specifically designed for these purposes, and with very few exceptions, these were all landings rather than opposed assaults. Even during the Age of Steam and the early modern period, when new ship types were cropping up constantly, little thought was given to designing ships for this role and landings continued to be made from merchantmen and standard warships using ships' boats. One exception for landing craft occurred during the era of paddle wheelers when specially designed boats called paddle box boats were used. D. K. Brown writes: "These boats carried about one hundred men for landing parties and were stowed, upside down, on the paddle boxes which the boats were shaped to fit."[2] Another exception might be the two Italian *Italia*-class predreadnoughts, completed in 1885 and 1887, that were designed with the capability of transporting a ten-thousand-man infantry division.

World War I

It was not until World War I that serious thought was given to designing amphibious landing craft (although not ships), and had it been up to First Lord of the Admiralty Winston Churchill, there might have been several assaults. Even before the war broke out, Churchill had ordered studies for landings on the Dutch, Danish, and Scandinavian coasts, as well as Germany, to help bottle up the German fleet. These proposals were met with only luke-warm enthusiasm (especially against the neutral countries) and none were carried out.[3] When Admiral Fisher returned to the Admiralty in 1914, how-ever, among his first building programs for new ships were orders for two hundred large and sixty small landing barges complete with steel shields for protection.[4]

In November 1914 proposals were made for a landing on the Belgian port of Zeebrugge, then being used by German submarines. In 1918 the Royal Navy finally mounted an assault on Zeebrugge using the old cruiser *Vindic-tive* converted with side ramps and machine guns for protection. Although a few blockships were sunk, the Germans easily beat off the attack and then quickly dredged around the sunken ships.

The only major amphibious assault during the war was the ill-fated Gal-lipoli operation proposed by Winston Churchill to open a second front by invading Turkey. The campaign started in January 1915 with battleship operations, followed by the main assault on 25 April. With one exception, however, as had been the practice throughout history, the ships used were merchantmen or other warships. That one exception was the former small collier *River Clyde* converted into an amphibious ship with gangways fitted to her sides and "sally ports" cut into her side for off-loading troops. For protection and covering fire, sandbag machine-gun placements were mounted on her superstructure. Thus to the *River Clyde* usually goes the honor of being the world's first amphibious ship, but her use was less than successful. She ran aground in water too deep for the troops to disembark and came under heavy Turkish fire. A barge was brought alongside, but after a few futile attempts to off-load troops, the operation was called off until darkness. British casualties on the *River Clyde* were seven hundred dead or wounded in this first assault.

Although the *River Clyde* was the only major amphibious ship built or con-verted during the war, smaller amphibious craft were used. For the later Gal-lipoli landing at Suvla Bay on 8 August, the Royal Navy hurriedly built nearly two hundred 160-ton craft with armor and ramps called X-Lighters. Also used were the specialized armored landing barges, nicknamed "beetles," that Fisher had originally ordered for Baltic operations. Later Y-Lighters, which were simply pontoon barges with outboard motors, were used. Whereas the original 25 April landing had met stiff resistance and quickly bogged down, the Suvla landing was successful, but unfortunately the British general failed to exploit the situation. Turkish troops were rushed to the area, and the momentum was lost and landing stalemated. The Allies finally evacuated in January 1916. Gallipoli was a disaster. Lord Fisher resigned, and Winston Churchill was forced out of the cabinet.

Other countries also developed a few amphibious ships. The Russians converted some shallow-draft merchant ships with gangways for operations in the Black Sea. They also built small craft called "Russud" with ramps for off-loading. The Germans similarly built some small craft with ramps for their Baltic operations, but most of these still fell into the "jury-rig" category.[5]

More important for the future of amphibious warfare were the supposed lessons from Gallipoli that operations against fortified positions with modern weapons such as better artillery and machine guns were simply not feasible. Turkish gunners had indeed had a field day against the *River Clyde,* and even though both major initial assaults had been successful, the Allies were never able to penetrate the Turkish defenses. Historians have found a variety of reasons, including timid leadership on the part of the British generals, especially for failing to exploit the successful second flanking movement at Suvla Bay on 8 August. While part of that success was attributed to surprise, it was also the first to use the specialized landing craft, the X-Lighters and "beetles." But the immediate lesson following World War I—like that following World War II—was that amphibious warfare was dead.

The Interwar Period

Despite the generally accepted lessons of Gallipoli, amphibious operations were not completely forgotten during the interwar period. The United States Marine Corps is usually cited as the main supporter of continuing amphibious operations, and it did conduct many of the major studies and exercises of the period, but Britain also continued some interest.[6] A seminal event came in a 1921 report when the eccentric Major Earl H. "Pete" Ellis wrote a fifty-thousand-word plan to the commandant of the Marine Corps recommending a Pacific island-hopping strategy for the Marines complete with reef-crossing vehicles. He had written this report upon returning from a secret mission to the Pacific. Ellis died in 1923 while on another trip to the Pacific Islands under mysterious circumstances. There were some suspicions that he was poisoned by the Japanese, but more likely his death was alcohol-related.[7] His recommendations were accepted, and from 1922 on, the Marines concentrated on the development of amphibious doctrine conducting annual landing exercises. As usual, most were with the ship's own boats.

Starting in 1924, the Marines began experimenting with two different types of amphibious landing craft: one with a bow ramp and the other an amphibious tractor. After doctrine, development of these landing craft would be the Marines' greatest contribution. The first accomplishment was the adoption of the Higgins boat as a landing craft. In 1926 a New Orleans boat builder named Andrew Jackson Higgins had built a shallow-water boat called *Eureka* for use on the lower Mississippi River. In 1936 the Marines tested the boat, which they and Higgins eventually developed first into the 37-foot LCP(L) for landing craft personnel (large), capable of carrying thirty-six troops or four tons of cargo and later in 1941 the LCP(R) with a ramp. Further developments and experiments with the LCPs led to the more famous LCVP, landing craft vehicle and personnel, thousands of which were built during the war. LCVPs are still carried on some amphibious ships.

The other major accomplishment was the development of "amtracs," the LVT "landing vehicle, tracked" or "alligators." In the early 1920s the Marines experimented with an early design by J. Walter Christie that proved unsatisfactory. In the 1930s, however, Donald Roebling developed a tracked vehicle for rescue work in the Florida Everglades swamps. The Marines tested the vehicle and in 1940 started producing LVT "alligators," which proved crucial in certain landings in the Pacific because of their capabilities to cross coral reefs and move troops and supplies actually on the beach. In the United States, the whole amphibious force is often called the "gator" force. LVT-1 started joining the fleet in the summer of 1941, just in time for the war. Later, LVT(A)s (for armored) with first 37 mm and later 75 mm guns would be built.

The U.S. Navy did build one amphibious ship during the interwar period. In 1936 the old "four piper" destroyer *Manley* was converted into a "fast transport," designated APD. Her torpedo tubes and some machinery were removed to make room for 120 troops and four LCPs. Later, thirty-six more destroyers and ninety-six destroyer escorts would be converted to APDs. The APDs would prove useful for raiding parties during World War II.

Japan also studied amphibious warfare for its own island-hopping plans in the Pacific and holds the honor of building the first truly amphibious ship. This was the 8,100-ton, 492-foot-long *Shinshu Maru*, built in 1933 for the army, not the navy. She was truly a revolutionary ship, the precursor of today's LSDs and even LPDs. The *Shinshu Maru* had stern doors and room for twenty landing craft and originally carried float planes with space for catapults, although they were never installed. The United States Navy would not complete an LSD until 1943 or a limited air capable LPD until 1960. During the war, Japan would convert four other former liners and merchant ships into similar LSD-type ships. Two, the *Akitsu Maru* and *Nigitsu Maru,* had flight decks to transport aircraft. Japan also built smaller landing craft with bows, the best known of which was the 46-foot *Daihatsu*. It was after seeing a picture of one of Japan's landing craft that Higgins and the Marines developed the LCP(R).

Despite the fiasco at Gallipoli, the Royal Navy did not give up completely on amphibious warfare and it holds the honor—or at least the shared honor—of developing the most famous of the World War II amphibious ships: the LST, officially known as landing ship tank but sarcastically—although affectionately—called "large slow targets" by their crews because their top speed was typically only 10 to 12 knots. As early as 1921, the Royal Navy formed a Landing Craft Committee, which led to a small motor landing craft (MLC) in 1926 and an improved design in 1929 capable of carrying a 16-ton truck. Only minor progress was made during the 1930s, but that changed when the war began for England in 1939. In 1940 England developed the LCA, landing craft assault, to be carried on larger troop ships and then the larger LCM, landing craft mechanized, capable of carrying a light tank.

After the Dunkirk evacuation, there was need for a larger craft to carry more tanks. In July 1940, after much prodding by Winston Churchill, the Admiralty ordered the LCT, or landing craft tank. These first LCTs were 226 tons, 152 feet long, capable of carrying three tanks. Later versions were slightly larger but still more or less in the "craft" size of ships. The LCT is usually cited as the forerunner of the famous LST developed during the war.

World War II

By 1940, when the war had started in Europe but was still a year away in the Pacific, there were only a handful of amphibious ships and construction of smaller landing craft and boats was barely under way. The ships were the Japanese *Shinshu Maru* and the American APD *Manley*. Only five more destroyers were converted before Pearl Harbor. The British were in the process of converting some merchantmen into troop transport landing ship infantry, large or LSI(L). The situation was not much better for landing craft. The Japanese had some *Daihatsu*, but the British were just starting to build LCAs, LCMs, and larger LCTs and the Americans LCPs and LVTs. Yet, as shown in table 11.1, before the war's end, hundreds of ships and thousands of landing craft would be built.

In 1940 the British had started building LCTs, and although subsequent models were larger, there was still a need for an even larger, seagoing version, or what became known as an "Atlantic LCT." As an interim measure, the Royal Navy converted three shallow-draft tankers originally built to pass over the sandbars of Lake Maracaibo, Venezuela. The "Maracaibo" LSTs

Table 11.1 Amphibious Ship Balance in World War II

Type	Britain	U.S.	Japan
LST	226	982	90
LSM/LCT-size	1,487	1,992	
LCI-size	420	1,139	
LSD	4	27	4
APD	0	132	22
AKA	7	108	
APA	32	241	
Command	5	17	
TOTAL	2,181	4,638	116

NOTES: LSM/LCT = Medium sized with some ocean capabilities (RN: LCT) (USN: LSM). AKA = Attack cargo transports carriers (RN: LSS, LSG & LSC) (USN: AKA). APA = Attack transports for personnel (RN: LSI series) (USN: APA).

were finished in July 1941, giving these conversions the honor of being the first LSTs. At the same time, the British also began work on a new design later designated LST(1). They were not actually laid down until 1942, the first not commissioned until 1943, and only three were ever built. These were 3,600 tons, 390 feet long, capable of carrying twenty medium tanks and almost two hundred troops.

Although there was a definite need for these large LSTs, the English shipbuilding facilities were taxed to the limits, so the scene shifted to the United States, leading to some confusion as to who should get the ultimate credit for the LST. In November 1941 a British delegation arrived to consult with the U.S. Navy on a new LST design. An American designer, John Niedernmair, in November had seen a brief outline of the British proposal but is usually credited with the new design that became known as LST (2). Regardless, USS LST-1 was finally laid down on 10 June 1942 and completed only six months later in December 1942.[8] This new design LST was 2,370 tons, 328 feet, capable of carrying about twenty medium tanks and 160 troops. Vehicles were off-loaded via a ramp in the bow doors. It was one of the most successful ship designs in history, with 1,052 authorized and 982 actually built before the war's end.

Several other smaller, similar important types were built that fall in between the amphibious ship and craft range. The most numerous were 240-ton, 158-foot-long LCI(L), landing craft infantry (large), of which a thousand were built during the war in the United States with many sent to Britain on lend-lease arrangements. The first was completed on 9 October 1942. They did not have a ramp, but rather beached and discharged their troops from gangways. LCTs landing craft were built throughout the war in ever-increasing sizes. In the United States the LCT(7) was designated LSM, landing ship medium. They were 520 tons and 196 feet, and about 550 were built. And there were several variations of these modes such as LSM(R)s and LCI(R)s with rockets for fire support.

Several other amphibious ship types were built or converted during the war. Both the British and Americans converted former merchantmen to amphibious roles. The British built large LSIs, converted merchantmen. In the United States two modes were built, attack transport (APA) and attack cargo (AKA) ships. These ships would off-load cargo with cranes from the AKA, with the troops going down nets on the APA into landing craft such as LCVPs or the larger LCM "mike" boats. This was a slow process that led to the most innovative of the World War II amphibious ships, the landing ship dock, LSD. The LSDs had 252-foot-long well decks that could accommodate three LCTs or fourteen LCMs. The well decks were flooded so the LCTs or LCMs could be easily driven out. Although originally a British idea, they were built only in the United States. The first was the 4,000-ton, 458-foot *Ashland* (LSD-1) commissioned in June 1943.

Finally, both the United States and England built amphibious command ships, designated LSH (landing ship headquarters) in the Royal Navy and AGCs in the U.S. Navy. It was discovered very early on that trying to conduct complex amphibious operations with a normal ship's communications system, even those found on larger warships such as battleships and cruisers, was virtually impossible because of all the communications and control requirements.

Although Japan had built the world's first amphibious ship and the *Daihatsu* landing craft in the interwar period, most of its amphibious conquests in the 1941–42 period were made with converted merchantmen rather than specialized amphibious ships. During the war the Japanese converted twenty-one old destroyers to fast transport (similar to the American APDs) with ramps at their sterns to launch landing craft. These fast transports were useful for resupplying the Japanese islands during the war. Also during the war Japan built a small LST-type vessel.

Germany built and converted some small craft for amphibious roles. For Operation Sealion to invade England, Germany gathered almost four thousand small craft. The most numerous were some nineteen hundred river barges (prahms) modified with bow ramps to carry tanks. The operation was called off in September 1941, much to the relief of the German army and navy.

AMPHIBIOUS WARFARE is invariably associated with the many landings by the Marines in the Pacific, but in fact, some of the largest assaults were conducted by the Army in the European theater. There were six major amphibious operations, five in the Mediterranean. The Mediterranean amphibious assaults were Operation Torch, the North African invasion on 8 November 1942; Operation Husky on Sicily on 10 July 1943; Operation Avalanche to invade Italy on 9 September 1943; followed by Operation Shingle at Anzio on 22 January 1944 to outflank the Germans; and finally the Allied invasion of southern France, Operation Dragoon, on 15 August 1944. With the possible exception of Anzio, all of these were considered very successful. At Anzio, as at Suvla Bay in 1915, the landing was successful, but the commanding general failed to exploit the situation and got bogged down. Operation Husky in Sicily in July 1943 was important as the first in which LSTs took part in any number.

The largest amphibious landing by far in World War II was Operation Overlord, the invasion of Europe at Normandy on D-Day, 6 June 1944. In that landing there were almost 2,300 landing ships and large landing craft, including 236 LSTs, 502 LCAs, 248 LCIs, and 837 LCTs. Twelve command ships were required for that complex operation. Even with all these ships and craft, Allied leaders felt they needed more. One of the reasons the landing had been delayed from 1942 to 1943 and finally 1944 was the lack of the crucial LSTs, causing Winston Churchill to write to General George Marshall: "The whole of this difficult question only arises out of the absurd shortage of L.S.T.s. How is it that the plans of two great empires like Britain and the United States should be so much hamstrung and limited by a hundred or two of the particular vessels will never be understood in history?"

It was in the Pacific island-hopping strategy of the United States, however, where the amphibious ships and craft became crucial for the conduct of the war, not just for initial landings as in Europe. With the exception of the August 1942 Guadalcanal landing, which was carried out by nonamphibious ships (although some craft were used), all the other assaults were by amphibious ships. At Guadalcanal, fortunately, the "gators" were not needed because the Japanese were totally surprised. Unfortunately, that element of surprise never occurred again, and they were certainly needed for the other landings. The first major appearance of LSTs was the landing at Rendova Island (opposite the Japanese air base on New Georgia) on 30 June 1943. Five months later came Tarawa—bloody Tarawa—that would have been bloodier without the amtracs. The landing boats got hung up on reefs, forcing the Marines

LSTs land troops on Bougainville during the Solomons campaign. These ships, nicknamed "large, slow targets," were indispensable for the many amphibious landings during World War II.
(U.S. Naval Institute)

to wade ashore under intense fire. Only the amtracs were able to operate. Kwajalein, Saipan, Peleliu, Iwo Jima, Okinawa, and the many other dozens of amphibious landings would have been impossible without these hastily built amphibious ships and craft.

Including river crossings, raids, and both small- and large-scale assaults, there were approximately six hundred amphibious landings during World War II.[9] Many, if not most, could not have been carried out without the specialized ships and landing craft that, as shown in table 11.1, numbered in the thousands at the end of the war. These numbers are even more amazing considering that in 1939, even 1941, many of these ships had not even been designed.

Post–World War II Period

The dawning of the atomic age raised questions about the future of navies and seapower, and in no area were those questions and doubts more acute than for the future of amphibious operations because their concentration of ships made seemingly tempting targets for nuclear weapons. The July 1946 Bikini tests, witnessed by Marine generals, seemed to prove that thesis. The second detonation was actually set off under an LSM landing ship, which instantly disintegrated. Head of the Manhattan Project Army Major General Leslie Groves wrote, "The tests clearly established that atomic weapons could easily rout any major beach attack" and Marine Corps Lieutenant General Roy Geiger agreed, writing to the commandant, "I cannot visualize another landing such as was executed at Normandy or Okinawa."[10]

The Marines did not give up, and in December 1946 they decided to test two concepts that eventually led to a postwar revolution in amphibious operations. These were the use of seaplanes, which did not work out, and the use of helicopters, which did. The seaplane firm Convair was given funds to produce a "flying LST," designated the R3Y Tradewind. The large, four-engine Tradewind, with a takeoff weight of 175,000 pounds, could carry one hundred troops and had the capabilities to taxi up to the beach to discharge her troops and small vehicles through an upward-lifting bow door. Eleven were built following initial tests in February 1954, but the plane had continuous mechanical problems and was eventually dropped. Besides, helicopters as an alternative were looking more attractive.

The Marines had actually tested a helicopter predecessor called the autogiro in 1931 against guerrillas in Nicaragua, but it had not proven effective. Helicopters were developed in the later years of World War II. The first Marine experimental helicopter assault took place in January 1948, when five HO3S helicopters successfully airlifted sixty-six Marines from the escort carrier *Palau*. This use of helicopters became known as "vertical envelopment." Exercises continued, and in May 1955 the *Thetis Bay* (CVE-90) was converted into a helicopter assault aircraft carrier designated CVHA-1. Completed in 1956, she proved successful, leading to the laying down in 1959 of the first of seven *Iwo Jima* class designated LPH, popularly called a "landing platform helicopter" but officially an amphibious assault ship. These ships are 18,000 tons full load, 602 feet long, and capable of carrying twenty-five helicopters and nineteen hundred troops.

While the LPHs were considered successful ships, they were criticized for being one-dimensional with no facilities for landing craft. This fault led to the building of twelve more amphibious assault ships with well decks. There were five *Tarawa*-class LHAs built from 1971 through 1980, followed by seven similar LHD *Wasp* class started in the mid-1980s. Ships from both classes are approximately 40,000 tons full load and 840 feet long with 268-foot-long well decks and are capable of carrying a variety of landing craft, from large LCUs to LCMs and LVTPs. Both also have capabilities for carrying V/STOL planes such as the Harrier as well as helicopters. The main difference in capabilities between the LHAs and LHDs is that the latter were specifically designed to carry V/STOL planes and air-cushion landing craft (LCACs), another major postwar development in amphibious warfare. The LCACs can travel at over 40 knots, four times the speed of previous landing craft. The United States is also starting to build the V-22 Osprey so-called tilt-rotor airplane that takes off like a helicopter and then tilts its rotor forward to fly like a conventional plane with about twice the speed and range of helicopters. In sum, with the V/STOL Harrier, tilt-rotor Osprey, and air-cushion LCACs, the amphibious force for the first time will be able to conduct operations over the horizon (OTH).

There have also been other improvements. The U.S. Navy's main amphibious goal in the 1950s was to build a fast "20-knot" force. Attempts were made to overcome the "slow" LST problem with two postwar classes, the *Terrebonne Parish* (LST-1156) class built in the early 1950s making 15 knots and the *Suffolk County* (LST-1173) class in the late 1950s making about 17, but the bow door configurations limited speed. Finally the Navy gave up, building the *Newport* (LST-1179) class in the mid-1960s, which had a hideous bow horn arrangement for lowering a ramp over the pointed bow instead of using bow doors. These LSTs are now being phased out, much to the chagrin of many because their departure will leave the U.S. Navy with no beaching capabilities except for smaller landing craft.

LSDs continue to be built, with the latest version the almost 16,000 tons full load, 610-foot-long *Whidbey Island* (LSD-41) class built during the 1980s. These were followed by the *Harpers Ferry* (LSD-49) "cargo variant," which has a smaller well deck but increases cargo capacity from the 500 cubic feet of the *Whidbey Island* class to 40,000 cubic feet. A somewhat similar ship, designated LPD for amphibious transport dock but sometimes unofficially called "landing platform dock" since they have limited helicopter capabilities, was also built. The first three were almost 14,000 tons full load, 521-feet-long *Raleigh* class, laid down in the 1960s, followed by twelve larger approximately 17,000-ton, 569-feet-long *Austin* class built from 1963 through 1971. The main difference between an LSD and LPD is that the latter has the well deck enclosed, allowing for a helicopter landing area and a small hangar. Currently the United States Navy is building a new, sophisticated LPD-17 class.

Other major navies have built amphibious ships in the post–World War II era. Although none have matched the U.S. Navy's gator force, there have been some interesting designs. The Royal Navy also recognized the utility of helicopters and after experimenting with old light carriers *Ocean* and *Theseus* in 1956 converted the newer light carriers *Albion* and *Bulwark* into "commando ships" in the late 1950s. Starting in the early 1960s, the Royal Navy built several amphibious ships, including two assault ships similar to American LPDs, the *Fearless* and *Intrepid,* and six *Sir Lancelot*–class LSL, logistic landing ships, similar to LSTs but with stern doors as well as bow doors. Ironically, the Royal Navy was in the process of retiring some of these ships when the Falklands War started.

In the late 1950s France built five *Trieux*-class LSTs, followed by two 8,500 tons full load LPD-type ships, the *Ouragan* and *Orage,* designated TCD for *Transport de Chalands de Debarquement.* Their design is unique with the bridge to one side to make room for helicopters. France is building two larger 11,800-ton *Foudre*-class TCDs with the capabilities for carrying fourteen hundred troops. Italy built three 5,000-ton, 437-foot-long LPD-type *San Giorgio*–class ships in the late 1980s with both a well deck and bow doors, allowing cargo to be off-loaded at either end. Japan has built the 11,000-ton *Oosumi* dock landing ship (which actually resembles a small carrier) that can accommodate helicopters and LCACs, and both the Netherlands and Spain have built 12,750-ton LPDs with multiple capabilities. Many of these multicapable ships are referred to as LSD "dock" landing ships in the literature, but because they have helicopter capabilities they should probably be called LPDs—or in some cases, since they resemble mini-carriers with well decks, LHAs.

The Soviet Union started building amphibious ships in the late 1950s and early 1960s, eventually creating some of the most interesting designs. In the beginning, these were essentially LST-type ships such as the small 770-ton "Polnocny" class built in Poland. These were followed by larger 3,200-ton "Ropucha" and 3,400-ton "Alligator" classes, which, like the British LSL, had both bow and stern ramps for off-loading. In 1978 the large 11,000-ton, 518-foot-long *Ivan Rogov* was launched. They have sometimes been compared to American LHAs because they have both well decks and helicopter capabilities, but the Russian craft are more limited. The *Ivan Rogov*s caused quite a stir in Western naval circles at the time, but only three were

The Italian LPD *San Giorgio*. Many countries have now built these multicapable amphibious ships with facilities for helicopters, landing craft, and well decks.
(U.S. Naval Institute)

ever built. At about the same time the Soviet navy started deploying overseas, sending some of these amphibious ships to Third World areas. Reports of a bombardment of Eritrean positions by an Alligator in 1978 were seen as a very ominous sign.

The Soviet navy built two other interesting types. In the 1970s, it built some very large air-cushion landing craft similar to the British craft that cross the English Channel. They had both bow and stern doors. The Soviets also tested the "wing-in-ground" (WIG) concept, essentially an airplane that skims just above the waves. One, dubbed the "Caspian Sea Monster," was powered by eight turbojets and reportedly had a speed of 300 knots and a range of 3,000 miles. They are sometimes compared to the American "flying LST" experiments, but that was a seaplane.

Smaller navies operate amphibious ships, but in most cases they are former American and British ships and craft. World War II–era LSTs and larger landing craft such as LCTs, LSIs, and LCUs can still be found in some navies, a great testimony to the durability of ships and craft very hurriedly built during wartime conditions.

CONTRARY TO ALL the gloomy predictions in the immediate post–World War II period, amphibious operations did not disappear. One of the more famous pessimistic predictions was General Omar Bradley's comment in 1949 before a congressional committee: "I am wondering if we shall ever have another large-scale amphibious operation." A year later, in September

1950, during the Korean War, General of the Army Douglas MacArthur would conduct his flanking Inchon assault, one of the most famous amphibious landings in all history. Once again, it was the LSTs that proved crucial. Although there has not been such a large landing since 1950, there have been numerous smaller assaults, all considered important.

Another gloomy assessment came in the mid-1970s after the Vietnam War in a book entitled *Where Does the Marine Corps Go from Here?* which predicted, once again, that amphibious operations were passé.[11] Yet again, during the 1980s and 1990s, there have been numerous amphibious operations. The most famous was the British assault during the Falklands War, which came just before the Royal Navy was about to retire several of its amphibious ships. Had the Argentineans waited six months, Britain might not have been able to mount the assault. As it was, the British force was a jury-rigged fleet including the famed liner *Queen Elizabeth* requisitioned into service as a troop transport. More recent examples include the American-led United Nations intervention in Somalia in 1991, and almost every year there is at least one rescue attempt using amphibious ships.[12]

Currently the United States Navy keeps two Amphibious Ready Groups (ARGs) in forward areas, one in the Pacific and the other in the Mediterranean or Persian Gulf areas. Finally, although not amphibious ships per se, the U.S. Navy also operates three civilian-manned Maritime Prepositioning Ship (MPS) squadrons of three to four ships apiece around the world that carry weapons and equipment and vehicles for the Marine Corps with similar ships for the Army. More important, with the demise of the old Soviet fleet, the strategy of the U.S. Navy is now focused on littoral areas, which is essentially a quasi-amphibious strategy. Besides aircraft carriers, nothing differentiates the U.S. Navy from other navies more than its large amphibious capabilities.

Conclusion

Amphibious warfare and warships have gone through four stages of development. First was what might be called the ad hoc stage, that is, simply using regular warships and merchantmen for troop carriers put ashore by the ship's regular boats. This was the way amphibious operations were conducted throughout most of history. Second was the specialized stage with ships and landing craft built specifically for amphibious assaults. This really did not start until the eve of World War II, and many specialized ships and craft were built during the war.

Third came the limited over-the-horizon stage in the late 1950s, when helicopters and special helicopter amphibious ships such as LPHs and commando ships were built. This gave the commanders limited over-the-horizon capabilities, although the bulk of material still needed to be landed by land-

Table 11.2 Amphibious Ship and Craft Comparisons

Class	Type	Navy	Year	Displacement	Dimensions	Characteristics
Ships						
Shinshu Maru	LSD	Jp	1935	9,000/11,800	492 × 72 × 27	20 landing craft, 20 airplanes
Glenearn	LSI(L)	RN	1940	9,800	511 × 67 × 32	24 LCA, 3 LCM, 1090 troops
LST 1	LST	USN	1942	2,370/4,080	328 × 50 × 4	20-25 tanks, 163 troops
Ashland	LSD	USN	1942	4,000/8,000	458 × 72 × 16	LCTs or LCMs, 250 troops
Haskell	APA	USN	1943	14,800 full	455 × 62 × 24	22 LCVP, 2 LCM, 1561 troops
Andromeda	AKA	USN	1943	14,000 full	459 × 63 × 26	16 LCVP, 8 LCM, 4450 tons cargo
Suffolk County	LST	USN	1956	3,860/7,850	442 × 62 × 13.5	LCU, LCVP, Amtracs, 635 troops
Raleigh	LPD	USN	1962	8,050/13,750	513 × 84 × 20.5	LCU, LCMS, helos, 930 troops
Sir Lancelot	LSL	RN	1963	3,270/5,670	412 × 60 × 13	16 tanks, vehicles, helos, 534 troops
Ouragan	LSD	Fr	1963	5,800/8,500	489 × 71 × 18	18 LCMs, helos, 470 troops
Ivan Rogov	LPH	USSR	1978	11,000/13,000	518 × 79 × 27	10 tanks, APCs, helo, 550 troops
Whidbey Island	LSD	USN	1983	11,125/15,750	609.5 × 84 × 20	Four LCAC or 20 LCMs, 440 troops
San Giorgio	LPD	It	1987	5,000/7,670	437 × 67 × 17	LCM, LCVPs, helos, 345 troops
Wasp	LHD	USN	1987	28,250/40,500	844 × 140 × 26	LCAC, 30 helos, 6 V/STOL, 1850 troops
Craft						
X-Lighter	Beach	RN	1915	160	105.6 × 21 × 3.6	men, horses, light equipment
Daihatsu	Ramp	Jp	1935	20	48 × 11 × 2.5	70 men or one tank
LCVP	Ramp	USN	1941	8	36 × 11 × 3	38 men or small vehicle
LCM	Ramp	USN	1942	23/52	50 × 14 × 2	1 tank or 60 troops

NOTES: Year = year completed. Displacement = standard/deep load in tons. Dimensions = overall length by width by draft in feet. Characteristics = Example of loads.

ing craft. Starting in the 1980s and continuing today, amphibious warfare has entered the fourth, and probably last stage, the complete over-the-horizon stage, with helicopters now joined by air cushion vehicles (LCACs) allowing for complete over-the-horizon assaults. In addition, V-22 Osprey tilt-rotor airplanes are now joining the U.S. Navy's inventory. They will allow for even further over-the-horizon assaults. Although no other navies have matched these American capabilities, most major fleets contain at least one or two larger, multicapable amphibious ships, with both helicopters and landing craft.

In sum, amphibious warfare has progressed constantly since World War II. And although the days of a Normandy D-Day, Okinawa, or even Inchon might be over, barely a year goes by without some amphibious operation requiring these specialized ships and landing craft. Contrary to all the gloomy predictions, amphibious warfare is alive and well.

Service Ships　　　　　　12

WHEN NAVALISTS WRITE about "blue" or deep-water warships and fleets, they invariably mean large vessels such as battleships, cruisers, and aircraft carriers that can operate far from shore. What really makes a so-called blue water fleet blue, however, are not these large combatants, but the oilers and storeships that support them. Even large warships cannot go long without the "beans, bullets, and black oil" supplied by the oilers and the ammunition and supply ships, the service force. This service force is particularly crucial for the smaller yet necessary screening destroyers and frigates that need to be refueled, "topped off," every three or four days.

This force has been known by many different names—the fleet train, auxiliaries, base force, support ships, and service force. In this author's opinion, the latter is the more appropriate term, describing their function as "servicing the fleet" rather than simply a merchantman or tanker that might happen to be bringing supplies to a ship or forward base. In general, there are two basic types of service ships: the under-way replenishment ships that service the fleet at sea under way and those found in ports or forward areas such as repair ships and tenders. Both are crucial for any modern navy.

Early Precedents

There are virtually no precedents for service ships in either the Ages of Galleys or Sail, although in some cases they would have been useful. During the Age of Galleys, merchantmen sometimes accompanied the fleets, but the normal practice was for the war galleys to operate alone, putting in to shore every night for both food and safety reasons. Besides, there was little room on the galleys jammed with rowers and marines to carry stores. There is at least one historic event from the Age of Galleys, however, when a service force might have been useful. As noted in chapter 2, Athens's reign as the major sea power ended when that city-state's sailors and marines were away forging for food, leaving the ships unguarded. Casson blames this on a "boneheaded" admiral, but a service force might have solved the problem.[1] The lack of room for stores with no service force did limit a galley's flexibility.

At the Battle of the Spanish Armada, usually considered the beginning of the Age of Sail, the smaller English galleons actually ran out of ammunition and had to give up their chase so that is at least one instance when a service force would have been useful during this period. Later, when larger ships of the line were built, and throughout most of the Age of Sail, warships were outfitted with sufficient supplies to last six months. Cannonballs and black powder did not take up much room. Refrigerated store ships would have helped solve the problem of scurvy, but that was handled by having ships go into port for fresh stores. One exception came during the Napoleonic wars, when at times the Royal Navy established a resupply system for its ships blockading French ports. There is some indication of an in port service force with older ships converted into "hulks," or what today would be considered tenders to support the fleet. In 1694 the *Chantam Hulk* was purposely built for this role.[2] There were other harbor craft, including hoys and lighters, dredgers, and camels, as well as hospital ships.[3]

A service force did not really become necessary until the Age of Steam, and the driving impetus was not for ammunition or food but for coal. These early warships could not steam for more than a few days on coal, which was the main reason sail was carried up to the late 1880s. Even then, the accepted solution was not service coaling ships, although a few called colliers were built, but rather land-based coaling stations, which was one of the rationales behind the scramble for land during the late nineteenth-century Age of Imperialism. England had the most elaborate system, with coaling stations around the world from Gibraltar and Malta in the Mediterranean, the Suez Canal, and then Aden, followed by stations in India and Ceylon, Singapore, and Hong Kong. Other countries, when they could, established similar coaling stations at strategic distances. Coaling ships, called colliers, were built, but in most cases they were simply merchant ships carrying bags of coal.

One of the earliest formations of a real service force was during the American Civil War, when the Union navy chartered merchant ships to support its warships on station blockading the Confederate States. The large paddle steamers *Connecticut* and *Rhode Island,* for example, would fill up in northern ports with fresh food, beef, vegetables, and other supplies, then sail south to Texas, replenishing the blockading ships as they went. For coal, the ships normally went into port.[4] Unfortunately, this system was abandoned after the Civil War, and the United States Navy returned to sailing warships. Not only was this advanced system abandoned, but as a disincentive, captains had to pay for coal out of their own pockets if they exceeded their allowance. That was one way to eliminate the need for a service force!

The best, or perhaps more appropriately worst, example of the need for a service force during the Age of Steam was the long voyage by the Russian European fleet to the Pacific, where it was decimated by the Japanese at the

Battle of Tsushima during the Russo-Japanese War. One of the major contributing factors for this Russian "fleet that had to die" was exhaustion from the long journey, exacerbated by fueling difficulties, especially after England had refused their requests.[5] Further complicating the situation was that the coal piled on board limited battle practice. During the interwar period, strategists calculated that a fleet lost 10 percent of its efficiency for every thousand miles it had to steam, and that would certainly seem to have been the case with the Russian fleet.

The American Navy also experienced this problem when its Great White Fleet made a trip around the world in 1908, usually seen as its "coming out party" as a modern fleet. But with no coaling stations, the fleet was at the mercy of local merchants and colliers, mostly British. Despite its worldwide coaling station system, England also established the Royal Fleet Train, a civilian-manned service force, during this period. Refrigerator ships started to appear at the end of the nineteenth century, solving the problem of fresh supplies. Colliers were improved from merchantmen carrying bags of coal to specifically designed ships with elaborate rigs to move the coal, but coaling a ship was still a slow, filthy process always done at anchor or in port. The general rule of thumb was that it took one day for each battleship. That eased somewhat with the switch to oil, and oilers replaced colliers, but fueling was still done in port or at anchor. In 1912, the United States Navy authorized two fuel ships. On the eve of World War I, however, few navies had more than a handful of colliers, oilers, or storeships.[6]

World War I

Although there had been some progress in organization and design of service ships before the Great War, it was limited. This should not be surprising because naval actions were expected to take place in the near waters of the North Sea or the closed waters of the Mediterranean, with home ports less than a day away. And with few exceptions that was the case. One of the exceptions was the problems facing German raiders and their warships caught outside European waters when the war began. The largest force was Vice Admiral's Spee's fleet of six warships in China that required support from eight colliers and store ships. For a time he was supported by Japanese colliers, but when Japan entered the war, that source was eliminated, which was one of the reasons Spee headed for South America.[7]

The German raiders had even more problems, which they solved by taking coal from captured ships, sometimes even bringing them along as ad hoc colliers. Germany also established an elaborate Etappe supply system around the world, with local German representatives and some 130 ships trying to keep their raiders supplied.[8] To a German raider probably goes the honor of making the first under-way replenishment. An auxiliary cruiser, the former liner *Kronprinz Wilhelm,* was able to stay at sea for over eight months without anchoring by coaling at sea "while steaming slowly ahead, accepting the risks and damage this entailed as liner and collier came together in the swell."[9] She finally put into Hampton Roads on 11 April 1915 for fresh food and was interned there. The German raiders' problems were not limited to worrying about Royal Navy cruisers hunting them down but also included where they were going to get necessary supplies.

The other major exception was the United States Navy, which also required a service force when it entered the war. The two fuel ships *Kanawha* and *Maumee,* authorized in 1912, were finally completed in 1915 and 1916 respectively, just in time to service the American fleet in World War I. These ships were 5,400 tons light, 14,500 full load, with an overall length of 476 feet, capable of making 14 knots. While called "fuel ships" and sometimes "oil carriers," they still operated like colliers, refueling ships moored alongside. In July 1917, however, the *Maumee* began experimenting with refueling destroyers under way using a procedure known as riding abeam (later called "broadside").[10] This procedure was developed by a team including then-lieutenant Chester A. Nimitz, who later headed the World War II Pacific Fleet, where refueling at sea was critical for the final victory. Nimitz would continue to play a key role in development of the service force. The destroyers sent overseas were refueled using this method. This development of the broadside under-way replenishment (UNREP) procedure is considered one of the seminal events, not just for the service force but in modern naval history.

Tenders were also important in certain areas. Germany converted two former liners, the *General* and the *Corcovada,* interned at Turkey, into depot ships to support its battle cruisers and cruisers. In 1917 a United States tender was sent to Queenstown, Ireland, to support the American destroyers. This is often seen as another seminal event for forward support. Even today, modern ships cannot go long without needing major repairs beyond the capacity of the ship's own company.

Although the Royal Navy had naval facilities in England and the Mediterranean, it still needed hundreds of service ships to support the fleet. According to *Conway's* for the period, the Royal Navy had eleven destroyer depot ships or tenders, twenty-one submarine tenders, three fleet repair ships, three torpedo depot ships, approximately one hundred oilers of various sizes, and well over two hundred other support ships listed as water tankers, store carriers, and squadron supply ships.[11] A few were built for the purpose, but most were converted merchantmen or old warships. Other countries also had service ships, but unfortunately, there is little detailed information available on any of these vessels or their operations.

The Interwar Period

The lessons of World War I for a service force were not forgotten during the interwar years; but because the budgets for all navies were cut, when the choice was between building either a warship or a service ship, the former was usually chosen. As a result, few service ships were built until war became imminent in the late 1930s, although planning continued and some progress was made. Such plans are apparent in War Plan Orange documents, the U.S. strategy to defeat Japan. Planning against Japan can be traced back to 1897, but it intensified during the interwar period.[12] The need for service ships was clear in the planning estimates over the years. In 1925 it was calculated that 163 service ships were needed, including 88 oilers; in 1928 that number rose to 248 with 100 tankers; and on the eve of World War II in 1938, the need for 379 ships with 121 oilers was projected.[13]

Some operational, procedural progress was also achieved. In April 1923 the oiler *Cuyama* fueled two ships at the same time. In 1925 tests with fueling astern began, which demonstrated its feasibility, but this process was slow and it was finally dropped by the U.S. Navy in 1931 (although other countries continued using this method). In 1930, refueling tests were conducted between the carrier *Saratoga* and destroyers. By 1931, refueling destroyers had become routine.[14] In short, during the 1920s and early 1930s, very important experiments were run by the United States Navy that would prove crucial in the Pacific during World War II.

Nevertheless, no service ships were being built. In 1933, the U.S. General Board set requirements for fast oilers to keep up with the fleet but then in 1934 recommended against building auxiliaries so as not to detract from building combatants. Once again, service ships would lose out to combatants. A breakthrough finally came in 1936, with the establishment of the U.S. Maritime Commission, followed by an agreement between the commission and Standard Oil to build oilers with naval features. The result was the *Cimarron,* completed in March 1939. Twelve *Cimarron* "T3" class were eventually built. These oilers were 7,000 tons light, 23,000 tons full load, 553 feet long, with a cargo capacity of 147,000 barrels of oil. More important, they had a speed of 18 knots. In 1940, a slightly smaller and slower (14 knots) "T2" design was started, of which 481 variants were built during the war. New techniques, especially welding instead of using rivets, allowed these ships to be constructed in as little as twenty-eight days.[15]

Other countries did not completely neglect service ships, although none really had the same need as the United States, especially its requirements in the vast Pacific. England's Royal Fleet Train was continued, but the Royal Navy still had bases throughout the world for support. Lack of service ships was not a problem for the British until Royal Navy carriers were sent to the

Pacific after Germany was defeated to assist the U.S. fleet commanders, who, incidentally, did not really want them because they would require American support. Similarly, the Japanese did not need a massive service force because they had bases spread throughout the Pacific.

The Germans, however, were faced with the same problem they had in World War I since the Royal Navy still controlled the seas. They came up with a new type of ship that was to have profound effects. Since Germany did not have the luxury of building single-purpose oilers, ammunition ships, and supply ships, it built multiproduct or multipurpose ships. The first was the *Dithmarschen,* built in 1938 with five more finished before the war. She was 10,900 tons light, 22,000 tons full load, and 582 feet long. The *Dithmarschen* is considered the world's first multipurpose replenishment ship, although the replenishment was done at anchor, not under way. She was taken over by the United States Navy after the war and became the test-bed for the modern, postwar multipurpose ships.[16]

World War II

Although considerable planning had been done with replenishment techniques developed in the interwar period, in 1939, when war broke out in Europe, there were still only a handful of service ships in any of the navies of the world. As shown in table 12.1, that situation would change drastically, as most countries took over merchantmen for service ships. Nowhere would that change be more dramatic than in the U.S. Navy, where the service force

Table 12.1 Service Force Balance in World War II

Type	U.S.	Britain	Germany	Japan
Oilers (AO)	108	54		79
Gasoline tankers (AOG)	75	20		
Ammunition ships (AE)	20	2		3
Store ships (AF)	47	4		8
Cargo ships (AK)	221			
Hospital ships (AH)	19	3		4
TENDERS				
Destroyer (AD)	36	2		
Repair ship (AR)	19	11	1	5
Submarine (AS)	26	3	6	6
Seaplane (AV)	18			

NOTES: Designations are USN designations. U.S. Navy data taken from *Fahey's Victory Edition* (1945) and are probably fairly accurate. Japanese data from Jentshura et al., *Warships of the Imperial Navy, 1869–1945,* and are probably also fairly accurate. British and German data from *Conway's* and *Jane's* which unfortunately do not give detailed breakdowns of service forces. In addition to these, all countries used their merchant fleets for some of these duties.

became crucial to support Pacific operations, especially after the Philippines and Guam had been captured by the Japanese.

Operations of the U.S. Navy's service force can be roughly divided into three levels or stages of support: oilers, the establishment of advanced bases using support ships, and finally complete under-way support. The most important function was the fleet support by the oilers in both the Atlantic and Pacific. Although barely mentioned in most books on the naval war in the Atlantic, oilers were needed to support the convoy screening destroyers, destroyer escorts, and frigates. During the war more than a hundred oilers were built or converted from commercial tankers. The most numerous were the T2 and T3.

Although certainly important in the Atlantic, oilers were absolutely crucial in the Pacific. By late 1943 they finally started joining the fleet in sufficient numbers. The Gilberts operations in November of that year were the first entirely refueled at sea. During this operation, 114 service ships were involved. Despite their numbers and importance, the support force was commanded by a captain. As Thomas Wildenberg, one of the few historians who has written about service forces in depth, comments, "It is an interesting commentary on the navy's command policy during World War II that command of the At-Sea Logistics Group at this time was not considered worthy of flag rank. . . . [It] is further evidence of the second-class status of the service force."[17]

Also important were the various support ships and tenders. In the United States Navy the primary store ships were ammunition ships (AE), general storeships (AKS), refrigerated and foodstuffs support ships (AF), and aviation supply ships (AVS). In most cases these were converted merchantmen, many Liberty Ships. There were four kinds of tenders and supply ships: general repair (AR), destroyer tenders (AD), submarine tenders (AS), and three categories of seaplane tenders: large (AV), small (AVP), and converted destroyers (AVD). Tenders were one of the main exceptions to the rule in that several were purpose-built rather than converted merchantmen. Four *Vulcan*-class ARs, five *Piedmont*-class ADs, and seven *Fulton*-class ASs were all built to a similar design of approximately 9,000 tons and 492 feet long. There were also others, including important floating dry docks. A first small prototype dock was built in 1936, but by the end of the war there were thirty, including three large enough to accommodate battleships.

There was a difference between prewar and wartime practices for this base force. Since there were never enough base force ships, the U.S. Navy developed a sequential, stepping-stone solution, initially using ships until base facilities could be built ashore, with the support ships moving to the next forward island. The bases were prepackaged, called Lions. The exception was the floating dry docks that would be moved to the next base.[18]

What might be called the complete under-way replenishment stage occurred near the end of the war. Up until 1944, while oilers refueled at sea, the ammunition and storeships refueled in port. This was not really a problem because the early island-hopping operations were fairly slow, ships were able to return to bases easily, and the ships could carry enough ammunition and supplies. In late 1944, however, U.S. Navy ships began to stay at sea longer while expending increasing amounts of ordnance. Some oilers started carrying limited amounts of ammunition and supplies, but not enough for sustained operations. Thus, in November 1944, the Navy formed a Logistic Support Group, and within a short time ammunitions and storeships also began under-way replenishment. Replenishment at sea became so perfected that a fleet could be completely replenished in about two days versus the ten to twelve it had normally taken to return to a base.[19]

Other countries built or converted some support ships, but neither their size nor procedures compared to those of the American force. Most of the major fleets had depot ships and tenders and even oilers, but they did not develop an under-way replenishment service force similar to that of the U.S. Navy. The Royal Navy almost had to break off its famous chase of the *Bismarck* for lack of oilers. The British still had bases around the world, and replenishment at sea did not really become a problem until they deployed to the Pacific. Italy had few logistics problems because its operations were in the Mediterranean, nor did the Japanese with their island bases. Only the Germans had major problems which they tried to solve with multiproduct ships.

Post–World War II Period

The end of the war did not diminish the U.S. Navy's need for a service force. If anything that need increased because of the United States's increased commitments and the diminishing strength of the Royal Navy. In addition, as the Korean War soon proved, the new jet aircraft required more than three times as much fuel as the old piston engine–driven planes. The biggest change, however, came in the move toward multiproduct ships developed in both the U.S. Navy and the Royal Navy after they had experimented with the former German World War II multiproduct ships. After the war, the Royal Navy received the *Nordmark,* renamed *Bulawayo,* and the U.S. Navy took over the *Dithmarschen,* renamed *Conecuh.*

The Royal Navy operated the *Bulawayo* as a multiproduct ship through 1955. Because of its success, in 1954 the Royal Navy laid down the first of three "Tide" class replenishment ships, the first of which, the *Tidewater,* was finished in 1955. They were 9,000 tons light, 26,000 full load, 583 feet long, and capable of 17 knots. These would be the world's first modern replenishment oilers, AORs. In the 1960s most navies would start building AORs. The Netherlands, for example, built its first AOR, the *Poolster,* in 1962, Canada

The Royal Navy's *Tidespring,* a "Tide"-class AOR. Note the helicopter hangars and deck. Most large navies have built at least a few AORs for their fleet. (Maritime Photographic)

the *Prowler* in 1963, and Australia a "Tide" class, the *Supply,* in 1962. Another new procedure developed in the 1960s was the use of helicopters for vertical replenishment (VERTREP) of stores. Today, AORs with helicopters are by far the most common type of replenishment ship and most major navies have at least two or three.

The U.S. Navy took a different tack, at least initially. After successfully testing the *Conecuh,* commissioned in 1953 as AOR-110 and reequipped with under-way refueling rigs, the U.S. Navy decided to build "fast combat support" ships, later designated AOE. The first of four was the *Sacramento,* AOE-1, laid down in 1961 and commissioned in 1964, built to combine the capabilities of an AO, AE, and storeships AKS. These are the world's largest under-way replenishment ships at 795 feet, 54,000 tons full load, with a speed of 26 knots, designed to operate with the battle fleet. They are capable of carrying 156,000 barrels of fuel, 2,100 tons of ammunition, 250 tons of dry stores, and 250 tons of refrigerated stores. They also have a large helicopter deck with three hangars. Even the U.S. Navy found these large ships too expensive so in the late 1960s they were followed by seven smaller, 41,000 tons full load, 659 foot-long *Wichita*-class AOR replenishment oilers. The multiproduct AORs have been followed by larger 49,000-ton, 755-foot-long *Supply*-class AOEs built in the 1990s.

USS *Sacramento* (AOE-1) refueling both USS *Kitty Hawk* (*right*) and USS *Sample*.
(U.S. Naval Institute)

Single-product replenishment ships have not been completely abandoned. Many navies still operate oilers, AOs, and storeships. The U.S. Navy has five large 38,000-ton full load, 708-foot-long *Cimarron*-class AOs in the active fleet and eighteen more slightly smaller *Henry J. Kaiser*–class fleet oilers built to commercial specifications operated by civilian crews. The U.S. Navy still also operates ammunition ships, AEs, and combat storeships, AFS, most of the latter now operated by civilian crews. The normal practice is for these single-product ships to act as "shuttle" ships to the forward areas to replenish the AORs and AOEs that then operate with the fleet. For the twenty-first century, the U.S. Navy is looking at a ship to combine both functions.

Virtually all navies now operate AOR-type ships for their fleets and some still operate the occasional AO or storeship, but none have the capacity of the U.S. Navy. For a time, it looked as though the Soviet navy might be developing a large service force. In the late 1960s the Soviets starting building *Boris Chilikin*–class AORs. What really got the attention of Western observers, however, was the large 36,000-ton full load, 695-foot-long replenishment oiler *Berezina*, completed in 1978. The Soviet navy seemed finally to be developing a blue water capacity, but that vessel turned out to be one of a kind. For this reason, even though the old Soviet Union built large warships, including cruisers and carriers, most Western strategists never really considered the Soviet surface fleet a major, long-term threat because of their lack of logistical support. Also, although the Soviet navy did develop under-way replenishment capabilities, its normal practice was to lay moored in isolated anchorages where the ships would replenish at anchor, which also made them potentially easy targets.

Many larger navies still operate repair ships and submarine and destroyer tenders, although they are disappearing now that most fleets stay in home ports. Even the United States Navy is retiring many of its tenders. And there are many, many more types of ships. Besides those mentioned, currently the United States Navy has salvage ships (ARS), salvage and rescue ships (ATS), submarine rescue ships (ASR), and oceangoing tugs (ATF). The Navy and U.S. Maritime Administration also operate fast sealift ships (FSS), which are modified merchant ships intended to carry Army mechanized and tank divisions. Others in this force include auxiliary crane ships, vehicle cargo ships, barge carrying ships, cargo ships, gasoline tankers, transport tankers, and troop transports. These are in the Ready Reserve Force (RRF) to be broken out quickly during emergencies such as the Desert Storm operation against Iraq in 1990–91.

Another trend in the 1990s is the increasing use of civilian crews to man service ships. In the United States these crews are under the Military Sealift Command (MSC), and other countries have similar (though less elaborate) organizations. The Royal Navy has a civilian-manned "red flag" Royal Fleet Auxiliary. England also has a program known as STUFT, "ships taken up from trade," civilian merchantmen brought under Royal Navy control during emergencies. The old Soviet merchant marine was always considered an auxiliary of the Soviet navy, and many of their crews were reservists. Merchant ships are still an important part of a country's emergency force. But more important are navy-designed ships such as AORs able to operate and directly supply the fleet.[20]

Conclusion

Service ships were not used or needed for most of the history of warships, but that changed when coal and oil replaced sail, requiring colliers and oilers. The problem was further exacerbated during World War II when the need arose to support far-flung fleets with both foodstuffs and ammunition, requiring vast fleets of store and ammunition ships. Service ships are now an important, integral part of the modern navy but unfortunately do not get their proper due. There are a few books on the role of the service force in World War II[21] and even one recent book on the history of tankers in the U.S. Navy from 1912 to 1992.[22] But though a typical book on World War II might make a passing reference to their role in the Pacific, they are, in general, virtually ignored in the literature. Nevertheless, the service force was just as crucial in defeating the Japanese as were the carriers, which could not have operated without them.

Even today they are slighted, yet as one analyst points out, during two major postwar conflicts, "Auxiliary warships have become so important that . . . there have been nearly as many auxiliary warships as combatants taking part." During the Falklands War, sixteen Royal Fleet Auxiliaries and twenty-five merchant ships taken up from trade were needed to support two carriers and twenty-five surface combatants, and during Desert Shield/Desert Storm the U.S. Navy had twenty-seven Navy and thirty civilian-manned MSC ships to support eight carriers and sixty-eight other combatants.[23] One reason many analysts questioned whether the old Soviet navy was ever really a blue water threat even when it was building battle cruisers and aircraft carriers was its lack of service ships. In short, the ships that really make blue water navies blue are those of the service force.

Mine Ships

13

MINES ARE THE most cost-effective naval weapons ever invented. Just the mere threat of mines has closed ports and stopped shipping. During both world wars mines costing a few hundred dollars sunk million-dollar ships and the fear of mines was a major factor denying the Royal Navy a decisive victory at Jutland, the only major battle between the dreadnoughts. During Desert Storm in 1991, Iraqi mines of a World War I design costing a few thousand dollars were able to put two U.S. Navy warships, worth $1 billion apiece, out of action. In the post–World War II period, more U.S. Navy warships have been lost to mines than any other source.

Yet throughout the history of mines, which can be traced back to the last days of the Age of Sail, the development of mine countermeasure craft was generally ignored until World War I for several reasons. Mines have been seen as both "unchivalrous" and the "weapons of the weak" with the result that regular officers often looked upon those involved with minesweeping as "no better than lavatory attendants," as expressed by some Royal Navy officers in World War I.[1] As a consequence, most mine craft in both wars were hurriedly built and manned by reservists. That attitude, shared by many professional naval officers, came back to haunt those regulars during both world wars, the Korean War, and Desert Storm in the 1990s.

Historically, mine ships, or crafts as they historically were called, fall into two categories—minelayers and minesweepers. Today, minelayers have disappeared from the seas, but minesweepers and countermeasure ships still play an important role in all navies.

Early Precedents

The origins of mine warfare can be traced back to the last days of the Age of Sail, and mines were used extensively throughout the Age of Steam and Ironclads. The first recorded use of mines was by the Dutch against the Spanish at Antwerp in 1585, when they used a flat raft floating mine, but that was an isolated incident. The origins of mine warfare are usually traced to 1777, during the American Revolutionary War, when David Bushnell tried using both a line of cabled mines and later floating keg mines to sink British warships. While Bushnell's efforts were unsuccessful, the hazards of minesweeping soon became apparent. In both instances, the mines were spotted by the British. In the first minesweeping effort, however, several British sailors were killed when the mines went off as the cable was being hauled in, and in the second, more British sailors were killed retrieving the floating kegs. Unfortunately, two inquisitive boys were also killed retrieving keg mines.

At the turn of the eighteenth century, Robert Fulton tried to interest both the French and the English in mines. British prime minister Pitt was interested, but the professional Admiralty was not. Similar sentiments would be echoed throughout the history of mine warfare. Even Fulton's successful demonstration sinking of the brig *Dorothea* in 1805 failed to sway the admirals. Fulton returned to the United States, where he tried to interest the U.S. Navy and Congress, again to no avail. A test in 1810 against a ship was thwarted when the ship's captain hung a net, foiling the floating mines, and Congress concluded that they were not a threat.

Rather than floating mines, several inventors suggested using moored, controlled mines set off from shore. In 1812 Russian Baron Pavel Schilling carried out a demonstration in St. Petersburg; in 1829 Samuel Colt (of revolver fame) began experiments; and in 1833 an American professor of chemistry, Robert Hare, suggested controlled mines for coastal defense. In the early 1840s Samuel Colt destroyed several ships in experiments but still failed to win funding from Congress. A controlled minefield was laid but not used during the 1848–51 Schleswig-Holstein War. The Russians laid some contact mines during the 1854–56 Crimean War, damaging a few British ships, and a proposed attack on Kronstadt in 1855 was canceled when British reconnoitering ships spotted minefields.[2]

Mines were used extensively by the Confederates during the American Civil War, leading to the development of countermeasures by the Union forces. Early in the war, in 1861, the Confederates established a Torpedo Bureau (as mines were then called) under Matthew Fontaine Maury, better known as the founder of naval oceanography. The first major Union loss came in December 1862, when the large river gunboat *Cairo* was sunk by a mine. The Union countered by developing a "torpedo catcher," also known as a "torpedo rake" or "devil." This rakelike device extending 20 feet from the bows of ships was designed to scoop up mines in the ship's path. The Union also used small boats with sailors using grappling hooks to snare mines and later they developed a jury-rigged sweeping device consisting of a chain towed between two boats weighed in the center to catch cables anchoring mines. Another method was simply to set off contact mines with rifle fire. Cutting mine cables and setting them off by gunfire is a technique still used today.[3]

Mines were also involved in one of the most famous sayings in American naval history during Rear Admiral David Glasgow Farragut's dashing assault into the mined Mobile Bay. When the monitor *Tecumseh* hit a mine and sank instantly, the lead ship, the sloop *Brooklyn,* hesitated, causing Farragut on the flagship *Hartford* to shout his famous, "Damn the torpedoes! Full speed ahead." While not taking anything away from Farragut's bravado, as one analyst notes, in fact Union boats had done a fairly thorough job before the attack of sweeping or neutralizing the Confederate mines.[4]

During the Civil War thirty-six ships were lost to mines, thirty-two Union and four Confederate. Three Confederate ships were sunk by their own mines, foreshadowing a continuing problem throughout the history of mine warfare. More important was the appearance of the first mine vessels with mine catchers for warships and small boats used to snag or cut cables, but these all fall into the jury-rig category. The ingenious John Ericsson was ordered to design a mine destroyer, which might have become the world's first, but he was too busy with his other projects.

Mines were used in all the late nineteenth-century naval wars, including the 1865–70 war between Paraguay, Argentina, and Brazil; the 1870 Franco-Prussian War; the Russo-Turkish War of 1877–78; and the War of the Pacific from 1879 to 1880. In 1873, the Royal Navy established a Torpedo Committee, and by the early 1880s most countries had established torpedo corps. It was during this time that the term *mine* came into use. Previously, *torpedo* had been used as a generic term for all underwater devices, but with the invention of the Whitehead torpedo in 1866, it became customary to designate nonpropelled weapons as *mines* and the new self-propelled weapons as *torpedoes.*[5]

The most famous mining event of the late nineteenth century never occurred, but nevertheless it illustrates their influence, especially on public opinion. This was the sinking of the U.S. battleship *Maine* in Havana Harbor, which led to the Spanish-American War of 1898. Originally thought to have been caused by a mine placed by the "dastardly" Spaniards, the sinking of the *Maine* is now generally accepted to have been an accidental internal explosion.[6] But the American yellow journalism of the day was able to whip up war hysteria fanned by this supposed unchivalrous act of mining.

The power of mines was clearly demonstrated during the Russo-Japanese War of 1904, when sixteen ships, including battleships and cruisers, were sunk by mines. The worst case was when Russian Admiral Stephan Makarov in his battleship *Petropavlovsk* knowingly and foolishly led his ships through a minefield. The admiral and his ship were lost to mines, and another battleship was seriously damaged. That would be the last time an admiral would "damn the torpedoes."[7]

The Modern Era: 1906–1914

Although there was both a long history of mine warfare and the introduction of several new ship types throughout the Age of Steam, new vessels for mine warfare were virtually ignored. There were several ad hoc, jury-rigged solutions such as putting mine catchers on Civil War gunboats or using boats or tugs, as both the Japanese and Russians did during their war, but no specially designed ships appeared. Part of the reason for this void was the still prevailing bias against mines among the professional naval officers. Another reason was the 1907 Hague Convention that restricted the use of mines during wartime, causing some to believe the problem solved.

The problem was not completely ignored. In 1906, the start of the modern era, the Royal Navy began experimenting more seriously with mine warfare and in 1908 purchased some fishing trawlers, converting them into minesweepers. Britain would later convert some old gunboats to mine craft. In 1907 England also formed a Trawler Reserve force of fishermen and their trawlers for minesweeping.[8] Thus the British were the first to form a mine force in peacetime and would set the precedent of using reserves for this arduous duty, a practice followed by many navies to this day. In 1910 France also converted some fishing boats to mine craft, and in 1913 the U.S. Navy rigged two fleet tugs, the *Patapsco* and *Patuxent,* for clearing mines.

The first purpose-built mine countermeasure ships were constructed by the Russians. In 1910 they launched five 150-ton, 148-foot-long *Fugas*-class minesweepers. Four would be lost to mines in World War I. Also in 1910 Russia built two smaller 106-ton, 86-foot-long *Albatros* class. Other countries would not lay down new mine craft until the war started.

While minesweeping craft were generally ignored, all the major countries made plans for minelaying, usually converting older ships for that role. Between 1907 and 1910, for example, the Royal Navy converted seven old 3,400-ton *Apollo* second-class cruisers built in 1890–91 into minelayers. In 1912 Russia became the first nation to build a submarine for minelaying.

World War I

Despite some prewar planning, only a handful of mine craft existed when war broke out in 1914. The Royal Navy had only ten old torpedo gunboats and thirteen trawlers rigged with sweeps; other countries had fewer. Yet by the end of war, hundreds of mine vessels were either built or converted. Mines would play an important part throughout the war, including crucial roles in the two most famous naval battles, the Dardanelles campaign and Jutland. As soon as the war started, all the countries laid minefields. Among the most effective were the mine barriers laid by Russia in the Baltic, resulting in the loss of four German cruisers and seven torpedo boats. Even Denmark laid mines to protect its neutrality.

All minelaying during the war was accomplished by converted warships and merchantmen, and for that reason, with the exception of the Royal Navy, whose mine craft have been chronicled by one scholar, detailed information is limited in most naval works. Before the war the Royal Navy had converted seven older cruisers to minelayers. During the war, forty-nine more larger ships, including some paddle wheelers, would be refigured for laying mines. Thirteen more cruisers, two turn-of-the-century *Diadem* class, seven newer *Arethusa,* and four *Boadicea* class, and the old battleship *London,* were also altered to lay mines. The large 19,000-ton light battle cruiser *Glorious* was converted but never used. Ten merchantmen, nine paddle wheelers, and fifteen trawlers were also refigured for minelaying. In addition to these larger ships, coastal motorboats and some former American and Canadian motor launches were also used, as were some landing craft "X" lighters.[9] Other countries also converted former warships and merchantmen. The United States, for example, used the old cruisers *San Francisco* and *Baltimore* and seven former liners.

During the war the Royal Navy converted 286 fishing trawlers, drifters, tugs, gunboats, small merchantmen, yachts, and paddle wheelers to minesweepers. More than a hundred were former trawlers; 81 were smaller paddle wheelers. In addition to these, the Royal Navy built 229 new minesweepers. These included 24 *Acadia* class, first ordered in January 1915, followed by 12 similar *Azalea* and 36 *Arabis* classes. These ships, classified as fleet sweeping sloops, were all around 1,250 tons, 250 feet long, built to a simple design. Some were turned out in only twenty weeks. The Royal Navy also built 24 *Ascot*-class paddle wheelers. The largest minesweeper class in number was the smaller 91-ship, 820-ton, 235-foot-long *Aberdare* class, first launched in 1918 (only 32 were finished by war's end, however).

Germany built three large minesweeping classes in the 425- to 500-ton range, all around 180 feet long, and two smaller coastal minesweeping class, one only 18 tons, 58 feet in length, used for harbor clearance. Russia built 35 new and converted another 194 craft to auxiliary minesweepers. When the United States entered the war in 1917, it used a previously approved 950-ton, 189-foot-long "Bird"-class dual-purpose minesweeper/fleet tug. Fifty-four were ordered. They would be used to clear minefields after the war.

Table 13.1 shows the approximate mine craft balance in World War I, compiled from *Conway's* and *Jane's* for the period. With the possible exception of the Royal Navy craft verified by other sources, these numbers are probably low.[10] Some conversions both formal and especially ad hoc are missing from these standard reference works. For example, at various times destroyers were rigged to clear mines. Though perhaps somewhat inaccurate,

Table 13.1 Mine Craft Balance in World War I

Type	Britain	France	Italy	Russia	U.S.	Japan	Germany	Austria
Minelayers	55		1	18	9	14	1	5
Minesweepers								
Built	229	18	57	26	54	13	242	10
Converted	286	69	65	229			N.L.	N.L.
TOTAL	570	87	123	273	63	27	243	15

NOTES: Except for RN data from M. P. Cocker, *Mine Warfare Vessels of the Royal Navy, 1908 to Date,* these numbers are probably low. Most European participants in WWI used conversions not always listed in *Conway's* and *Jane's*. Also, many destroyers and torpedo boats were converted to minesweepers at various times. The table still illustrates numbers involved. N.L. = Nonlisted but indications that some existed.

table 13.1 is still useful since it gives some idea of the number of new and converted mine craft involved in World War I.

MINES PLAYED KEY ROLES in two of the major naval engagements of the war. In the 1915 Dardanelles campaign, the original plan was for the Allied fleet to force its way through to the Black Sea. Initial minesweeping was conducted by slow converted trawlers manned by fishermen, and when that did not work, jury-rigged faster, better armed destroyers were used. The Allies finally tried to force their way through on 18 March, but after a French battleship was sunk, a British battleship badly damaged, and two British cruisers also sunk, most by mines, the operation was called off, leading to the disastrous amphibious assault on Gallipoli.[11]

Mines also played at least an indirect role at Jutland. Earlier in the war Admiral Jellicoe had stated, "If, for instance, the enemy battle-fleet were to turn away from an advancing fleet, I should assume that the intention was to lead us over mines and submarines; and should decline to be so drawn." Many analysts have taken that statement as the reason Jellicoe did not pursue the German fleet when it turned away at Jutland. No doubt the recent Dardanelles and even Russian experience from the Russo-Japanese War only a decade earlier was still fresh in Jellicoe's mind.

More important than these key battles was the role mines played throughout the war. They were, in short, a constant concern not just for Admiral Jellicoe at Jutland but for all ships, both warships and merchantmen. Estimates are that some 240,000 mines were laid by both sides. Allied losses were 87 warships, 585 merchantmen, and 152 small craft. The Central Powers lost 129 warships and an unknown number of merchantmen.[12] More ships were lost to mines than to any other single source in World War I. Clearing mines was also dangerous, and the Royal Navy lost 26 minesweepers and Germany 33.[13]

The Interwar Period

In the immediate postwar period, minesweepers were busy removing the minefields, but after that task was completed, mine forces fell on hard times. The reservists who manned the bulk of the mine forces returned to civilian life, most mine craft were retired, and the regulars stayed away from mine warfare, seeing little chance for promotion. This was particularly true in the U.S. Navy, which viewed mine warfare as "unpleasant work for a naval man, an occupation like that of rat-catching." [14] By 1919, the U.S. Navy had only a small organization headed by a lieutenant. Up to 1939 there was little interest, with the head of the mine warfare desk, a civilian, and only two scientists involved. In 1928, the U.S. Navy commissioned the submarine *Argonaut,* designed for minelaying, although during the war she was used as a supply and troop carrier. By the end of the 1920s, only two "Bird"-class minesweepers remained on active duty in the U.S. Navy.

Fortunately, the Royal Navy maintained an interest and conducted some important research and development during the interwar period. Probably the most important was the invention of the process for reducing a ship's magnetic field, known as "degaussing," named after Karl Friedrich Gauss, a mathematician who had done work on magnetic fields. Most World War I mines were "contact" mines, although late in the war the British came up with a magnetic mine dubbed the "M Sinker" that was able to lie on the ocean's floor and was set off when steel warships passed over it. This is why most minesweepers were eventually made out of wood or composites. Degaussing tremendously reduced a ship's magnetic signature. This development was fortunate because the Germans developed a magnetic mine for World War II.

The Royal Navy also laid down the first purpose-built minelayers. In 1922, it launched the 6,740-ton, 520-foot-long cruiser-minelayer *Adventure,* capable of carrying 280 mines. She was originally built with a transom stern for dropping mines, but it proved unsatisfactory and was later replaced. The *Adventure* was damaged twice by mines in World War II. Considered more successful were six 2,650-ton, 418-foot-long *Abdiel*-class fast minelayers, capable of carrying up to 156 mines, started in 1939. Three of the six *Abdiel* class were sunk during the war in the dangerous business of laying mines. Though called cruiser-minelayers, the *Adventure* carried only four 4.7-inch guns and the *Abdiel*s six 4-inch guns. In 1937 the smaller 805-ton *Plover* coastal minelayer was commissioned. The Royal Navy launched the submarine minelayer *Porpoise,* capable of carrying 50 mines, in 1932.

With two exceptions, no new English minesweepers were converted or laid down until the eve of World War II. One exception was China river gunboats adapted for minesweeping after the undeclared war between China and Japan began in 1932. The other exception was twenty-one 825-ton, 245-foot-long

Halcyon-class minesweepers built from 1933 through 1939. One, the *Seagull*, launched in 1937, was the first all-welded major warship in the Royal Navy. A few small 32-ton, 75-foot-long Thornycroft motor minesweepers were also built in 1937. With these few exceptions, most of the hundreds of mine craft built and converted by the Royal Navy for World War II were not started until 1939.

Japan also took a major interest in mine warfare. In 1929 the Japanese launched three minelayers. One, the large 2,000-ton, 341-foot-long *Itsukushima,* patterned after the British cruiser-minelayer *Adventure,* was capable of carrying 400 mines. Also built were the medium-sized 1,400-ton *Shirataka* and two smaller 450-ton *Kamome* class. During the 1930s a dozen more minelayers were built. Most were smaller ships, but two were large cruiser-minelayers, the 4,400-ton *Okinoshima* launched in 1935 and the 4,000-ton *Tsugaru* launched in 1940. Japan also built new minesweepers. Four 615-ton, 244-foot-long W1 class were launched from 1923 to 1924, followed by two slightly larger 620-ton W5 class in 1928. During the 1930s a dozen more were built. Thus Japan built by far the most modern minelaying and minesweeping force during the interwar period yet did not effectively use them, sowing mostly defensive minefields during World War II. Had Japan been more aggressive, there is no telling what damage mines might have caused the U.S. Navy, especially in some of the closed, narrow waters around the South Pacific islands.

Italy built ten minesweepers in the mid-1920s in the 600-ton, 200-foot range and during the late 1930s three more smaller craft. Russia built two smaller coastal minesweepers in the 1920s, followed by sixteen 434-ton, 203-foot-long *Tral* class starting in 1935. In the late 1920s Germany started building some small 60-ton motor minesweepers. These were followed by a slightly larger 115-ton craft in the mid-1930s built in eight various modes through the end of the war. Then, in 1935, Germany finally started building the larger 685-ton, 224-foot-long "Mob" type, constructing sixty-nine by 1941. France did not start its 630-ton *Elan* class until the eve of the war in 1938, although none were ever deployed as mine craft but rather used as coastal escorts.

Starting in 1930, the United States converted eight old flush-decker destroyers into light minelayers (DM) and in 1938 laid down two *Raven*-class mine craft (AM) commissioned in 1940. In 1940, the U.S. Navy began building the slightly larger 890-ton, 220-foot-long *Auk* class, of which ninety-seven were built during the war.[15]

World War II

Although there was only a handful of jury-rigged mine craft before World War I, on the eve of World War II there were two handfuls. More important, they were new craft and more were being built so it was fairly easy to continue churning out more. The United States continued building the *Auk* class throughout the war. In addition, over a hundred smaller 850-ton, 185-foot-long *Admirable* class, based on a patrol class design, were also built during the war. The Royal Navy began the *Bangor* class in 1940, built in three modes, all around 600 tons, followed by three slightly larger classes. Both the United States and Britain built trawlers for minesweeping, and many other trawlers and similar types were taken over and converted into minesweepers. Table 13.2 shows the approximate minesweeper balance during World War II. As is true of the numbers for the World War I balance, these figures are probably low, omitting some conversions (especially for the Axis navies). Table 13.2 also does not include smaller craft that were used in multiple roles. For example, more than one hundred of the British Commonwealth–built, ubiquitous Fairmile patrol boats (see chapter 14) were used for both minelaying and sweeping.

The large numbers were needed because the mine problem became considerably more complex during World War II. The Germans developed the magnetic mine, which they used initially to great effect. Fortunately, the British recovered a German mine dropped in error on a beach and were able to counter them by generating false magnetic signatures. Doing so required larger boats with auxiliary generators. Another solution was the move to wooden boats. The Germans reacted with more sophisticated modes, including acoustic mines set off by sound and "counters" that would go off only after so many passes, making sweeping even more tedious. Acoustic-magnetic combination mines were also fabricated. The most devious mine built, however, was the pressure or oyster mine detonated by the pressure from a ship's hull. Both sides developed pressure mines in 1940 but, because they were unsweepable, were afraid to use them. Hitler finally ordered their use against the 1944 D-Day invasion and the Americans used them against Japan late in the war.[16]

Table 13.2 Mine Craft Balance in World War II

Type	England	U.S.	Russia	France	Germany	Italy	Japan
MINELAYERS							
Interwar	5	8	18		3	10	18
War	51	65	0				17
MINESWEEPERS							
Interwar	23	2	80	12	38	3	18
New	754	845	160		235		36
Converted	835	67	N.L.	N.L.	N.L.		104
TOTAL	1668	987	258	12	276	13	193

NOTES: As with Table 13.1, except for RN data from Crocker, *Mine Warfare Vessels of the Royal Navy*, these numbers are probably low. Most countries used conversions not always listed in *Conway's* and *Jane's*. The table is still useful to illustrate the numbers involved. N.L. = Nonlisted but there probably were some.

Although there was no single dramatic application of mines in World War II such as their direct effect at Gallipoli or indirect one as at Jutland in World War I, they were, once again, a constant worry. Estimates are that some 631,000 mines were laid, resulting in almost 1,600 German ships and 1,075 Japanese ships being lost or damaged by mines. Mines were the fourth major cause of warship losses.[17] There is one important "might have been" concerning mines. The Americans started Operation Starvation against Japan in March 1945, dropping approximately 12,000 mines in Japanese waters and another 13,000 over a wider area. Within five months, almost all shipping to Japan was cut off. After the war, Japanese naval officers stated that had the mining begun earlier, Japan would have had to surrender before August— that is, before the dropping of the atomic bombs.[18] Although the laying of a minefield is not as exciting as a *Bismarck-Hood* exchange or a Battle of Midway, their importance equals those of the carriers and submarines.[19]

Post–World War II

With the major demobilization after the war, the mine force again fell on hard times, especially in the U.S. Navy, and this would result in one of the most embarrassing moments in its history. There was even a feeling that mine warfare was a thing of the past because longer-range aircraft made minelaying dangerous. In 1947 the United States Navy even did away with the mine man rating.

That situation changed with the Korean War. Fortunately, only a few mines had been laid at Inchon, and they had no effect on that famous amphibious landing. Considering the narrow channel and other obstacles at Inchon, a few well-placed mines might have wreaked havoc. But the North Koreans apparently learned their lesson well. A month later, the United States planned another end-run landing at Wonsan on the east coast but found the harbor extensively mined. On 12 October two minesweepers, the *Pirate* (AM-275) and *Pledge* (AM-277), were sunk by mines and the operation was postponed, causing Rear Admiral Allen E. "Hoke" Smith to send a message: "We have lost control of the seas to a nation without a Navy, using pre–World War I weapons, laid by vessels that were utilized at the time of the birth of Christ." Before the mines were swept, the U.S. Navy would lose four sweepers and a tug and have five destroyers damaged.[20] Adding to the insult, by the time the Marines landed, the Army had taken Wonsan and was being entertained by Bob Hope!

The Allies learned their lessons from Korea, and thus began the greatest peacetime mine craft buildup in history, resulting in the building of five hundred vessels between 1952 and 1961. From the Korean War experience, it was learned that the new Russian magnetic-influence mines could defeat degaussing, making steel-hulled sweepers obsolete. Accordingly, in 1951 the Royal Navy authorized the 360-ton, 152-foot-long "Ton" class (named after villages that ended in "ton" such as the *Coniston*) and launched 115 from 1952 through 1959. An additional 93 were built by other countries. They were aluminum framed with a wooden hull and nonmagnetic fittings. In addition, 93 smaller inshore 120-ton, 107-foot-long "Ham" class (named after villages that ended with "ham" such as the *Inglesham*) were built. Others were built by foreign governments.

In 1951 the United States started two new classes. The first was the large 640-ton, 172-foot-long oceangoing MSO (minesweeper, ocean) *Agile* class of which 93 were built through 1956. (In 1955, the U.S. Navy changed the designation for large mine craft from AM to MSO.) The U.S. Navy retained 58 MSOs and transferred the rest to allies. Also started was a smaller 360-ton, 145-foot-long coastal MSC *Bluebird* class of which 159 were built and 20 retained by the United States. Both the *Agile* and *Bluebird* classes were wooden hulled. By 1960, the Western allies had some 500 modern mine craft. Unfortunately, the downside of this large buildup, especially for the United States, was that few were built for the next thirty years, into the 1980s, when the MSOs and MSCs were clearly obsolete, creating a classic block obsolescence dilemma as all these ships reached the end of their useful lives at the same time.

U.S. Mine Division 43, consisting of four oceangoing MSOs, steams in formation on 20 July 1962 off Cape Henry, Virginia.
(U.S. Naval Institute)

The Soviet navy built the largest minesweeping fleet. From 1960 through 1973, it built sixty-five 200-ton, 132-foot-long *Vanya*-class coastal mine craft, followed by sixty-five more 450-ton, 160-foot-long *Sonya* class from 1973 through 1980. Throughout most of the Cold War period, the Soviet navy maintained the largest mine force by far, numbering two to three hundred. Other countries have also built mine craft, although none matched the Soviet navy in numbers. One of the most successful were thirty-five French-Dutch-Belgian 520-ton, 161-foot-long "Tripartite" class built from 1981 through 1990. In 1985 the Italians started the 485-ton, 164-foot-long *Lerici* class. The U.S. Navy adopted that basic design for its slightly larger 500-ton, 188-foot-long *Osprey* coastal mine craft built in the 1990s. The U.S. Navy has also built fourteen very large 1,100-ton, 224-foot-long *Avenger* class, the largest in the world.

Minelaying vessels have nearly disappeared from the sea. In 1967 the Royal Navy built the 1,375-ton, 265-foot-long HMS *Abdiel* as a support ship and exercise minelayer, now retired, and several Scandinavian countries and the Soviet Union have built a few. Today, most mines are laid by aircraft, submarines, or regular ships, both warships and merchantmen. The infamous Red Sea mining in 1983 by Libya was done by a "Ro-Ro" (roll on–roll off) merchantman and the Persian Gulf mines were probably laid by Iranian motorboats.

There have been other changes in mine warfare since World War II. As mines have become more sophisticated, old-fashioned sweeping is no longer sufficient. Mines must now be hunted down. The first mine hunter was the United States Navy's mine-hunter, coastal (MHC) *Bittern,* built in 1955, designed to locate or hunt mines rather than sweep them. She was the first built without any mine-destruction capabilities. Most hunting is now done by sophisticated sonar and remote-controlled sleds. Another major change was use of helicopters for minesweeping developed by the United States. Experiments were run as early as 1952, but in the 1960s the U.S. Navy transferred some medium-lift CH-53 helicopters to the minesweeping role. The U.S. Navy has converted a former *Iwo Jima*–class helicopter-carrying amphibious assault ship (LPH) into a mine support ship to operate helicopters (and also to provide tender services to the surface mine ships). The advantage, of course, is that the helicopters cannot be blown up by mines. In that regard, both air-cushion craft and catamarans have also been used to reduce the risk of accidentally setting off mines.

Mines have played a major role in post–World War II operations. As noted above, they caused tremendous problems in Korea. Mines were used by both sides during the Vietnam War, and most observers believe it was the mining of Haiphong Harbor by the United States that finally brought the North Vietnamese to the negotiating table. Just a very few mines closed that harbor. Mines laid by Libya closed the Red Sea, with no merchantmen dar-

The Belgian mine hunter *Dianthus*, one of the successful "Tripartite" class of mine craft built with France and the Netherlands between 1981 and 1990.
(Courtesy of Belgian Navy)

ing to damn the very few mines actually laid. And they were particularly effective in the Persian Gulf, where three American ships, the frigate *Samuel Roberts*, Aegis cruiser *Princeton*, and amphibious assault ship *Tripoli* all were put out of action by mines. Fortunately, the Western countries have learned their lessons and most navies now maintain modern mine countermeasure ships on active duty.[21]

Conclusion

Even though mines have been deadly, cost-effective weapons since the mid-nineteenth-century Age of Ironclads, mine countermeasure ships were long ignored for several reasons, some good, some bad. Part of this had to do with the "unchivalrous" nature of mines, an attitude still prevalent to a certain degree, but there were also some good—or at least understandable—reasons. Other craft were fairly easily converted to minesweepers, and new vessels usually were built in a matter of months. Therefore, even though only a handful of mine craft were in the pre–World War I and II fleets, they were built or converted quickly, eventually numbering in the hundreds. Also, most were manned by hastily trained reservists, who did a superb job.

Over the years there has also been a general sameness to mine countermeasure ships. Most coastal minesweepers were in the 150-ton, 150-foot range and most oceangoing ones were around 500 tons, 250 feet long. And sweeping methods changed little from the Civil War through World War II. Although the basic method of sweeping mines has remained the same, the mechanics have changed from Civil War soldiers with grappling hooks to paravanes and now remote-controlled sleds. Another change came with the development of more complex mines requiring not just minesweepers but hunters with sophisticated sonars. Perhaps the biggest change has been in perceptions. Most navies have learned their lessons and now keep at least small fleets of mine countermeasure ships in their active force with others in the active reserves. It appears that the days of ignoring mine warfare might finally be over.

Small Combatants   14

T<small>HERE HAVE ALWAYS</small> been two groups of enthusiasts for small
combatants. First and foremost are dashing young naval officers
hoping to make a name for themselves, and second are frugal old
politicians hoping to save money. Mature, professional naval officers have always been more skeptical of their value. All three have invariably
been wrong. With very few exceptions, young officers found drudgery rather
than glory while frugal politicians found they could not buy defense on the
cheap. Professional naval officers, however, discovered that small combatants
did have certain missions and, more important, could be turned out in great
numbers during wartime. Small combatants have also performed another
important task as experimental prototypes. Better to make a mistake with a
small combatant than a large dreadnought.

Historically there have been three categories of small combatants: coastal
patrol, small gunboats, and, sometimes forgotten, river craft. In modern
times two more categories have been added: the fast attack craft, first torpedo
boats but later missile boats, and small escort ships, mostly for antisubmarine warfare. Although many escort ships such as the 110-foot sub-chasers
of both world wars were definitely in the small combatant category, the line
between some larger patrol escort combatants (such as sloops and corvettes)
and destroyer escorts and frigates usually considered in the "ship" category
has often been a fine one. Small escorts were generally slower, single-mission
vessels, under 1,500 tons, less than 300 feet long, but there are no clear distinctions. Small escorts have virtually disappeared from the seas, but they
played major roles during both world wars. A sixth type, mine craft, are
often included as small combatants, but these specialized ships really fall into
a separate category. Amphibious craft are also sometimes included, especially when they were converted into small gunboats as happened during the
Indo-China and Vietnam Wars.

Small combatants probably do not get the credit they deserve. It can be
reasonably argued that the first modern warships were small combatants and
most of the major naval engineering advances were first incorporated on
small craft. Small combatants, coastal patrol and gunboats, and not dreadnoughts, were the ships used for constant patrols, and during both world

wars hundreds were built. Today they still play important roles and are by far the most numerous types of warships in two general categories: fast attack craft, or FACs, and coastal patrol, now often called OPV, offshore patrol vessels. And they still are important as prototypes for new ideas such as testing hydrofoils, air-cushion, and SWATH concepts.

Early Precedents

Throughout history there have always been larger and smaller warships although it would be hard to cite any real precedents during the Age of Galleys for small combatants as we know them today. Most galleys were themselves small by today's standards, and anything much smaller would have had difficulty using the boarding tactics of the day. There were smaller galleys such as the *lembos,* but comparatively the differences were slight and certainly not like those between the torpedo boats and battleships of the Modern Age. During the Age of Sail the smaller warships such as the brigantines, snows, cutters, and others would fall into the small combatant category. The most famous small combatants from the Age of Sail are probably "Mr. Jefferson's gunboats," which were small coastal gunboats with a few cannon that President Thomas Jefferson forced on the early U.S. Navy to save money. They were quickly found inadequate and are usually cited as an example of a politician trying to buy defense on the cheap. The large navies of the day did use small gunboats for certain missions such as coastal defense, but they were backed up by ships of the line.

The real precedent for the modern small combatant came during the Age of Ironclads, and it can be argued that the first truly modern ships, that is, those without any sail, were small craft. During the Crimean War, from 1853 to 1856, the Royal Navy produced several different classes of small steam gunboats, most carrying 68-pounders. The largest number were ninety-eight 232-ton *Albacore* class with one each 68- and 32-pounder. Although these Crimean War gunboats carried one or two large guns and might be considered "monitors," they were still in the small craft range in size. As was typical during this stage of the Age of Ironclads, a hodgepodge of various gunboat types were built by the Royal Navy through the end of the nineteenth century. One of the largest classes were thirty so-called flatiron gunboats laid down between 1867 and 1881, followed by twenty-six similar *Ant, Gadfly,* and *Bouncer* classes. All were in the 250-ton, 85-foot-long range, armed with one 10-inch muzzle loader.[1] Most other powers of the day also built small gunboats during this time, especially for colonial duty.

The major small combatant innovation of this era was the motor torpedo boat. They first appeared during the American Civil War. Both sides used small craft with spar torpedoes that had to be attached to the sides of ships. The Confederates operated semisubmergible "Davids," the most famous use of which was the 1863 attack that damaged the Union ironclad *New Iron-*

sides. In 1864 Union Lieutenant William B. Cushing fulfilled every young naval officer's dream by using a steam launch with a spar torpedo to sink the Southern ironclad *Albemarle.* The first purpose-built small combatant was the Union torpedo vessel *Spuyten Duyvil* of 1864. Never used in battle, she was an interesting design with a turtleback deck, the ability to flood down for a very low freeboard, and a reloadable spar torpedo run out underwater.

Pre-Dreadnought Era

The start of the pre-dreadnought or premodern era in small combatants can be traced to 1871, when the British builder Thornycroft designed the *Miranda* for experimentation and in 1872 built what is usually considered the world's first true torpedo boat, the *Rasp,* for Norway. Originally constructed with a towing torpedo, the *Rasp* was changed to carry a spar. By the mid-1870s, most countries had acquired similar craft. During the 1877–78 war against Turkey, Russia converted some fast launches to carry spar torpedoes.

Two inventions brought about the progression to the most famous of the small combatants, the fast torpedo boat. First was the development of fast river launches. Thornycroft and other builders started building fast launches in the 1860s, which happened to coincide with the invention of the self-propelled torpedo, leading inevitably to the fast torpedo boat. Up to this time, all torpedoes had been either towed or were spar torpedoes. The Royal Navy's first premodern torpedo boat was the 32-ton, 87-foot-long *Lightning* (TB-1) completed in 1877. Originally, the torpedoes were lowered into the water and fired, but a bow firing tube was developed in 1879. Thus in a space of about twenty years from 1860 to 1880, the fast launch was coupled with the self-propelled torpedo to produce the motor torpedo boat (MTB).

The Royal Navy built two classes of torpedo boats: large seagoing first class and smaller second class to be carried on cruisers and depot ships. The first-class torpedo boats were built in four basic sizes through the end of the nineteenth century: first, 28-to-32-ton 87-footers until 1885, followed by 125-footers until 1892, then 140-footers through the 1890s, and finally, more-than-100-ton 160-footers at the turn of the century. Smaller second-class torpedo boats meant to be carried on cruisers were started in 1878. They were all in the 10- to 20-ton range, around 60 feet long. Two specialized torpedo boat depot ships were built, the *Hecla,* launched in 1878, and the *Vulcan* in 1889. The *Hecla* was a converted merchantman, but the *Vulcan* was a purpose-built cruiser-type ship. Starting with the *Lightning* in 1877, the Royal Navy built 128 first-class and 69 second-class torpedo boats through 1904.

During the latter part of the Age of Ironclads no country embraced the concept of using small torpedo boats more than did France. This was the era of the *jeune école,* and its main proponent, Admiral Aube, became Minister of Marine in 1884. Like England, France built both small and large torpedo boats in varying sizes from 1876 to the turn of the century. The first craft were built by Thornycroft and Yarrow, but starting in 1877 the French began building a 27-meter type followed by larger 33- and 35-meter modes in the 20- to 40-ton range. Considered one of the most successful was the 126 design, a 71-ton, 118-foot-long boat capable of 21 knots first built in 1889. During this period France built some 350 torpedo boats. One of the largest classes was a 37-meter (121 foot) type in the 85-ton range of which 91 were built in slightly varying modes between 1897 and 1904.

Russia also embraced the small torpedo boat and most other major countries also built them. Exceptions were the United States and Japan, which were far from the more closed European waters. After the turn of the century, however, torpedo boats fell out of favor and were replaced by the new torpedo boat "destroyer." As noted in chapter 8, starting in the mid-1880s torpedo boat "catchers" and then TBD torpedo boat "destroyers" started to be built. The early catchers in the 200-foot range fall into the small combatant category, but the 1890s destroyers eventually evolved into ship size, although the difference between larger torpedo boats and early destroyers was often slight. Germany continued to use the term *torpedo boat* through World War I, but most analysts considered them destroyers. Thus, on the eve of the modern era, the old torpedo boat was being overtaken by the equally fast and larger torpedo boat destroyer and most countries were phasing out the former.[2]

Modern Age: To 1914

In 1904 the Frenchman Count Récoupé built what is sometimes considered the first modern, authentic torpedo boat with an integral bow-firing torpedo tube, but in general the early modern era was not kind to the development of small combatants for two reasons. First, this was the golden era of dreadnoughts and increasing emphasis was being placed on ever larger battleships and battle cruisers, and second, the smaller warships, light cruisers, and especially destroyers were now as fast and in some cases even faster than the torpedo boats. The torpedo boats were no match for the new destroyers with their larger, quick-firing guns. Moreover, the destroyers also carried torpedoes, making the smaller MTBs unnecessary. Thus, by 1910, with few exceptions, the hundreds of torpedo boats built in the late nineteenth century were either retired, placed in reserve, or used for coastal patrol, which became their main function during World War I.

Ironically, while small boats generally fell out of favor, major developments using small craft were started, many of which are still considered futuristic designs. These were the hydroplane, hydrofoil, and air cushion, all designed to overcome the resistance of the normal displacement hull to high speeds. Major increases in speed had been achieved in the mid-1890s. In 1896 the French boat *Forban* became the first to make over 30 knots, and the same year the British experimental *Turbina* reached 34 knots, but the classic monohull restricted greater speeds.

In 1905, however, the French built the first "planing" boat, which would eventually lead to fast boats in the 40-knot range, giving them an advantage over larger warships. Planing is the condition when a small boat with a light hull and flat, beamy bottom is forced out of the water by the hydrodynamic lift generated by fast speeds. This reduces resistance, resulting in the boat skimming or "planing" along the surface. Planing was understood as far back as 1840. Experiments were conducted in 1887, when Escher Wyss built the first planing boat, *Le Rapide,* in Zurich, but it barely lifted. It was not until 1905 that the first true planing boat was built by the Frenchman Campet. In 1910 the English *Miranda IV* made 35 knots, and she would have great influence on the Royal Navy's World War I fast boats.[3]

Two other designs still usually considered futuristic made their first appearance during this period. These were the hydrofoil and air cushion. The hydrofoil was demonstrated as early as 1891 by Count de Lambert with a boat using four transverse hydroplanes, but it barely lifted. During the early years of the modern era, however, several countries carried out experiments with hydrofoils, including a series by Alexander Graham Bell (of telephone fame) that began in 1909 and led to various designs tested through 1919. One reached 60 knots. Further experiments on hydrofoils were carried out in the interwar period, and Germany had a major program during World War II, including building two large boats for quickly resupplying General Erwin Rommel in North Africa, but none ever joined the fleets. It was not until the 1960s that truly successful hydrofoils were built.

The idea for an air cushion can be traced to 1883, when Gustave Laval of France had an idea to blow air through slits in the bottom of a boat. In 1911 the sea-sled, a hybrid planing–air-cushion craft with a W-shaped hull, was designed by the Canadian W. Albert Hickam, but the major testing came during World War I. In 1915 Austrian Lieutenant Dogobert von Müller-Thomamühl developed a concept to blow air under a flat-bottomed hull with twin bilge keels, and several experiments were actually carried out. The concept was abandoned by the Austrian government, which saw little use for such a boat. Not until the 1970s would successful air-cushion boats be built. Thus, while the pre–World War I years were generally difficult times for small combatants, such craft still continued to play key roles as experimental prototypes.[4]

World War I

World War I brought the small combatant back into prominence for four reasons: mines, submarines, dreadnought gridlock, and simply because they could be turned out in large numbers. Immediately after the war began, mines were sown, which stimulated the construction and conversion of hundreds of mine craft. Some of those converted were old torpedo boats, and often the same design was used for both new mine craft and escorts, so there is a definite overlap between the small combatant and mine craft categories.

Like mine warfare, submarine warfare had also been underestimated, requiring the building or converting of hundreds of antisubmarine escort ships. The Royal Navy responded by building a dual-purpose "Flower" class (named after flowers, e.g., *Acacia* and *Azalea*) for both minesweeping and escort duty. Although most were slated for minesweeping, twelve 1,250-ton, 268-foot-long *Aubrietia* class built in 1916, followed by twenty-five similar sized *Anchusa* class in 1917, were classified as convoy sloops. Both carried two 4-inch guns. France also received some British "Flower"-class escort sloops as well as building some of her own design. France's largest class were six 570-ton, 256-foot-long *Marne*-class sloops. Thirty larger 850-ton, 246-foot *Amiens* class were started but not finished until 1919.

By far the largest number of escort ships were built by the United States for both its own and Allied use. In 1915 the Royal Navy contracted with the Electric Launch Company (ELCO) to build 75-foot launches. After fifty were delivered, five hundred more were ordered in a slightly longer 80-foot version, and the 80-foot ELCO became the largest class built in World War I. They were made of wood and simple to build, designed along the lines of pleasure craft. The ELCOs clearly illustrate the small craft's biggest advantage— speed of building. Using mass-production techniques, 550 were turned out in 488 days, or an average of one per day. France operated 40 ELCOs and ordered 12 more and Italy 110. ELCOs were followed by another successful small craft, 110-foot submarine chasers, also built of wood with one 3-inch gun and one ASW Y-gun. The first was completed in August 1917, and 440 eventually were built for the United States Navy and its allies. In 1918 the United States also began building a larger open-ocean ASW escort known as Eagle Boat patrol vessels. They were 500 tons, 201 feet long, with two 4-inch guns and one Y-gun. PE-1 was commissioned on 28 December 1918, and most were completed in 1919. Sixty were eventually built; several were transferred to the U.S. Coast Guard after the war.[5] All told, more than a thousand small craft were built by the United States in approximately three years, an average of about one per day.

Fast attack boats also made a comeback in World War I. Frustrated by what might be called dreadnought gridlock with the fleets sitting in port, in 1915 two young British sublieutenants suggested the building of small, fast boats to be carried on cruisers for transporting to the German coast, where they could be released to attack the German fleet in port. This idea led to the building of the fast coastal motorboat (CMB) based on the 1910 *Miranda IV*. The 40-foot CMB-1, capable of 33 knots and carrying one torpedo, began trials in 1916. A longer 55-foot version was introduced in 1917 capable of carrying two torpedoes, followed by a 70-foot version for laying the new "M-Sinker" magnetic mine. Five were completed after the war ended. Contrary to the sublieutenants' wishes, however, the CMBs were used mostly for local operations and only a few were ever carried on ships. The CMBs' greatest success actually came after the war, in July 1919, when CMB-4 sank the Russian cruiser *Oleg* off Kronstadt. Ninety-one CMBs were completed during the war. After the war, several ended up in the United States, used to catch rum-runners during Prohibition.

The most famous small combatants of World War I were the Italian motor antisubmarine (MAS) boats, which despite their usual antisubmarine designation were completed as either motor torpedo boats or motor gunboats.[6] Unlike the fast Royal Navy hydroplane CMBs, the MAS boats were a more conventional and slower design. The first MAS boats, launched in 1915, were 12 tons, 52 feet long, with a speed of only 23 knots. MAS boats were built throughout the war in various modes, all around the same size with top speeds of about 28 knots, fairly slow for fast attack boats. But the MAS boats had spectacular successes during the war, sinking two Austrian-Hungarian battleships: the old *Wien* on 10 December 1917 and then Austria's most modern battleship, the *Szent Istvan,* on 10 June 1918. The sinking of the *Szent Istvan* was captured on film and is invariably shown in all World War I shows. MAS-15, which sank the *Svent Istvan,* is still preserved in Rome.

Germany also built some small, faster boats to eliminate the antisubmarine and antitorpedo boat net barriers laid by the British. First called "L-boats" (*Luftschiffmotorboote,* or airship-engined boat), its designation was changed to LM in 1919 to differentiate it from the "L" designation given airships. The LMs were smaller boats, all around 49 feet long, and had only limited success. Neither France nor Russia built any special coastal craft during the war, which is ironic considering their enthusiasm in the late nineteenth century.[7]

And there were many, many more in the small combatant range too numerous to mention, either built or converted during the war. Italy, for example, bought forty-seven Japanese fishing boats, equipped them with one or two 3-inch guns, and converted them into "Vedette boats." England built twelve "Fly" class river gunboats for operations on the Tigris and Euphrates against Turkey. Small gunboats for colonial duty were still in most navies. Most countries also took over private yachts and converted small merchantmen and fishing boats for coastal patrol duties. One of the more interesting types was the 8-ton Italian *Grillo*-class "naval tanks," which had lateral caterpillar chains for overcoming harbor barriers. The *Grillo* was damaged by Austrian gunfire while forcing the barrages at Pola.[8]

Table 14.1 shows the approximate naval balance for small combatants during World War I. The numbers might be slightly off because prewar craft use is sometimes unclear and detailed information on some smaller craft types is missing altogether, but the table clearly illustrates the numbers

Table 14.1 Small Combatant Balance in World War I

Type	Britain	France	Italy	Russia	U.S.	Germany	Austria
1914							
Torpedo boats	40	135	10	34			6
Gunboats	59	3	2	12	2	2	4
BUILT							
TBs	36		86	98		85	
CMB/MAS	100		200~			33	6
Escort	40	48			20		
ELCOs	400	40	110				
Subchasers		50			50		
TOTAL	675	276	408	144	72	120¹	16

NOTES: This table is used for illustrative purposes only for several reasons, since small combatant categories were different in each navy. Many of the prewar torpedo boats and gunboats were converted to minesweepers. TB = Torpedo boats, usually in the 100- to 200-ton range. CBM = In the under 50-ton range.

involved, and these were just the purpose-built. Including auxiliary craft, all told the Royal Navy operated some 3,700 small craft.[9] Although there were only a very few spectacular actions such as MAS-15 sinking the modern Austria dreadnought *Szent Istvan,* small combatants were still important in carrying out day-to-day coastal patrols.[10]

Interwar Period

After the war, small combatants again fell on hard times, mostly for financial reasons. Hundreds of escort and fast patrol craft were either retired, placed in reserves, or sold. By the end of the 1920s the Royal Navy had only two CMBs left on the books. The United States returned to its prewar attitude, often referring to small boats as "suicide boats" or "poor men's warships." In the early 1930s interest in smaller combatants was revived, but it was not until the late 1930s and early 1940s that construction began again in any numbers.

There were exceptions to this general attitude toward small combatants. Germany, restricted by the Versailles Treaty, in 1920 began a small secret program that eventually led to the development of the *Schnellboot* (or E-Boat as the Allies called it) of World War II. In 1926 they launched the experimental boat *Narwal,* which at 27 tons was the largest hydroplane of her day. In 1928, development began on another boat commissioned as a guard boat (*Wachboot*) W.1, eventually reclassified as *Schnellboot* S.1 in 1932. The E-boats' main characteristic was two integral bow torpedo tubes. By the mid-1930s, they were about 92 tons with a speed of 39 knots. The E-boats' large size gave them good sea-keeping characteristics and allowed them to operate beyond coastal and channel waters.[11]

The other exception was the Soviet Union, which in the 1920s became enamored of the *jeune école* (at least partially for budgetary reasons) and in 1926 authorized eighteen 450-ton, 235-foot *Uragan*-class coastal patrol torpedo boats built between 1929 and 1935. These were the first surface ships built by the new Soviet government. The same program also authorized thirty-six 11-ton 59-foot MTBs patterned after the British CMBs. The Soviets continued building these and other classes and by 1936 had 190 boats in service with 43 more building, giving the Soviet Union the largest inventory of active small combatants during this period.[12]

In 1928 the Royal Navy launched two 1,045-ton, 266-foot *Bridgewater*-class sloops as replacements for the World War I "Flower" class, but they were intended for foreign service and minesweeping. These were followed by four similar *Hastings* class launched in 1930 and eight slightly larger *Shoreham* class launched from 1930 to 1932. All three classes had two 4-inch guns and speeds around 17 knots. Starting in 1933 the first of twelve (four for Australia) 990-ton, 266-foot *Grimsby* class were launched, followed by nine smaller 520-ton *Kingfisher* and *Shearwater* coastal class escorts in the late 1930s. And in 1936 the Royal Navy launched the first of twelve "motor torpedo boats" designated MTB rather than the CMB (coastal motorboat) used in World War I. They were 18 tons, 60 feet, with a speed of 35 to 38 knots and were the first MTBs built since World War I. Finally, in 1939 the Royal Navy laid plans for a new 1,200-ton, 205-foot "Flower" class corvette and had sixty on order when the war started.

Other countries also planned to build small combatants before the war started. In 1937 the United States began looking for a new 110-foot submarine chaser, with prototypes built by 1940. In 1938 a program began that led to the famous PT boats of World War II. Italy, which had continued building a few MAS boats through the interwar period, developed a 500 series launched in 1936 that became the standard for all subsequent boats. It was 22 tons, 56 feet, with a top speed of 44 knots. Italy also built some escort classes. France in the mid-1930s built twelve 680-ton, 249-foot *La Melpomène*–class torpedo boats. Japan launched four 535-ton, 259-foot *Tomozuru* torpedo boats in 1933 followed by eight 945-ton, 284-foot *Otori* class launched from 1935 to 1937. Although called torpedo boats, they were built along destroyer escort lines and should not be confused with the MTB motor torpedo boats.[13]

World War II

Unlike in World War I, when production did not really begin for two years, all the countries had small combatants building or at least in the planning stages so new ships were turned out almost immediately. This was fortunate for the Allies because small escort ships were desperately needed for the deadly antisubmarine Battle of the Atlantic. During the war, including DEs and frigates, the Allies would build almost two thousand small escorts.

In the Royal Navy, the largest class of ocean escorts consisted of 151 1,100-ton, 208-foot "Flower" class corvettes with one 4-inch gun, depth charges, and hedgehogs built in two modes. These ships were launched from 1940 through 1944. There was actually a larger class of 218 small 560-ton, 148-foot-long "Admiralty" class trawlers built like fishing trawlers that were used for both escort and mine duties. Although the trawlers were the most numerous, they were considered marginal for escort duty. Considered more suitable were the larger corvettes, sloops, frigates, and smaller destroyers. The "Flower" class corvettes were followed by the 1,400-ton, 301-foot-long "River" frigate class with two 4-inch guns, hedgehogs, and depth charges. Sixty-two "River" class were launched starting in 1942, and more were built in Canada. Most of these escort ships were built along commercial lines, but two classes, *Black Swan* class sloops and "Hunt" class destroyers, were built to warship specifications. The "Hunt" class destroyers (called DEs by *Conway's*) were only 1,000 tons, 280 feet, but they carried four 4-inch guns and probably fall into the escort category, but the *Black Swan* class sloops built in various modes were about 1,350 tons, 376 feet long, with six 4-inch guns and, although considered escorts, probably more properly fall into a destroyer category. Counting these smaller destroyers, frigates, and larger sloops as well as the corvettes and trawlers, the Royal Navy built 945 escort ships in twenty-three new classes during World War II. Many were constructed in Canada.[14]

The United States built 961 escort ships (1,136 including AMs that were used as escorts as well as for minesweeping). Of these, over half, 570, were destroyer escorts (DEs) in the 1,400-ton, 300-foot-long range with three 3-inch guns. With speeds of only 20 knots, these are more probably in the escort rather than multipurpose destroyer ship category, but the line between small combatants such as corvettes and DEs is a fine one. To add to the confusion, the United States also built 77 even larger 1,500-ton, 302-foot-long *Asheville* and *Tacoma* class listed as patrol class frigates (PF) based on the Royal Navy's "River" class. The largest number of small escorts were 354 patrol craft (PCs) designed as coastal escorts and submarine chasers. They were around 400 tons, 173 feet long, with one 3-inch gun and various ASW weaponry. Also built were 63 slightly larger patrol craft escorts (PCE). Eighteen 925-ton patrol gunboats (PGs) were also constructed for England and Canada. All told, the United States built six major classes and eleven subclasses of escorts.[15] In addition to these larger escort ships, as in World War I, the United States built a 110-foot subchaser.

The Axis forces built only a handful of escorts. Germany had ten 712-ton, 249-foot-long F class listed as fleet escorts launched starting in 1935 but built no more after the war began. In the mid-1930s Italy built thirty-two 620-ton

269-foot-long *Spica* class designated torpedo boats but used as escorts during the war. These were followed by four *Pegaso* class similar to the British "Hunt" class in the late 1930s. During the war Italy constructed fifteen *Ciclone* class similar to the *Pegaso* and then sixteen *Ariete* class similar to the *Spica* class. In addition, fifty-nine 660-ton, 211-foot-long *Gabbiano* class corvettes were launched during 1942–43. Many of these Italian ships were seized by the Germans when Italy surrendered in 1943. Before the war Japan built a few small subchasers and larger 860-ton, 250-foot-long *Shimushu* class escorts. During the war Japan built two classes of escorts, eighteen *Matsu* class and fourteen *Tachibana* class, both around 1,270 tons, 321 feet long, with three 5-inch guns. Japan also built 281 smaller escorts all in the 700- to 900-ton range with two or three 4.7-inch guns.

Although the escort and patrol craft were probably more important, the more romantic fast torpedo boats have always gotten the most attention. Perhaps the most famous are the American PT boats celebrated in the great World War II John Wayne movie *They Were Expendable,* based loosely on the life of Vice Admiral (then Lieutenant) John Bulkeley, who won the Congressional Medal of Honor for his exploits in the Philippines during the dark days of early 1942. President John F. Kennedy's heroic deeds on PT-109, also documented in a movie, added even more luster. Several different models of

U.S. Navy PT boats return to base after a mission.
(U.S. Naval Institute)

PT boats were built during the war. These were the 77-foot ELCO of which 29 were built, followed by an 80-foot ELCO of which 160 were completed. In addition, 131 78-foot Higgins boats were built. Most had four 21-inch torpedo tubes, one or two 40 mm guns, and various machine guns.

The Royal Navy built several classes of MTBs and MGBs (motor gunboats) all in the 60- to 70-foot range with speeds up to 38 knots. The Royal Navy also built the most ubiquitous of all small combatants, the Fairmile, completing more than 800 in various modes. The Fairmile company had proposed a simple wooden boat based on a motor launch. After a few experimental "A" models were completed, some 650 "B" models were built operating as everything from coastal patrol to minesweepers to coastal convoy escorts. They were followed by faster "D" models that operated as MTBs and had two torpedo tubes and various smaller guns. Fairmiles were also built by, and served in, many Commonwealth countries.[16]

Japan finally started building MTBs in 1943 and by the end of the war had some 314. They were generally in the 14- to 20-ton range, 50 to 60 feet long, with two torpedo tubes. Italy once again built MAS boats, as well as a large MS boat and antisubmarine VAS boat. Italy also built some very small "explosive motorboats" in the 1-ton, 20-foot range. They were designed to be carried by larger ships with two-man crews who would jump off before the boat hit its target. The German S (or E) boats were probably the most famous Axis MTB. By the end of the war they were up to around 100 tons and 114 feet long, making them almost escort size and very seaworthy. All told, 249 S-boats were commissioned. Table 14.2 shows the approximate small combatant balance during World War II. The numbers might be slightly inaccurate because numbers of small craft are sometimes inexact, but they are indicative of the importance of small combatants.

Small craft played important roles in World War II. Although it was not until the escort carriers appeared in the spring of 1943 that the Battle of the Atlantic was finally won by the Allies, the hundreds of small ocean escorts played crucial roles in the interim. While they sank some German U-boats, their primary role and mission was simply presence, which in many cases was sufficient. Most submarine attacks were carried out on the surface, so even the presence of a slow corvette or trawler would often deter an attack.[17]

The fast attack boats scored some successes. The American PT boats were credited with sinking two Japanese destroyers, severely damaging two more, and participating in the destruction of a cruiser and two destroyers. Their greatest contributions were probably "barge-busting," attacking Japanese small craft and barges carrying reinforcements to islands. After a while, torpedo tubes were taken off some PT boats and replaced by more and larger guns for this purpose. In the Royal Navy one of the MTBs' primary roles was rescuing downed fliers. The Italians never repeated their success of World War I in sinking a battleship, although six explosive boats launched from

Table 14.2 Small Combatant Balance in World War II

Type	Britain	U.S.	France	Russia	Germany	Italy	Japan
MTBs							
Interwar	25	0	2	269	25	63	2
WW II	403	417	3	130	224	63	482
TOTAL	428	417	5	399	249	126	484
ESCORTS							
Interwar							
DE/FF	36	0	0	0	0	4	0
Corvette	9	0	12	22	18	33	16
PC	0	3	4	88	0	4	15
World War II							
DE/FF	313	499	0	0	15	16	32
Corvette	421	75	4	2	25	75	242
PC	1,100	908	17	115	0	62	324
TOTAL	1,879	1,482	37	227	58	194	692

NOTES: MTB = Motor torpedo boats, PT boats, MAS, S-boats, and other fast launches. DE/FF = Destroyer escorts, frigates, and others over 1,000 tons. Corvette = Corvettes, gun boats, torpedo boats, and others from 500 to 1,000 tons. PC = Patrol craft, submarine chasers, and others under 500 tons.

destroyers did sink the Royal Navy cruiser *York*. One of the German E-boats' major kills was the catching and sinking of some LSTs practicing D-Day landings. This tragic, embarrassing episode was covered up for many years. Generally, however, MTB operations were disappointing. Axis MTBs found increasingly tough sledding as the Allies gained control of the skies, requiring them to operate only at night. But they were a constant threat that could not be ignored.[18]

Post–World War II Period

In the post–World War II period, most of the hundreds of small combatants built during the war were retired, given away to smaller powers, or broken up. In the United States the first batch of small DEs commissioned in 1942–43 were broken up in 1946–47—a four-year life span. A few PT boats were kept for experimental purposes and then retired. The Royal Navy gave away or sold its many Fairmiles, and they could be found, especially in Commonwealth navies, well into the 1960s.

Although small ocean escorts have just about disappeared from the seas in the 1990s, many were still built during the 1950s. The United States, for example, built small DEs such as the 1,300-ton *Dealey* and *Claud Jones* classes through the early 1960s that were a throwback to the small World War II escorts. The Royal Navy built the 1,180-ton second rate utility

Blackwood class in the late 1950s. Most, however, operated as destroyers and were soon found to be inadequate for the destroyer's multipurpose roles. The *Blackwood*s, for example were called "second rate futility." [19] Since the mid-1960s, the United States has built only larger DEs (redesignated frigates) for ocean escort, and most other countries have followed suit. Ships with the primary role of ocean escort are still built, but most are well over 2,000 tons, outside the small combatant category.

More common are small coastal patrol corvettes such as the 1,100-ton, 262-foot-long *D'Estienne D'Orves* class built by France from the mid-1970s through the early 1980s. Considered one of the best recent designs is the American-built Israeli 1,100-ton "Saar 5" class corvette with harpoon missiles and a helicopter. Currently, and in keeping with using smaller boats for experiments, some of the most intriguing stealth designs are being conducted on corvettes.

Since World War II, the leader in coastal patrol combatants has been the Soviet Union, which, unlike most countries, has continued to build smaller frigates in the 1,000-ton range as well as corvettes. In the early 1950s the Soviets built sixty-eight 1,160-ton, 295-foot-long *Riga* class frigates, followed by the even smaller 950-ton *Petya* class frigates in the 1960s and the 750-ton *Grisha* class corvettes in the early 1970s. They are currently building a 910-ton *Grisha V* class for light antisubmarine missions. Although many were considered an old design and were used simply for border patrol, others are considered quite capable, such as the 800-ton *Nanuchka*-class missile corvettes first launched in the mid-1960s. Currently the Russian Navy has the largest corvette fleet, numbering more than 100.

The vessels that have gotten the most attention have been the Soviet fast attack craft missile boats, first the 62-ton, 83-foot-long "Komar" class built in the mid-1950s, followed by the "Osa" class in the late 1950s and 1960s. The *Komar* class represented the first missile attack boats. Hundreds of *Komar* and *Osa* class were built, with many transferred to Soviet client states. They gained fame with the sinking of the Israeli destroyer *Elath* in 1967 by a Styx missile fired from an Egyptian Komar. In addition, the Soviet Union continues to build both fast torpedo and gun boats.

Other countries have also built FACs. Germany, for example, built thirty 184-ton, 140-foot-long *Jaguar*-class gunboats designated as Schnellboot 5 in the late 1950s, followed by ten larger 173-ton, 140-foot-long *Zobel* class in the early 1960s and twenty even larger 234-ton, 154-foot-long S-41 class in the early 1970s. Germany's latest are ten 398-ton, 189-foot-long S-71 class. Most countries have built only a few FACs, but they are still considered useful in certain waters. The Scandinavian countries, for example, all operate FACs, some with torpedoes, for their closed waters. The United States has built only a handful that could be classified as FACs. The most interesting

A "Komar"-class guided missile craft from the Soviet Union. Missiles from an Egyptian "Komar"-class ship sank the Israeli destroyer *Elath* on 27 October 1967. (U.S. Naval Institute)

were six 230-ton, 147-foot-long *Pegasus*-class hydrofoil ships commissioned from 1977 through 1982. Although they were supported by Admiral Elmo Zumwalt, junior officers, and many in Congress, the U.S. Navy was never enthusiastic about them and they were retired in 1993.

A sometimes forgotten category of small combatants reemerged during the French Indo-China and Vietnam Wars. This was the riverine force. During the Vietnam War, the United States built more than twenty-five different types of riverine craft, many former amphibious craft converted into gunboats. The best known were the 32-ton, 65-foot-long "Swift" boats built of aluminum based on a commercial craft used to support offshore drilling platforms in the Gulf of Mexico. About 125 were built for both coastal and riverine patrol. More numerous, with more than five hundred built, were smaller 8-ton, 32-foot-long PBR boats with fiberglass-reinforced plastic hulls. During the late 1960s the United States Navy also built seventeen 225-ton, 165-foot-long *Asheville*-class gunboats for coastal and blockade missions, but they were soon decommissioned after the war.[20]

IT COULD BE ARGUED that the only major sea battles in the post–World War II era have involved small combatants. During the 1973 Arab-Israeli Yom Kippur War, there were several such engagements. On the first night of the war, five Israeli units fought the first missile-versus-missile surface action in naval history against Syrian units, sinking three. In another engagement thirteen Israeli FACs armed with Gabriel launchers defeated twenty-seven Arab Osa and Komar boats mounting longer-range Styx missiles.

FACs also played a key role in the Vietnam War. On 2 August 1964 three North Vietnamese patrol boats attacked the destroyer USS *Maddox* (DD-731) in the Gulf of Tonkin. Three days later, on 5 August, North Vietnamese boats once again attacked the *Maddox,* this time in company with the *Turner Joy* (DD-951). This incident led to the Gulf of Tonkin Resolution, used by President Lyndon Johnson to justify retaliating against North Vietnam and considered a key element escalating U.S. involvement in the Vietnam War. Ironically, it is now generally agreed that there was in fact no attack on 5 August but that the radar tracks were caused by atmospherics. During Persian Gulf operations, Iranian speedboats were a constant concern; several were sunk by the U.S. Navy.

Conclusion

Although overshadowed by the larger warships, small combatants have been the most numerous ships throughout modern history. There have been literally hundreds of different types and classes, from less than 10 to approximately 1,500 tons and with missions ranging from border patrol to taking on dreadnoughts. In the late nineteenth century hundreds of motor torpedo boats were built on the premise that they could defeat the larger ships, but they were instead subdued by the larger, faster torpedo boat destroyer. During both world wars, however, fast boats again were found useful for some missions. Perhaps more important in both world wars were small escorts such as corvettes that could be turned out quickly for ASW and other escort duties.

Today, while the large ships, the carriers, cruisers, and destroyers, still get the most attention, small combatants are by far the most numerous in two general classes, fast attack craft or coastal patrol, now often called offshore patrol vessels, or OPVs. The value of OPVs should not be underestimated. As shown in appendix D, Israeli OPVs have been extremely successful in dealing with terrorist attacks. Even the smallest country has at least one and probably several OPVs. Although many have only a few light guns, others are quite capable with sophisticated electronics and missile and even helicopter capabilities. Perhaps more important, most new hull and engineering experiments are still being carried out on small craft. And even in this era of shrinking fleets, small combatants still offer command opportunities and visions of glory for junior officers.

Futuristic Warships   15

BEFORE CONTEMPLATING WHAT the future might hold, it is necessary to comment on a certain irony regarding the labeling of the various ages of warships. That is, the different ages have not been defined by their distinct war-fighting capabilities and weaponry, but rather by their means of propulsion. It is the Age of Galleys, not the Age of the Ram; the Age of Sail, not the Age of Muzzle Loaders; the Age of Steam, not the Age of Shell or Torpedoes, although those terms are sometimes also added. Only in the Modern Age is the label not usually attributed to propulsion although the post–World War II era is often known as the Nuclear Era with the double reference to both nuclear weapons and propulsion. In short, when looking into the future, the first stop must be on propulsion and then the related subject of hull design before looking at weaponry and new designs for each specific warship type.

New Ship Propulsion Systems

According to the precedent of characterization by propulsion, the current period should actually be called the Gas Turbine, not the Nuclear or even the Missile and Electronics era. It seemed that nuclear power might be the answer after the U.S. Navy's submarine *Nautilus* got "under way on nuclear power" in 1955. The *Nautilus* was quickly followed by other nuclear submarines and several nuclear-powered surface ships. In 1961 the first three U.S. nuclear-powered surface ships were completed: the aircraft carrier *Enterprise,* cruiser *Long Beach,* and merchant ship *Savannah.* More nuclear-powered cruisers followed in the 1960s and 1970s, and Congress even passed a resolution that all future major U.S. Navy surface combatants should be nuclear powered. Nuclear propulsion, however, has proven costly although incredibly "long-legged." Safety and environmental concerns have also been raised, although none have yet proven legitimate. Except for carriers, nuclear propulsion has proven too complex and expensive for continued use with surface combatants. It remains a main power source for submarines despite the higher costs because it allows them to stay submerged indefinitely.

Rather, the major propulsion advance since the end of World War II has been the replacement of steam boilers with gas turbine and combined systems. When World War II ended, most major warships were still steam driven; a few were diesel powered. Diesels were easier to maintain and cheaper, but they were relatively large and heavy. They had also proven disappointing for high speeds, which was exacerbated by the vibration problems of their pistons. Steam plants also had two major drawbacks. First, they were complex and manpower-intensive for operation and maintenance. That mattered less when manpower was relatively cheap or during emergency wartime conditions but became increasingly important in the cost-conscious postwar period. Another major issue was that it took hours to light off steam plants so they could not get under way without considerable lead time.

The answer to both problems was gas turbines. Gas turbines can be traced back to the 1930s, but major developments did not begin until after the war, when the Royal Navy was the first to develop operational modes. It began trials in 1947 and converted the first gas turbine warship, the gunboat *Grey Goose,* in 1953. The first U.S. gas turbines were on the *Asheville* gunboat class launched in 1966, with the first on large ships being the *Hamilton*-class Coast Guard cutters commissioned starting in 1967. The Soviet Union's *Kara*-class cruiser, laid down in 1968, was the first major warship with gas turbines. In the 1970s, high-powered aircraft service proven marine gas turbine sets were placed on the large U.S. Navy *Spruance*-class destroyers.

Although gas turbines are faster and more efficient at a designed fixed high speed, they are less efficient at any other speed. To seek offsets gaining increased efficiency, another major change was to build combined systems, including steam and gas turbine (COSAG), diesel *or* gas (CODOG), diesel *and* gas (CODAG), and both cruise and high-speed (COGOG) gas turbine. In most cases, the steam plants or diesels are used for normal cruising with the gas turbines used for high speed. Currently, most warships are now either combined or gas turbine systems.[1]

While studies continue on alternatives, no major breakthroughs or changes in ship propulsion are expected in the near future, and no serious propulsion set research and development is under way. There is still some hope for the development of cheaper nuclear plants and/or combined nuclear–gas turbine systems. Other alternatives such as the use of solar power have so far proven disappointing and unreliable, especially for a warship. But both nuclear and solar power might eventually come into use when oil reserves start getting more depleted in the mid-twenty-first century. (During the oil crisis of the 1970s there were some thoughts of returning to sail for commercial ships, and a few interesting but disheartening experiments were conducted.)

The major change undergoing study is the move to gas turbine–powered all-electric drive. The U.S. Navy had plans to move to all-electric drive in the late 1980s and studies are ongoing, but once again capital costs have prevented that change. The U.S. Navy's SC-21 family of surface combatants is scheduled to have all-electric drive. Thus for the immediate future, changes in propulsion will be evolutionary with better, more efficient gas-turbine and combined systems.

New Hull Designs and Configurations

New propulsion systems have solved some problems, but they still have not resolved two others—speed and stability—and they probably cannot. Both are limited by the nature of the classic monohull design of the ship's hull. The water resistance generated by monohulls has generally restricted a ship's top speed to less than 42 knots (and nominally to around 35 knots for full displacement) no matter what the engine type or horsepower, and the problem gets worse at higher speeds. For example, a 10 percent increase in speed at 20 knots requires roughly a 30 percent increase in horsepower, but at 30 knots, a 10 percent increase requires more than a 50 percent increase in horsepower, and it has been calculated that a 10 percent increase at 40 knots would require a 100 percent increase in horsepower. As a result, the increased speed has not been worth the expense. In fact, because of these extra costs, ship speeds have actually decreased in many cases. Both World War I and II destroyers could steam at about 35 knots, but many of today's modern destroyers and frigates barely make 30.

Stability has also been generally restricted by the inherent characteristics of the monohull. One solution to increase stability has been simply to increase the size and fullness of the monohull, which is fine for large passenger cruise ships and today's huge tankers for which a range of speeds is secondary, but that has never been considered a viable option for warships. Thus the solution for both greater speed and stability was either to change the shape of the hull in some manner or to reduce resistance by lifting the hull out of the water. Five options have been tried over the years. As shown in figure 15.1, these are the catamaran, SWATH, hydrofoils, surface effect ships (SES), and air-cushion vehicles (ACV).

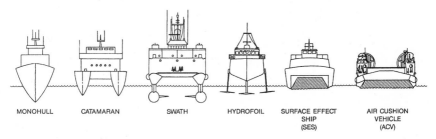

MONOHULL   CATAMARAN   SWATH   HYDROFOIL   SURFACE EFFECT SHIP (SES)   AIR CUSHION VEHICLE (ACV)

FIGURE 15.1 Advanced technology ship comparisons.
(Drawing by William Clipson)

CATAMARAN

The oldest method to get around the restrictions of a monohull was to have twin hulls with a platform between them. There is some speculation that the large Age of Galley polyremes, the twenties, thirties, and especially the one large forty, were catamarans. A few modern catamaran warships have been built, including cable-layers. The twin hull eases the laying of cable. While often used for stability, catamarans can also have increased speed. Some modern sailboats, for example, are catamarans and there are even a few trimarans, three-hulled. Since there were no prohibiting rules, Dennis Connor used an extremely light, planing catamaran to defeat what was considered the most advanced, sleekest, monohull sailing craft ever built to win the America's Cup.

SMALL WATERPLANE AREA TWIN-HULL (SWATH)

A design similar to that of the catamaran is the small waterplane-area twin hull, or SWATH, configuration. The SWATH consists of two submarine-shaped hulls below the water that support a hull above the water by means of long, slender struts. The buoyancy parts of the ship and propulsion units are below the water, while the hull that contains the auxiliary equipment, personnel, and weaponry is above. The SWATH's strongest attribute is stability, especially in higher sea states. For that reason, the SWATH design was used for the U.S. Navy's civilian manned ocean surveillance ships (AGOS) that were designed to operate in the often rough North Atlantic. They have also been proposed for small SWATH carriers.

HYDROFOIL

There are three alternatives, not necessarily to change the shape of the hull but to lift it out of the water. The oldest, dating back to before World War I, is the hydrofoil. The hydrofoil works in a manner similar to the airplane's airfoils or wings in that it lifts the boat out of the water, thus reducing resistance. This is a high-technology design requiring expensive, aircraftlike materials, and special welding techniques, equipment, and machinery. The U.S. Navy built a small squadron of hydrofoils in the late 1970s, but their limited endurance and high cost caused them to be operationally limited so they were retired. Several commercial hydrofoil ships operate throughout the world.

SURFACE EFFECT SHIP (SES)

Instead of holding up the hull by the displacement of submerged hulls or the dynamic lift of hydrofoils, another proposal was to sit on a cushion of air generated by powerful fans thrusting downward. There were two methods for smaller and larger ships. The larger surface effect ship (SES) has catamaranlike hulls forming the sides, which give it greater additional support for greater payloads. A few small SES ships have been built for experimental reasons, but a larger 3,000-ton SES frigate proposed for years has yet to be built.

AIR-CUSHION VEHICLE (ACV)

The smaller static lift versions are the air-cushion vehicles (ACVs) that literally skim along the water on an air cushion, even allowing them to operate briefly over land. For this reason, they have been adopted for amphibious roles. The best known are the U.S. Navy's 102-ton, 81-by-43-foot LCACs (landing craft air cushion) that have been operational since 1993. Other countries have also operated ACVs, and the Soviet navy has several large versions.[2]

WITH THE EXCEPTION of the ACVs for smaller craft, all of these new designs for warships have proved disappointing for various reasons. Proponents blame the conservatism of professional naval officers, and there might be some truth to that charge. A rectangular-shaped, squat SES frigate, for example, simply does not have the same sleek warship look of a monohull

One of the Soviet navy's large air-cushion landing vehicles.
(U.S. Naval Institute)

destroyer or frigate. On the other hand, experiments on these new types have been ongoing since before World War I, with most proving to be either technological disappointments or too expensive to operate. For example, the U.S. Navy's SWATH AGOS did not prove as stable as predicted and follow-on AGOSs have been monohulls. The U.S. Navy's patrol hydrofoils were expensive to operate and had only limited open-ocean capabilities. They might have been useful in closed waters such as the Persian Gulf. In short, with limited funds in most navies to experiment compounded by the natural conservatism of most professional naval officers, the classic monohull appears very secure for at least the initial years of the twenty-first century.

There are, however, two other proposals regarding the shape of future warships that warrant brief mention. These are the search for commonality of design and then stealth.

COMMONALITY

One effort to cut costs and improve efficiency has been to find a common hull for all surface types from frigates to aircraft carriers. In the late 1980s the U.S. Navy's David Taylor Research Center had conceptual building plans for future ships, recommending only one or two basic types for different missions. The researchers suggested building a carrier dock multimission (CDM) ship with variants for everything from the next generation of amphibious ships and aircraft carriers to a carrier dock guided missile (CDG) ship. One of the problems was that it was built along commercial, rather than warship, lines with the result that it did not "look" like a navy ship. For the future the U.S. surface navy is looking at an SC-21, "Surface Combatant for the Twenty-first Century," which is described as a family of ships to replace current frigates, destroyers, and cruisers and which may include features that make it adaptable for future carriers and amphibious ships.

A related concept is to use more modularity in shipbuilding. Using this approach, whole ship sections can be reconfigured or one basic type can be built initially, with different weapon or combat system suites inserted to meet varying mission requirements. This also eases improvements and modernization. The German "Meko" frigate has different packages, and several European countries are looking at building common frigates, but with perhaps different weapon and electronic suites.

STEALTH

There is one major hull modification that is proceeding in most major navies. This is the adoption of stealth techniques, which generally means more streamlined hulls and superstructures, radar-absorbent material, and other improvements such as special geometric attention that reduce the radar sig-

A model of Vosper Thornycroft's new Sea Wraith stealth corvette design. This futuristic design looks more like a spaceship than a sea ship.
(U.S. Naval Institute)

nature of ships. The U.S. Navy's new DDG-51 Aegis-class destroyers have some reduced signature features. The most advanced stealth design being built in the late 1990s is the French *Lafayette*-class frigate with the sides of the hull and superstructure inclined at ten degrees and the superstructure and masts coated with radar-absorbent paint. Virtually all new warships being built today have some new stealthlike features. Futuristic proposals, such as Thornycroft's Sea Wraith, actually look more like spaceships. The United States Navy is testing a very stealthy experimental ship called, appropriately, "Sea Shadow."

New Weaponry

GUNS

While the era of the big gun may be over, smaller guns are still an important part of most ships' weaponry. The United States evaluated resurrecting an 8-inch major-caliber lightweight gun (MCLWG) and conducted tests on the destroyer *Hull* in the mid-1970s. Although considered successful, the program was abandoned because it was too costly. Today, the largest guns afloat and active are a few old 6-inchers on an old Dutch cruiser still carried on the Peruvian Navy's books. The most common large guns today are the U.S. Navy's 5-inch and 4.7- or 4.5-inch guns found in several other navies of the world. Their range is from 8 to 15 miles. Most ships actually carry smaller guns, with the 76 mm (3-inch) being extremely common throughout the world.

Guns still play an important role for three reasons: cost, size, and their necessity for certain missions. First, they are cheap to operate compared to missiles; second, ships can carry considerably more shells than missiles; and finally, they still have some crucial missions. Marines still like the precision gunfire support capabilities of guns and remain the biggest proponents of recommissioning the battleships for that reason. Guns are still useful for local self-defense, especially in closed waters such as the Persian Gulf. During both the Vietnam War and the more recent war in the Gulf, ships hurriedly jury-rigged small-caliber guns for self-protection.

For the twenty-first century there are programs to extend both the range and accuracy of guns. The U.S. Navy has a program to develop a rocket-assisted extended-range guide munition (ERGM) for the 5-inch gun that could give it a range of approximately 100 miles. Also, there are programs to increase accuracy such as using the current Global Positioning System (GPS) to reduce the circular error probability (CEP) to less than 20 yards. Another idea is laser-guided munitions. New technologies in guns themselves, such as an electrothermal chemical (ETC) gun and a vertical-gun advanced system (VGAS), are also under investigation. And the era of the big (or at least bigger) gun may not be over: the U.S. Navy is studying the feasibility of a 155 mm (6.1-inch) gun. Both VGAS and perhaps the 155 mm gun are under consideration for the DD-21, the first of the SC-21 family, to be completed around 2010. Because the cost of more advanced "smart" shells would still be in the thousands of dollars (as opposed to at least $1 million for most missiles), guns will continue to be an important part of most ships' inventories well into the twenty-first century.

MISSILES

Of course, the greatest revolution in weaponry since the end of World War II has been in missiles. A few crude guided missiles were used in World War II, but development began in earnest after the war with surface-to-air (SAMs) appearing in the mid-1950s and surface-to-surface (SSMs) in the 1970s. Missiles have gone through three generations. The first generation had to be guided from a parent station, usually the ship or airplane. Then in the early 1970s at the end of the Vietnam War came the so-called smart missiles with television cameras that allowed them to be guided right on target. Later so-called fire and forget missiles were developed that required no guidance from a mother ship. Missiles are now entering what is often called the "brilliant" phase with greater accuracy allowing them to search and seek targets. During Desert Storm operations against Iraq, one of the favorite briefing gimmicks was to show missiles going through windows right on target. It has been estimated that whereas in World War II it took a thousand "dumb" bombs to destroy a target, today it might take only one smart or brilliant missile to provide a similar effect. Another trend is faster missiles. Whereas the first generations of missiles flew at Mach 1 or 2, modern missiles can reach speeds of Mach 3 or even 4. Cruise missiles like the Tomahawk, which were subsonic, are now becoming supersonic.

Thus, even though missiles are considerably more expensive to build and operate, they often prove more cost-effective in the long run while also reducing casualties and losses. American pilots still have bitter memories of losing multi-million-dollar jets to knock out thousand-dollar bridges in Vietnam. Missiles will continue to become more and more accurate and to have greater and greater ranges at faster and faster speeds. The trick will be to also make them less and less expensive.

EXOTIC WEAPONS

When writing about the future, many people think about so-called exotic weapons like the use of directed-energy weapons such as laser beams and particle beams. At least to date, most experiments in truly effective exotic weapons have proven disappointing for several reasons. One is the ever more burdensome and limiting problem of costs. Research and development in exotic weapons is extremely expensive. Another problem, especially for a ship, is miniaturization. The energy source required for many of these new systems is usually large and beyond the capacity of shipboard equipment. The final problem is simply taking advantage of, and overcoming, the laws of physics. Most work on exotic weapons is classified, but work does proceed in all these areas even if limited by funds. Nonetheless, truly revolutionary weapons beyond better guns and missiles are probably many years away.

ELECTRONICS

The most sweeping post–World War II revolution has not been in weaponry but in electronics. Electronics became important in World War II, with many analysts concluding that Allied "sensing" systems such as sonar, radar, and direction finding played as large a role as any factor in defeating the Axis forces. System development has matured greatly in the postwar period thanks to better detection systems. The latest trend is extending electronics into command, control, and decision support.

In the 1970s tacticians came to realize that the most important element in the fast-paced world of supersonic missiles and jet aircraft was not this new weaponry per se but how to control them. This became known as command and control, or C^2. Over the years the requirements of this concept have gotten considerably more complex, as can be seen in the change of terminology and acronyms. It was soon realized the command and control was not inclusive enough but also needed to include communications, hence C^3, command, control, and communications. That terminology soon changed to C^{3}I, for command, control, communications, and intelligence and later the acronym C^{4}I^2, command, control, communications, computers, intelligence, and information. The latest acronym is C^{4}ISR for command, control, communications, computers, intelligence, surveillance, and reconnaissance, but tomorrow some other acronym or superior number(s) will probably be added—and for good reason.

In the United States a field of study known as RMA, "revolution in military affairs," has emerged, a combination of new strategies, tactics, and weapons, all controlled by an "electronic battlefield" of which C^{4}ISR is the most important element, more important than the weapons themselves. The changes are everywhere. While the ship's combat information center, or CIC, became increasingly more important during World War II, today it is the absolute nerve center from which the captain or executive officer controls operations instead of from the bridge. While the U.S. Navy's Aegis-class cruisers and destroyers look—at least on the surface—very underarmed with only one or two visible 5-inch guns showing, these "all-big-electronics" ships with their sophisticated electronic suites are as revolutionary today as the all-big-gun HMS *Dreadnought* was in 1906.

DEFENSE SYSTEMS

As can be expected, with the increased sophistication of weaponry, ships' defense has become more important and difficult. Perhaps somewhat ironically, and as proponents of recommissioning the battleships like to point out, old-fashioned armor is still useful as a defense against some of the new missiles, which actually have relatively small warheads, but the days of slab armor are over. Thus most ships have both active and passive defense. Active systems usually consist of either fast-firing guns such as the U.S. Navy's CIWS (close-in weapon system), which uses depleted uranium shells to explode the incoming missile or anti-missile-missile systems. There are also passive systems like filling the air with chaff to confuse the missile's detection systems.

And with electronics increasingly important, defensive electronic countermeasures (ECM) are used. Unfortunately, although radar and active sonar are great detection devices, their signals are easily picked up, as are many of those same C^{4}ISR systems now so necessary for the modern battlefield. Critics have been predicting the vulnerability of ships since the end of World War I but so far have always been proven wrong. With the increased sophistication of smart and brilliant weapons, however, those predictions may be coming true. Fortunately, the United States has never faced a really sophisticated enemy, but that could well change in the twenty-first century. Thus the real challenge in the next century could be the race between offensive and defensive systems, similar to that of the late nineteenth and early twentieth centuries between guns and armor.

UNMANNED VEHICLES

There is an increasing trend toward the use of unmanned systems. UAVs, small unmanned air vehicles used for surveillance, are now available in most major countries' inventories. There has even been some speculation that the next generation of airplanes that will be built in the early twenty-first century could well be the last manned aircraft and that they will be followed by unmanned craft. American proponents of the revolution in military affairs now claim that they can target anything, anywhere in the world, limited only by the range of current manned weapon systems. Whether the result will also be unmanned warships remains to be seen, although there are proposals for autonomous unmanned submarines (UUVs) for some missions, and remote devices are currently used for mine hunting and clearance.

Future of Major Warship Types

SURFACE COMBATANTS: CRUDESGATES

Although a last-ditch effort is being made to save one or two U.S. Navy battleships for gunfire support, officer training, and a NATO flagship, even if successful (which is extremely doubtful), the halcyon days of the traditional dreadnought are definitely over. These large ships that can trace their ancestry back centuries are now viewed as too expensive to operate. Unfortunately, it seems as though cruisers and even destroyers might not be far behind. Only four countries currently operate cruisers, with none building. Although newer cruisers will remain in Russian and American fleets for many years, it would not be surprising if they were the last. Even large destroyers are now rare, with most fleets becoming frigate navies.

Many of today's frigates, however, are quite sophisticated and considerably more capable than destroyers and even some of the older, smaller cruisers of the 1970s. Spain, for example, is building a 6,000-odd-ton Aegis frigate that certainly falls into the destroyer range in size and will be more capable than most 1970-era guided missile cruisers. In short, the line between some of these ships is a fine one. During the late 1970s, when large U.S. frigates were being redesignated as cruisers, the U.S. Navy was building destroyers larger than some cruisers with smaller destroyer escorts (DEs) designated frigates, this author wrote a semi-tongue-in-cheek article about building ships called CRUDESGATES. The new Spanish Aegis frigate and the proposed U.S. Navy SC-21 family of surface combatants might well fall into that category. But more countries are building small frigates, and while they are generally adequate for today's missions there is some question as to whether they will be sufficient for tomorrow's.

Aircraft Carriers

The U.S. Navy has plans for only one more large-deck *Nimitz*-class carrier, described as a "transitional" type for a new CVX design. There are two proposals: build either a smaller, conventional carrier to save money, or perhaps move to V/STOL carriers, depending on the progress of ASTOVL planes. But even the United States is finding building large-deck carriers too expensive. France had plans for two CVNs but now is struggling to pay for one. Russia, which was on the verge of joining the exclusive carrier club with several carriers, is attempting to keep just one afloat. China has wanted to build a carrier for years but keeps putting it off for budgetary reasons.

Although there has been something of a renaissance in smaller V/STOL carriers, even they are rare because of their expense. The Royal Navy carries three on the books, but only two are kept in active service at any one time. There are plans to replace the three V/STOL carriers with two mid-size CTOL carriers, but costs may prove prohibitive. Spain, Italy, and Thailand operate modern small V/STOL carriers. Though adequate for these countries' needs, these V/STOL carriers are too small for major operations—especially against land aircraft. Those operations can be conducted only by the large-deck carriers and their more sophisticated CTOL aircraft. Large-deck carriers will remain in the French and American fleets well into the twenty-first century, and no one really questions their utility or capabilities, but they may eventually fall victim to the budget cutters. The future really depends on a new generation of advanced V/STOL planes (ASTOVL). If new ASTOVL aircraft can match the capabilities of CTOL planes, a wide spectrum of possibilities would open up, from small SWATH carriers to midsized conventional carriers.

Submarines

The major new submarine developments involve their propulsion plants. New AIP systems finally give conventional submarines a modicum of the unlimited submerged capabilities of nuclear submarines. Though they are considerably slower than SSNs, if that problem were ever solved, conventional AIP submarines could be the wave of the future. The most critical factor in submarine warfare is quietness, and improvements are constantly needed. These tend to be incremental changes, but they are necessary to allow the first real stealth platforms to remain so. The real key could be the future of ASW. If (as many have predicted since the end of World War I) the seas truly do become "transparent," the days of the submarine could be over—or at least severely limited.

AMPHIBIOUS SHIPS

The classic beaching LST amphibious ships of World War II fame have just about disappeared from most fleets although medium-size beaching ships are still found in some navies. While the U.S. Navy still maintains a fairly wide spectrum of amphibious types, most other major navies have moved to multipurpose LPD or LPH types with capabilities for both helicopters and flooding well decks for small landing craft or even air-cushion vehicles. Amphibious warfare ships could well end up where they started as the current types are not much different from the first Japanese ships of the interwar period. But contrary to all the gloomy predictions after both world wars, amphibious warfare has remained important, with most countries recognizing the need for at least one or two of these flexible warships.

SERVICE SHIPS

The main change since World War II has been the move to multiproduct replenishment ships. Most countries have a few AORs that have both alongside and helicopter replenishment capabilities. The other major trend is the move to civilian-manned service forces; while these may be adequate for peacetime conditions, their use during times of hostility remains a concern. The biggest problem facing the service force will be the old one of competing with warships for funds. Invariably, when a ship has to be cut, it is always the service ship.

MINE CRAFT

The major change in mine craft in the last few years has been the move from minesweepers to mine hunters as a result of the increasing sophistication of mines. This is also one of the few warship types in which there has been some innovation in hull designs. Countries have experimented with both catamaran and air-cushion designs, and unmanned remote vehicles are playing ever-increasing roles. The latest trend is the move toward organic antimine detection and avoidance systems on all warships.

SMALL COMBATANTS

As has usually been the case since the Age of Steam, most of the new experiments are still being carried out by ships in the small combatant category. All of the new hull configurations such as SWATH and air-cushion vehicles are smallish craft. Many of the new stealth configurations are also small combatants. Sweden, for example, is currently building new, very sleek, stealthy patrol boats. With ship costs escalating, smaller countries find they can afford only small combatants. It should be pointed out that while most of the small combatants now being built fall into the OPV category, useful only for border patrol, some new corvettes are quite sophisticated. Their guns, missiles, and even helicopter capabilities can be quite deadly in certain situations, such as closed waters like the Persian Gulf.

OTHER

Will there be completely new, even radical, types in the twenty-first century? Radical hull configurations have, at least to date, proven disappointing, although some interesting experiments continue. The only truly different type of ship on the boards was the U.S. Navy's arsenal ship, envisioned as a sleek, low-profile ship full of missiles, but it was canceled for lack of funds. Its proponents once again blame conservatism for the demise of the arsenal ship, but the Navy claims that many of its characteristics (such as more missiles) will be on the proposed DD-21. The demise of the old Soviet Union has dealt a blow to some of the most radical proposals for new ship designs. The old Soviet leaders were often portrayed as traditional and conservative, but they actually came up with some of the most radical designs. These included several large air-cushion craft and wing-in-ground (WIG) effect vehicles. Although the post–Cold War period of relative peace with no major war predicted for years to come might be the best time to experiment with radical designs and new "dreadnoughts" with the potential to make all else obsolete, with the combination of lack of funds, traditional naval conservatism, and perhaps lack of imagination, none seem forthcoming.

Comments: Tomorrow's Warships

The new warships built in the early twenty-first century will probably not look significantly different from those sailing today. They will be more streamlined in appearance to provide enhanced stealth characteristics, but at least on the outside, tomorrow's frigate will resemble today's. Somewhat ironically, and generally bucking the trend since the 1850s, with few exceptions the new ships might actually be smaller and slower. Larger and faster ships are simply too expensive to build. They will also look underarmed with only one or two guns showing (and if the vertical gun systems are developed, perhaps none at all). However, although the ships might look underarmed, with new belowdeck vertical launch systems, advanced gun munitions, and an increasingly large array of missiles, they will pack the wallop of a dreadnought.

The major changes will be internal with ever more sophisticated electronics for both command and control and internal weaponry. Some "dumb" weapons will undoubtedly still exist because of their lower costs and their utility for certain situations, but weapons will move from their current smart modes to a more brilliant phase. This will present increasing challenges to warship builders to devise ways to defend against these weapons, a problem navies have seldom faced since the end of World War II. This race between offense and defense may become the dominant characteristic of the twenty-first century.

COMMENTS AND CONCLUSIONS

Summaries, Ironies, Myths, and Lessons 16

Summaries

THE AGES AND THEIR ERAS

As summarized in table 16.1, there have been four broad ages of warships and at least twenty discernible suberas. Not surprisingly, the majority of these suberas, eight of the twenty, occurred during the over 4,000-year history of the Age of Galleys that lasted from approximately 2500 B.C. to the Battle of Lepanto in 1571, usually cited as the end of that age, although galleys still played minor roles into the nineteenth century. Most of these galley types were built in the Mediterranean during seven distinct eras: first, the early types of which the most common were the penteconters, followed by the development of the bireme along with the ram, the weaponry that would dominate the Age of Galleys. Next came the Greek trireme, probably the most famous of the ancient galleys, although it was dominant for one of the shorter eras. Triremes were overtaken by the polyremes, whose era was in some respects the height of the Age of Galleys with "fours" and "fives" all the way up to gigantic "twenties" and even one "forty."

Following the Battle of Actium in 31 B.C. came the smaller Roman triremes and liburnians that played such a large factor in maintaining Pax Romana, the two hundred-odd years of peace after the birth of Christ. The medieval period saw two more basic types, first the Byzantine dromons and then the Venetian galleys, each of which went through at least two versions. Galleys were built in other places. The most famous and distinct were the Viking longboats, but it was in the Mediterranean where galley development reached its zenith.

Table 16.1 Summary of the Ages and Eras of Warships

Age of Galleys: 2500 B.C.–A.D. 1571

Pentecounters and other early warships	2500–900 B.C.
Biremes and rams	900–500 B.C.
Greek triremes	725–400 B.C.
Polyremes	400–31 B.C.
Roman triremes and liburnians	31 B.C.–A.D. 450
Dromons	450–1250
Viking longboats	750–1200
Venetian galleys	1250–1571

Age of Sail: 1200–1850

Fighting cogs	1200–1400
Carracks	1400–1525
Galleons	1525–1650
Ships of the line	1650–1850

Age of Steam, Ironclads, and Steel: 1815–1905

Early Period	1815–1860
Paddle wheelers	1815–1845
Screw and conversion era	1845–1860
Ironclads, steel, and other innovations	1860–1890
Early ironclads	1860–1875
Experimental era	1860–1890
Steel and other innovations	1875–1890
Premodern era	1890–1905

Modern Age: 1906–Present

Dreadnought era	1906–1945
Missile and electronics era	1946–Present

The Age of Sail is usually dated to the Armada battle in 1588, but its beginnings can be traced to around A.D. 1200 when early northern European merchantmen were converted into "fighting cogs." The major change came with the invention of the three-masted full-rigged carrack around 1400, considered one of the greatest inventions of all times. With some justification, one historian even considers the invention of the three-masted full rig as important as the discovery of the wheel and fire. That development led to the Age of Discovery in the fifteenth and sixteenth centuries, the galleon about 1525, and finally the classic ship of the line around 1650. The Age of Sail was without doubt the Golden Age of the influence of warships, a time when worldwide empires were won and lost through seapower, sometimes just a single sea battle.

Next came the Age of Steam, Ironclads, and Steel, the transition period from the Age of Sail to the Modern Age. This age started slowly with first paddle wheelers and then the conversion of classic wooden sailing ships into screw vessels. More dramatic changes occurred after 1860. Although difficult to summarize because of the hodgepodge of different ship types built, especially during the experimental era from 1860 to 1890, this age saw the greatest progress and change in warship design. In this thirty-year period, the warship was transformed from wooden sailing ships to steel pre-dreadnoughts. Most of today's warships can be traced back to the late nineteenth-century pre-dreadnought era, which more properly should be called the premodern era. This was also the century of Pax Britannia, the hundred years of relative peace from the end of the Napoleonic Wars in 1815 to World War I in 1914.

The Modern Age began with the launching of HMS *Dreadnought* in 1906. This age is usually broken down into two eras: the dreadnought or big gun era that lasted through World War II and the postwar nuclear or missile and electronics era that continues to this day. The dreadnought era was another golden age for warships—not necessarily because of their influence on history, although they were certainly important in both world wars, but because so many different types of warships were built. Even today, though many of the pre–World War II types are long gone, navalists still refer to them in their characterizations of ships. In the missile and electronics era warships no longer bristle with guns and even look underarmed, but that is deceiving because they carry powerful and accurate belowdeck missiles and, perhaps even more important, sophisticated electronics to control the battle scene.

WARSHIP CONSTRUCTION

Naval construction has gone through three broad phases. First was the shell method of construction in which a ship's planks were laid to form the shape of the ship with frames inserted later for strength. The planks were held together in an edge-to-edge or carvel technique with a very intricate tongue-in-groove mortise and tenon method. This method has been found in the earliest boats and lasted throughout much of the Age of Galleys. A slight variation was found in northern shipbuilding where an overlapping or clinker method of planking was used rather than the carvel technique. This shell method started to change around A.D. 1000.

Then, starting around A.D. 1200 or so, the skeleton or frame method was begun with a ship's framing constructed first with planks attached to the frames as most ships are constructed today. This was a major step forward because it allowed ships to be better shaped and lengthened. All wooden ships, however, had a problem of the ends sagging or hogging, which generally restricted their lengths to the 150- to 200-foot range. This hogging problem was not fully solved until the early nineteenth century with new diagonal framing techniques, but improved wooden ships were soon overtaken by the first ironclads in 1860 and then steel ships in the 1870s in the last major phase in shipbuilding.

Besides these broad areas of construction techniques, there are two other major milestones. First was the invention of the three-masted full-rig ship around 1400, considered a seminal event in history that led to the Age of Discovery and later the classic ship of the line. The second major milestone was the development of steam engines in the early nineteenth century. Two other innovations that bear mention are the development of the rudder around 1200 and the introduction of oil around 1900.

NAVAL WEAPONS

Naval weapons have gone through five major phases, as summarized in table 16.2. The first, and by far the longest, was the boarding era, starting in ancient times and lasting throughout the Age of Galleys; boarding was still considered the main tactic until around 1650, during the Age of Sail. Fighting at sea was essentially little different from fighting on land. There were a few exceptions. The invention of the ram around 900 B.C. made ramming an option; then came catapults, first placed on ships around 400 B.C. But even these tactics were usually considered complementary to boarding. Greek fire, initially used around in the late seventh century A.D., was another exception. Second was the muzzle-loading gun era. Even though guns were first placed on board ships around 1325 and side gun ports date to around 1500, it was not until the Anglo-Dutch War of 1653 and the development of the three-decker with broadside ports that guns truly replaced boarding as the main fighting tactic. The muzzle loader dominated ship's weaponry until midway through the Age of Steam in 1870.

Around 1870, two major developments occurred that led to the big gun and torpedo era. First, breech loaders finally replaced muzzle loaders, allowing for more rapid-fire rates with quick-firing guns developed in the 1880s. Also around 1870 came the development of the self-propelled or locomotive torpedo that made both small torpedo boats and eventually submarines deadly weapons. The period from 1870 through World War I was the golden age of the big guns and torpedoes, and they still played major roles through World War II. Mines were also important during this period, although they were not shipboard weapons per se.

The fourth phase, the warplane era, began during World War I, but major developments did not begin until after the war. There was some question whether big guns or airplanes would be more important in World War II, but that debate ended in December 1941. Today, airplanes are still considered the premier at-sea weapon, although they are being increasingly challenged

Table 16.2 Summary of Naval Weapon Eras

Boarding Era: 2500 B.C.–A.D. 1650

Rams	900 B.C.–A.D. 1000
Catapults	400 B.C.–A.D. 1300~
Greek fire	A.D. 700–A.D. 1200

Muzzle-Loading: 1650–1870

Appearance of guns	1325
Gun ports	1500
Broadside tactics	1650

Big Gun and Torpedo Era: 1870–1945

Breech loaders replace muzzle loaders	1870
Development of locomotive torpedo	1870
Development of quick-fire guns	1880
Submarine	1900

Warplane Era: 1920–Current

First aircraft carriers	1914
First flattops	1920

Missile and Electronics Era: 1940–Current

Electronics:	
Sonar	1918
Radar	1930s
Missiles	1950s
C^2I developments	1970s

by missiles and electronics. The fifth, and current, phase of naval weaponry, the missile and electronics era, can be traced to World War II, when sonar and radar became increasingly more important, but missile development did not really become important until the mid-1950s and even 1960s. While guns, torpedoes, and airplanes are still very important warship weapons, missiles and increased electronics sophistication may become dominant in the twenty-first century.

IRONIES, MYTHS, AND LESSONS

As the brief summary above illustrates, the history of warships, their construction methods, and weaponry has been long and complex, but what are some of the lessons of that history? There are a dozen lessons and observations, but also, perhaps more interesting, three ironies as well two myths. Some have already been mentioned, but they bear repeating briefly.

THE IRONIES

Ages Defined by Propulsion, Not Weaponry

The most meaningful irony is that the various ages of warships have been defined by propulsion, not weaponry. It was the Age of Galleys, not the Age of Rams; the Age of Sail, not the Age of Muzzle Loaders; and the Age of Steam, not the Age of Shell or Torpedoes (although those terms are sometimes added to this multinamed age). Only in the Modern Age is the direct reference to a propulsion description dropped. In some respects this should not be too surprising because propulsion is so important.

Greatest Progress Often Came at End of Ages

Another irony is that in many cases, the greatest developments and progress came at the end of the age when they were no longer needed and, in some cases, were obsolete. There is some evidence of this phenomenon at the end of the Age of Galleys with the large Venetian great galleys and galleasse at Lepanto, but the clearest examples are at the end of the Age of Sail and the end of the dreadnought era. The greatest progress in sailing ships of the line came during the early Age of Steam period from 1814 to 1850 when Sir Robert Seppings solved many of the problems facing wooden ships, allowing for larger ships with heavier guns. Also, the best dreadnoughts and cruisers (especially heavy cruisers) were built in the late 1930s and early 1940s, when they were becoming obsolete. Whether this means the large-deck aircraft carrier and large nuclear submarine will go the same way remains to be seen, although in those cases it may be more cost than capabilities that threaten their existence.

Greatest Utility for Warships During Peacetime

Finally, the greatest need for and utility of warships might actually be during peacetime. Obviously, warships are necessary during wartime, but they made their greatest contributions during times of peace. At least one author claims that the galleys were more important during the Pax Romana than originally thought, and virtually all historians agree on the crucial roles of warships during the century of Pax Britannia. This irony and lesson has implications for the current period and will be explored in more detail in chapter 17.

THE MYTHS

Ships Built for Missions

Contrary to a popular saw that warships are never used for the purposes for which they were originally built, throughout history most warships were, in fact, used for the purposes for which they were built. This was the case throughout the Ages of Galleys and Sail and even for most types during the Age of Steam and the Modern Age. The most significant exception was the mighty dreadnoughts built for the decisive Mahanian battle, which were instead mostly used for shore bombardment. And while it is true that many modern warships such as cruisers, submarines, and aircraft carriers were originally built to support the dreadnought as screening eyes of the fleet, their missions quickly changed. Other modern types such as amphibious ships, mine craft, and the service force are built and used for very distinct missions. While modern surface combatants are flexible ships that perform important day-to-day duties and show-the-flag missions, they are also designed for specific missions.

Usually a Spectrum of Ships

There has developed a myth, at least in the world's dominant navy, the U.S. Navy, that there are only two levels of sophistication for warships. This has become known as the "high-low" mix of building a few, high-end, very sophisticated, and unfortunately very expensive ships, usually offset by a low end of less sophisticated and costly types. With very few exceptions, however, there has always been a wide spectrum of ship sizes since the Age of Galleys.

Starting with the Age of Sail, there was actually a spectrum of eight size or ratings. In the Age of Sail these were the six ship-of-the-line rates, from large 100-gun ships to smaller frigates, plus sloops/brigs and small craft such as cutters. In the Modern Age there were also eight levels: battleships, heavy cruisers, light cruisers, large destroyer leaders, destroyers, frigates and DEs, corvettes, and patrol craft. These were built for cost but also for mission reasons. Even during most of the post–World War II era there was a four-level spectrum of cruisers, destroyers, frigates, and smaller corvettes. Most navies still have a spectrum of a few larger destroyers or frigates, with more smaller frigates and a few corvettes or patrol boats. The exception has been the U.S. Navy, which since the late 1980s has built only sophisticated ships.

A Dozen Lessons

While the ironies and myths are interesting, more important are the lessons. These can be broken down into three categories.

GENERAL

Warships as Complex, Sustainable Machinery

Throughout their long, over 4,500-year history, warships have been the most complex pieces of machinery known to mankind. It has only been in the twentieth century that first airplanes and then a few spacecraft have challenged the warship in sophistication and intricacy. Thus the history of warships is really not just that of naval or even military weaponry but rather encompasses the entire record of technological progress. Even today, warships are still the most complex, sophisticated, *self-sustaining* pieces of machinery in existence. While airplanes, helicopters, trucks, and tanks can operate for hours, only warships can operate for days, weeks, and, with a little support from service ships, even months on end. This simple fact, though seemingly self-evident, has often been forgotten, but it has clear strategic implications for the future when placing troops ashore will be an increasingly unappealing option and airplane presence, at best, ephemeral.

Importance of Industrial Base

The importance of a good industrial base has been demonstrated time and time again and is even more important in modern times. During ancient times Athens's shipyards and sheds were one of its great advantages and one reason they were quickly destroyed by its enemies. Venice had its great arsenal that was as valuable as the fleet. Although France often built better warships during the Age of Sail, it could never match England's shipbuilding. The industrial base has been of greatest importance during more modern times. During the Age of Steam, France, the United States, or Italy often made the first innovations, but with her great industrial base, England was always able to catch up and then surpass these countries quickly.

Japan might have made a terrible blunder pulling out of the London Naval Treaty in 1935 because it did not have the industrial capability to match the United States, which was then no longer restricted. It was the U.S. Navy ships started after the Second London Conference in the late 1930s that won the war in the Pacific. Today with the increased sophistication and cost of weaponry, once that industrial base is lost it will probably never be rebuilt.

"Come as You Are" Wars

Although an industrial base is important, most wars are essentially "come as you are" wars. Once a war begins, virtually no new large ships are built for reasons of both time and economy. During both world wars, only a handful of ships larger than destroyers were started and completed before the war ended. Even during the best of wartime conditions, working around the clock, it takes about three years to build larger ships. This does not diminish the need for an industrial base because shipyards can still turn out smaller craft in a matter of months, filling gaps in defense needs, and they are also needed for repair and modernization. There are always surprises that require the industrial base for quick fixes.

There is one small exception that also points to the need for a spectrum of ship types. A main difference between World War I and World War II shipbuilding was that in the former, small craft were not being built or planned;

therefore, it took two years to gear up. Early in World War II some small-craft construction was already under way, so that additional craft could be turned out almost immediately.

Importance of Propulsion

Although naming the ages after propulsion and not weaponry may at first glance seem somewhat ironic, it should not be entirely surprising since throughout history a warship's greatest limitations have been its mobility, not weaponry. One scholar even goes so far as to assert that the limitations of galleys prevented them from "controlling the seas" in the classic sense.[1] Another scholar equates the invention of the full-rigged three-masted ship which gave ships flexibility with the discovery of fire and the invention of the wheel. While these conclusions might be slightly overstated, there is an element of truth to both assertions. Up to World War II, a ship's mobility and speed were crucial in battle. It was only in World War II and the Battle of Coral Sea, the first fought between fleets that never saw each other, that propulsion could be considered secondary, although still important. Even today, a warship's greatest limitations are not weaponry or food but fuel.

Relationship of Warships to Weapons

Direct Relationship with Weaponry

Despite the naming of the ages of warships based on propulsion rather than their war-fighting capabilities, there is also a direct relationship with weaponry. The invention of the ram for the first time differentiated warships from simply armed merchantmen, and the development of broadside tactics during the Anglo-Dutch War of 1653 meant that armed merchantmen could no longer stand in the battle line. Similarly, the development of exploding shells doomed the wooden ship, leading to the need for ironclads, and the last half of the nineteenth-century Age of Ironclads saw a race between bigger guns and better armor. Torpedoes also had a great effect, leading to the development of the small torpedo boat and making submarines deadly weapons. Today, ships are designed to accommodate the latest electronic suites as well as the latest weapons. In short, even though the ages are named after propulsion, the development of weaponry has also had a direct effect on warship construction.

Influence of New Weaponry Ephemeral

Another lesson sometimes forgotten is that while the introduction of new weaponry was significant, the impact was usually temporary and any advantage quickly dissipated by the enemy copying, adapting, or countering the new weapon system. This can be seen from the introduction of the corvus by the Romans, which temporarily caught the Carthaginians by surprise, to the introduction of the torpedo and torpedo boat, which were fairly quickly thwarted by the torpedo boat destroyer and quick-firing guns, to the initial uses of submarines and aircraft carriers. It is, in short, a constant back and forth between offense and defense, and those in search of "silver bullets" or "revolutions in military affairs" to solve all their problems are invariably disappointed, or worse.

Mixture of Quality and Quantity Needed

Another lesson is that a mixture or both quantity and quality is usually needed, especially for any sustained conflict. Numbers can be offset to a certain extent by better weapons, and, of course, the opposite is true, but usually some mixture is needed for both economic and mission reasons. French sailing warships were often considered better than English ships, but France could never match the Royal Navy's strength. The Germans during World War II had some of the best weapons but could not counter the large Soviet advantage in manpower and the U.S. advantage in weapon numbers. The solution could be more, sophisticated weapons, but very few countries, even the richest, have ever had that advantage.

Mixture of Weaponry, Skill, Readiness, and Luck

Victory comes about for many reasons but is usually a combination of weaponry, skill, readiness, and plain, ordinary good luck. The best of weaponry is of little use without good training. What set apart the Athenians, Romans, and Royal Navy from the others of their day was not necessarily better ships but better training. During World War II both the Germans and Japanese ran out of skilled pilots, not airplanes. And one of these days it will dawn on Third World countries that having the latest Russian or American weaponry is no substitute for good training. This is why the current U.S. military rightly places such a high premium on training and readiness. But there is also the element of luck. The Athenians were lucky at Salamis, less lucky at Syracuse.

STRATEGY LESSONS

The Flexibility of Ships and Seapower

The greatest lesson from seapower is its flexibility, as noted by a famous quote from Francis Bacon: "But this much is certain; that he that commands the sea is at great liberty, and may take as much and as little of the war as he will." The greatest practitioner of this flexibility was England, which took as much and as little of war for over three hundred years generally, avoiding major commitments on the continent and then using its navy to advantage. Even when temporarily stymied and subdued, as during the Napoleonic Wars and, worse, during World War II, England was able to survive using the flexibility of seapower. Moreover, the flexibility of seapower allows that practitioner the ability to strike where he so desires.

The Clout and Leverage of Seapower

Close to the idea of flexibility is the notion of the leverage of seapower. Some, like well-known naval strategist Colin Gray, use the terms somewhat synonymously, but there is, at least in this author's opinion, a slight yet significant difference.[2] Leverage means more than just flexibility. Rather, leverage means the ability, usually of smaller countries, to increase their power using seapower. There are several examples, including the small Italian city-states of Venice and Genoa during the Middle Ages, Portugal during the Age of Discovery, and the Netherlands during the seventeenth century. They were all comparatively small powers that probably would have fared poorly in major land conflicts with their larger neighbors, but they were able to use the leverage of seapower to become major actors in the international arena. Spain, Portugal, and the Netherlands were also able to sustain overseas empires for years through seapower.

In more recent times, the old Soviet navy was able to use the leverage provided by seapower. During the late 1960s the Soviet navy started to deploy around the world using friendly countries as bases in the Mediterranean, on the east and west coasts of Africa, in the Indian Ocean, and in the South China Sea. While this never represented a true military threat, there were concerns that the Soviet Union was trying to encircle the West.

Symbolism of Warships

There is great symbolism to warships that is not pertinent to other weaponry. Often the largest ships carry their country's name or are named for the country's greatest battles and heroes. Ships are often used for diplomatic reasons for similar reasons. The first port visit is usually considered very important as a major stepping-stone in relations between two countries. At the end of the Cold War, U.S.-Russian port visits and U.S.-Chinese port visits were widely reported in the press as major diplomatic steps. Large bombers have sometimes been named to try to capture that symbolism, but it does not have the same meaning. Unfortunately, that can also have a downside as when a well-known ship such as the *Hood* was lost or when one named for its country is sunk, which is why Hitler changed the name of the pocket battleship *Deutschland* to *Lutzow*. Part of the reason for the symbolism of warships goes back to the first lesson on self-sustainability. Warships were not just fighting machines like tanks and planes, in which men also fought and died, but were also places where those men lived as well. In that sense, a warship is not just a weapon but a living, breathing symbol of that country's power.

Utility During Peacetime

The final lesson—and also, as noted, an irony—is that a warship's greatest utility may actually come during peacetime or at times of crises and not necessarily during wartime. Ancient Athens was able to survive during its cold war with Sparta by keeping supplied through seapower. Clear examples are the unappreciated use of ships to maintain Pax Romana and the much appreciated use of ships by England to maintain Pax Britannia. The role of seapower has not always been appreciated during the Cold War, which leads into the future of seapower to be explored in more depth in the final chapter.

The Future of Seapower and Warships: 17
Another Golden Age?

THE TRENDS FOR warship types seem certain for at least the initial years of the twenty-first century, although whether these are the right designs remains to be seen. The real question, however, has to do with the future of seapower in the post–Cold War era of uncertain world conditions. This could, and perhaps should, actually be another golden era for seapower and warships. During times of relative peace, navies, not armies or air forces, have been the lead service maintaining that peace, and these interwar periods have also provided golden opportunities to experiment with new warship types.

The Golden Ages of Seapower and Warships

Before reflecting on whether this will be another golden age of seapower and warships, first a review of past golden ages and their relationships to warships is needed. There have been five such ages.

GOLDEN AGE OF OVERALL INFLUENCE

Without question, the golden age for the overall influence of warships and seapower on world events came during the Age of Sail, which coincided with the Age of Discovery and the building of overseas empires that could be maintained only by men-of-war. During this time even relatively minor sea battles such as the French defeat of the English fleet at the Battle of Virginia Capes could have a major impact. This golden age began with the invention of the full-rigged, three-masted ships that had the necessary power and flexibility for exploration during the Age of Discovery, and it also led to the development of the classic ship of the line. In short, there was a direct relationship to the type of ship and its effect on history.

GOLDEN AGE OF DIRECT INFLUENCE

What might be called the golden age of direct influence or dominance of seapower and warships came during the century of Pax Britannia after the Napoleonic Wars that lasted until World War I. It is not coincidental that this was also the Age of Steam and Ironclads, when England was at the height of its industrial strength following the industrial revolution. Although other countries often came up with new ideas and warship types first—the French with shell guns and the first ironclad, the Americans with the first steam warship *Demologos* and the first modern warship *Monitor,* Italy with the first big-gun pre-dreadnoughts and early battle cruisers, Austria with torpedoes—England with her greater industrial strength always quickly regained any temporary lost advantage and remained dominant. England skillfully maintained that dominance through seapower even when new powers such as Germany, Italy, the United States, and Japan emerged during the late nineteenth century, which most historians view as the golden age of balance-of-power politics.

Golden Age of Leverage

The Golden Age of Leverage came during the late stages of the Age of Galleys and the early Age of Sail when relatively small states such as the Italian city-states of Venice and Genoa and then later small countries like the Netherlands and Portugal were able to extend their influence through seapower. Also, through the leverage of seapower, small states like the Netherlands, Portugal, and later Spain, when it became a second-rate power in the nineteenth century, were able to maintain some elements of their far-flung empires into the twentieth century.

Golden Age of Warship Types

The golden age for warship types came during the dreadnought era from 1906 through the end of World War II. Besides the development of battleships, cruisers, and destroyers, which had precedents in the earlier ages, this period also saw the building of completely new types, including aircraft carriers, mine craft, amphibious ships, and a service force as well as the transition of submarines from experimental prototypes to deadly weapons. During this time more distinct types, many never seen before, were built than at any other time in history. Most navalists still refer to these categories when describing ships.

Golden Age of Progress

The era of greatest progress was the experimental period of the Age of Steam and Ironclads that lasted from approximately 1860 to 1890. During this thirty-year period, ships, which in some respects had not changed for hundreds, even thousands of years, were refashioned from wood of old to the modern type we know today. Although the introduction of airplanes at sea during World War I was also a significant change, as was the introduction of electronics in World War II and then missiles in the 1950s, overall even these major advancements pale in comparison to the radical change from the wooden three-deckers that dominated until 1860 to the pre-dreadnought and other types of 1890. Today, it takes at least ten and usually twenty years to go from the drawing board to deployment. This was the Victorian era, often seen as the height of cultural conservatism, but there was nothing conservative about the Victorian naval officers.

The Future of Seapower

Although in many respects the conditions seem ripe for another golden age for seapower and warships at the turn of the century, there are three major problems: budgetary restraints, interservice mission competition, and a lingering post–World War II lack of appreciation for seapower.

BUDGETARY RESTRAINTS

The major problem facing all navies, and indeed the military in general, is declining defense budgets in all countries. With the end of the old Soviet peril and new major threats probably not emerging until at least 2015, probably much later, there is a natural inclination to cut military budgets. Navies have responded by either building fewer or smaller ships, with, in most cases, frigates replacing destroyers. Most navies, however, still maintain a spectrum of intra-warship types with, for example, a few sophisticated frigates many with destroyer (even cruiser) capabilities, offset by smaller frigates and corvettes. To maintain a balance, many countries have resorted to smaller V/STOL carriers while building one or two medium-size amphibious ships with both helicopter and landing craft capabilities.

The major exception has been the United States Navy, which currently builds only sophisticated and, unfortunately, very expensive ships. Until the 1980s the U.S. Navy also built a spectrum of ships with a few cruisers, more destroyers, and then many DEs and later frigates. That changed in the 1980s and probably for good reasons. Starting in the late 1970s the quality of Soviet ships finally started to match their quantity; the Soviet navy added quiet submarines, capable cruisers, and even aircraft carriers. In response, the United States was correct to switch from building a spectrum of warships to more sophisticated types. While current U.S. Navy warships are admittedly more capable, there is now some question of their need in the post–Cold War environment. The result is that only a very few ships are currently being built by the U.S. Navy.

The U.S. Navy's early twenty-first century force structure calls for a 300-odd ship navy. Since warships last approximately thirty years, that requires a building rate averaging about 10 ships per year. Unfortunately, since the early 1990s and planned through the early years of the twenty-first century, rates will average only about 5 to 7 ships, indicating an eventual 150- to 210-ship navy. The Navy is worried about the so-called bow-wave effect of force structure goals not matching procurement, but after ten years that problem may not just be a passing bow wave that can be easily corrected but a sustained tsunami that will eventually swamp the world's only remaining sea power.

Other navies are facing similar problems. For years the Royal Navy's goal was 50 surface combatants, but each year that goal gets lowered. France wants to build two CVNs but will probably build only one. China, with aspirations of entering the front ranks of naval powers, has plans for carriers, but they keep getting postponed. As shown in appendix C, fleets are a shadow of their World War I and II strengths, but that might still be the proverbial good news. Starting after the turn of the century, the many ships built in the 1970s and 1980s to match the increasingly capable Soviet navy will reach block obsolescence and few funds will be available for replacements—certainly not on a one-for-one basis.

INTERSERVICE MISSION RIVALRY

The second problem facing navies is mission competition over which forces are most appropriate for current threats. As happened after both World Wars I and II, airpower advocates are now claiming that they can fulfill the peacekeeping and crisis-response operations that traditionally have been naval functions. No navy has suffered more from this claim than the once mighty Royal Navy, which continues to play second fiddle to the Royal Air Force. Worse, some countries have even passed anti-navy laws. Italy, for example, has given all airplane responsibilities to its air force, which forced the navy to beg it for a few V/STOL planes. Other countries such as Russia and China have traditionally been land powers, which creates even more problems for their navies.

The United States passed the Goldwater-Nichols Act in the mid-1980s that mandates "joint" operations regardless of the situation. This law went into effect in 1986 just when it was becoming obvious that the Soviet Union was starting to crumble. Politicians like to accuse generals and admirals of "fighting the last war," but Goldwater-Nichols may be a classic case of "legislating the last war." The absurdity of this law was clearly demonstrated during the 1993 intervention against the island-nation of the Dominican Republic when a large-deck attack aircraft carrier's airplanes were off-loaded to make way for Army helicopters. Even though the Navy had twelve large amphibious assault ships specifically designed for helicopter operations as well as the Marine Corps, which has trained specifically for island operations since the 1920s, the Dominican Republic operation was conducted and controlled by the Army for the sake of "jointness." About once a year, for the sake of jointness, bombers are sent halfway around the world to release cruise missiles—the same cruise missiles that are found on warships already patrolling off the coast of the target country. Interservice rivalry is always a factor to some degree, and in some cases this competition can actually be healthy. But legislating strategy and tactics, especially in a time of scarce resources, may be as foolish as King Canute's attempt to hold back the waters.

LACK OF APPRECIATION OF SEAPOWER

The greatest problem facing navies might be a lack of understanding as regards seapower, compounded perhaps by a slight inferiority complex. Some have been predicting the end of navies since the invention of the airplane. This happened after World War I, but navies would soon play crucial roles in the Battle of the Atlantic and the Battle in the Pacific was one of the few truly naval wars in all history. With the invention of the atom bomb, again many predicted the end of navies after World War II, only to find out five years later how crucial seapower was in Korea. Then, after the launch of Sputnik in October 1957, predictions came fast that the new missile age would finally render navies obsolete. This author vividly remembers that prediction, which came only four months after being sworn in as a midshipman, and wondering whether his might be the shortest naval career on record. Only a few years later the backbone of that missilery force—which continues to this day—was the SSBNs, the fleet ballistic nuclear submarines.

Now, in the post–Cold War period navies face similar problems. Just when everyone was writing about "the end of history" and wars with the demise of the Soviet Union and most countries were starting to demobilize, Saddam Hussein of Iraq in 1990 made the classic blunder of underestimating Western resolve, which resulted in the largest concentration of allied warships, armies, and airplanes since World War II. Tank warfare, which some considered obsolete, proved itself again, and despite all the talk of a revolution in military affairs, old-fashioned soldiering was still required. Proponents of airpower have claimed that they could have won the war all by themselves, and in that particular case of fighting in the open desert, they might have been right. While there were no great sea battles, the role of navies was also important. The Navy and Marine Corps were the first to go in and the last to come out. And while most armies and air forces have long since left, the U.S. Navy (with occasional help from allied navies) still patrols the Persian Gulf region.

As history tells us and Operation Desert Storm against Iraq reminds us, at some future time and in some future place there will be another war and probably more great land and air battles. The world is, in short, in another interwar period. But there will be no more great sea battles—no more Battles of Salamis, or Trafalgar, or Jutland, and not even another Coral Sea or Midway. There was some thought that when the Soviet navy started to deploy worldwide in the early 1970s and then began to build sophisticated cruisers and aircraft carriers in the late 1970s to early 1980s it might challenge the U.S. Navy on the open seas. The U.S. Navy responded with its maritime strategy to "challenge the bear north of the G-I-UK gap." Thus it appeared that there might once again be—however brief—some great sea battles. But those days are over. Even the possibility of a third Battle of the Atlantic against the massive Soviet submarine fleet has passed, at least for the near term.

Yet seapower is not irrelevant, especially for today's conditions and those that will prevail for at least for the foreseeable future in the early years of the twenty-first century. There will be smaller wars and conflicts, and as shown in appendix D, navies have played key roles and often paid the price. More important than these conflicts will be the constant crises and the necessary crisis response, and as has been proven time and time again, those are navy missions: "Throughout the postwar period the United States has turned most often to its Navy when it desired to employ components of the armed forces in support of political objectives. Naval units participated in 177 of the 215 incidents, or more than four out of every five. . . . In short, the Navy clearly has been the foremost instrument for the United States' political uses of the armed force: at all times, in all places, and regardless of the specifics of the situation."[1]

That assessment, from the Brookings Institution book *Force without War,* written in the mid-1970s, has been verified many times over since that time, and the number of crises now numbers about three hundred. While a few situations such as the breakup of Yugoslavia will require troops on the ground, the typical crisis response will be conducted by the Navy and Marine Corps. Moreover, the days of stationing troops overseas are probably numbered. It would be very surprising to see more than a few token U.S. troops in Europe or South Korea much after the turn of the century. This will put even more pressure not just on the U.S. Navy but on all navy forces.

There is no question that the next major war—like most wars throughout history—will be fought by armies with support from air forces and navies, but, fortunately, major wars are very few and very far between. In the fifty years since World War II there have been only three major regional wars—those in Korea, Vietnam, and Iraq. And with the demise of the Soviet Union, there are no major power threats projected until at least sometime after 2015. And when that next major regional war does come, the first on the scene, the last to leave, and the force that will remain on patrol will be the navy. Constant crises will arise, however, and most will be controlled by navies.

The Future of Warships

The turn of the twenty-first century, a generally peaceful interwar era, could, and should, be another golden age for seapower, especially for the world's remaining superpower, the United States Navy. The question arises, What kind of peaceful, or pax, era will it be: a Pax Britannia or a Pax Romana? The question is important because it has implications for the type of warships built. Pax Britannia required ever more sophisticated ships but Pax Romana did not.

There is a natural inclination for navalists to cite Pax Britannia for several reasons. It is more recent, and, indeed, there will still be people alive in the early twenty-first century who have firsthand memories of Pax Britannia. The types of ships from that era are also familiar, not, in some respects, much different in overall size and shape from those today. But there are also two significant differences. First, although England was by far the dominant sea power, it was not the only major power. The nineteenth century was also the golden age of balance-of-power politics with several major, and generally equal, powers competing. Second, the nineteenth century was also the golden age of progress with the constant development of new types of ships and weapons. In short, although England was the dominant sea power, it was by no means the dominant power and had to keep ahead of its rivals by constantly building increasingly sophisticated ships.

Thus, in some respects the conditions of Pax Romana might be more applicable. The United States, like Rome, is not only the dominant sea power but the dominant military power. There are no other threats, no power likely to emerge with a new, revolutionary weapon. Today progress is more evolutionary than revolutionary. Though certainly possible, it is highly unlikely that a "dreadnought" in the year 2006 will appear, "making all else obsolete" and if it does, it will probably be an American dreadnought.

This has direct implications for future warships. Most major countries are building smaller frigates that may be adequate for today's environment. The sophisticated U.S. Navy ships, or at least all of them, might not be needed. The U.S. Navy has also gotten into the fashion of building very large classes of the same basic design, which eliminates diversity. The Navy is currently looking at building a "one size fits all" SC-21 surface combatant that may or may not be productive in the long run. By building smaller ships in smaller classes the lesser navies still have money left over for experimentation. Many of the new experiments are being conducted by navies other than the U.S. Navy. The use of ski jumps for V/STOL carriers, new submarine propulsion systems, new stealth frigates, corvettes, and patrol craft, and new-design medium-sized amphibious ships are being built by European navies, not the U.S. Navy. In short, the U.S. Navy's building philosophy may turn out to be more conservative than that of the Victorians.

On the other hand, current U.S. Navy ships have no equals. While the capabilities and characteristics between different navies' battleships, cruisers, destroyers, submarines, and aircraft carriers were slight through World War II, today no other navy's carrier can match a *Nimitz,* nor can any destroyer match an *Arleigh Burke,* nor can any amphibious ship match the *Wasp.* And though the warships of other navies might be adequate for the turn-of-the-century conditions, they might not be for the more sophisticated 2015 time frame.

While no one can predict the future, history tells us that in warships there must be a balance of quality and quantity. But one thing is certain: despite all the dire predictions the age of warships is far from over, and the best guide for the future is still an understanding of the past.

Appendix A

Warship Balance in World War I

Type	England	France	Italy	U.S.	Japan	Russia	Germany	Austria
Pre-dreadnoughts	41	21	15	25	8	11	20	6
Battleships	33	13	3	10	2	4	15	6
Battle cruisers	14				8		5	
Large cruisers	43	25	10	22	14	17	14	5
Light cruisers	99	36	9	15	11	3	54	10
Destroyers	517	102	60	163	76	125	249	30
Submarines	201	80	62	74	16	62	367	27
TOTAL	948	277	159	309	135	222	724	84

NOTE: Totals include all those on hand and built and commissioned during the war.

Appendix B

Warship Balance in World War II

Type	England	U.S.	France	Russia	Germany	Italy	Japan
Battleships	17	25	8	3	6	6	8
Battle cruisers	3	2	2		2		2
Aircraft carriers							
Large	11	28	1				13
Light	13	9					7
Escort	44	76					4
Heavy cruisers	18	27	10		6	7	18
Light cruisers	73	52	7	9	6	15	44
Destroyers	412	541	66	73	56	96	156
Frigates and DEs	349	499			15	20	32
Submarines	228	298	85	177	1210	152	182
TOTAL	1168	1557	179	262	1301	296	466

NOTE: Totals include all those on hand and built and commissioned during the war.

Appendix C

Warship Balance in the Year 2000

Type	U.S.	Russia[a]	China	England	France	Germany	Italy	Japan
Aircraft carriers								
CVN	10 + 2				1			
CV	2	1			1			
V/STOL	(11)[b]			3			1	
Cruisers								
CG	27	3						
Other					1		1	
Destroyers								
DDG	30	10	2	12	4	2	4	9
DD	24	7	19		10			30
Frigates								
FFG	36		2					
FF		14	24	24	4	12	16	14
Submarines								
SSN	50	30	4	12	6			
SSBN	16	18	(1)[c]	4	4			
SS		24	70			12	8	16
Minecraft	26	100	64	23	13	20	12	38
Amphibious ships								
LPH-type	11			1			3	1
LSD/LPD	23	1			3			
Other	2	20	15	5				
Service ships	34	12	4	13	4	6	3	4
TOTAL	291	240	204	97	51	52	48	112
Personnel:								
(thousands)	373	180	170	34	58	20	39	43

NOTE: Approximate strength of active duty forces in navies based on late 1990s plans and normal retirements.

[a] Current status of Russian Navy unclear; carrier *Kuznetsov* has not been operable since a 1996 refit, cruisers carried on book, but inactive, etc.

[b] USN LPHs have V/STOL capabilities.

[c] Chinese SSBN has probably been retired.

Appendix D
Warship Casualties since World War II

Date	Country	Casualty	Results and Cause
Conflict Related			
1945–47	United Kingdom	7 patrol & 4 merchantmen	Mined/damaged by Jewish "Palmach" frogmen
22 Oct. 1946	United Kingdom	DD *Saumarez*	Mined in Corfu channel, 36 killed, damaged beyond repair
22 Oct. 1946	United Kingdom	DD *Volage*	Mined in Corfu channel, 8 killed, damaged, but repaired
Korean War			
2 July 1950	North Korea	Three PT boats	Sunk by cruisers USS *Juneau* and HMS *Jamaica,* frigate HMS *Black Swan*
25 July 1950	United States	Hospital Ship *Benevolence*	Sinks in collision with SS *Mary Luckenback;* recommissioned for Korea
29 Sept. 1950	United States	Minesweeper *Magpie*	Mined and sunk, 21 missing in action; first USN ship lost in war
30 Sept. 1950	United States	*Mansfield* (DD-728)	Mined and damaged, five MIA
12 Oct. 1950	United States	Two minesweepers	*Pirate* (AM-275) and *Pledge* (AM-277) sunk in Wonsan Harbor
2 Feb. 1951	United States	Minesweeper *Partridge*	Sunk sweeping mines north of Wonsan, last minesweeper lost in Korea
12 June 1951	United States	*Walke* (DD-723)	Damaged by mine off Hungam, North Korea, 26 men killed
14 June 1951	United States	DMS *Thompson*	Extensive damage from shore battery, three killed
7 Oct. 1951	United States	*Small* (DDR-838)	Mined, extensive damage with 27 casualties
26 Apr. 1952	United States	DMS *Hobson*	USN destroyer minesweeper sunk with loss of 176 in collision with *Wasp*

Date	Country	Casualty	Results and Cause
27 Aug. 1952	United States	ATF *Sarsi*	Fleet tug sunk by mine. Last USN ship lost in Korean War
16 Sept. 1952	United States	*Barton* (DD-722)	Mined, major damage with 11 casualties
11 July 1953	United States	*Saint Paul* (CA-73)	Severe underwater damage by shore battery, no casualties
1950–53	United States	80 other USN ships	Besides five sunk and seven seriously damaged noted above, 80 other USN ships suffered minor damage, mostly from North Korean shore batteries

ISRAEL: WAR OF INDEPENDENCE (1948–1949)

Date	Country	Casualty	Results and Cause
10 Apr. 1948	Syria	Freighter *Lino*	Mined and sunk by "Palmach" frogmen in Port of Bari, Italy
27 Aug. 1948	Syria	Freighter *Argiro*	Loaded with weapons; seized en route by Israeli Navy off Crete, sunk
22 Oct. 1948	Egypt	Sloop *El Emir Farouk*	Egyptian Navy's flagship; sunk by Israeli Naval Commandos' boats
22 Oct. 1948	Egypt	Minesweeper B.Y.M.S.	Seriously damaged; put out of service by Israeli Naval Commandos' boats
30 Nov. 1948	Lebanon	Gunboat MS *Igris*	2560 ton (once Hitler's yacht) mined and damaged by Israeli frogmen

SINAI CAMPAIGN (1956)

Date	Country	Casualty	Results and Cause
31 Oct. 1956	Egypt	DD *Ibrahim el Awal*	Captured in battle off Bay of Haifa by Israel; in Israeli Navy as ISN *Haifa*
1 Nov. 1956	Egypt	Frigate *Domiat*	Sunk by HMS cruiser *Newfoundland*—last surface action
Nov. 1956	Egypt	Four MTBs	Sunk by RN carriers during Suez crisis

SIX-DAY WAR (1967) AND "WAR OF ATTRITION"

Date	Country	Casualty	Results and Cause
8 June 1967	United States	AGTR *Liberty*	USN ship attacked by Israeli planes and torpedo boats, 34 killed
11 July 1967	Egypt	2 P-183 FACs	Sunk by Israel DD *Eliat* and two torpedo FACs
21 Oct. 1967	Israel	DD *Elath*	Sunk by 3 Styx missiles fired by Egyptian Komar—first in history

Date	Country	Casualty	Results and Cause
8 Sept. 1969	Egypt	2 P-183 FACs	Mined, sunk by Israeli frogmen at Suez prior to amphibious operation
16 Nov. 1969	Israel	2 civilian freighters	Mined and damaged by Egyptian frogmen in Port of Eilat, Israel
6 Feb. 1970	Israel	LC Bat-Sheba	Mined and damaged by Egyptian frogmen in Port of Eilat, Israel
6 Feb. 1970	Israel	Navy aux. Bat-Galim	Mined and damaged by Egyptian frogmen in Port of Eilat, Israel
6 Feb. 1970	Egypt	Minesweeper	Sunk by Israeli planes in the Port of Hurgada, Egypt
13 May 1970	Israel	Civilian fishing boat	Sunk by Styx missiles fired by Egyptian Komar offshore Northern Sinai
16 May 1970	Egypt	DD *El Qaher*	DD & landing craft sunk by Israeli planes in Port Ras-Banas, Red Sea
13 Aug. 1973	Egypt	De-Castro Patrol Boat	Hit, out of order by Israel PCs while attempting to shell Israeli naval base

"YOM KIPPUR" WAR (1973)

Date	Country	Casualty	Results and Cause
6 Oct. 1973	Egypt	Osa missile boat	Sunk by Israeli aircraft off Romani, north of Sinai
6 Oct. 1973	Egypt	1 PC, 2 Commando boats	Sunk by Dabur patrol boats within Egyptian port in Gulf of Suez
6 Oct. 1973	Syria	Osa missile boat	Sunk by Israeli Gabriel missiles from missile boats, offshore Syria
6 Oct. 1973	Syria	2 Komar missile boats	Sunk by Israeli Gabriel missiles from missile boats, offshore Syria
6 Oct. 1973	Syria	K-123 torpedo boat	Hit by guns and sunk by Israeli missile boats, offshore Syria
6 Oct. 1973	Syria	T-43 minesweeper	Sunk by Israeli Gabriel missiles from missile boats, offshore Syria
8 Oct. 1973	Egypt	3 Osa missile boats	Hit by Israeli Gabriel missiles from missile boats, two sunk, one beached
8 Oct. 1973	Egypt	De Castro patrol boat	Sunk by two Dabur patrol boats, one damaged by Egyptian shore guns

Date	Country	Casualty	Results and Cause
10 Oct. 1973	Syria	2 Osa missile boats	Hit by Israeli Gabriel missiles from missile boat, one sunk, one damaged
10 Oct. 1973	Egypt	Komar missile boat	Mined and destroyed by Israeli frogmen in Port Hurgada, Red Sea, Egypt
10 Oct. 1973	Egypt	Oil tanker *Marifella*	Greek tanker working for Egypt hit Egyptian mine, badly damaged
14 Oct. 1973	Egypt	3 big, 12 small fishing	Carry munitions; hit and sunk by Israeli Dabur patrol boats
16 Oct. 1973	Egypt	Osa, two smaller PCs	Mined, damaged by Israeli frogmen in Port of Said, two frogmen missing
22 Oct. 1973	Egypt	Komar missile boat	Hit and destroyed by Israeli commandos with anti-tank rockets in Port Hurgada
22 Oct. 1973	Egypt	2 mobilized fishing craft	Hit and sunk by guns from Israeli missile boats during a shelling
24 Oct. 1973	Egypt	De Castro patrol boats	Hit and sunk by Israeli tanks during occupation of Naval Base of Adabia
24 Oct. 1973	Egypt	2 K-123 patrol boats	Captured by Israeli Dabur patrol boats during occuption of Adabia
24 Oct. 1973	Egypt	2 Bertram patrol boats	Captured by Israeli Dabur patrol boats during occuption of Adabia
26 Oct. 1973	Israel	Oil tanker *Siris*	Hit and destroyed by Egyptian mine; no casualties

Terrorist Activities in the Arab-Israeli Conflict

Date	Country	Casualty	Results and Cause
1971–1993	Terrorists	101 ships and boats	In 58 incidents, Israeli forces have sunk or damaged 36 fishing boats, 26 motor boats, 20 freighters, 17 Zodiac boats, one tug and one sea motorcycle involved in terrorist activities

Indo-Pakistani Wars and South Asia

Date	Country	Casualty	Results and Cause
18 Dec. 1961	Portugal	Sloop *A. De Albuquerque*	Sunk by Indian cruiser *Mysore* and destroyers during invasion of Goa
Dec. 1961	Portugal	*Antares* and *Regulus*	Coastal patrol boats sunk by Indian forces during their invasion of Goa

Date	Country	Casualty	Results and Cause
4 Feb. 1971	Pakistan	SS *Ghazi*	Probably sunk by own mine, also claimed by Indian ASW forces (Former US *Diabolo*)
5 June 1971	Pakistan	Minecraft *Muhafiz*	Sunk by Indian Navy
5 Dec. 1971	Pakistan	DD *Khaibar*	Sunk by Indian 'Osa' class FAC
9 Dec. 1971	India	Frigate *Khukri*	Torpedoed and sunk by Pakistani submarine *Hangor* [First since WW II]

VIETNAM WAR

Date	Country	Casualty	Results and Cause
1 May 1964	United States	USNS *Card*	Former escort carrier used as transport sunk at pier at Saigon by mine
5 Aug. 1964	North Vietnam	Patrol boats	25 patrol boats damaged or destroyed, first USN strike on North Vietnam
14 Feb. 1966	United States	PCF 4	First Swift boat lost in action sunk by mine; four killed, two wounded
11 May 1966	North Vietnam	Freighter	USN and USCG forces sink largest steel-hulled freighter supplying South
1 July 1966	North Vietnam	Three PT boats	Sunk by USN aircraft after they had approached destroyers
7 July 1966	North Vietnam	Four PT boats	USN aircraft sank two, damaged two near Haiphong
6 Aug. 1966	North Vietnam	Five PT boats	USN aircraft sank four, damaged one near Haiphong
11 Aug. 1966	United States	CG *Point Welcome*	Accidentally attacked by friendly forces, two killed including CO
13 Aug. 1966	North Vietnam	Two PT boats	Sunk by USN aircraft near Haiphong
23 Aug. 1966	North Vietnam	Three PT boats	One sunk, two damaged by USN aircraft
23 Aug. 1966	United States	MSTS *Baton Rouge*	Freighter under charter strikes mine, seven killed with ship beached
29 Aug. 1966	North Vietnam	Three PT boats	One sunk, two damaged by USN aircraft from Constellation
29 Aug. 1966	China	Two merchantmen	China claimed USN sank one, damaged one. US claims fired on first
11 Sept. 1966	United States	River patrol boats	Ambushed, one killed, first American fatality in Operation Game Warden

Date	Country	Casualty	Results and Cause
26 Oct. 1966	United States	*Oriskany* (CVA-34)	During battle action, flare accidentally ignites ammunition, kills 44
31 Oct. 1966	North Vietnam	57 junks and sampans	Largest riverine action of war in Mekong River, no USN losses
31 Oct. 1966	United States	MSB-54	Mined and sank on Long Tau river; 2 killed; first sinking of minesweeper
23 Dec. 1966	United States	*O'Brien* (DD-725)	Hit by North Vietnam shore battery, two killed, first direct hit
4 Nov. 1966	United States	*Braine* (DD-630)	Received minor splinter damage from shore battery, no casualties
6 Nov. 1966	North Vietnam	Torpedo boat	Sunk by aircraft from *Constellation*
5 Dec. 1966	United States	*Ingersoll* (DD-652)	Slight damage from shore battery, no casualties
23 Dec. 1966	United States	*O'Brien* (DD-725)	Hit twice by NV shore battery, two killed, four wounded, first DD direct hit
31 Dec. 1966	United States	*Mahnomen County*	(LST-912) ran aground, split in two by waves
9 Jan. 1967	United States	*Jamaica Bay*	Viet Cong sink 170-ft dredge, two civilians killed
9 Jan. 1967	United Kingdom	*Haustrum*	Tanker hit while proceeding to Saigon, one killed, one wounded
20 Jan. 1967	North Vietnam	Five patrol craft	*Benner* (DD-807) and *Stoddard* (DD-566) damage five craft
4 Feb. 1967	United States	PBR 113	First of class lost to enemy; damaged beyond repair by grenade
1 Mar. 1967	United States	*Canberra* (CAG-1)	North Vietnam shore batteries score two minor hits; no casualties
11 Mar. 1967	United States	*Keppler* (DD-765)	Hit by shore fire on forward mount, none killed, six injured
17 Mar. 1967	United States	*Stoddard* (DD-566)	Major hit above waterline by shore battery, but none injured
25 Mar. 1967	United States	*Ozbourn* (DD-846)	Two minor hits from shore battery, no injuries
5 Apr. 1967	United States	*Duncan* (DDR-874)	Light damage from shore battery, no injuries
7 Apr. 1967	United States	*Waddell* (DDG-24)	Light damage from shore battery, no injuries

Date	Country	Casualty	Results and Cause
15 May 1967	United States	*Providence* (CLG-6)	Slight damage from shore fire; no injuries
27 May 1967	United States	*Edson* (DD-946)	Hit by shrapnel from shore fire, ten injured, three seriously
29 July 1967	United States	*Coconino County*	LST-603 has mysterious explosion in Vietnam, one wounded
30 July 1967	United States	*Ault* (DD-698)	Minor damage from shore battery, none injured
31 July 1967	United States	*Ault* (DD-698)	Minor damage from shore battery, no casualties
2 Aug. 1967	United States	*Saint Paul* (CA-73)	Minor damage from air burst from shore battery, one wounded
18 Oct. 1967	Australia	*Perth*	Slight damage from N.V. shore battery, four wounded
11 Nov. 1967	United States	*Goldsborough* (DDG-20)	Minor damage from N.V. shore battery, no injuries
18 Dec. 1967	United States	*McCormick* (DDG-8)	Superficial damage from fragments from shore battery, no injuries
6 May 1968	United States	*T. E. Chandler* (DD-717)	Direct hit from shore battery, one slightly wounded
19 May 1968	U.S.–U.K.	*Anchor Queen*	British tanker fired on Saigon river, five U.S. sailors wounded
28 May 1968	United States	*Harwood* (DD-861)	Hit by N.V. shore batteries, minor damage, two hurt
29 May 1968	United States	*Buchanan* (DDG-14)	Superficial damage from shore batteries, no injuries
3 June 1968	United States	*Wilson* (DDG-7)	Direct hit from shore battery, one slightly wounded
16 June 1968	United States	*Boston* (CAG-1)	Slightly damaged by friendly fire from USAF plane
16 June 1968	Australia	DDG *Hobart*	Slightly damaged by friendly fire from USAF plane; 2 killed, 7 wounded
16 July 1968	United States	*Blue* (DD-744)	Hit by shore fire, minor damage, no injuries
16 July 1968	United States	USNS *Private Merrell*	Hit by small fire on river, no damage or casualties
22 Aug. 1968	United States	USNS ships	*Lt. Robert Craig* and *Santa Monica* hit with rockets, no casualties
24 Aug. 1968	United States	*Brule* (AKL-28)	Attacked on river, two wounded

Date	Country	Casualty	Results and Cause
30 Aug. 1968	United States	MSTS *Transglobe*	Hit by fire, one civilian killed
7 Oct. 1968	United States	*Furse* (DD-882)	Hit by shore battery, three injured
12 Sept. 1968	United States	*Hunterdon Cty* (LST-838)	Attacked on river, 2 killed, 25 wounded
1 Nov. 1968	United States	*Westchester Cty* (LST-1167)	Underwater explosion; 5 killed, 27 wounded
15 Mar. 1969	United States	*Harnett Cty* (LST-821)	Hit by recoiless rifle, minor damage, four wounded
21 Mar. 1969	United States	*Caddo Cty* (LST-515)	Hit by rocket-grenade, minor damage, no casualties
8 July 1969	United States	*Boston* (CA-69)	Five inch shell explodes accidentally during gunfire support, six injured
9 Sept. 1969	United States	*Noxubee* (AOG-56)	Mined by enemy swimmers at anchor, 18-inch hole, but no casualties
3 Oct. 1969	United States	*Boston* (CA-69)	Five inch barrel blows off, four slightly injured, second accident
13 Jan. 1970	United States	*New London Cty* (LST-1066)	has minor damage from exploding mine, no casualties
11 Sept. 1970	United States	*Lloyd Thomas* (DD-764)	Accidental explosion kills three, injures ten while firing in support
11 Oct. 1972	United States	*Newport News* (CA-148)	Explosion in 8-inch mount during fire mission kills 20, injures 9
1966–70	United States	Others	North Vietnamese batteries hit 19 allied ships, none sunk, 6 dead
16 Oct. 1966	China	Four gunboats	Nationalist Chinese sank two, damaged two, in sea battle off Matsu Is.
19 Jan. 1967	South Korea	Patrol boat	Sunk by North Korean shore battery leading 70 fishing boats in N.K. waters
29 July 1967	United States	*Forrestal* (CVA-59)	Rocket goes off accidentally causing eight-hour fires with 134 killed
22 Jan. 1968	United States	AGER *Pueblo*	USN intelligence ship seized by North Koreans; one died of injuries
9 June 1969	North Korea	Spy boat	Sunk by South Korean Coast Guard

Date	Country	Casualty	Results and Cause
22 July 1974	Turkey	*Kocatepe* (D-354)	Sunk in error by Turkish Air Force mistaking it for Greek during Cyprus

FALKLANDS WAR

Date	Country	Casualty	Results and Cause
2 May 1982	Argentina	CL *General Belgrano*	Torpedoed, sunk by RN submarine *Conqueror* [Former USN CL *Phoenix*]
10 May 1982	United Kingdom	DDG *Sheffield*	Hit by Exocet and scuttled
22 May 1982	United Kingdom	FF *Ardent*	Damaged and sunk by rockets
24 May 1982	United Kingdom	FF *Antelope*	Bombed and sunk
25 May 1982	United Kingdom	DDG *Coventry*	Bombed and sunk
8 June 1982	United Kingdom	LSL *Sir Galahad*	Bombed and scuttled
8 June 1982	United Kingdom	LSL *Sir Tristram*	Bombed, but survived
24 Mar. 1986	Libya	Waheed missile boat	Sunk by USN A-6 Harpoons and Rockeyes in Gulf of Sidra
24 Mar. 1986	Libya	Nanuchka II corvette	Sunk by USN A-6 Harpoons and Rockeyes in Gulf of Sidra
25 Mar. 1986	Libya	Ean Mara corvette	Sunk by USN A-6 Harpoons and Rockeyes in Gulf of Sidra

PERSIAN GULF WAR

Date	Country	Casualty	Results and Cause
17 May 1987	United States	*Stark* (FFG-31)	Hit by two Exocet missiles fired by Iraqi plane, 37 men killed
8 Oct. 1987	Iran	Speedboats	One sunk, two captured by USA helicopter flying off *Ford* (FFG-54)
14 Apr. 1988	United States	*Roberts* (FFG-58)	Severely damaged by contact mine
18 Apr. 1988	Iran	*Joshan* fast patrol boat	Sunk by USN ships, *Wainwright* and *Simpson* after she had fired Harpoon
18 Apr. 1988	Iran	Boghammar speed boats	Five attack a merchantman, one sunk by USN A-6s
18 Apr. 1988	Iran	Frigate *Sahand*	Sunk by USN planes
18 Apr. 1988	Iran	Frigate *Sabalan*	Severely damaged by USN planes
22 Jan. 1991	Iraq	T-34 minelayer & PC	Sunk by 4 USN A-6 aircraft; a patrol boat disabled
23 Jan. 1991	Iraq	Hovercraft & PC	Sunk by USN A-6 aircraft
24 Jan. 1991	Iraq	Minelayer & PC	Sunk by USN A-6 aircraft
24 Jan. 1991	Iraq	Minelayer	Sunk after hitting own mine
24 Jan. 1991	Iraq	Four PC	Damaged by A-6 and F-18 strikes on Umm Qasr Naval Base

Date	Country	Casualty	Results and Cause
24 Jan. 1991	Iraq	Minelayer	Sunk by Saudi warship with Harpoon missile
26 Jan. 1991	Iraq	TNC-45 patrol boat	Sunk by USN aircraft, in Kuwait harbor
27 Jan. 1991	Iraq	Patrol boat	Sunk by USN aircraft
29 Jan. 1991	Iraq	4 small boats	Sunk by USN helicopters
30 Jan. 1991	Iraq	7 patrol boats	Sunk by USN aircraft and helicopters
1 Feb. 1991	Iraq	Patrol boat	Sunk at oil terminal
2 Feb. 1991	Iraq	4 patrol boats	Sunk by USN A-6 and helicopters
7 Feb. 1991	Iraq	2 patrol boats	Heavily damaged
7 Feb. 1991	Iraq	15 boats	Sunk or damaged by USS *Wisconsin* (BB-64)
8 Feb. 1991	Iraq	Frigate and PC	Neutralized by A-6
9 Feb. 1991	Iraq	Zouk patrol boat	Damaged by A-6
10 Feb. 1991	Iraq	2 patrol boats	Damaged by A-6s
14 Feb. 1991	Iraq	Osa patrol boat	Sunk in Kuwait harbor by A-6
20 Feb. 1991	Iraq	Gunboat	Sunk by USN S-3
Jan–Feb 1991	Iraq	Ships & boats	70 ships and boats sunk or damaged, includes 15 by *Wisconsin*, BB-64
18 Feb. 1991	United States	*Princeton* (CG-59)	Hit by mine, loses power, but survives
18 Feb. 1991	United States	*Tripoli* (LPH-10)	Amphibious assault ship hit by mine, remains on station

MAJOR INCIDENTS AT SEA

10 May 1967	U.S.–USSR	*Walker–Besslednyi*	Bumping incident in Sea of Japan with minor damage
11 May 1967	U.S.–USSR	*Walker–*Soviet DD	Bumping incident in Sea of Japan with minor damage
1960–1970	U.S.–USSR	Near misses, buzzing, etc.	Approximately 82 incidents at sea reported including airplane buzzing and near misses between various U.S. and Soviet ships

Major Operational Accidents

3 Dec. 1946	Canada	Mine craft *Middlesex*	Wrecked near Halifax
20 Dec. 1946	United Kingdom	FF *Aire*	Wrecked
23 Apr. 1949	United States	*United States* (CVA-58)	Sunk by unfriendly fire by Secretary of Defense Johnson

Date	Country	Casualty	Results and Cause
26 Aug. 1946	United States	*Cochino* (SS-345)	Lost off the coast of Norway
21 Nov. 1947	United Kingdom	SS P-511	Lost at sea with all hands
22 Jan. 1949	Portugal	Gunboat *Fataca*	Wrecked
12 Jan. 1950	United Kingdom	SS *Truculent*	Sunk in collision with Swedish tanker *Dvina* with heavy loss of life
26 Apr. 1952	United States	*Hobson* DMS-26	Lost in collision with *Wasp;* 176 lives lost
23 Sept. 1952	France	*Sibylle* (S-614)	Lost off Toulon (Former RN *Sportsman*) (P1, 42)
16 Oct. 1953	United States	*Leyte* (CV-32)	Explosion and fire kill 37 men
4 Apr. 1953	Turkey	*Dumlupinar* S-344	Sunk by Swedish freighter *Naboland,* 95 lost. (Former USN *Blower*)
25 Mar. 1954	Spain	Minesweeper *Guadalete*	Foundered in storm off Gibraltar while employed as Coast Guard vessel
26 May 1954	United States	*Bennington* (CV-20)	Explosion and fire off Newport kills 103, injures 201
29 Oct. 1955	Soviet Union	BB *Novorossiysk*	Sunk by old German mine
28 June 1957	United Kingdom	DE *Cleveland*	Wrecked
28 May 1958	United States	*Stickelback* (SS-415)	Sunk without loss of life in collision with *Silverstein* (DE-534)
19 May 1959	Soviet Union	S-99	Explosion, not repaired, experimental boat like German Walter subs
16 June 1959	United Kingdom	*Sidon* (S-59)	Torpedo accidentally went off while in port, sinking Sidon
16 June 1960	United States	*Hartley* (DE-1029)	Collides with merchantman, loses power, towed to Norfolk, no injuries
19 July 1960	United States	*Ammen* (DD-527)	Collides with *Collett* (DD-730), eleven killed, damaged beyond repair
19 Nov. 1960	United States	*Constellation* (CV-64)	Fire while under construction kills 50 workers, injures 150
16 Apr. 1961	United Kingdom	Submarine *Affray*	Snorkel accident, all lost
10 Apr. 1963	United States	*Thresher* (SSN-593)	Lost at sea, cause unknown; probably reactor shut-down during dive
10 Feb. 1964	Australia	*Voyager* D-04	Sunk in collision with carrier *Melbourne*

Date	Country	Casualty	Results and Cause
18 July 1965	United States	*Knox* (DDR-742)	"Knox on the rocks" in South China Sea; took five weeks to free
27 Aug. 1965	United States	*Newman Perry* (DD-883)	Collides with USS *Shangri-La* (CVA-18) in Mediterranean, 1 killed
7 Dec. 1965	United States	*Kitty Hawk* (CVA-63)	Fire in machinery room kills 2, injures 28
5 Feb. 1966	United States	*Bass–Waddell*	(DD-887) and (DDG-24) collide. 3 killed in rescue failure
25 Feb. 1966	Spain	*Ariete* (D-36)	Grounded and total loss
25 June 1966	United States	*Stalwart* (MSO-493)	Caught fire and capsized alongside pier in San Juan, no injuries
14 Sept. 1966	Germany	SS *Hai*	Training submarine sank in North Sea, 19 (of 20) lives lost
3 Nov. 1966	United States	*Tiru* (SS-416)	Ran aground off Australia, moderate damage
10 Nov. 1966	United States	*Nautilus-Essex*	Underwater collision during an exercise. Both had minor damage
20 Jan. 1967	United States	MSB-43	Struck underwater dolphin and sank near Charleston
31 Jan. 1967	United States	*McMorris–Tombigbee*	DE-1036 and AOG-11 collide with two in *McMorris* killed
29 July 1967	United States	*Forrestal* (CVA-59)	Major fire killing 132, 2 missing, 60 injured; 21 planes destroyed
18 Aug. 1967	Soviet Union	Submarine K-3	Fire, 39 men died
23 Dec. 1967	United States	*Kearsarge* (CVS-33)	Fire kills three crewman, two seriously burned
25 Jan. 1968	Israel	Submarine *Dakar*	Lost in Med with all hands (69) while on passage from England
27 Jan. 1968	France	*Minerve* (S-647)	Lost in Med with all hands (52). One of two *Daphne* class patrol subs lost
6 Feb. 1968	United States	*Bache* (DD-470)	Grounded. Broke up and stricken from registry
Apr. 1968	Soviet Union	Golf II submarine	North Pacific accident, all lost
8 Mar. 1968	Soviet Union	Submarine K-129	Ballistic submarine suffered internal explosion and sank
21 May 1968	United States	*Scorpion* (SSN-589)	Lost with entire crew 400 miles southwest off Azores, cause unknown

Date	Country	Casualty	Results and Cause
16 Oct. 1968	United States	*Alvin*	Experimental deep diving submarine lost off Spain, none on board
14 Jan. 1969	United States	Carrier *Enterprise*	Rocket goes off accidentally causing fire, 27 dead, 65 injured
15 May 1969	United States	*Guitarro* (SSN-665)	Sinks at dockside while being built
23 May 1969	United States	*King* (DLG-10)	Fire kills four
2 June 1969	United States	*Frank E. Evans* (DD-754)	Cut in two in collision with Australian carrier *Melbourne*, 74 U.S. lives lost
8 July 1969	United States	*Boston* (CA-69)	Five inch shell explodes, six injured
4 Sept. 1969	United States	*Dewey* (DDG-14)	Boiler explosion and fire kills three, three injured
3 Oct. 1969	United States	*Boston* (CA-69)	Five inch barrel blown off, four slightly injured, second accident
6 Oct. 1969	United States	*Avenge* (MSO-423)	Extensive damage from fire, no injuries
23 Oct. 1969	Canada	DE *Kootenay*	Explosion in engine room kills eight, injures nine
10 Jan. 1970	United States	*Shangri-La* (CVA-58)	Fire kills one, injures two
11 Feb. 1970	United States	*Semmes* (DDG-18)	Greek freighter sideswipes nest of four USN ships, DDG-18, heavy damage
12 Feb. 1970	United Kingdom	SS *Auriga*	Explosion injures ten
4 Mar. 1970	France	*Eurydice* (S-644)	Lost in Med, second of two Daphne class patrol subs lost, all 57 crew lost
12 Apr. 1970	Soviet Union	November class SSN	Fire, sank 400 miles off Spanish coast. Crew taken off
26 Aug. 1970	USSR–Sweden	*Sundfsvall*	Swedish frigate rammed by Soviet DD in Swedish waters, minor damage
11 Sept. 1970	United States	*Lloyd Thomas* (DD-764)	Accidental explosion kills three, wounds ten, while firing off Vietnam
4 Nov. 1970	United States	*Goldsborough* (DDG-20)	Boiler explosion kills two, injures two
9 Nov. 1970	U.K.–USSR	*Ark Royal–Kotlin*	Collided in Mediterranean, two Russian sailors killed
28 Nov. 1970	United States	*Canopus* (AS-34)	Fire on this Polaris tender at Holly Loch kills three
2 July 1971	United Kingdom	SS *Artemis*	Sank at mooring, three trapped, but later rescued after ten hours

Date	Country	Casualty	Results and Cause
11 Oct. 1972	United States	*Newport News* (CA-148)	Explosion in 8-inch turret kills 20, injures 9 on Vietnam fire mission
25 Sept. 1973	United States	USNS *Pendelton*	Ran aground and abandoned
9 Nov. 1975	Soviet Union	FFG *Storozhevoy*	Mutiny by some of crew, forced back by other Soviet units
22 Nov. 1975	United States	*Belknap* (CG-26)	Severely damaged in collision with *John F. Kennedy* (CV-67), 8 killed
14 Sept. 1976	United States	*Bordelon* (DD-881)	Collides with carrier *John F. Kennedy,* damaged beyond repair, 6 injured
20 Sept. 1976	United Kingdom	Mine craft *Fittleton*	Sunk in collision; 12 lives lost
20 Oct. 1978	United States	CG *Cuyahoga*	Coast Guard cutter sunk in collision with freighter, 11 killed
10 Jan. 1980	United States	CG *Blackthorn*	Coast Goard buoy tender sinks in collision with tanker, loss 23
9 Apr. 1981	United States	*G. Washington* (SSBN-598)	Collides with Japanese merchantman with loss of two
24 Sept. 1981	Israel	Sa'ar 3 missile boat	Grounded, repaired, and returned to active service, no casualties
24 Oct. 1981	Soviet Union	Submarine S-178	Sank after collision with a refrigerator ship
27 Oct. 1981	Soviet Union	Submarine S-137	Ran aground in Sweden, famous "Whisky on the rocks"
June 1983	Soviet Union	Charlie class sub	Sank off Kamchatka, 16 lost
1 Nov. 1983	United States	*Ranger* (CV-61)	Six killed, 35 injured when fire breaks out in engine room
17 Nov. 1983	U.S.–USSR	*Fife–Razyashchiy*	Soviet frigate collides with USN destroyer, no injuries, minor damage
21 Mar. 1984	U.S.–USSR	*Kitty Hawk*–Victor	USN carrier collides with surfacing Soviet submarine, minor damage
22 Mar. 1986	United States	Tug *Secota*	Sinks with loss of two lives in collision with *Georgia* (SSBN-729)
6 Oct. 1986	Soviet Union	Yankee class sub	Sank east of Bermuda after missile explosion, some deaths
12 Feb. 1988	U.S.–USSR	"Bumping" incident	*Yorktown* (CG-48) and *Caron* (DD-970) bumped by Soviet ships

Date	Country	Casualty	Results and Cause
24 Apr. 1988	United States	*Bonefish* (SS-582)	Last USN diesel submarine wracked by explosion and fires, beyond repair
7 Apr. 1989	Soviet Union	Komosolmelts	Fire, sank off Norway, 42 died
19 Apr. 1989	United States	*Iowa* (BB-61)	Turret explosion, kills 47 officers and men
11 Oct. 1989	United States	*Iwo Jima* (LPH-2)	Two killed by rounds fired from Phalanx aboard *El Paso* (LKA-117)
8 May 1990	United States	*Conyngham* (DDG-17)	Fire in boiler room kills one, 18 injured
20 June 1990	United States	*Midway* (CV-41)	Explosions set off by fire kills two seamen
Oct. 1992	Turkey	DD *Muavenet*	Two Sea Sparrow missiles fired accidentally from USS *Saratoga* strike bridge, kill captain and four sailors and wound 14 others
24 Mar. 1995	Israel	Dabur patrol boat	Grounded in rough seas on offshore reef, no casualties

SOURCES: Korean War data from Malcolm W. Cagle and Frank A. Manson, *The Sea War in Korea.* (Annapolis, Md: Naval Institute Press, 1957.)
Israeli War of Independence and Arab–Israeli War data compiled by Rear Admiral Ze'ev Almog, Israeli Navy (Ret.). Printed with his permission.
Conway's All The World's Fighting Ships, 1922–1946, and *Conway's All The World's Fighting Ships, 1947–1995.*
Naval and Maritime Chronology, 1961–1971. (Annapolis, Md: Naval Institute Press, 1973.)
Jack Sweetman, *American Naval History: An Illustrated Chronology,* 2d ed. (Annapolis, Md: Naval Institute Press, 1991.)
NOTE: This list does not include those sunk as targets or while under tow.

Notes

Chapter 2. The Age of Galleys

1. R. C. Anderson, *Oared Fighting Ships: From Classical Times to the Coming of Steam* (1962; new ed., London: Argus Books, 1976), p. v.

2. Detlev Ellmers, "The Beginnings of Boatbuilding in Central Europe," in *The Earliest Ships: The Evolution of Boats into Ships,* ed. Arne Emil Christensen (Annapolis, Md.: Naval Institute Press, 1996), pp. 11–12.

3. For a good summary of this early period, see Sean McGrail, *Rafts, Boats, and Ships: From Prehistoric Times to the Medieval Era* (London: Her Majesty's Stationery Office, 1981), pp. 12–14.

4. Clark G. Reynolds, *Command of the Sea: The History and Strategy of Maritime Empires* (New York: William Morrow, 1974), p. 19.

5. For a good description of this period, see Lionel Casson, *Ships and Seamanship in the Ancient World* (1971; rpt., Baltimore: Johns Hopkins University Press, 1995), pp. 11–29.

6. Ibid., p. 8.

7. For a detailed discussion of these methods, see Basil Greenhill, *The Evolution of the Wooden Ship* (New York: Facts on File, 1988), pp. 29–34.

8. Fik Meijer, *A History of Seafaring in the Classical World* (New York: St. Martin's Press, 1986), pp. 1–2.

9. Lionel Casson, *The Ancient Mariners: Seafarers and Sea Fighters of the Mediterranean in Ancient Times* 2d ed. (Princeton: Princeton University Press, 1991), p. 20.

10. John Morrison, *Long Ships and Round Ships: Warfare and Trade in the Mediterranean, 3000 B.C.–500 A.D.* (London: Her Majesty's Stationery Office, 1980), p. 51.

11. Casson, *Ships and Seamanship in the Ancient World,* pp. 54–55.

12. Lionel Casson, *Ships and Seafaring in Ancient Times* (Austin: University of Texas Press, 1994), p. 48.

13. Ibid.

14. N. K. Sanders, *The Sea Peoples: Warriors of the Ancient Mediterranean* (London: Thames and Hudson, 1978).

15. Helmut Pemsel, *A History of War at Sea* (Annapolis, Md.: Naval Institute Press, 1976), p. 11.

16. Anderson, *Oared Fighting Ships,* p. 1.

17. For the best description of biremes, see Casson, *Ships and Seamanship in the Ancient World,* pp. 49–60.

18. Casson, *Ancient Mariners,* pp. 72–73.

19. This reconstruction has been described in J. S. Morrison and J. F. Coates, *The Athenian Trireme: The History and Reconstruction of an Ancient Greek Warship* (Cambridge: Cambridge University Press, 1986).

20. Casson, *Ships and Seamanship in the Ancient World,* pp. 92–93.

21. For good discussion of the trireme, see ibid., pp. 77–96, and Morrison and Coates, *Athenian Trireme.* Also, John Morrison, "The Trireme," in *The Age of the Galley: Mediterranean Oared Vessels Since Pre-Classical Times,* ed. John Morrison (Annapolis, Md.: Naval Institute Press, 1995), pp. 49–65.

22. Casson, *Ships and Seafaring in Ancient Times,* pp. 70–71.

23. Casson, *Ships and Seamanship in the Ancient World,* p. 100.

24. Casson, *Ships and Seafaring in Ancient Times,* p. 86.

25. For a good discussion of all the possibilities, see Meijer, *History of Seafaring in the Classic World,* pp. 115–26.

26. Casson, *Ships and Seamanship in the Ancient World,* pp. 128–29; John Morrison, "Hellenistic Oared Warships, 399–21 B.C.," in *Age of the Galley,* ed. Morrison, p. 74.

27. Casson, *Ships and Seamanship in the Ancient World,* p. 127.

28. For more details on this period, see John S. Morrison and R. T. Williams, *Greek and Roman Oared Warships, 399–31 B.C.* (Oxford: Oxford University Press, 1994).

29. Casson, *Ships and Seamanship in the Ancient World,* p. 145.

30. Boris Rankov, "Fleets of the Early Roman Empire, 31 B.C.–A.D. 324," in *Age of the Galley,* ed. Morrison, p. 79.

31. Quoted in John H. Pryor, "From Dromon to Galea: The Mediterranean Gireme Galleys, A.D. 500–1300," in *Age of the Galley,* ed. Morrison, p. 101.

32. Frederick M. Hocker, "Late Roman, Byzantine, and Islamic Galleys and Fleets," ibid, p. 95.

33. Ibid., p. 96.

34. Ibid., p. 99.

35. David Lyon, "Underwater Warfare and the Torpedo Boat," in *Steam, Steel, and Shellfire: The Steam Warship, 1815–1905,* ed. Andrew Lambert (Annapolis, Md.: Naval Institute Press, 1992), p. 134.

36. For a good discussion of weaponry and tactics, see Hocker, "Late Roman, Byzantine, and Islamic Galleys and Fleets," in *Age of the Galley,* ed. Morrison, pp. 98–100.

37. Frederic Chapin Lane, *Venetian Ships and Shipbuilders of the Renaissance* (Baltimore: Johns Hopkins University Press, 1934), pp. 1–34.

38. Anderson, *Oared Fighting Ships,* p. 67.

39. Jan Glete, "The Oared Warship," in *The Line of Battle: The Sailing Warship, 1650–1840,* ed. Brian Lavery (Annapolis, Md.: Naval Institute Press, 1992), p. 99.

40. Anderson, *Oared Fighting Ships,* pp. 72–73.

41. Morrison and Coates, *Athenian Trireme,* p. 16.

42. Uwe Schnall, "Early Shiphandling and Navigation in Northern Europe," in *Earliest Ships,* ed. Christensen, p. 123.

43. For a good summary of the Viking ships, see Donald Macintyre and Basil W. Bathe, *Man-of-War: A History of the Combat Vessel* (New York: McGraw-Hill, 1969), pp. 21–23.

44. Anderson, *Oared Fighting Ships,* p. 44.

45. For a good summary of oared warships during the Age of Sail, see Glete, "The Oared Warship" in *Line of Battle,* ed. Lavery, pp. 98–105.

46. Anderson, *Oared Fighting Ships,* p. 99.

47. Reynolds, *Command of the Sea,* pp. 98–104.

48. Chester G. Starr, *The Influence of Sea Power on Ancient History* (New York: Oxford University Press, 1989), pp. 5–6.

49. J. H. Rose, *The Mediterranean in Ancient Times* (Cambridge: Cambridge University Press, 1933), p. 120, quoted from ibid., p. 68.

Chapter 3. The Age of Sail

1. Casson, *Ships and Seafaring in Ancient Times,* p. 14.

2. Ibid., pp. 21, 36.

3. For a good overview of the use of sail during the Age of Galleys, see Romola Anderson and R. C. Anderson, *The Sailing-Ship: Six Thousand Years of History* (New York: Norton, 1963), pp. 17–86.

4. Owain T. P. Roberts, "Descendants of Viking Boats," in *Cogs, Caravels, and Galleons: The Sailing Ship, 1000–1650,* ed. Richard W. Unger (Annapolis, Md.: Naval Institute Press, 1994), pp. 11–18.

5. Timothy J. Runyan, "The Cog as Warship," in ibid., p. 47.

6. Detlev Ellmers, "The Cog as Cargo Carrier," in ibid., p. 37.

7. Anderson and Anderson, *The Sailing Ship,* p. 87.

8. Runyan, "The Cog as Warship," pp. 43–44.

9. Ibid., p. 49.

10. Unger, *Cogs, Caravels, and Galleons,* p. 184.

11. Alan McGowan, *Tiller and Whipstaff: The Development of the Sailing Ship, 1400–1700* (London: Her Majesty's Stationery Office, 1981), p. 4.

12. Ian Friel, "The Carrack: The Advent of the Full Rigged Ship" in *Cogs, Caravels, and Galleons,* ed. Unger, pp. 78–79; and Anderson and Anderson, *The Sailing Ship,* p. 117.

13. Friel, "The Carrack," p. 77.

14. Quoted in ibid.

15. McGowan, *Tiller and Whipstaff,* p. 15.

16. Macintyre and Bathe, *Man-of-War,* p. 30.

17. Archibald R. Lewis and Timothy J. Runyan, *European Naval and Maritime History, 300–1500* (Bloomington: Indiana University Press, 1990), p. 84.

18. Anderson and Anderson, *The Sailing Ship,* p. 129.

19. Martin Elbl, "The Caravel and the Galleon," in *Cogs, Caravels, and Galleons,* ed. Unger, p. 91.

20. Ibid., p. 92.

21. McGowan, *Tiller and Whipstaff,* p. 17.

22. Anderson and Anderson, *The Sailing-Ship,* p. 124.

23. Elbl, "The Caravel and the Galleon," p. 95.

24. Carla Rahn Phillips, "The Caravel and Galleon," in *Cogs, Caravels, and Galleons,* ed. Unger, p. 99.

25. Frederic C. Lane, *Venice: A Maritime Republic* (Baltimore: Johns Hopkins University Press, 1973), p. 361.

26. McGowan, *Tiller and Whipstaff,* pp. 22–24.

27. Bryce Walker, *The Armada* (Alexandria, Va.: Time-Life Books, 1981), p. 85.

28. Pemsel, *History of War at Sea,* p. 42.

29. Phillips, "The Caravel and the Galleon," p. 106.

30. Anderson and Anderson, *The Sailing Ship,* p. 140.

31. Ibid., p. 141.

32. Brian Lavery, *The Ship of the Line,* vol. 1 (Annapolis, Md.: Naval Institute Press, 1983), p. 8.

33. Brian Lavery, "The Ship of the Line," in *Line of Battle,* ed. Lavery, p. 11.

34. Constructed from the "Glossary," ibid., pp. 195–204.

35. For a good summary discussion of guns, see Macintyre and Bathe, *Man-of-War,* pp. 38–45.

36. Lavery, *Ship of the Line,* passim.

37. Alfred Thayer Mahan, *The Influence of Sea Power upon History, 1660–1793* (Boston: Little, Brown, 1890).

38. Robert Gardiner, "The Frigate," in *Line of Battle,* ed. Lavery, p. 27.

39. Anderson and Anderson, *The Sailing Ship,* pp. 164–65.

40. Gardiner, "The Frigate," p. 27.

41. Ibid., pp. 27–45.

42. For a good description of this system, see John Keegan, *The Price of Admiralty: The Evolution of Naval Warfare* (New York: Viking, 1988), pp. 20–26.

43. For a history of American frigates, see Henry E. Gruppe, *The Frigates* (Alexandria, Va.: Time-Life Books, 1979).

44. For a good description of all these types, see Robert Gardiner, "Sloop of War, Corvette, and Brig," and Karl Heinz Marquardt, "The Fore and Aft Rigged Warship," in *Line of Battle,* ed. Lavery, pp. 46–84. See also Howard I. Chapelle, *The History of the American Sailing Navy* (New York: W. W. Norton, 1949).

45. Chris Ware, "Fireships and Bomb Vessels," in *Line of Battle,* ed. Lavery, pp. 85–89.

46. Ibid., pp. 89–95.

47. Brian Lavery, "Support Craft," in *Line of Battle,* ed. Lavery, pp. 106–14.

48. N. A. M. Rodger, *The Wooden World: An Anatomy of the Georgian Navy* (New York: Norton, 1996), p. 11.

Chapter 4. The Age of Steam, Ironclads, and Steel

1. For a good summary of these and other early experiments and proposals, see D. K. Brown, *Before the Ironclad: Development of Ship Design, Propulsion, and Armament in the Royal Navy, 1815–1860* (Annapolis, Md.: Naval Institute Press, 1990), pp. 44–60; and Macintyre and Bathe, *Man of War,* pp. 75–76.

2. William Hovgaard, *Modern History of Warships* (1920; rpt. Annapolis, Md.: Naval Institute Press, 1971), pp. 1–2.

3. Andrew Lambert, "The Introduction of Steam," in *Steam, Steel, and Shellfire,* ed. Lambert, p. 18.

4. D. K. Brown, *Paddle Warships: The Earliest Steam-Powered Fighting Ships* (London: Conway Maritime Press, 1993), pp. 25–41.

5. For a good description of the river paddle wheelers, see Donald L. Canney, *The Old Steam Navy: Ironclads, 1842–1885* (Annapolis, Md.: Naval Institute Press, 1993), pp. 35–45.

6. R. D. Layman, *Before the Aircraft Carrier: The Development of Aviation Vessels, 1849–1922* (Annapolis, Md.: Naval Institute Press, 1989), p. 13.

7. Brown, *Before the Ironclad,* pp. 99–102.

8. For more detail, see ibid., pp. 108–20.

9. Andrew Lambert, "The Screw Propeller Warship," in *Steam, Steel, and Shellfire,* ed. Lambert, p. 41.

10. For a good discussion, see Brown, *Before the Ironclad,* pp. 135–60.

11. Andrew Lambert, "Iron Hulls and Armour Plate," in *Steam, Steel, and Shellfire,* ed. Lambert, pp. 47–48.

12. David Lyon, *Steam, Steel and Torpedoes: The Warship in the Nineteenth Century* (London: Her Majesty's Stationery Office, 1980), p. 20.

13. Brown, *Before the Ironclad,* p. 97.

14. Hovgaard, *Modern History of Warships,* p. 7.

15. For a detailed study on the *Warrior,* see Andrew Lambert, *Warrior: The World's First Ironclad, Then and Now* (Annapolis, Md.: Naval Institute Press, 1987).

16. Charles O. Paullin, *History of Naval Administration* (Annapolis, Md.: Naval Institute Press, 1986), p. 280.

17. There are several good books on Civil War ships, including Canney, *The Old Steam Navy,* and Paul H. Silverstone, *Warships of the Civil War Navies* (Annapolis, Md.: Naval Institute Press, 1989).

18. David K. Brown, "The Era of Uncertainty, 1863–1878," in *Steam, Steel, and Shellfire,* ed. Lambert, pp. 75–94.

19. Oscar Parkes, *British Battleships: "Warrior" 1860 to "Vanguard" 1950, A History of Design, Construction, and Armament* (Annapolis, Md.: Naval Institute Press, 1990), pp. 44–45.

20. Sigfried Breyer, *Battleships and Battle Cruisers, 1905–1970* (Garden City, N.Y.: Doubleday, 1973), p. 19.

21. Hovgaard, *Modern History of Warships,* p. 29.

22. For a good discussion of all these various arrangements, see ibid., pp. 8–58.

23. John Roberts, "Warships of Steel, 1879–1889," in *Steam, Steel, and Shellfire,* ed. Lambert, pp. 96–98.

24. Breyer, *Battleships and Battle Cruisers,* pp. 36–37.

25. For a good summary, see Macintyre, *Man-of-War,* pp 78–83.

26. See David Lyon, "Underwater Warfare and the Torpedo Boat," in *Steam, Steel, and Shellfire,* ed. Lambert, pp. 134–46.

27. For a good discussion, see Theodore Ropp, *The Development of a Modern Navy: French Naval Policy, 1871–1904* (Annapolis, Md.: Naval Institute Press, 1987), pp. 155–80.

28. Breyer, *Battleships and Battle Cruisers,* p. 35.

Chapter 5. Overview of the Modern Age

1. For its impact on World War II, see Kenneth Poolman, *The Winning Edge: Naval Technology in Action, 1939–1945* (Annapolis, Md.: Naval Institute Press, 1997).

Chapter 6. Battleships and Battle Cruisers

1. For a good summary of precedents during the Age of Sail and early Age of Steam eras, see Anthony Preston, *Battleships* (London: Bison Books, 1981), pp. 6–39.

2. For a good summary of this era, see John Roberts, "The Pre-Dreadnought Age, 1890–1905," in *Steam, Steel, and Shellfire,* ed. Lambert, pp. 112–26.

3. Richard Hough, *Dreadnought: A History of the Modern Battleship* (New York: Macmillan, 1964), pp. 15–16.

4. Parkes, *British Battleships,* pp. 466–83.

5. Jon T. Sumida, *In Defense of Naval Supremacy: Finance, Technology, and British Naval Policy, 1889–1914* (Boston: Unwin Hyman, 1989).

6. For more information on U.S. battleships of this period, see Norman Friedman, *U.S. Battleships: An Illustrated Design History* (Annapolis, Md.: Naval Institute Press, 1985), pp. 51–170, passim.

7. Pemsel, *History of War at Sea,* p. 107.

8. There are dozens of books on Jutland. For a good summary, see Paul G. Halpern, *A Naval History of World War I* (Annapolis, Md.: Naval Institute Press, 1994), pp. 310–28.

9. Thomas H. Buckley, *The United States and the Washington Conference, 1921–22* (Knoxville: University of Tennessee Press, 1970).

10. Robert O. Dulin Jr. and William H. Garzke Jr., *Battleships: Axis and Neutral Battleships in World War II* (Annapolis, Md.: Naval Institute Press, 1990).

11. William H. Garzke Jr. and Robert O. Dulin Jr., *Battleships: United States Battleships, 1935–1992,* rev. and updated ed. (Annapolis, Md.: Naval Institute Press, 1995).

Chapter 7. Cruisers

1. M. J. Whitley, *German Cruisers of World War II* (London: Arms and Armour Press, 1985), p. 7.

2. Anthony Preston, *Cruisers: An Illustrated History, 1880–1980* (Englewood Cliffs, N.J.: Prentice-Hall, 1980), p. 6.

3. *Conway's All the World's Fighting Ships, 1860–1905* (London: Conway Maritime Press, 1979), p. ii.

4. Whitley, *German Cruisers,* p. 7.

5. David Lyon, *The Ship: Steam, Steel, and Torpedoes, the Warship in the 19th Century* (London: Her Majesty's Stationery Office, 1980), p. 36.

6. For a good summary of this period, see John Roberts, "Cruising ships," in *Steam, Steel, and Shellfire,* ed. Lambert, pp. 105–10.

7. Hovgaard, *Modern History of Warships,* p. 174; Preston, *Cruisers,* p. 7.

8. Hovgaard, *Modern History of Warships,* pp. 170, 203.

9. *Conway's All the World's Fighting Ships, 1860–1905,* p. 62.

10. Richard Hough, *Fighting Ships* (New York: G. P. Putnam's Sons, 1969), p. 251.

11. Noted in Norman Friedman, Introduction to *German Warships of World War I: The Royal Navy's Official Guide* (Annapolis, Md.: Naval Institute Press, 1992).

12. Preston, *Cruisers,* pp. 7–8.

13. *Conway's All the World's Fighting Ships, 1906–1921* (London: Conway Maritime Press, 1985), p. 1.

14. Hector C. Bywater, *Cruisers in Battle: "Light Cavalry" Under Fire, 1914–1918* (London: Constable, 1939).

15. Preston, *Cruisers,* p. 13.

16. Compiled from *Jane's Fighting Ships of World War I* (1919; rpt., New York: Military Press, 1990).

17. For a good description of these and all American cruisers, see Norman Fried-

man, *U.S. Cruisers: An Illustrated Design History* (Annapolis, Md.: Naval Institute Press, 1984).

18. Quoted in Arnold Toynbee, *Survey of International Affairs, 1927* (London: Humphrey Milford, 1929), p. 59.

19. David Carlton, "Great Britain and the Coolidge Naval Disarmament Conference of 1927," *Political Science Quarterly* 4 (December 1968): 573.

20. Preston, *Cruisers,* p. 41.

21. Comdr. Marc Antonio Bragadin, *The Italian Navy in World War II* (Annapolis, Md.: Naval Institute Press, 1957), p. 359.

22. Ibid., p. 361.

23. Pemsel, *History of War at Sea,* p. 139.

Chapter 8. Destroyers and Frigates

1. Casson, *Ships and Seamanship in the Ancient World,* p. 127

2. Anthony Preston, *Destroyers* (Englewood Cliffs, N.J.: Prentice-Hall, 1977), p. 9.

3. For a good summary of this early period, see David Lyon, "Underwater Warfare and the Torpedo Boat," in *Steam, Steel, and Shellfire,* ed. Lambert, pp. 134–45.

4. Preston, *Destroyers,* p. 10.

5. Peter Smith, *Hard Lying: The Birth of the Destroyer, 1893–1913* (Annapolis, Md.: Naval Institute Press, 1971).

6. For a good discussion of all American destroyers, see Norman Friedman, *U.S. Destroyers: An Illustrated Design History* (Annapolis, Md.: Naval Institute Press, 1982).

7. *Conway's All the World's Fighting Ships, 1860–1905,* p. 99.

8. For a description of British destroyers, see Capt. T. D. Manning, *The British Destroyer* (London: Putnam, 1961).

9. Peter K. Kemp, *H.M. Destroyers* (London: Herbert Jenkins, 1956), pp. 91–105.

10. Preston, *Cruisers,* pp. 21–23.

11. Halpern, *Naval History of World War I,* pp. 139–78.

12. For a description of interwar and World War II–era destroyers, see M. J. Whitley, *Destroyers of World War II: An International Encyclopedia* (Annapolis, Md.: Naval Institute Press, 1988).

13. For a good description of German destroyers and their use in World War II, see M. J. Whitley, *Destroyer! German Destroyers in World War II* (Annapolis, Md.: Naval Institute Press, 1983).

14. Preston, *Cruisers,* p. 110.

15. Ibid., pp, 162–63.

16. For more detail on U.S. destroyer operations, see Theodore Roscoe, *United States Destroyer Operations in World War II* (Annapolis, Md.: Naval Institute Press, 1953).

17. Samuel Eliot Morison, *The Two-Ocean War: A Short History of the United States Navy in the Second World War* (Boston: Little, Brown, 1963), pp. 584–85.

18. Eric Grove, "Major Surface Combatants," in *Navies in the Nuclear Age: Warships Since 1945,* ed. Norman Friedman (Annapolis, Md.: Naval Institute Press, 1993), p. 51.

Chapter 9. Submarines

1. For a history of this early period, see Alex Roland, *Underwater Warfare in the Age of Sail* (Bloomington: Indiana University Press, 1978).

2. Erminio Bagnasco, *Submarines of World War II* (1973; rpt. Annapolis, Md.: Naval Institute Press, 1991), p. 13. According to *Conway's All the World's Fighting Ships, 1906–1921,* p. 206, the *Narval,* also launched in 1899, was the first with a periscope.

3. For a good summary of this premodern era, see Michael Wilson, "Early Submarines," in *Steam, Steel, and Shellfire,* ed. Lambert, pp. 147–57.

4. For a good summary of World War I operations and data, see Bagnasco, *Submarines of World War II,* pp. 18–24.

5. For a more detailed history of submarine operations in World War I, see Richard Compton-Hall, *Submarines and the War at Sea, 1914–1918* (London: Macmillan, 1991).

6. There is some controversy over the exact meaning of ASDIC. Most agree that "ASD" stands for "Anti-Submarine Detection," but there is some question about the meaning of "IC"—possibly "Investigation Committee."

7. For a good summary of this period, see Michael Wilson, "The Submarine," in *The Eclipse of the Big Gun: The Warship, 1906–1945,* ed. David K. Brown (Annapolis, Md.: Naval Institute Press, 1992).

8. For more detail on these boats see, John D. Alden, *The Fleet Submarine in the U.S. Navy* (Annapolis, Md.: Naval Institute Press, 1979).

9. Bagnasco, *Submarines of World War II,* p. 24.

10. For German U-boat use, see V. E. Tarrant, *The U-Boat Offensive, 1914–1945* (Annapolis, Md.: Naval Institute Press, 1989). For Royal Navy use, see Alastair Mars, *British Submarines at War, 1939–1945* (Annapolis, Md.: Naval Institute Press, 1971).

11. See Carl Boyd and Akihiko Yoshida, *The Japanese Submarine Force and World War II* (Annapolis, Md.: Naval Institute Press, 1995).

12. Mars, *British Submarines at War,* p. 96.

13. In 1955 the Soviet Union tested a Scud A missile fired from a "Zulu" submarine in what is sometimes considered the world's first ballistic missile launch, but this system did not become operational until 1962.

14. For a good summary of submarine construction in the post–World War II era, see Norman Friedman, "Submarines," in *Navies in the Nuclear Age,* ed. Friedman.

15. For a good history of all Russian and Soviet submarines, see Norman Polmar and Jurrien Noot, *Submarines of the Russian and Soviet Navies, 1718–1990* (Annapolis, Md.: Naval Institute Press, 1991).

Chapter 10. Aircraft Carriers

1. Layman, *Before the Aircraft Carrier,* p. 15.

2. Ibid., p. 13.

3. Ibid., p. 14, 115.

4. For a good history of this early period, see Anthony Preston, *Aircraft Carriers* (New York: Grosset & Dunlap, pp. 6–11; also Richard Humble, *Aircraft Carriers: The Illustrated History* (Seacaucus, N.J.: Chartwell Books, 1982), pp. 6–11.

5. Quoted in Layman, *Before the Aircraft Carrier,* p. 9.

6. R. D. Layman, *Naval Aviation in the First World War: Its Impact and Influence* (Annapolis, Md.: Naval Institute Press, 1996), pp. 25, 36.

7. For a good history of carrier operation during the Great War, see Layman, *Naval Aviation in the First World War.*

8. For a good history of British carriers, see Norman Friedman, *British Carrier Aviation: The Evolution of the Ships and Their Aircraft* (Annapolis, Md.: Naval Institute Press, 1988).

9. Most give the *Hosho* the honor of being the first, but one author claims there is "strong evidence" she was originally laid down as an oiler. See Roger Chesneau, *Aircraft Carriers of the World, 1914 to the Present: An Illustrated Encyclopedia* (Annapolis, Md.: Naval Institute Press, 1984), p. 157.

10. Preston, *Aircraft Carriers,* p. 43.

11. For a good description of all these carriers, see Chesneau, *Aircraft Carriers.*

12. Gordon W. Prange, *Miracle at Midway* (New York: McGraw-Hill, 1982).

13. There are many books on the air war in World War II, but generally considered one of the best is Clark G. Reynolds, *The Fast Carriers: The Forging of an Air Navy* (Annapolis, Md.: Naval Institute Press, 1992).

14. For a good discussion of this whole period, see Jeffrey G. Barlow, *Revolt of the Admirals: The Fight for Naval Aviation, 1945–1950* (Washington, D.C.: Naval Historical Center, 1994).

15. For a good summary of this era, see David Steigman, "Aircraft Carriers," in *Navies in the Nuclear Age,* ed. Friedman.

Chapter 11. Amphibious Ships

1. For the history of early amphibious warfare, see Merrill L. Bartlett, ed., *Assault from the Sea: Essays on the History of Amphibious Warfare* (Annapolis, Md.: Naval Institute Press, 1983), pp. 3–141.

2. Brown, *Paddle Warships,* p 79.

3. Halpern, *Naval History of World War I,* p. 101.

4. Ibid., p. 36.

5. Brian Fried and Robert Gardiner, "Amphibious Warfare Vessels," in *Eclipse of the Big Gun,* ed. Brown, pp. 140–42.

6. For a history of this period, see Kenneth J. Clifford, *Amphibious Warfare Development in Britain and America from 1920–1940* (Laurens, N.Y.: Edgewood, 1983).

7. For a history of Ellis's life, see Dirk A. Ballendorf and Merrill L. Bartlett, *Pete Ellis: An Amphibious Warfare Prophet, 1880–1923* (Annapolis, Md.: Naval Institute Press, 1996).

8. Norman Polmar and Peter Mersky, *Amphibious Warfare: An Illustrated History* (London: Blandford Press, 1988), pp. 59–61.

9. Ibid., p. 7.

10. Quoted in ibid., p. 133.

11. Martin Binkin and Jeffrey Record, *Where Does the Marine Corps Go from Here?* (Washington, D.C.: Brookings Institute, 1976).

12. For a history of post–World War II operations, see Joseph H. Alexander and Merrill L. Bartlett, *Sea Soldiers in the Cold War: Amphibious Warfare, 1945–1991* (Annapolis, Md.: Naval Institute Press, 1995).

Chapter 12. Service Ships

1. Casson, *Ships and Seafaring in Ancient Times*, p. 71.

2. Brian Lavery, "Support Craft," in *Line of Battle*, ed. Lavery, pp. 106-7.

3. Ibid., pp. 106-15.

4. James L. George, "Naval Auxiliary and Support Ships," in *International Military and Defense Encyclopedia*, vol. 4 (Washington, D.C.: Brassey's, 1993), p. 1923.

5. Richard Hough, *The Fleet That Had to Die* (New York: Pantheon, 1958).

6. Unfortunately, there is no good history of this early period. For a brief summary, see Norman Friedman, "The Fleet Train," in *Eclipse of the Big Gun*, ed. Brown, pp. 165-67.

7. Halpern, *Naval History of World War I*, p. 72.

8. Ibid., p. 67.

9. Ibid., pp. 81-82.

10. Thomas Wildenberg, *Gray Steel and Black Oil: Fast Tankers and Replenishment at Sea in the U.S. Navy, 1912-1992* (Annapolis, Md.: Naval Institute Press, 1996), pp. 8-13.

11. *Conway's All the World's Fighting Ships, 1906-1921* (London: Conway Maritime Press, 1985), p. 104.

12. Edward S. Miller, *War Plan Orange: The U.S. Strategy to Defeat Japan, 1897-1945* (Annapolis, Md.: Naval Institute Press, 1991).

13. Ibid., pp. 128, 283.

14. For a good history of this period, see Wildenberg, *Gray Steel and Black Oil*, pp. 27-45.

15. Ibid., pp. 56-145.

16. For an overview of this period, see Friedman, "Fleet Train," pp. 165-71.

17. Wildenberg, *Gray Steel and Black Oil*, p. 188.

18. Friedman, "Fleet Train," pp. 168-69.

19. Wildenberg, *Gray Steel and Black Oil*, pp. 190-210.

20. For a good overview of service ships in the post–World War II era, see David Steigman, "Naval Auxiliaries," in *Navies in the Nuclear Age*, ed. Friedman, pp. 121-32.

21. See, for example, Worral R. Carter, *Beans, Bullets, and Black Oil* (Washington, D.C.: Department of the Navy, 1953), on the Pacific, and Worral R. Carter and Elmer E. Dual, *Ships, Salvage, and Sinews of War* (Washington, D.C.: Department of the Navy, 1954), on the Atlantic and Mediterranean.

22. Wildenberg, *Gray Steel and Black Oil*.

23. Steigman, "Naval Auxiliaries," p. 121.

Chapter 13. Mine Ships

1. Halpern, *Naval History of World War I*, p. 34.

2. Capt. J. S. Cowie, RN, *Mines, Minelayers, and Minelaying* (London: Oxford University Press, 1949), pp. 7-23.

3. For a good history of Civil War mine warfare, see Tamara Moser Melia, *"Damn the Torpedoes": A Short History of U.S. Naval Mine Countermeasures, 1777-1991* (Washington, D.C.: Naval Historical Center, 1991), pp. 9-16.

4. Ibid., pp. 1-4.

5. Gregory K. Hartmann, with Scott C. Truver, *Weapons That Wait: Mine Warfare in the U.S. Navy* (Annapolis, Md.: Naval Institute Press, 1991), pp. 32-33.

6. H. G. Rickover, *How the Battleship* Maine *Was Destroyed* (Annapolis, Md.: Naval Institute Press, 1995).

7. For good histories of this early period, see Hartmann, *Weapons That Wait,* pp. 17–42; Melia, *"Damn the Torpedoes,"* pp. 7–28; and Cowie, *Mines, Minelayers, and Minelaying,* pp. 7–43.

8. K. D. McBride, "Mine Warfare and Escort Vessels," in *Eclipse of the Big Gun,* ed. Brown, p. 110.

9. M. P. Cocker, *Mine Warfare Vessels of the Royal Navy, 1908 to Date* (Shrewsbury, Eng.: Airlife Publishing, 1993), pp. 26–35.

10. Ibid.

11. Halpern, *Naval History of World War I,* pp. 109–23.

12. Hartmann, *Weapons That Wait,* p. 15.

13. For a good history of mine operations in World War I, see Cowie, *Mines, Minelayers, and Minelaying,* pp. 43–87.

14. Melia, *"Damn the Torpedoes,"* p. 40.

15. For a good summary of the interwar period, see Cowie, *Mines, Minelayers, and Minelaying,* pp. 88–118. For U.S. developments, see Melia, *"Damn the Torpedoes,"* pp. 41–50.

16. For a discussion of all these different mine types, see Hartman, *Weapons That Wait,* pp. 66–70.

17. David Brown, *Warships Losses of World War II* (Annapolis, Md.: Naval Institute Press, 1990), pp. 228–29.

18. Melia, *"Damn the Torpedoes,"* pp. 63–64.

19. For more detail on World War II operations, see Cowie, *Mines, Minelayers, and Minelaying,* pp. 119–67.

20. Malcolm W. Cagle and Frank A. Manson, *The Sea War in Korea* (Annapolis, Md.: Naval Institute Press, 1957), pp. 527–28.

21. For a good overview of post–World War II mine craft, see David K. Brown, "Mine Countermeasures Vessels," in *Navies in the Nuclear Age,* ed. Friedman, pp. 89–97.

Chapter 14. Small Combatants

1. Gunboats are virtually ignored in the literature on small combatants. For a brief description, see *Conway's All the World's Ships, 1860–1905,* pp. 107–13.

2. For a good history of this early period, see David Lyon, "Underwater Warfare and the Torpedo Boat," in *Steam, Steel, and Shellfire,* ed. Lambert, pp. 134–46.

3. Harald Fock, *Fast Fighting Boats, 1870–1945: Their Design, Construction, and Use* (Annapolis, Md.: Naval Institute Press, 1978), pp. 14–16.

4. Ibid., p. 50.

5. For a good description of the U.S. Navy's World War I–era small combatants, see Norman Friedman, *U.S. Small Combatants: An Illustrated Design History Including PT-Boats, Subchasers, and the Brown-Water Navy* (Annapolis, Md.: Naval Institute Press, 1987), pp. 19–46.

6. The term *MAS* went through several iterations. It originally meant *Motobarca armata SVAN,* from the name of the yard at which they were built. Later, MAS meant *Motobarca anti-sommergibile* (antisubmarine motor launch), *Motobarca armata silurante* (torpedo-armed motor launch), and finally *Motoscafo anti-sommergibile* (antisubmarine motorboat, or subchaser).

7. For the best description of fast boats in World War I, see Fock, *Fast Fighting Boats,* pp. 23–62.

8. For an overview of small combatant operations during World War I, see Anthony Preston, *Strike Craft* (New York: Bison Books, 1982), pp. 9–13.

9. Halpern, *Naval History of World War I,* p. 26.

10. For a good overview of all small craft during this period, see Al Ross, "Coastal Forces," in *Eclipse of the Big Gun,* ed. Brown, pp. 124–25, 128–29.

11. Fock, *Fast Fighting Boats,* pp. 107–24.

12. Ibid., pp. 75–78.

13. For a good overview of this period, see Ross, "Coastal Forces," pp. 129–34.

14. Peter Elliot, *Allied Escort Ships of World War II: A Complete Survey* (Annapolis, Md.: Naval Institute Press, 1977), foreword and pp. 130–322 passim.

15. Ibid., foreword and pp. 419–94.

16. For a good history of the remarkable Fairmile, see John Lambert and Al Ross, *Allied Coastal Forces of World War II,* vol. 1, *Fairmile and U.S. Submarine Chasers* (Annapolis, Md.: Naval Institute Press, 1990).

17. For a history of escort operations, see Peter Kemp, *Decision at Sea: The Convoy Escorts* (New York: Elsevier-Dutton, 1978).

18. For a good summary of motor torpedo boat actions in World War II, see Preston, *Strike Craft,* pp. 16–41.

19. Eric Grove, "Coastal Combatants and Austere Frigates," in *Navies in the Nuclear Age,* ed. Friedman, p. 53.

20. Victor Croziat, *The Brown Water Navy: The River and Coastal War in Indo-China and Vietnam, 1948–1972* (Poole, U.K.: Blandford Press, 1984).

Chapter 15. Futuristic Warships

1. For a good summary of post–World War II propulsion systems, see Norman Friedman, "Propulsion," in *Navies in the Nuclear Age,* ed. Friedman, pp. 199–210.

2. For a good discussion of all these, see Reuven Leopold, "Surface Warships for the Early Twenty-First Century," in *Problems of Sea Power as We Approach the Twenty-First Century,* ed. James L. George (Washington, D.C.: American Enterprise Institute, 1978), pp. 272–77.

Chapter 16. Summaries, Ironies, Myths, and Legends

1. John Francis Guilmartin, *Gunpowder and Galleys: Changing Technology and Mediterranean Warfare at Sea in the Sixteenth Century* (London: Cambridge University Press, 1974).

2. Colin S. Gray, *The Leverage of Sea Power: The Strategic Advantage of Navies in War* (New York: Free Press, 1992).

Chapter 17: The Future of Sea Power and Warships

1. Barry M. Blechman and Stephan S. Kaplan, *Force Without War: U.S. Armed Forces as a Political Instrument* (Washington, D.C.: Brookings Institution, 1978), pp. 38, 39.

Bibliography

Naval History

Potter, E. B., and Chester W. Nimitz, eds. *Sea Power: A Naval History.* Englewood Cliffs, N.J.: Prentice-Hall, 1960.

Reynolds, Clark G. *Command of the Sea: The History and Strategy of Maritime Empires.* New York: William Morrow, 1974.

———. *Navies in History.* Annapolis, Md.: Naval Institute Press, 1998.

Silburn, P. A. *The Evolution of Sea Power.* London: Longmans, Green, 1912.

Stevens, William Oliver, and Allan Westcott. *A History of Sea Power.* New York: Doubleday, 1948.

History of Warships

Angelucci, Enzo, and Attilio Curari. *Ships.* New York: McGraw-Hill, 1975.

Cowburn, Philip. *The Warship in History.* New York: Macmillan, 1965.

Hough, Richard. *Fighting Ships.* New York: G. P. Putnam's Sons, 1969.

———. *A History of Fighting Ships.* London: Octopus Books, 1975. (This is an abridged version of *Fighting Ships.*)

Hovgaard, William. *Modern History of Warships.* 1920. Reprint. Annapolis, Md.: Naval Institute Press, 1971.

Ireland, Bernard. *Warships: From Sail to the Nuclear Age.* London: Hamlyn, 1978.

Landstrom, Bjorn. *The Ship: An Illustrated History.* New York: Doubleday, 1961.

Macintyre, Donald, and Basil W. Bathe. *Man-of-War: A History of the Combat Vessel.* New York: McGraw-Hill, 1969.

Perlmutter, Tom, ed. *War Machines, Sea: From Phoenician Galleys to Polaris Submarines.* London: Octopus Books, 1975.

Polmar, Norman, and Norman Friedman. *Warships: From Early Steam to Nuclear Power.* London: Octopus Books, 1981.

Whitehouse, Arch. *Fighting Ships.* Garden City, N.Y.: Doubleday, 1967.

Willmott, H. P. *Warships: Sea Power Since the Ironclad.* London: Octopus Books, 1975.

Ships and Seapower

Gates, P. J. *Surface Warships: An Introduction to Design Principles.* London: Brassey's Defense Publishers, 1987.

Till, Geoffrey. *Modern Sea Power: An Introduction.* London: Brassey's Defense Publishers, 1987.

War at Sea

Brodie, Bernard. *Sea Power in the Machine Age.* Princeton: Princeton University Press, 1941.

Bruce, George. *Sea Battles of the Twentieth Century.* London: Hamlyn Publishing Group, 1975.

Keegan, John. *The Price of Admiralty: The Evolution of Naval Warfare.* New York: Viking, 1988.

McKee, Alexander. *Against the Odds: Battles at Sea, 1591–1949.* Annapolis, Md.: Naval Institute Press, 1991.

Pemsel, Helmut. *A History of War at Sea.* Annapolis, Md.: Naval Institute Press, 1976.

Richmond, H. W. *Naval Warfare.* London: Ernest Benn, 1930.

Warner, Oliver, et al. *The Encyclopedia of Sea Warfare.* New York: Thomas Y. Crowell, 1975.

The Eras

The Age of Galleys

Anderson, R. C. *Oared Fighting Ships: From Classical Times to the Coming of Steam.* 1962. New ed. London: Argus Books, 1976.

Casson, Lionel. *The Ancient Mariners: Seafarers and Sea Fighters of the Mediterranean in Ancient Times.* 2d ed. Princeton: Princeton University Press, 1991.

———. *Ships and Seafaring in Ancient Times.* Austin: University of Texas Press, 1994.

———. *Ships and Seamanship in the Ancient World.* 1971. Reprint. Baltimore: Johns Hopkins University Press, 1995.

Christensen, Arne Emil, ed. *The Earliest Ships: The Evolution of Boats into Ships.* Annapolis, Md.: Naval Institute Press, 1996.

Greenhill, Basil. *The Evolution of the Wooden Ship.* New York: Facts on File, 1988.

Guilmartin, John Francis. *Gunpowder and Galleys: Changing Technology and Mediterranean Warfare at Sea in the Sixteenth Century.* London: Cambridge University Press, 1974.

Haywood, John. *Dark Ages Naval Power: A Reassessment of Frankish and Anglo-Saxon Seafaring Activity.* New York: Routledge, 1991.

Herm, Gerhard. *The Phoenicians: The Purple Empire of the Ancient World.* New York: William Morrow, 1975.

Hourani, George, F. *Arab Seafaring in the Indian Ocean in Ancient and Early Medieval Times.* 1951. Revised and Expanded by John Carswell. Princeton: Princeton University Press, 1995.

Lane, Frederic Chapin. *Venetian Ships and Shipbuilders of the Renaissance.* Baltimore: Johns Hopkins University Press, 1934.

Lewis, Archibald R., and Timothy J. Runyan. *European Naval and Maritime History, 300–1500.* Bloomington: Indiana University Press, 1990.

McGrail, Sean. *Rafts, Boats, and Ships: From Prehistoric Times to the Medieval Era.* London: Her Majesty's Stationery Office, 1981.

Meijer, Fik. *A History of Seafaring in the Classical World.* New York: St. Martin's Press, 1986.

Morrison, John S. *Long Ships and Round Ships: Warfare and Trade in the Mediter-*
ranean, 3000 B.C.–500 A.D. London: Her Majesty's Stationery Office, 1980.

——, ed. *The Age of the Galley: Mediterranean Oared Vessels Since Pre-Classical*
Times. Annapolis, Md.: Naval Institute Press, 1995.

Morrison, John S., and J. F. Coates. *The Athenian Trireme: The History and Recon-*
struction of an Ancient Greek Warship. Cambridge: Cambridge University Press,
1986.

Morrison, John S., and R. T. Williams. *Greek Oared Ships, 900–322 B.C.* Cambridge: Cambridge University Press, 1966.

——. *Greek and Roman Oared Warships, 399–31 B.C.* Oxford: Oxford University
Press, 1994.

Rogers, Vice Adm. William L., USN (Ret.). *Greek and Roman Naval Warfare.*
Annapolis, Md.: Naval Institute Press, 1964.

——. *Naval Warfare Under Oars: 4th to 16th Century.* Annapolis, Md.: Naval
Institute Press, 1967.

Sanders, N. K. *The Sea Peoples: Warriors of the Ancient Mediterranean.* London:
Thames and Hudson, 1978.

Starr, Chester G. *The Influence of Sea Power on Ancient History.* New York: Oxford
University Press, 1989.

——. *The Roman Imperial Navy, 31 B.C–A.D. 324.* New York: Barnes and Noble,
1960.

Thubron, Colin. *The Venetians.* Alexandria, Va.: Time-Life Books, 1980.

Wernick, Robert. *The Vikings.* Alexandria, Va.: Time-Life Books, 1979.

THE AGE OF SAIL

Anderson, Romola, and R. C. Anderson. *The Sailing Ship: Six Thousand Years of*
History. New York: Norton, 1963.

Archibald, E. *The Wooden Fighting Ship of the Royal Navy.* London: Blandford,
1968.

Chapelle, Howard I. *The History of the American Sailing Navy.* New York: W. W.
Norton, 1949.

Gardiner, Robert. *The Heavy Frigate: Eighteen Pounder Frigates,* Vol. 1, *1778–*
1800. Annapolis, Md.: Naval Institute Press, 1995.

Greenhill, Basil, ed. *The Evolution of the Sailing Ship, 1250–1580.* London: Conway
Maritime Press, 1995.

Gruppe, Henry E. *The Frigates.* Alexandria, Va.: Time-Life Books, 1979.

Howarth, David. *The Men-of-War.* Alexandria, Va.: Time-Life Books, 1978.

Kirsch, Peter. *The Galleon: The Great Ships of the Armada Era.* Annapolis, Md.:
Naval Institute Press, 1990.

Lambert, Andrew. *The Last Sailing Battlefleet: Maintaining Naval Mastery, 1815–*
1850. London: Conway Maritime Press, 1991.

Lavery, Brian. *The Arming and Fitting of English Ships of War, 1600–1815.* Annapolis, Md.: Naval Institute Press, 1987.

——, ed. *The Line of Battle: The Sailing Warship, 1650–1840.* Annapolis, Md.:
Naval Institute Press, 1992.

——. *Nelson's Navy: The Ships, Men, and Organization, 1793–1815.* Annapolis,
Md.: Naval Institute Press, 1989.

——. *The Ship of the Line.* Vol. 1, *The Development of the Battlefleet, 1650–*
1850. Annapolis, Md.: Naval Institute Press, 1983.

McGowan, Alan. *Tiller and Whipstaff: The Development of the Sailing Ship, 1400–1700.* London: Her Majesty's Stationery Office, 1981.

Rodger, N. A. M. *The Wooden World: An Anatomy of the Georgian Navy.* New York: Norton, 1996.

Unger, Richard W. *The Ship in the Medieval Economy, 600–1600.* London: Croom Helm, 1980.

———, ed. *Cogs, Caravels, and Galleons: The Sailing Ship, 1000–1650.* Annapolis, Md.: Naval Institute Press, 1994.

Walker, Bryce. *The Armada.* Alexandria, Va.: Time-Life Books, 1981.

Ware, Chris. *The Bomb Vessel: Shore Bombardment Ships of the Age of Sail.* Annapolis, Md.: Naval Institute Press, 1995.

Whipple, A. B. C. *Fighting Sail.* Alexandria, Va.: Time-Life Books, 1978.

The Age of Steam and Ironclads

Alden, John D. *The American Steel Navy.* Annapolis, Md.: Naval Institute Press, 1972.

Baxter, J. P. *The Introduction of the Ironclad Warship.* 1933. Reprint. Hamden, Conn.: Archon Books, 1968.

Brown, D. K. *Before the Ironclad: Development of Ship Design, Propulsion, and Armament in the Royal Navy, 1815–60.* Annapolis, Md.: Naval Institute Press, 1990.

———. *Paddle Warships: The Earliest Steam Powered Fighting Ships, 1815–1850.* London: Conway Maritime Press, 1993.

Canney, Donald L. *The Old Steam Navy: Ironclads, 1842–1885.* Annapolis, Md.: Naval Institute Press, 1993.

Conway's All the World's Fighting Ships, 1860–1905. London: Conway Maritime Press, 1979.

King, J. W. *The Warships and Navies of the World, 1880.* 1880. Reprint. Annapolis, Md.: Naval Institute Press, 1982.

Lambert, Andrew. *Battleships in Transition: The Creation of the Steam Battlefleet, 1815–1860.* Annapolis, Md.: Naval Institute Press, 1984.

———. *Warrior: The World's First Ironclad, Then and Now.* Annapolis, Md.: Naval Institute Press, 1987.

———, ed. *Steam, Steel, and Shellfire: The Steam Warship, 1815–1905.* Annapolis, Md.: Naval Institute Press, 1992.

Lyon, David. *Steam, Steel, and Torpedoes: The Warship in the 19th Century.* London: Her Majesty's Stationery Office, 1980.

Ortzen, Len. *Fighting Ships in the Age of Steam.* London: A. Barker, 1978.

Silverstone, Paul H. *Warships of the Civil War Navies.* Annapolis, Md.: Naval Institute Press, 1989.

Sumida, Jon T. *In Defense of Naval Supremacy: Finance, Technology, and British Naval Policy, 1889–1914.* Boston: Unwin Hyman, 1989.

The Modern Era — General

Brown, David K., ed. *The Eclipse of the Big Gun: The Warship, 1906–1945.* Annapolis, Md.: Naval Institute Press, 1992.

Friedman, Norman. *Modern Warships: Design and Development.* New York: Mayflower Books, 1979.

———, ed. *Navies in the Nuclear Age: Warships Since 1945*. Annapolis, Md.: Naval Institute Press, 1993.

Lyon, Hugh. *The Encyclopedia of the World's Warships: A Technical Directory of Major Fighting Ships from 1900 to the Present Day*. London: Salamander Books, 1978.

WORLD WAR I

Bennett, Geoffrey. *Naval Battles of the First World War*. London: Batsford, 1968.

Coletta, Paolo E. *Sea Power in the Atlantic and Mediterranean in World War I*. Lanham, Md.: University Press of America, 1989.

Conway's All the World's Fighting Ships, 1906–1921. London: Conway Maritime Press, 1985.

Fitzsimons, Bernard, ed. *Warships and Sea Battles of World War I*. New York: Beekman House, 1973.

Halpern, Paul G. *A Naval History of World War I*. Annapolis, Md.: Naval Institute Press, 1994.

———. *The Naval War in the Mediterranean, 1914–1918*. Annapolis, Md.: Naval Institute Press, 1987.

Hoehling, A. A. *The Great War at Sea: A History of Naval Action, 1914–18*. New York: Thomas Y. Crowell, 1965.

Hough, Richard. *The Great War at Sea, 1914–1918*. London: Oxford University Press, 1983.

Jane's Fighting Ships of World War I. 1919. Reprint. New York: Military Press, 1990.

The Interwar Period

Buckley, Thomas H. *The United States and the Washington Conference, 1921–22*. Knoxville: University of Tennessee Press, 1970.

Conway's All the World's Fighting Ships, 1922–46. London: Conway Maritime Press, 1980.

Gordon, G. A. H. *British Seapower and Procurement between the Wars: A Reappraisal of Rearmament*. Annapolis, Md.: Naval Institute Press, 1988.

Hall, Christopher. *Britain, America, and Arms Control, 1921–37*. New York: St. Martin's Press, 1987.

Kaufman, Robert. G. *Arms Control During the Pre-Nuclear Era: The United States and Naval Limitation Between the Two Wars*. New York: Columbia University Press, 1990.

O'Connor, Raymond G. *Perilous Equilibrium: The United States Navy and the London Naval Conference of 1930*. Lawrence: University of Kansas Press, 1962.

Pelz, Stephan W. *Race to Pearl Harbor: The Failure of the Second London Naval Conference and the Onset of World War II*. Cambridge, Mass.: Harvard University Press, 1974.

Roskill, Stephen. W. *Naval Policy Between the Wars*. Vol. 1, *The Period of Anglo-American Antagonism, 1919–1930*. New York: Walker, 1968.

———. *Naval Policy Between the Wars*. Vol. 2, *The Period of Reluctant Rearmament, 1930–1939*. Annapolis, Md.: Naval Institute Press, 1976.

WORLD WAR II

Bennett, Geoffrey. *Naval Battles of World War II*. London: Batsford, 1975.

Brown, David. *Warship Losses of World War II*. Rev. ed. Annapolis, Md.: Naval Institute Press, 1995.

Conway's All the World's Fighting Ships, 1922–1946. London: Conway Maritime Press, 1980.

Dunnigan, James F., and Albert A. Nofi. *Victory at Sea: World War II in the Pacific*. New York: William Morrow, 1995.

Jane's Fighting Ships of World War II. London: Studio Editions, 1989.

Miller, Nathan. *The Naval Air War, 1939–1945*. Annapolis, Md.: Naval Institute Press, 1991.

———. *War at Sea: A Naval History of World War II*. New York: Scribner, 1995.

Morison, Samuel Eliot. *The Two-Ocean War: A Short History of the United States Navy in the Second World War*. Boston: Little, Brown, 1963.

Rohwer, Jurgen, and Gerhard Hummelshen. *Chronology of the War at Sea, 1939–1945: The Naval History of World War Two*. New ed., expanded and revised. Annapolis, Md.: Naval Institute Press, 1992.

Roskill, S. W. *White Ensign: The British Navy at War, 1939–1945*. Annapolis, Md.: Naval Institute Press, 1960.

Van der Vat, Dan. *The Atlantic Campaign: World War II's Great Struggle at Sea*. New York: Harper & Row, 1988.

———. *The Pacific Campaign: World War II, the U.S.-Japanese Naval War*. New York: Simon & Schuster, 1991.

Winston, John. *Air Power at Sea, 1939–45*. New York: Thomas Y. Crowell, 1977.

POST–WORLD WAR II

Blechman, Barry M., and Stephan S. Kaplan. *Force Without War: U.S. Armed Forces as a Political Instrument*. Washington, D.C.: Brookings Institution, 1978.

Brown, David. *The Royal Navy and the Falklands War*. Annapolis, Md.: Naval Institute Press, 1988.

Cagle, Malcolm W., and Frank A. Manson. *The Sea War in Korea*. Annapolis, Md.: Naval Institute Press, 1957.

Conway's All the World's Fighting Ships, 1947–82. 2 vols. London: Conway Maritime Press, 1983.

Friedman, Norman, ed. *Navies in the Nuclear Age: Warships Since 1945*. Annapolis, Md.: Naval Institute Press, 1993.

George, James L., ed. *Problems of Sea Power as We Approach the Twenty-First Century*. Washington, D.C.: American Enterprise Institute, 1978.

Grove, Eric. *The Future of Sea Power*. Annapolis, Md.: Naval Institute Press, 1990.

Schreadley, R. L. *From the Rivers to the Sea: The United States Navy in Vietnam*. Annapolis, Md.: Naval Institute Press, 1992.

Sokolsky, Joel J. *Seapower in the Nuclear Age: The United States Navy and NATO, 1949–1980*. Annapolis, Md.: Naval Institute Press, 1991.

General Country Works

AUSTRIA-HUNGARY

Greger, Rene. *Austro-Hungarian Warships of World War I*. London: Ian Allan, 1976.
Sokol, Anthony E. *The Imperial and Royal Austro-Hungarian Navy*. Annapolis, Md.: Naval Institute Press, 1968.
Sondhaus, Lawrence. *The Naval Policy of Austria-Hungary, 1867–1918: Navalism, Industrial Development, and the Politics of Dualism*. West Lafayette, Ind.: Purdue University Press, 1994.

FRENCH NAVY

Auphan, R. Adm. Paul, and Jacques Mordal. *The French Navy in World War II*. Annapolis, Md.: Naval Institute Press, 1959.
Jenkins, E. H. *A History of the French Navy*. London: MacDonald and Janes, 1973.
Labayle-Couhat, Jean. *French Warships of World War I*. London: Ian Allan, 1974.
Ropp, Theodore. *The Development of a Modern Navy: French Naval Policy, 1871–1904*. Annapolis, Md.: Naval Institute Press, 1987.

GERMAN NAVY

Bekker, Cajus. *Hitler's Naval War*. New York: Doubleday, 1974.
Groner, Erich. *German Warships, 1815–1945*. Vol. 1, *Major Surface Vessels*. Rev. English ed. Annapolis, Md.: Naval Institute Press, 1990.
Hansen, Hans J. *The Ships of the German Fleets, 1848–1945*. Annapolis, Md.: Naval Institute Press, 1987.
Lenton, H. T. *German Warships of the Second World War*. London: MacDonald and Janes, 1975.
Porten, Edward P. Von der. *The German Navy in World War II*. New York: Thomas Y. Crowell, 1969.
———. *Pictorial History of the German Navy in World War II*. New York: Thomas Y. Crowell, 1976.
Schmalenbach, Paul. *German Raiders: A History of Auxiliary Cruisers of the German Navy, 1895–1945*. Annapolis, Md.: Naval Institute Press, 1979.
Taylor, John C. *German Warships of World War I*. London: Ian Allan, 1969.
Thomas, Charles S. *The German Navy in the Nazi Era*. Annapolis, Md.: Naval Institute Press, 1990.

ITALIAN NAVY

Bragadin, Cmdr. Marc Antonio. *The Italian Navy in World War II*. Annapolis, Md.: Naval Institute Press, 1957.
Fraccaroli, Aldo. *Italian Warships of World War I*. London: Ian Allan, 1970.

JAPANESE NAVY

Dull, Paul S. *A Battle History of the Imperial Japanese Navy, 1941–45*. Annapolis, Md.: Naval Institute Press, 1977.
Jentschura, Hansgeorg, et al. *Warships of the Imperial Japanese Navy, 1869–1945*. Annapolis, Md.: Naval Institute Press, 1975.
Watts, Anthony J. *Japanese Warships of World War II*. Garden City, N.Y.: Doubleday, 1967.

Russian and Soviet Union Navy

Breyer, Siegfried. *Soviet Warship Development.* Vol. 1, *1917–1937.* Annapolis, Md.: Naval Institute Press, 1993.

George, James L., ed. *The Soviet and Other Communist Navies: The View from the Mid-1980s.* Annapolis, Md.: Naval Institute Press, 1986.

Herrick, Robert Waring. *Soviet Naval Strategy: Fifty Years of Theory and Practice.* Annapolis, Md.: Naval Institute Press, 1968.

Mitchell, Donald W. *A History of Russian and Soviet Sea Power.* New York: Macmillan, 1974.

Pavlovich, R. Adm. N. B., ed. *The Fleet in the First World War.* Vol. 1, *Operations of the Russian Fleet.* New Delhi: Amerind Publishing for the Smithsonian Institution, 1979.

Polmar, Norman. *Guide to the Soviet Navy.* 5th ed. Annapolis, Md.: Naval Institute Press, 1991. (Published periodically from 1970.)

Saunders, Cmdr. M. G., ed. *The Soviet Navy.* New York: Frederick A. Praeger, 1958.

United Kingdom (Royal) Navy

Archibald, E. H. H. *The Metal Fighting Ship in the Royal Navy, 1860–1970.* New York: Arco, 1971.

Dittmar, F. J., and J. J. College. *British Warships, 1914–1919.* London: Ian Allan, 1972.

Dolby, James. *The Steel Navy: A History in Silhouette, 1860–1963.* Rev. ed. London: MacDonald, 1965.

Kemp, Peter. *The History of the Royal Navy.* London: Arthur Barker, 1969.

Marcus, G. J. *A Naval History of England: The Formative Years.* Boston: Little, Brown, 1961.

Marder, Arthur J. *The Anatomy of British Sea Power: A History of Naval Policy in the Pre-Dreadnought Era, 1880–1905.* New York: Knopf, 1940.

———. *From the Dardanelles to Oran.* London: Oxford University Press, 1974.

———. *From the Dreadnought to Scapa Flow: The Royal Navy in the Fisher Era, 1904–1919.* 5 vols. London: Oxford University Press, 1961–70.

Roskill, Capt. S. W. *White Ensign: The British Navy at War, 1939–1945.* Annapolis, Md.: Naval Institute Press, 1960.

Sturtivant, Ray. *British Naval Aviation: The Fleet Air Arm, 1917–1990.* Annapolis, Md.: Naval Institute Press, 1990.

United States Navy

Baer, George W. *One Hundred Years of Sea Power: The U.S. Navy, 1890–1990.* Stanford: Stanford University Press, 1994.

Beach, Edward L. *The United States Navy: 200 Years.* New York: Henry Holt, 1986.

Field, J. A. *A History of United States Operations in Korea.* Washington, D.C.: U.S. Government Printing Office, 1962.

George, James L., ed. *The U.S. Navy: The View from the Mid-1980s.* Boulder, Colo.: Westview Press, 1985.

———. *The U.S. Navy in the 1990s: Alternatives for Action.* Annapolis, Md.: Naval Institute Press, 1993.

Hagan, Kenneth J. *This People's Navy: The Making of American Sea Power.* New York: Free Press, 1991.

Howarth, Stephen. *To Shining Sea: A History of the United States Navy, 1775–1991.* New York: Random House, 1991.

Isenberg, Michael T. *Shield of the Republic: The United States Navy in an Era of Cold War and Violent Peace, 1945–1962.* New York: St. Martin's Press, 1993.

Johnson, Robert Erwin. *Guardians of the Sea: A History of the U.S. Coast Guard, 1915 to the Present.* Annapolis, Md.: Naval Institute Press, 1987.

King, R. Adm. R. W., USN (Ret.), ed. *Naval Engineering and American Sea Power.* Baltimore: Nautical and Aviation Publishing Company of America, 1989.

Knox, Dudley. *A History of the United States Navy.* New York: Putnam, 1948.

Miller, Nathan. *The U.S. Navy: A History.* Rev. and updated ed. New York: William Morrow, 1990.

Morison, Samuel Eliot. *The Two-Ocean War: A Short History of the United States Navy in the Second World War.* Boston: Little, Brown, 1963.

Potter, E. B. *Illustrated History of the United States Navy.* New York: Galahad Books, 1971.

Silverstone, Paul H. *U.S. Warships of World War I.* London: Ian Allan, 1970.

———. U.S. Warships of World War II. Annapolis, Md.: Naval Institute Press, 1989.

Sweetman, Jack. *American Naval History: An Illustrated Chronology of the U.S. Navy and Marine Corps, 1775–Present.* 2d ed. Annapolis, Md.: Naval Institute Press, 1991.

Uhlig, Frank, Jr. *How Navies Fight: The U.S. Navy and Its Allies.* Annapolis, Md.: Naval Institute Press, 1994.

OTHER COUNTRIES' NAVIES

German, Cmdr. Tony, RCN (Ret.) *The Sea Is at Our Gates: The History of the Canadian Navy.* Toronto: McClelland and Stewart, 1990.

Scheina, Robert L. *Latin America: A Naval History, 1810–1987.* Annapolis, Md.: Naval Institute Press, 1987.

Modern Ships

GENERAL REFERENCE

Brassey's Naval Annual. Published since 1886 under various similar names.

Conway's All the World's Fighting Ships, 1860–1905. London: Conway Maritime Press, 1979.

Conway's All the World's Fighting Ships, 1906–1921. London: Conway Maritime Press, 1985.

Conway's All the World's Fighting Ships, 1922–1946. London: Conway Maritime Press, 1980.

Conway's All the World's Fighting Ships, 1947–1982. Part 1, *The Western Powers.* London: Conway Maritime Press, 1983.

Conway's All the World's Fighting Ships, 1947–1982. Part 2, *The Warsaw Pact and Non-Aligned Nations.* London: Conway Maritime Press, 1983.

Conway's All the World's Fighting Ships, 1947–1995. London: Conway Maritime Press, 1995.

Jane's Fighting Ships. Published annually since 1898.

Jane's Fighting Ships of World War I. 1919. Reprint. New York: Military Press, 1990.

Jane's Fighting Ships of World War II. 1947. Reprint. London: Studio Edition, 1989.

Warship. Published annually since 1978.

NAVAL JOURNALS

Naval Forces. Bimonthly since 1978.
Naval War College Review. Quarterly.
Warship International. Quarterly since 1964.
U.S. Naval Institute *Proceedings.* Monthly.

AIRCRAFT CARRIERS

Barlow, Jeffrey G. *Revolt of the Admirals: The Fight for Naval Aviation, 1945–1950.* Washington, D.C.: Naval Historical Center, 1994.

Chesneau, Roger. *Aircraft Carriers of the World, 1914 to the Present: An Illustrated Encyclopedia.* Annapolis, Md.: Naval Institute Press, 1984.

Friedman, Norman. *British Carrier Aviation: The Evolution of the Ships and Their Aircraft.* Annapolis, Md.: Naval Institute Press, 1988.

———. *U.S. Aircraft Carriers: An Illustrated Design History.* Annapolis, Md.: Naval Institute Press, 1983.

Humble, Richard. *Aircraft Carriers: The Illustrated History.* Secaucus, N.J.: Chartwell Books, 1982.

Layman, R. D. *Before the Aircraft Carrier: The Development of Aviation Vessels, 1849–1922.* Annapolis, Md.: Naval Institute Press, 1989.

———. *Naval Aviation in the First World War: Its Impact and Influence.* Annapolis, Md.: Naval Institute Press, 1996.

Melhorn, Charles M. *Two-Block Fox: The Rise of the Aircraft Carrier, 1911–1929.* Annapolis, Md.: Naval Institute Press, 1974.

Poolman, Kenneth. *Allied Escort Carriers.* Annapolis, Md.: Naval Institute Press, 1988.

Preston, Anthony. *Aircraft Carriers.* New York: Grosset and Dunlap, 1979.

Raven, Alan. *Essex-Class Carriers.* Annapolis, Md.: Naval Institute Press, 1988.

Reynolds, Clark G. *The Fast Carriers: The Forging of an Air Navy.* Annapolis, Md.: Naval Institute Press, 1992.

Terzibaschitsch, Stefan. *Aircraft Carriers of the U.S. Navy.* 2d. ed. Annapolis, Md.: Naval Institute Press, 1989.

AMPHIBIOUS SHIPS

Alexander, Joseph H., and Merrill L. Bartlett. *Sea Soldiers in the Cold War: Amphibious Warfare, 1945–1991.* Annapolis, Md.: Naval Institute Press, 1995.

Bartlett, Merrill L., ed. *Assault from the Sea: Essays on the History of Amphibious Warfare.* Annapolis, Md.: Naval Institute Press, 1983.

Burton, Earl. *By Sea and Land: The Story of Our Amphibious Force.* New York: McGraw-Hill, 1944.

Clifford, Kenneth J. *Amphibious Warfare Development in Britain and America from 1920–1940.* Laurens, N.Y.: Edgewood, 1983.

Croizat, Colonel Victor J. USMC (Ret.) *Across the Reef: The Amphibious Tracked Vehicle at War.* New York: Sterling, 1989.

Lorelli, John. *To Foreign Shores: U.S. Amphibious Operations in World War II.* Annapolis, Md.: Naval Institute Press, 1994.

Maund, R. Adm. L. E. H., RN. *Assault from the Sea.* London: n.p., 1949.

Polmar, Norman, and Peter Mersky. *Amphibious Warfare: An Illustrated History.* London: Blandford Press, 1988.

U.S. Navy. *Allied Landing Craft of World War Two.* Annapolis, Md.: Naval Institute Press, 1985.

U.S. Navy. Naval Amphibious Base. *A Brief Historical Sketch on Amphibious Operations.* Little Creek, Va.: Amphibious Training Command, 1948.

Vagts, Alfred. *Landing Operations: Strategy, Psychology, Tactics, Politics, from Antiquity to 1945.* Harrisburg: n.p., 1946.

Whitehouse, Arch. *Amphibious Operations.* Garden City, N.Y.: Doubleday, 1963.

BATTLESHIPS AND BATTLE CRUISERS

Breyer, Siegfried. *Battleships and Battle Cruisers, 1905–1970.* Garden City, N.Y.: Doubleday, 1973.

Burt, R. A. *British Battleships of World War One.* London: Arms & Armour Press, 1986.

———. *British Battleships, 1889–1904.* Annapolis, Md.: Naval Institute Press, 1989.

Campbell, N. J. M. *Battlecruisers: The Design and Development of British and German Battlecruisers of the First World War Era.* London: Conway Maritime Press, 1978.

Coward, B. R. *Battleships and Battlecruisers of the Royal Navy Since 1861.* London: Ian Allan, 1986.

Dulin, Robert O., Jr., and William H. Garzke, Jr. *Battleships: Allied Battleships in World War II.* Annapolis, Md.: Naval Institute Press, 1980.

———. *Battleships: Axis and Neutral Battleships in World War II.* Annapolis, Md.: Naval Institute Press, 1990.

———. *Battleships: U.S. Battleships in World War II.* Annapolis, Md.: Naval Institute Press, 1991.

———. *Battleships: United States Battleships, 1935–1992.* Rev. and updated ed. Annapolis, Md.: Naval Institute Press, 1995.

Friedman, Norman. *U.S. Battleships: An Illustrated Design History.* Annapolis, Md.: Naval Institute Press, 1985.

Hough, Richard. *Dreadnought: A History of the Modern Battleship.* New York: Macmillan, 1964.

Jordan, John. *An Illustrated Guide to Battleships and Battlecruisers.* New York: Arco, 1984.

Parkes, Oscar. *British Battleships: "Warrior" 1860 to "Vanguard" 1950: A History of Design, Construction, and Armament.* 1966. Rev. ed., Annapolis, Md.: Naval Institute Press, 1990.

Preston, Anthony. *Battleships.* London: Bison Books, 1981.

Raven, Alan, and John Roberts. *British Battleships of World War II: The Development and Technical History of the Royal Navy's Battleships and Battlecruisers from 1911–1946.* Annapolis, Md.: Naval Institute Press, 1976.

Reilly, John C., and Robert L. Scheina. *American Battleships, 1886–1923: Predreadnought Design and Construction.* Annapolis, Md.: Naval Institute Press, 1980.

Sturton, Ian, ed. *Conway's All the World's Battleships, 1906 to the Present.* Annapolis, Md.: Naval Institute Press, 1987.

Terzibaschitsch, Stefan. *Battleships of the U.S. Navy in World War II.* New York: Bonanza Books, 1977.

CRUISERS

Burt, R. A. *British Cruisers in World War One*. London: Arms and Armour, 1987.
Bywater, Hector C. *Cruisers in Battle: Naval "Light Cavalry" Under Fire, 1914–1918*. London: Constable, 1939.
Friedman, Norman. *U.S. Cruisers: An Illustrated Design History*. Annapolis, Md.: Naval Institute Press, 1984.
Lenton, H. T. *British Cruisers*. New York: Doubleday, 1973.
Musicant, Ivan. *U.S. Armored Cruisers: A Design and Operational History*. Annapolis, Md.: Naval Institute Press, 1985.
Poolman, Kenneth. *Armed Merchant Cruisers*. London: Leo Cooper, 1985.
Preston, Anthony. *Cruisers: An Illustrated History, 1880–1980*. Englewood Cliffs, N.J.: Prentice-Hall, 1980.
———. *Cruisers*. London: Bison Books, 1982. An abridgement of the above book.
Raven, Alan, and John Roberts. *British Cruisers of World War II*. Annapolis, Md.: Naval Institute Press, 1980.
Schmalenbach, Paul. *German Raiders: A History of Auxiliary Cruisers of the German Navy, 1895–1945*. Annapolis, Md.: Naval Institute Press, 1979.
Smith, Peter C., and John R. Dominy. *Cruisers in Action, 1935–1945*. Annapolis, Md.: Naval Institute Press, 1981.
Terzibaschitsch, Stefan. *Cruisers of the U.S. Navy, 1922–1962*. Annapolis, Md.: Naval Institute Press, 1988.
Whitley, M. J. *Cruisers of World War Two: An International Encyclopedia*. Annapolis, Md.: Naval Institute Press, 1995.
———. *German Cruisers of World War II*. London: Arms and Armour Press, 1985.

DESTROYERS AND FRIGATES

Alden, John D. *Flush Decks and Four Pipes*. Annapolis, Md.: Naval Institute Press, 1989.
Friedman, Norman. *U.S. Destroyers: An Illustrated Design History*. Annapolis, Md.: Naval Institute Press, 1982.
Kemp, Peter K. *H.M. Destroyers*. London: Herbert Jenkins, 1956.
Manning, Capt. T. D., RNVR. *The British Destroyer*. London: Putnam, 1961.
March, Edgar J. *British Destroyers: A History of Development, 1892–1953*. London: Seely Service, 1966.
Preston, Anthony. *Destroyers*. Englewood Cliffs, N.J.: Prentice-Hall, 1977.
Roscoe, Theodore. *United States Destroyer Operations in World War II*. Annapolis, Md.: Naval Institute Press, 1953.
Smith, Peter. *Hard Lying: The Birth of the Destroyer, 1893–1913*. Annapolis, Md.: Naval Institute Press, 1971.
Whitley, M. J. *Destroyer! German Destroyers in World War II*. Annapolis, Md.: Naval Institute Press, 1983.
———. *Destroyers of World War II: An International Encyclopedia*. Annapolis, Md.: Naval Institute Press, 1988.

MINE CRAFT

Cowie, Capt. J. S. *Mines, Minelayers, and Minelaying*. London: Oxford University Press, 1949.

Elliott, Peter. *Allied Minesweeping in World War II*. Annapolis, Md.: Naval Institute Press, 1979.

Hartmann, Gregory K., with Scott C. Truver. *Weapons That Wait: Mine Warfare in the U.S. Navy*. Updated ed. Annapolis, Md.: Naval Institute Press, 1991.

Lott, Arnold S. *Most Dangerous Sea: A History of Mine Warfare and an Account of U.S. Navy Mine Warfare Operations in World War II and Korea*. Annapolis, Md.: Naval Institute Press, 1959.

Marolda, Edward J., ed. *Operation End Sweep: A History of Minesweeping Operations in North Vietnam*. Washington, D.C.: Naval Historical Center, 1993.

Melia, Tamara Moser. *"Damn the Torpedoes": A Short History of U.S. Naval Mine Countermeasures, 1777–1991*. Washington, D.C.: Naval Historical Center, 1991.

SERVICE SHIPS

Ballantine, Duncan. *U.S. Naval Logistics in the Second World War*. Princeton: Princeton University Press, 1949.

Carter, Worral Reed. *Beans, Bullets, and Black Oil*. Washington, D.C.: Department of the Navy, 1953.

Carter, Worral Reed, and Elmer E. Dual. *Ships, Salvage, and Sinews of War*. Washington, D.C.: Department of the Navy, 1954.

Clephane, Lewis P. *History of the Naval Overseas Transportation Service in World War I*. Washington, D.C.: Naval History Division, Department of the Navy, 1969.

Dyer, George C. *Naval Logistics*. Annapolis, Md.: Naval Institute Press, 1960.

Hooper, Edwin B. *Mobility, Support, Endurance: A Story of Naval Operations Logistics in the Vietnam War, 1965–1968*. Washington, D.C.: Naval History Division, Department of the Navy, 1972.

Land, Emory, S. *Winning the War with Ships*. New York: Robert McBride, 1958.

Sigwart, E. E. *Royal Fleet Auxiliary Service: Its Ancestors and Affiliations, 1600–1968*. London: Adlard Coles, 1969.

Wildenberg, Thomas. *Gray Steel and Black Oil: Fast Tankers and Replenishment at Sea in the U.S. Navy, 1912–1992*. Annapolis, Md.: Naval Institute Press, 1996.

SMALL CRAFT

Chant, Christopher. *Small Craft Navies*. London: Arms and Armour, 1992.

Croizat, Victor. *The Brown Water Navy: The River and Coastal War in Indo-China and Vietnam, 1948–1972*. Poole, U.K.: Blandford Press, 1984.

Elliott, Peter. *Allied Escort Ships of World War II: A Complete Survey*. Annapolis, Md.: Naval Institute Press, 1977.

Fock, Harald. *Fast Fighting Boats, 1870–1945: Their Design, Construction, and Use*. Annapolis, Md.: Naval Institute Press, 1978.

Friedman, Norman. *U.S. Small Combatants: An Illustrated Design History Including PT-Boats, Subchasers, and the Brown-Water Navy*. Annapolis, Md.: Naval Institute Press, 1987.

Kemp, Peter. *Decision at Sea: The Convoy Escorts*. New York: Elsevier-Dutton, 1978.

Lambert, John, and Al Ross. *Allied Coastal Forces of World War II*. Vol. 1, *Fairmile Designs and U.S. Submarine Chasers*. Annapolis, Md.: Naval Institute Press, 1990.

———. *Allied Coastal Forces of World War II*. Vol. 2, *Vosper MTBs and U.S. Elcos*. Annapolis, Md.: Naval Institute Press, 1994.

Mariot, John, ed. *Brassey's Fast Attack Craft*. London: Brassey's, 1978.

Winston, John. *Convoy: The Defense of Sea Trade, 1890–1990*. London: Michael Joseph, 1983.

SUBMARINES

Alden, John D. *The Fleet Submarine in the U.S. Navy*. Annapolis, Md.: Naval Institute Press, 1979.

Bagnasco, Erminio. *Submarines of World War II*. 1973. Reprint. Annapolis, Md.: Naval Institute Press, 1991.

Blair, Clay, Jr. *Silent Victory: The United States Submarine War Against Japan*. Philadelphia: J. B. Lippincott, 1975.

Boyd, Carl, and Akihiko Yoshida. *The Japanese Submarine Force and World War II*. Annapolis, Md.: Naval Institute Press, 1995.

Burgess, Robert F. *Ships Beneath the Sea: A History of Subs and Submersibles*. New York: McGraw-Hill, 1975.

Busch, Harald. *U-Boat at War: German Submarine in Action, 1939–1945*. New York: Ballantine Books, 1955.

Carpenter, Dorr, and Norman Polmar. *Submarines of the Imperial Japanese Navy*. Annapolis, Md.: Naval Institute Press, 1986.

Compton-Hall, Richard. *Submarines and the War at Sea, 1914–1918*. London: Macmillan, 1991.

Friedman, Norman. *Submarine Design and Development*. Annapolis, Md.: Naval Institute Press, 1984.

———. *U.S. Submarines Through 1945: An Illustrated History*. Annapolis, Md.: Naval Institute Press, 1995.

Garrett, Richard. *Submarines*. Boston: Little, Brown, 1977.

Gibson, R. H., and Maurice Prendergast. *The German Submarine War, 1914–1918*. London: Constable, 1931.

Gray, Edwyn. *The Killing Time: The U-Boat War, 1914–1918*. New York: Scribner's, 1972.

Herzlett, Sir Arthur. *The Submarine and Seapower*. New York: Stein and Day, 1967.

Hoyt, Edwin P. *Submarine at War: The History of the American Silent Service*. New York: Stein and Day, 1984.

Mars, Alastair. *British Submarines at War, 1939–1945*. Annapolis, Md.: Naval Institute Press, 1971.

Middleton, Drew. *Submarine: The Ultimate Naval Weapon—Its Past, Present, and Future*. Chicago: Playboy Press, 1976.

Polmar, Norman. *The American Submarine*. Baltimore: Nautical and Aviation Publishing Company, 1983.

Polmar, Norman, and Jurrien Noot. *Submarines of the Russian and Soviet Navies, 1718–1990*. Annapolis, Md.: Naval Institute Press, 1991.

Preston, Anthony. *Submarines*. New York: Gallery Books, 1982.

Roland, Alex. *Underwater Warfare in the Age of Sail*. Bloomington: Indiana University Press, 1978.

Roscoe, Theodore. *United States Submarine Operations in World War II*. 1950. Reprint. Annapolis, Md.: Naval Institute Press, 1986.

Tarrant, V. E. *The U-Boat Offensive, 1914–1945*. Annapolis, Md.: Naval Institute Press, 1989.

Van der Vat, Dan. *Stealth at Sea: The History of the Submarine.* Boston: Houghton Mifflin, 1995.

Weir, Gary E. *Building American Submarines, 1914–1940.* Washington, D.C.: Naval Historical Center, 1991.

———. *Forged in War: The Naval-Industrial Complex and American Submarine Construction, 1940–1961.* Washington, D.C.: U.S. Government Printing Office, 1993.

Naval Weapon Systems

Boyce, Joseph C. *New Weapons for Air Warfare: Fire-Control Equipment, Proximity Fuses, and Guided Missiles.* Boston: Little, Brown, 1947.

Campbell, John. *Naval Weapons of World War II.* Annapolis, Md.: Naval Institute Press, 1986.

Devereux, Tony. *Messenger Gods of Battle: Radio, Radar, Sonar—The Story of Electronics in War.* London: Brassey's, 1991.

Fisher, David, E. *A Race on the Edge of Time: Radar—The Decisive Weapon of World War II.* New York: McGraw-Hill, 1981.

Grant, Robert M. *U-Boats Destroyed: The Effects of Anti-Submarine Warfare, 1914–1918.* London: Putnam, 1964.

Hackmann, Willem. *Seek and Strike: Sonar, Anti-Submarine Warfare and the Royal Navy, 1914–54.* London: Her Majesty's Stationery Office, 1984.

Jolie, E. W. *A Brief History of U.S. Navy Torpedo Development.* Newport, R.I.: Naval Underwater Systems Center, 1978.

Padfield, Peter. *Guns at Sea.* London: Hugh Evelyn, 1973.

Tucker, Spencer. *Arming the Fleet: U.S. Navy Ordnance in the Muzzle-Loading Era.* Annapolis, Md.: Naval Institute Press, 1989.

History of War and Weapons

Brodie, Bernard, and Fawn M. Brodie. *From Crossbow to H-Bomb.* Rev. and enlarged ed. Bloomington: Indiana University Press, 1973.

Dupuy, Col. T. N. *The Evolution of Weapons and Warfare.* Indianapolis: Bobbs-Merrill, 1980.

Fuller, Maj. Gen. J. F. C. *Armament and History.* New York: Charles Scribner's Sons, 1945.

———. *A Military History of the Western World.* Vol. 1, *From the Earliest Times to the Battle of Lepanto.* New York: Minerva Press, 1967.

———. *A Military History of the Western World.* Vol. 2, *From the Defeat of the Spanish Armada, 1588, to the Battle of Waterloo, 1815.* New York: Minerva Press, 1967.

———. *A Military History of the Western World.* Vol. 3, *From the Seven Days Battle, 1862, to the Battle of Leyte Gulf, 1944.* New York: Minerva Press, 1967.

Keegan, John. *A History of Warfare.* New York: Knopf, 1993.

Van Creveld, Martin. *Technology and War: From 2000 B.C. to the Present.* Rev. and expanded ed. New York: Free Press, 1991.

Wright, Quincy. *A Study of War.* 2d ed. Chicago: University of Chicago Press, 1965.

Index